DEEP RIVER

THE COMPLETE POEMS OF
ARCHIBALD RUTLEDGE

Archibald Rutledge is the author of 70 books. Among
best known of these are: "Home by the River," "Brimm
Tide," "Life's Extras," "The Heart's Citadel," "Those W
the Days," and "Rain on the Marsh." By legislative enactm
he has been Poet Laureate of South Carolina for 27 years.

ACKNOWLEDGMENTS

ı this collection of poems, the following first appeared in *The ies' Home Journal:* "The Source," "Spirit Dawn," and "Autumn ;."

ı *McCall's Magazine* appeared "The Favor," "Once to His Love," "Final Proof."

ı *The Saturday Evening Post* appeared "The Compass" and atchers."

ı *Mature Years* appeared "The Least of These."

ı *The New York Times* appeared "Rejoice."

The author is grateful to these magazines for their permission to int the poems mentioned.

EP
VER
E COMPLETE POEMS OF ARCHIBALD RUTLEDGE

E R. L. BRYAN COMPANY   COLUMBIA, S. C.
PUBLISHERS

PRINTED BY

THE R. L. BRYAN COMPANY

COLUMBIA, S. C.

DEDICATION

To

JOSEPHINE ALDRICH HARRIS,
Alabama's Wood Thrush,
dear faithful friend and perfect comrade

r generously helping me to bring this book to light, I owe
p and lasting debt of gratitude to these dear friends:

Mrs. Anna Hyatt Huntington

Mr. and Mrs. Avery Rockefeller

Mrs. Susie Abney

ACKNOWLEDGMENTS

For courteous permission to reprint certain poems in book, the author makes grateful acknowledgments to editors of *The Atlantic Monthly, Harper's Magazine, Christian Herald, The New York Times, Poetry, Good H keeping, The Fleming Revell Co.*, and other magazines.

CONTENTS

HEART OF THE WILDWOOD

CONTENTS—*Continued*

DEEP RIVER

CONTENTS—*Continued*

[xv]

CONTENTS—*Continued*

CONTENTS—*Continued*

SONNETS

CONTENTS—*Continued*

CONTENTS—*Continued*

CONTENTS—*Continued*

THE VALIANT

CONTENTS—*Continued*

CONTENTS—*Continued*

CONTENTS—*Continued*

Heart of the Wildwood

STRENGTH

Of weakness and of strength
How little can we tell!
I thought the wildflower's bell,
Beside the great oak's hardihood,
The frailest thing in all the wood;
Yet in the storm the wildflower stood.
It was the oak that fell.

SANCTUARY

Every wild wing of the harried, the hunted,
Every fleet foot of the stalked, the pursued,
Every bright eye of the fearful, the followed,
Solace may find in this blithe solitude.
Here the wing folds by the peace of the waters;
Here the feet pause in the woodland's bright calm;
Here the eye rests; for the woods and the waters
Friendly and welcoming, offer their balm.

Where the tree dips to the wide placid water,
Where the reeds bend to the stately slow tide,
Where the moon rises o'er leagues of dim marshland,
Glimmering greenly—here may they abide.
Hither they speed over moorland and mountain,
Wary and valiant, far-sighted and brave;
Hither they come to the call of compassion;
Here may they rest in the wood, on the wave.

Beautiful wings of the air and the river,
Wonderful eyes of the forest and glade,
Marvelous voices atune with the dawn-wind,
Welcome, ah, welcome, to sun and to shade!
Here you may have the desired, the cherished,
Only the warrant in freedom to live:
Here in this solitude stayed is the hand of man,
Opened the heart of man—refuge to give!

THE VEERY

When day is hushed and hidden,
And golden woods are mute,
The elegist of evening
Touches his silver lute.

As if the light were lyric
That from the first star gleams
Far through the dewy pinewood
The glimmering choral streams.

As if through lonely oriels
Of sundown's gorgeous fane
Resplendent dying beauty sang
Anthems of love and pain.

As if the rosebay's beauty
In music overbrimmed
Till all the fading forest hears
Her radiant vespers hymned.

As if a heart long harried,
And scourged by many a rod,
Had triumphed and were singing
Safe in the arms of God.

THE MOUTH OF THE SANTEE

The river flows through landscapes lost,
By storied ruins of the past;
The river finds the ancient coast,
The rolling surge, the ocean vast;
There where the craggy cedars mark
Through vistas, opening on the foam,
The floodtide flowing full and dark,
The pacing of the ebbtide home.

4

THE DARKENED TIDE

No moon or sun is burning
As beacon for its way,
And yet the tide keeps coming
Through darkened creek and bay.
The tide keeps flooding inland;
Nothing its course can stay.

Its valor is more steadfast
Than any mortal might,
Unfailing in fidelity
Even in deepest night,
Having a strength in darkness
Great as its strength in light.

WOOD THRUSH

About the setting of the sun,
When fevers of the day are done,
A wood thrush in the tawny light
Is caroling of coming night
Upon the harp he harps upon.

The cares that to the day belong
He sings away with mystic song.
His notes are few, but pure and deep,
Like magic music heard in sleep,
Like love that sorrow has made strong.

Such melody my spirit stills;
Celestial hope this voice fulfils.
And then my heart in rapture rallies
At visions of eternal valleys,
At cognizance of heavenly hills.

IN A FOREST

An orchestra with harps of gold
Makes music in this forest old:
I hear from dewy hill-hung firs
Dim melodies of dulcimers;
The regal cardinalis tall
Carols a scarlet madrigal;
The trumpets of the hidden stream
Are silver horns heard in a dream;
The wind's soft wand of lyric fire
Touches the copse into a choir;
The vireo 'mid the bloomy sprays
Fingers the flute Titania plays:
Such melody, surpassing art,
Brings deepest silence to my heart.

There comes a quiet to the wood,
As if it uttered solitude.
Demurely down the silent glade
Shimmers the reticence of shade;
Bright hauteurs virginally gleam
From cloistered oaks, from soundless stream;
A wild forsaken beauty shines
About the hushed momentous pines;
I did not dream that there could be
Such stillness of felicity.
The forest glimmers, mystic, mute,—
A veiled enchantress . . . There's no lute,
No harp, no cymbal, and no singing,
But in my heart wild bells are ringing.

THE RETURN TO THE OAK

But for the glimmering pillars, he had veiled
The house from view. Tall, twilight-dim he stands,
The guardian of lustrous summer lands,
In glory of his emerald armor mailed.

As when a boy his stalwart bulk I see,
The proud and ancient patriarch! His form
Has gathered grace from sun and power from storm,
Lone in the dusk he looms tremendously.

At sight of him, my heart is filled with joys;
The monarch-oak is standing, massive, grand—
Ah, no mere oak is he! I understand
The meaning of this steadfast giant's poise;

This vast glad strength, this purpose calm and deep,
This brow heroic that with stars confers
This rooted hardihood, this light that stirs
The foliage in its bright aereal sleep.

Lo, he had waited my return so long!
A thousand dawns of disappointment came;
Vainly he saw a thousand sunsets flame;
But ever he was watchful and was strong.

While I in far forgetful paths did roam,
This oak stood sure, devotion's faith to prove;
Pledge of the proud eternity of Love,
Powerful warder at the gates of Home.

THE SUNSET PINES

The pines give forth their evening hymn,
A wild sweet melody they weave;
The deep bass-horns are blowing dim,
The stormy tenor-trumpets grieve.

I hear in yonder forests lone
Tremendous music rolling free,
Where tall pines echo, tone for tone,
The tumult of the thundering sea.

A gray rain sweeps the pinewood through,
Yet gorgeously the sunset shines;
Now breaks above the happy blue,
And Splendor paces through the pines.

Far and more far the sunset shines,
The cool clear heavens are silver-gray;
The Moon is roaming through the pines
Alone upon her radiant way.

WOOD SONG

O walk into the wood with me,
And drink a wine of wizardry!
Nature's wild beauty brims the cup;
Tiptoe, Titania holds it up.
This innocent golden chalice drain
And come to peace beyond all pain;
To joy beyond the dreams of youth,
To insight elder than the Truth,
Vision more poignant, to descry
In the violet's little brimming eye,
In rockrose and in goldenrod
The mercy and the love of God.

8

BEACH BOY

With the salt marsh in my blood,
And the sea-wind in my heart,
With live-oaks and magnolias
Of all my life a part;

With the whistle of the willet
Above the breakers' roll,
And the calling of the curlew
A music in my soul;

With the pine trees and the jessamines
My friends from boyhood days,
No other land is homeland to
A child of creeks and bays.

O for the scenes I cherish,
A world I call my own!
The great wood ibis soaring
Above the hummock lone;

The wild dove in her dusky flight
The cedar trees along;
The eagle cruising down the coast,
Bold as a battle-song;

The brimming floodtide, strewing
The beach with sedge and foam;
The fishing boats returning,
The ebbtide pacing home.

Ah, for the olden voices
I love and understand:
The sea-wind in the yellow pines,
The sea-wave on the sand!

MY OLD HOUND PACK

Riverward they took him flying,
And they brought him sailing back,
All the merry music-makers
Of my yowling fox-hound pack.
Now they've gone above the pasture,
Swinging widely to the west;
Now he's heading up the mountain
For a stern and stubborn test.
And I stand and hearken, happy,
To that melody of sounds.
Is there any heavenly music
Like the voices of the hounds?

There's a short low tenor,
And a yipping ki-yi;
There's a bell-mouth ringing
That a fox has got to die.
There's a ding-dong chop-mouth,
Always in the noise;
There's a bass with no bottom,
And a rolling gong voice.
There's a bugle with a break,
And a bugle with a scream,
And a high wailing tenor
Like a trumpet in a dream!

Reynard now has quit his climbing,
And he's taken to the swamp.
To the deep low-thicket country,
Where it's always dark and damp.
Does he think my bawling yodlers
In that brake will let him hide?
Hear that clamor in the bracken?
Oh, they'll take him for a ride!
Now he's kiting for the wild woods,
Where there's many a misty glen;
And I ought to blow them off now,
But I hate to say just when!

When my hunting here is over,
From the tall harps' golden sounds
I will steal away to harken
To the voices of the hounds
When they start a phantom red fox
On a phantom heavenly hill,
And with me, a phantom huntsman,
Getting all the old-time thrill.
For a man who's bred to hunting
Must forever be that way;
And he'll never know it's heaven
Till he listens, and can say:

There's a short low tenor,
And a yipping ki-yi;
There's a bell-mouth ringing
That a fox has got to die.
There's a ding-dong chop-mouth,
Always in the noise;
There's a bass with no bottom,
And a rolling gong voice.
There's a bugle with a break,
And a bugle with a scream,
And a high wailing tenor
Like a trumpet in a dream!

UNTIL

Until you've traveled on the road,
And many a bramble broke,
And found the shade beneath the oak,
Advise not wayside folk.

MOUNTAINS AND VALLEYS

I

Hail to you, male mountains! The iron, the massive
In adamant morticed and based!
You hard-hearted, masculine, physical mountains,
I see you standing there and fearing not.
O excellent, obdurate Force! Naked and obstinate,
Bulwarked by boulders huge,
With flying-buttresses of granite bastioned,—
Thoughtful, vast, indomitable!
O Fortitude, Stubbornness, grimmest Tenacity!
Hale with a hardihood born out of fathomless courage!
Calm are you with an ancient savage strength.
Your battlemented fronts wear valor's visage.
Intrepid, sternly audacious,
You await all onslaughts of wrath.
When the mad cyclone comes screaming in your faces,
Unperturbed you break the back of the fiendish Thing.
Unappalled you meet the volleying thunders of storms.
With mighty thews you unhorse the hurricane,
The champion bareback-rider of heaven you overthrow.
—O silent ranks of rugged Titans!
Your tall legions are reviewed by the Morning;
Your veteran battalions parade in the sunset . . .
Dauntless you patrol the lofty loneliness,
The upper spaces where cruel wings beat, where black
      voices call,
The outer silences, the dreadful clutching darkness.
Resolute sentinels, fronting the frontiers of Fear,
Not once are you shaken, not once dismayed.
You stand guard at the gates of the valleys,
O elemental male mountains, tacit and strong,
Warriors of the earth, and soldiers of the sky!

II

Behold, far away, heart-breaking in beauty,
The Female Valley! O lovely, alluring,
Surely your beauty is glory enough for you!
But you, too, are conqueror, even of the mountains.
Almighty strength of tenderness is yours; for 'tis to
    you
The powerful mountains yearn.
The independent giants,—they longingly look toward
    you.
O delicate, feminine, exquisite Valley,
The buoyant, the lissome, the airy, the lithe,
Wearing your life like a garment of rainbows fashioned.

O virginal Valley! Wafted from you are fragrances
    poignant—
O modest and chaste,—mistily retiring,
Fair with a wildrose wonder and innocence,
Yet winsome-inviting and wise!
Far-calling, singing, beckoning, dancing,
Bright with light and laughter,
Beautiful, all a-shimmer with dew and with delight,
Shining softly, irradiating peace,
The sweet home with love illumining.
Haunting, mysterious Valley! Fruitful and quiet,
Tinged and tinted with the touches of immortal grace!
Glimmering with the premonitions of nameless bliss!
Inscrutable Valley! I fear you in fascination:
I love you,—I fear you!
- - - The bold and upright mountains are understood,
Those simple and candid and barbarous children,
Prideful in power,—I admire them, honor them,
Giving to strength its due.
But O Valley divine! I cannot know you!
O sacred one! Dear sweetheart Eve, you are to be loved
With love of the heart that is holiest mystery.

WORTH KNOWING

When I behold what changes grief has wrought
Deep in the soul: the tenderness it wakes,
The warm compassion and the loving thought
Although the eyes brim and the brave heart breaks.
Yet in the end the spirit is made strong,
Free of all selfishness, to others given.
It brings to life a clear and valiant song
That sounds as if it might have come from heaven.

I know the aisles of yew, with no light beaming,
The cold and broken tears grief sheds alone.
I know the sunset glow of farewell streaming,
My heart within me still as any stone.
Yet when the waters of grief have ceased their flowing
I am convinced that sorrow is worth knowing.

THE FAVOR

I would be wise to ask my Love a favor;
She of my dust a golden image made.
Lest her celestial image of me waver,
The gold be tarnished, and the colors fade,
"O Love," I shall appeal, "look not on me,
But on this idol, born of your sweet trust;
There fix your eyes with joyous constancy.
Behold your dream, regarding not my dust.

"And though unworthy, I may gaze with you,
And strive to be the wonder that you wrought;
Then, if my love is strong, if it be true
In act and purpose and in every thought;
If I can but be valiant to life's verge,
With my Love's image of me I may merge."

14

TWILIGHT SONG

Beautiful singer of the gorgeous rite
Of setting suns, calm elegist of Light!

If purple anthems from the pineland rolled,
Blown by the pines' rich organ-basses bold;

If music of undiscovered oceans tossed
On mystic shores, to all but dreamers lost;

If flowers, rosy with the dawn's caress,
Found utterance for their dewy loveliness;

If twilight, lingering in a fragrant dell,
Were lyric with the thought of life's farewell:

If these were tuned to love by heavenly art,
Divinely penetrative of the heart,

They would be vocal in thy poignant song,
Floating the holy woodland aisles along,

When, ere the magic star of evening gleams,
Thy mortal music builds immortal dreams.

GOD'S BRIDE

Is there anything at all
More magical, more mysterious,
Than a night-blooming cereus?
Reserving for the darkness,
For the dewy stillness
Of the glimmering deep night
Her beauty's delight?
O, intimate of dusky silence,
Of the silvery, secret stars,—
Out of man's sight
Your loveliness opens wide,
As if you were
God's bride.

15

HEART OF THE WILDWOODS

It was in mellow October, and the tinted woods were sifting red
    and yellow leaves,
As we walked up the old logging-road, my faithful setter and I.
Far-off we heard a soft reverberant drumming; insistent,
    penetrant, challenging;
It was the proud cock-grouse, standing upon his favorite mossy
    log (so I supposed),
And drumming his challenge - - - for it was too late to be a
    call of mating and love.
And I said to my dog, "Let us find him, this high-souled wood-
    land prince,
For he is one of the noblest patricians of the North American
    wilds.
His lineage is lofty and far-descended from the best blood of
    the past;
He carries armorial bearings of the ancient forest-world;
His 'scutcheon is gorgeous with wood-symbols and thrilling
    wood mysteries;
His arms are the beauties of virginal woodlands and of powerful
    silent mountains,
And of dusky laurelled gorges, glimmering, luring the heart
    away.
If we see him, we shall have seen the very soul of wild beauty,
The heart of the magical lonely woods, the spirit of solitude,
    the source of life."
And my dog listened to me and understood me; I am very sure
    he understood me;
For he looked at me with clear, faithful eyes, accepting my
    words and approving.
He is more intelligent and affectionate than many men I know;
He will follow me to the death; his greatest grief is when I
    must leave him.

So we stepped quietly forward on the wonderful glowing leaves,
Alert, expectant of the radiant apparition of a presence of
glory.
And the tattered gold of the yet-unfallen leaves, hanging
gorgeous and ruinous,
Seemed screens to veil a miracle, or arras marginal to mystery.
We were very careful - - - my dog more careful than I. He
did not trail or point,
But he stepped tense and ghostlike, his noble eyes ready for
the vision.
Then thro' a vista, shimmering far with sad and beautiful
autumnal lights,
Proud on a mossy log, unconscious of us, yet superbly wary,
valiant and brave,
Stood the cock-partridge!
His fan-tail was spread; his wings were lowered; he was
strutting.
The soft gleaming of woodland lights was on his plumage; I
could see the ruff,
The prince's black ruff, quiver in the stress of a challenger's
emotions.
All this my dog saw - - - and perhaps he saw more than I. He
was fast to a point.
- - - A man, a dog, a cock-grouse . . . We had no gun . . .
and did we regret it?
No. (For once we were not sorry, though we are hunters and
lovers of sport;)
For we had seen the heart of the beautiful lonely woods.
And we left it beautiful and unbroken.

RAVENSWOOD

Happy in dreams I stood
By quiet Ravenswood,
Close to the pacing flood
Of Awensdaw;
There Beauty's scene I viewed,
There my lost youth renewed,
There the far past reviewed,—
And there I saw

With boyhood's joy again
Marshes of Cape Romain,
Through which the mighty main
Makes with its tides.
Whatever storms befall
Through the years' interval,
Far Romain's tower tall
Faithful abides.

There by the beach's rim
Where the salt sea-tides brim,
Now with gray sea-mist dim,
Now with sun bright,
Solemn wise herons wade,
Fiddlers in ranks parade,
And in the cedars' shade,
Warblers delight.

Amber-hued Awensdaw,
Obeying ancient law,
Your mystic tides withdraw
From Wambaw wild;
Past dreamy Doe Hall going;
By Eagle Hummock flowing,
The sea, your mother, knowing,
Like a lost child!

Myrtles where nest the doves,
Live-oaks and sandy coves,
Shellbanks the curlew loves,
You do not change!

Nor does the olden song
Sounding the pines among,
Whose rolling anthems strong
Starward still range!

Yonder the home is seen
Through oaks' alluring screen,
Welcome-wide it has been
Ever to me;
Home, at whose open gates
Gentle affection waits,
Stronger than all the fates,
Deep as the sea!

Ravenswood, Ravenswood,
Near you in dreams I stood,
Nor in my waking could
Wish to depart.
Land, land with beauty bright,
Land of sweet love's delight,
Fade never from my sight,
Home of my heart!

Land, land where Beauty's spell
Evermore seems to dwell,
Lo, I have loved you well,—
Sometimes through tears;—
But all my love of you
Is naught but being true
To those whose love I knew
Lived through the years.

Where beats a heart for me,
There, there for aye I'd be,
Whether by land or sea,
Or shore or foam.
Life holds but little rest;
These gifts in it are best:
True hearts and tenderest,
Home-love and home!

A BURNS TWILIGHT

A hillside blue with gorse and heather blowing;
The tinted clouds are wandering far and free;
Below, a briared burn with waters flowing
Past wistful wildflowers swaying faerily.
A star above the hanging woods is showing
A beamy brightness. From the misty lea
A late and happy lark is skyward going
To magic shores of song by music's sea.

A wildrose with the early dew is gleaming;
A mountain breeze is on the bending wheat;
A line of whistling plover far is streaming
High o'er the vale where night and twilight meet.
With looks like love's the setting star is beaming;
With love's delight the world grows piercing sweet;
Deepens the burn's pure music with a dreaming
Of how love makes all life with joy complete.

The highland hills their starry thoughts are
        thinking;
The west remote a fading glory shows.
In violet sleep the valleys far are sinking;
Night's fragrance hale upon their faces blows.
Deep in the burn an antlered stag is drinking;
The warbling water round his fetlocks flows;
A bonny blink in yonder glen is winking,
Though night has veiled the mountains and the
        rose.

RED LEAF

From an autumnal leaf I learned
How beautifully one may go
In golden glory without grief,—
Though to be buried deep in snow.
For I have seen a red leaf fall,
Dancing upon its downward way,
As if the ending of the year
Were gayer than the spring is gay.

20

FEMALE ARIEL

She was rollicksome and witty,
She was gay and sweet and pretty.
Darken not her starry flight
With our sorrow's standard night.
For her let us not be grieving
Since to us her love she's leaving.
She, a debonair blithe dancer,
To our anguish was the answer.
Flaunting like an oriole,
Less by body than by soul,
All our hearts she gaily stole.
When she went from us afar,
Heaven gained another star.
I can see God smile to meet her,
And the angels, laughing, greet her.
Let not our forgiveness flout her,
Saying stupid things about her.
She was frolicksome and pretty,
She was gay and sweet and witty.
From her bosom you withhold
Nunlike lilies, icy-cold;
Yet when death's Dark Angel found her,
There were roses all around her.

AUTUMN MIGRANT SINGING

In dying autumn listening
I heard a gallant migrant sing.
Only one little song I heard
From this triumphant unseen bird.
I never heard it any more;
But on the everlasting shore
Of Memory, by Music's river,
My heart shall hear that song forever,—
Because it is most valiant to
Bequeath brave singing as we go,
Giving to life love's lyric lights
Between two mute mysterious nights.

21

THE COTTON FIELD

Looming black pines are deeply listening
To music in the voice of mystic night,
And stars have diademed their thoughtful brows.
Expectant of a miracle, the field,
The level field of cotton, stretches far,
Lucent in misty dew and glimmering bloom.
At last the moon, that fired the dusky forest,
Sails clear above the pines, and floods the land
With dreamlight that is beautiful as love.

Now, all night long shall sleep in golden light
The world beneath the glory of the moon.
In ghostly beauty the cotton-blooms shall glow
With secret lights. There shall the foliage shed
The fragrant dew all glistening to the ground.
And 'neath the luminous moonlight curtain vast,
Shall ripen flower and boll, and bring to pass
The splendor of the harvest that shall be.

Now o'er the western pines the moon descends;
Across the fields, chill, dewy, fragrant, full
Of night-renewed vigor and fresh youth.
A dawn-wind breathes. The day is near at hand.
Now fades the light on trees and field. The east,
Already rosy with the break of dawn,
The Star of Day's Annunciation wears.

RICHER OFFERING

Because of miracles to be,
I think I'll wait to hear and see,
Upon the borders of this wood,
The pines' Hungarian orchestra,
The moon's immortal maidenhood.

Waiting until these wonders come,
It may be I can carry home
A beauty from this life apart
To give to those who love me well
More mystic worship of my heart.

THE PINES

They have hands to be laid
On the wild and weary heart;
Cool green hands for my head . . .
All I need, they impart.
And, to still the pulses' start,
More divine than Music's art,
Silences like starlight shed.

Faint recoverings I feel
Of the hope I had resigned.
Theirs is love whose touch can heal
Mortal wounds of heart and mind.
Have I lost, They can find . . .
Since my trouble they've divined,
They can give me grace to kneel.

They have voices to be heard
By the heart whence music's fled;
Mighty are the gifts conferred
On the soul to rapture dead:
Peace, toward which the feet are led;
Calm, to which the spirit's wed;
Love, with resurrection word.

Only Love thus fathomed me,
Sweetly life's grave truth to teach
With a poignant sympathy:
In a language more than speech,
On the sky's eternal beach,
"Grief is not beyond love's reach,"
Hymns the Pines' melodious sea.

THE WILDFLOWER

As, fringed with folds of fragile lace,
You lift your exquisite pure face,
Far Beauty's presence I can trace
Sad-gleaming shine;
Frail haunting charm, pale magic grace,
Spirit divine.

If naught else in the world I saw
To teach me love and sacred awe,
Through you I understand the law
That hearts obey:
Your life and loveliness you draw
From far away.

To lift your virgin dewy eyes,
Younger than Eve's in sweet surprise,
To make you look upon the skies
Earth had no might;
It took the sun to make you rise
Into the light.

And never a heart but feels from far
The Power that ranges, star to star,
Whose gorgeous coming naught can bar:
It finds its own,
Mounting, where love's high altars are,
Its mystic throne.

OLD HUNTER

The oriole sings her hymn to God,
The bobwhite calls her brood,
While I forget the woods I trod,
The fields wherein I stood.
'Tis grief to know not night from morn,
But wilder grief I know:
I can but hear the hunter's horn
That once I used to blow.

AUTUMN SONG

O the horn, O the horn,
O the hunter's merry horn
That with music thrills the wildwood
And that carries through the corn,
Silvered, sere, and shivering brightly
In the frosty autumn morn!

O the hounds and the horn
And the buck that breaks from cover!
His flaunting tail is flashing high;
His black nose is a-quiver;
They'll be fleetest hounds that follow,
For he's running for the river!

O the golden gleam and glance
Of the sun on bronzing fell!
O the dewy pinewood purple,
And the ferny fragrant dell,
O the young hound's grieving tenor,
And the old hound's deep bass bell!

O bright in flaming beauty
Burn the berries in the bush!
And the scarlet of the sumac
Lures to feast the timid thrush;
(He will hymn the holy evening
When day's strident clamors hush.)

O the horn in distance fainting,
O the hounds beyond the hills!
O the strong stag o'er the river!
O rich music that fulfils
Autumn's beauty! 'Tis the veery
That like love the wildwood thrills.

THE GROUSE

With him the woodland wonders come;
Their beauties in his flight depart,
Or like far music fading sweet
They linger in the listening heart;
For all that wanders and is wild,
With faerie charms remote and dim,
Luring like rich autumnal lights,
Seems gathered to the soul of him.

To the lost wood he brings a soul;
A spirit to the glen he gives;
The silent and forsaken hill
To sudden rapture wakes and lives
As off he speeds upon those wings
That deftly thread the thicket's way;
Or does he merely cross the road?
The day becomes a magic day!

Of mountain-silence he's the tone,
The voice of hushed, seraphic places;
The meaning of the loveliness
That glimmers forth the forest-graces;
The haunting scenes of mountains grand,
The radiant peace of wonder-woods,
The mystery and marvel old
Abiding in the solitudes.

The hill-crest pines have runes of sleep;
The brawling brook has urgent speech;
The ocean's old unrest is loud
In rolling anthems of the beach;
But in this bird the wildwood sings
The only lyric to impart
A sense of all the silentness
And music of sweet Nature's heart.

MOONRISE

The wide marsh stirs from marge to marge,
A wind is freshening from the sea;
A red moon rises, low and large,
The flood is flowing deep and free.

Uncertain echoes fill the night;
The marsh-birds gather on the sedge;
The marsh is sinking out of sight,
The red moon watching from its edge.

The dim marsh drinks the waters warm,
Drinks them and drowns in moving bliss;
The sea is losing her love-charm,
The moon no longer leans to kiss.

Far as the farthest islands mark
The distant beaches, where the foam
Is thunderous, are waters dark,
Through which the silver moon will roam.

QUIET VALLEY

There is a quiet valley that I know
Far from the ocean. But by its brook I found
In yellow sands sea-shells of long ago.
Though now no billows make the air resound,
Here once the main was master; and once over
This meadowy calm the maned sea-breakers tolled.
Where dream this herdsgrass and this crimson clover
Great waters their reverberations rolled.

So sometimes when I look upon a face
Tranquil and beautiful, with life at peace,
I feel that out of storm has come a grace,
Life's music deepening as its clangors cease.
Of grief but few memorials remain;
Its sea surged here, but surges not again.

TOLD IN SONG

Across a river carolling
I heard two joyous cardinals sing.
So wild their music was, and free,
God's choristers they well might be.

Each to the other sent in songs
The beauty that to love belongs:
Far violets that the wildwood knows,
The garden's fragrant queen, the rose.

I never saw them cross that tide
(The river there is deep and wide);
Yet if they never spanned that river
Their story shall abide forever.

Long after I could hear them sing,
To love I heard love answering;
So let our loving be like theirs,
Song answering song through all the years.

PLANNED BEAUTY

Potential in an acorn slept this oak;
Instinctive in the feathery mast, this pine;
This magic dogwood in a berry woke;
And each has brought to triumph its design.
They stand as miracles revealed; and yet
There's deeper wonder, like a poignant pang,
If, in delighting, we shall not forget
The Hand that cradled them, the Heart that sang

Their being's song. In every golden bar
Of life's far music, God is imminent,
Inherent in the soul of tree and star,—
Children on whom His glorious care is spent.
Only the nervous, wild, unerring Hand
Of Everlasting Love such beauty planned.

MOUNTAIN LION

The fever of the day is done;
Red in the tree-tops swims the sun.
The panther, pacing in his rage
The limits of his cruel cage,
Beholds in dreams, beyond the bars,
His mountain pines, his canyon stars.

Deep in the primal pagan night
The lion's eyes are still alight.
The wild somnambulistic moon
Chants to his heart a passionate rune.
The occult dark, the tawny dew,
The royal stars his soul renew.

The sun is rising once again
Upon a world of strife and pain.
By argent amorous archery
The moon has set the panther free.
He's sleeping now behind the bars
Whose spirit spent the night with stars.

WHITE OAK

When I shall build my little house,
And so fulfil a dream,
I'll build it by an old white oak
Beside a quiet stream.
Since for a planted one to grow
I know I cannot wait,
My house shall be beside a tree
That is already great.

This stream remembers Indians.
They loved its gentle flow.
This oak was here before they came,
And shall be when I go.
I love this stream's eternal quest
To find its home, the river;
I love the way this monarch stands,
A symbol of Forever.

RAIN ON THE MARSH

Rain on the Romain Marsh,
And the sullen tide is low;
The barren flats are chill and bare;
The fitful rain-winds blow.
The tall blades of the marsh
Tremble and bend and sigh;
The weary fishing boats come in
Under the weary sky.

Silence and rain and mist
From the lone sea-marsh's rim
To the dripping plumes of the mournful pines
That fringe the forest dim.
My heart seems shut and still;
But my eyes with fear are free,
Peering across the reaches blind
That stretch forth to the sea.

The rain is over! A wind
Sweet from the pineland blows.
The sun has set, and the far deep west
Blooms like a gradual rose.
The mists from the marshes rise;
The marsh-blades lift and stir;
The floodtide sets in from the sea;
The west grows lovelier.

O ever and ever the light,
After the mist and the rain!
And beauty and joy and hope once more
After the fear and the pain!
Always a mightier Mind
Under great Nature's veil,—
Always a Heart to love my heart,
A Mercy that shall not fail.

A JUDGE OF FLOWERS

Lord, when I come to judge Your flowers,
Summoned by duty to decide
Which blooms are fairest to behold,
Which blossoms silver, which are gold,
What skill has set them on their throne,
Be You my counselor and guide,
Let me with justice like Your own
Abide.

With You I know I cannot err,
Let me be worshipful and still.
O may I from Your wisdom learn;
Give me the instinct to discern
How You would judge if You were I.
Hold fast my hand. Lead me until
My heart beats to all beauty by
Your will.

Give me the virtue and the grace
To honor merit, as I view
The loveliness You brought to be;
And with Your insight let me see
What is deserving of renown,
And be so near it shall be true
That I do not award the crown,—
But You.

POSSESSION

Deep in the sweet mysterious wood
The wildflowers in their beauty stood.
I longed to enter, and to be
One with their love's eternity.
I yearned to touch their tremulous grace,
Against their own to lay my face.
What stayed me? For I saw them shine
In mercy,—and they might be mine.
Perhaps all beauty is possessed
By them alone who let it rest.
And only as I leave it free
Its magic can belong to me.

31

PINE AND JASMINE

In the wildwoods of home, I well remember,
Out of a thicket of holly and of bay
Towered a solitary yellow pine
Momentously in glad primeval might,
Pagan and stalwart and of lonely valor;
Now a familiar of the sun, and now
The peer and intimate of choiring stars
Whose mansion is the dwelling-place of light.
Dawn he patrolled like some archangel tall,
Was warder of the azure deeps of day,
And evening's glimmering bivouac sentineled.
And to his strength there clung with clambering grace
A delicate jasmine, frail and feminine.
She wrapped him tenderly and thus arose
Out of the shadows to the radiances
Until the two seemed one. Secure through him,
Childlike she tossed her fragrant saffron showers,
By magic stayed in air. His power sustained her,
While he with beauty was adorned. It seemed
To be his own but really was of her.

Now many a year has gone. The giant pine,
Whose mailed and massive old renown I loved,
Again I see, the vine still banding him.
But he has suffered what we all must feel:
The failure of the flesh upon the bone.
A storm has shorn his dark mysterious crest,
Whose multitudinous harps were wont to mourn
Their astral melodies. Forlorn he stands,
A ruined champion, pregnable and sad.
But now supporting, clinging close, upholding
His failing strength, the jasmine's beauty climbs,
With unbound tresses covering his scars,
As if to shield from foes his impotence.
Just as a woman, wedded once to glory,
With love's incomparable loyalty,
Deeply, defensively loves what is left,
Loves all the more because of splendors gone.

And proud and broken might can be sustained
By love alone, and crashes gloomily
If ever once that tender comfort fail.
Whenever I see the jasmine and the pine,
They make me think of husband and of wife.

WHIPPOORWILL

When the dusk of spring is tawny green again,
And the locust blooms are falling in the lane,
From the hollow and the hill,
By the river and the rill,
You can hear the whippoorwill,
"Whippoorwill! Whippoorwill!"
Wild and sweet and sad and shrill,
Waking dreams of love I thought forever still,
Waking dreams that nothing can fulfil.
And the whipporwill is mourning, "Whippoorwill!"

When the deeper dark has hushed the valley wide,
And the mountains in a misty trance abide,
In the evening's dewy chill,
By the wildwood's ruined mill,
You can hear the whippoorwill,
"Whippoorwill! Whippoorwill!"
Sweet and sad and wild and shrill,
Waking dreams of love I thought no more could thrill,
Waking dreams no magic can fulfil.
And the whippoorwill is wailing, "Whippoorwill!"

When all the world's a realm of the night,
And the stars deliver dim seraphic light,
When dark's mysteries distil,
And the moon's a daffodil,
You can hear the whippoorwill,
"Whippoorwill! Whippoorwill!"
Sad and wild and sweet and shrill,
Waking dreams of love I thought forever still,
Waking dreams no waiting can fulfil,
And the whippoorwill is weeping, "Whippoorwill!"

THE BELL-BUOY

When silences like shadows fall
In night's majestic glimmering hall,
Beyond the coastline's sombre wall
Where pines have made a purple pall,
I hear her wild mysterious call
In darkness terrible and tall . . .
Her music takes my heart in thrall:
I question, and she answers all.

She's manacled to White Shark Bank
Where the proud *Indian Princess* sank . . .
Against her chain she haggles lank,
Whimpering a wet and dreary clank,—
Her glossy-gleaming female flank
With beryl cascades streaming dank:
Now drowned and dazed, now heaving blank,
Bowing to breakers, rank on rank.

Slow-nodding to the raveled rips,
She plunges, poises, bleakly sips
A pledge to proudly passing ships . . .
She checks; she dips; her bosom drips,
Adown a sliding canon slips;
Then as she reels and madly strips
Green draperies from breast and hips,
A requiem is on her lips.

Crying like some long-captured thing,
Groined to the mud, with soul awing,—
Shackled, she has the heart to sing!
I find my spirit listening
To what that wild sea-bell may ring,
What grim defiance she may fling,
What mortal message she may bring,—
Groined to the mud, with soul awing!

From you, O mystic wild sea-bell,
Lyric in your lone citadel,
Unutterable secrets swell:
To me at last are audible
The language still of hope's farewell,
The words that in brave silence dwell,
Tears of the heart that never fell,—
All that love feels, but cannot tell.

Nobly the music from her came:
(What tether can the spirit tame?)
Her dauntless comradeship I claim:
Suffering a torment none can name,—
Like me, like me,—our fate the same,
Fellows in fate's gigantic game,—
Tossing for aye 'twixt heaven and shame,—
Chained to the mud, with soul aflame!

Far-off, far-off I hear the moan
Or her immortal music lone:
Though trembling on a mortal throne,
Eternal things are in her tone.
Where never a guiding light has shone,
Deep in the night, the night alone,
Her heart has fathomed the Unknown,
And all she finds, she makes my own.

Dim chantress of the rolling years,
Divinely knelling mortal fears,—
I hearken: and to me appears
The light eternal beauty wears;
My heart the shore immortal nears,
Where sounds, amid the starry spheres,
Such music as the spirit hears
When Love has touched life's Harp of Tears.

I know not how to capture
This fragrant wildwood's rapture,
The magic of these dells
Where silent beauty dwells,
Were noble strength and power
In oak and pine tree tower.
But when from these I come,
I hope to carry home
Some spirit not yet had
To keep me strong and glad,
Something from oak and pine
To be forever mine;
When from these woods I part,
Some wildflower in my heart.

UNSOUGHT TRIBUTE

When the great star had risen,
Night's diadem,
Proud roses thought it would
Shine upon them.
Lilies illustrious
Dreamed that its light
Would be illumining them
Through the long night.

But clouds intervened,—
Oak, elm, pine;
Not on one haughty bloom
Would the star shine.
To what, ere its setting,
Did such splendor yield?
To a field-flower forsaken
In a wild field.

FOUNDERED BULL

Had he been old or loveless or alone!
But O the green meadow where his harem cows
Grazed waitingly! His power overthrown,
Up to his weeping eyes, his pitiful brows
The treacherous sands their sinister battle fought.
The great bull foundered, and his huge bulk sank,
The mire mastering his might,—who sought
The waters of life. But the waters of death he drank.

Had it been night! But shockingly and full
In vivid view was all that he found fair,
Desirable, his, and very beautiful:
Love, life, the shade and sun, the grass and air,
From these he was withdrawn. Though but a bull,
He understood our meaning of despair.

LOITERER

Just where the wood and marshland meet
I linger, for the air is sweet;
And I may hear before I go
The viol of the vireo.

Listening for the flute the plover plays,
I loiter through the reedland's ways;
Or the melodious seashore note
Wild-bubbling from the curlew's throat.

Of dawn's wildrose and lilac mist
The cardinal is lutanist.
The mourning dove's soft dulcimer
Murmurs of love and grief that were.

This orchard oriole's caroling
Has made me late with listening!
Yet I must stay until I've heard
The lyre of the mockingbird.

THE LAW

It makes the mountains bide.
Its rein is on the tide;
And where the far worlds ride
In vasty heaven,—
To lone Arcturus bright,
To Neptune in his might,
Plunging through ancient night,
One law is given.

Deftly the Hand Divine
Lifted the towering pine,
And taught the helpless vine
Clambering grace.
Sea-beach and dell's repose,
River and virgin rose,
In order did dispose,
Each in its place.

Bournes of the sunset far
Under the evening star,
Glens where the kalmia
Blushes alone,—
Rapt spirit-lands withdrawn,
Deep sources of the dawn,
Hills with mist-mantles on,
One law have known.

To its almighty wand
Wildflowers and worlds respond;
And human hearts are bond
Unto its might,—
Whose purpose is to bless,
Whose strength is gentleness,
Whose hand is a caress,
Whose word is light.

Through it all Truth is taught;
By it all joy is brought;
All striving comes to naught
With it at war;
And it abides, although
All else to dust shall go.
Be still, O heart, and know
Love is the Law.

GRAY HERALDS

Though the hillsides harbor snows,
Every heart wild gladness knows
As northward through the misty night
The clanging chorus goes.
Ranging through the vaulted deep,
Gray battalions grandly sweep
Through the fields of stars and azure,
Up the glimmering stairs of sleep.

Fog-mysterious village lights
Turn them from their tingling heights
As over house and garden pass
The dark bewildered flights,—
Bringing news of bursting vines,
Roses, myrtles, jessamines,
Southshore springtime, far green glimpses
Of bright bayoux fringed with pines.

Valiantly the streaming wedges
Graze the wild moon's icy edges.
By tomorrow they'll be sporting
In the Athabascan sedges!
Daring trumpeters who bring
Summons to the heart to sing;
For they van the march triumphant
Of the legions of the spring.

ORATORIO

It seems that everywhere I turn
Of some new melody I learn,
Hearing wild minstrelsy awake
From tree and dew-bespangled brake.
Across the marshes stretching free
A redwing's whistling, O-gl-ee.
A little wren, of his delight,
Is caroling with main and might.
Where emerald field and forest meet,
A bobwhite's whistling clear and sweet.
A chat is chuckling at his joke;
A thrasher chants high in an oak
His aria from the topmost spire.
An oriole leads the orchard choir.
A blithe lark serenades the meadows;
A woodtrush gives from dusky shadows
Eternity an utterance.
A cardinal's lilting of romance.
A robin trills his roundelay.
A dove is mourning far away.
A harper's harping in the wood—
A veery, voicing solitude;
While from the misty, fading hill
Laments a phantom whippoorwill.
Deep in the dark the heaven stirs
With dim, mysterious trumpeters.
It seems that everywhere I go
I hear an oratorio.

My cardinal, forgetting
How far my music's fled,
Upon a flame-azalea sings
Love-songs above my Dead.

FAIRIES IN OUR GARDEN

Yonder, see the fairies
Twinkling in the foxgloves,
Glittering in the cyclamen,
Bleeding in the bleeding heart,
Flickering in the wild phlox,
Sparkling in the larkspur,
Shimmering in the hyacinth,
Dawning in the dahlias,
Shining in the bluebells,
Glinting in the violets,
Gleaming in the rosebay,
Flaring in the trumpet-vine,
Glimmering in the moonflower.

Roguish, they are everywhere!
Tripping through the honeysuckle,
Leaning from the ladyslippers,
Swaying in the columbines,
Climbing in the morning-glories;
Romping, pert and dapper,
In the amaryllis,
Frisking under daisies,
Pirouetting gaily,
Dancing in the daffodils,
Skipping on the water-lilies,
Swinging from the lotus-blooms,
Beckoning from forget-me-nots.

Listen to the fairies
Playing on their elf-harps
High in the jewel-weeds;
Blowing on their elf-horns
From the yellow jasmine;
Laughing from the pansies,
Singing from lobelias;
In the snowy cascades
Of the chaste syringa
Caroling, caroling;
Lilting in the laurels,
Merry in the marigolds,
In the rose rejoicing!

WOOD VIOLETS

By the home avenue,
Shadowed by vines,
Gleaming with dreams and dew,
Perfumed by pines,
Fair in this woodland old
Young beauty shines.

Here the wood-violets
Radiant rise,
Turn toward the fathomless
Blue of the skies
All the deep azure of
Fathomless eyes.

From the mold's midnight dead
By the dim road
Here the wood-violets
Lift through the sod
Beauty most mystical,
Brimming with God.

So near is He, the wood
Trembles with grace;
And now for joy is still
In His embrace:
Loveliness is His form,
Beauty, His face.

In my heart every voice
Of hate is dumb;
In my heart Love's sweet voice
Cries, "He is come!"
So near is He, my heart
Might be His home.

Ah, but I sought Him far!
Vain ways I've trod.
He's in the violets,
Here by the road.
Beauty is everywhere
Giving us God.

ALLIES

Imperious and dreadful need had I
For friends to meet my foemen in the gate.
I sought in nature whosoe'er was great;
As henchmen, whosoe'er had valor high.
Of granite bastions, shouldering out the sky,
Aid I implored against my imminent fate;
Brave hills beheld my want importunate,
And forest giants heard my rallying cry.

But solitary with my foes malign
I found myself. No armed and shaggy oak,
No darkly splendid monumental pine,
No hero mountain to my rescue woke . . .
But when your little hand was laid on mine,
All, all my enemies fell at a stroke!

EDEN AGAIN

The fairy fingers of the rain
Came tapping on my window-pane.
The rose beneath my window-sill
Trembled in beauty, and was still.
Loudly, at lulling of the shower,
My clock kept arguing the hour.
Then suddenly, in quiet awe,
A wonder in the heavens I saw:
An elfin gleam of azure sky
As narrow as a needle's eye.
Then all the clouds were swept away
As darkness is at break of day.
Once more wild birds were on the wing,
Their joyous carols choiring.
Miraculously after rain
The earth was Eden once again.

43

GREAT SMOKIES

Always to me
The Great Smoky Mountains
Are like a mad and monstrous sea,
Are like a massive wild ocean
That suddenly
Has lost all motion.
They are fabulously tall frozen fountains.
The valleys, mist-filled,
Abruptly were stilled;
The crests of the thundering waves
Became silent as ancient graves.
In a moment of day or of night
All the tumult was muted;
The might
Of the wild-maned sea-breakers,
The plunging shore-shakers,
The wrath and the roar of the deep
Fell asleep;
Fell asleep in a storm at its height,
Fell asleep for all darkness and light;
And hence do these mountains seem
Like a turbulent sea in a dream;
Like a vision stayed,
For immortality arrayed.
The massively pagan, primeval
Valley and hill,
With tormented breast
Must have found rest;
Must have heard
The Word,
"Peace, be still!"

INTRUSION

I did not know that,
Moldering in the Cambodian jungle far away,
In the ruined temple of Ankhor-Vat,
Two huge hamadryads,
Slithering and lush,
Had made their secret mating-place;
And that this was their time to be alone,
Creating life, permitting none to come.
Terrible and sublime,
Lethal and vigilant,
With sex their religion,
Against the world they held their wild love-home.

The fault was mine.
Mortal and ignorant, I intruded
Into this sacred serpent-shrine.
The furious female, outraged,
Lashed amain.
There was no need for her to strike again.
I barely saw that venomous face and flat;
Yet because of it, even to this very day,
I lie far, far away
In lonely Ankhor-Vat,—
While quite beyond my sight,
In the jungle night
The glimmering huge hamadryads
Perform their secret and their sacred rite.

BLUE GROSBEAK

Among my cardinals to feed,
A blue imperial bird has come,
A stranger, lovely and in need.
I think it must be far from home.

I never saw this bird before.
This alien I had never met.
Although I may not see him more,
His beauty I shall not forget.

How often to the heart arrives
Some loveliness we had not known;
Nor can we guess how Fate contrives
To make that loveliness our own.

THE DREAMING MAST

He towered to the tempest and the sun
A hundred years upon the mountain-crest;
Was tinged with silver when the day begun,
Stood black against the blazing of the west;
Then from his blue imperial throne was taken
To be the mainmast for a vessel proud;
To be by alien winds and thunders shaken,
To bear the canvas and the straining shroud.

High in the heavens, soaring dark and strong,
Conferring with the clouds and with the stars,
He hears the waves as his lost forest song;
And when the moonbeams sleep along the spars,
He dreams, while swaying o'er the lonely foam,
That he is rocking in his mountain home.

THE GARDEN I MADE

Whenever I think of
Life's lights that must fade,
The gleam and the glow
That must pass into shade;
When hopes that I had
Now but leave me afraid—
With joy I remember
The garden I made.

The redbuds and dogwoods
I planted will grow;
The flaming azaleas
Will blossom, I know;
The chaliced syringa's
Wild beauty will snow
When I shall be one with
The long, long ago.

The glimmering gardenias,
The wildflowers wan,
The red rose, the lily
As white as a swan:
The garden I made
Will keep blossoming on
When life with its fevers
Is faded and gone.

OLD BUCK

Now hound and horn are silent,
And the pines roll like the sea,
The old buck of Wambaw
Still wanders wild and free.
The hunters have gone home at last.
They had to let him be.

His royal diadem is yet
Rained on by morning dews.
Upon his tawny rack the pine
Her whispering needles strews.
About him is the woodland's peace,
And over him, the blue's.

Wild lover of the wilderness,
Your magic to enfold,
The myrtles draw their curtains close,
And occult oak-trees old.
The hickory hangs upon your horns
Tributes of tattered gold.

Your eyes are full of quietness
Now that the hunt is gone.
Tranquil you pace the moonlit trails,
Mysterious and wan.
Your antlers give the questing stars
Beauty to sparkle on.

THE OLD GARDEN

I have loved since dewy childhood
That old garden of the wildwood
Where the woodbine weeps its wonder,
And the stargrass glints thereunder.
There the vagrant violet's glowing.
And the random lily's snowing . . .
Shadow-winged the wood-winds move,
Fragrant as the thought of love.
With the charm of disarray
Accidental lures waylay.
By Man's diligence unmarred
Magic ways are blossom-barred.
In her sunlit boudoir dreaming,
Unadorned, with tresses streaming,
In her negligee reclining,
Innocence about her shining,
Beauty, past the range of art,
Captives my joyous heart.
In that garden wild and olden
Jasmines blow their trumpets golden,
While the silvery silence listens
Where the lustral live-oak glistens.
Unofficial, gay, unordered,
Careless trails are blossom-bordered . . .
Glad neglect begets a grace
That the spirit can embrace.
Astral wood-lights, gleaming wan,
Tinge the leaves they linger on.
There the bee in blooms carouses,
And the wild buck bells and browses
Where the dewdrops hang delicious
From the sweet-bay's cup capricious.
Vistas dim, with views disheveled,
Grass uncut and paths unleveled,
Tress that trespass, wilds untrod . . .
And the gardener is God.

A SANTEE MOONRISE

Gloom, and the glamour of night,
The purple, imperial night,
The black and powerful night!
Hushed are the fields and the woods,
And the river's song is of rest.
God, what a moment divine,
Expectant of heavenly things!
And now with a silence that swoons
In the arms of ineffable love,
The empress-queen of the air,
The goddess divine of the dark,
Arrives to a worshipping world.
Behold what in beauty is wrought
By the touch of the lovely light,
By the mystical wand of the moon.
The bush and the briar and clod,
By daylight obscure and unknown,
Unlovely and heartless,—lo, now,
In virginal marble are wrought,
Are statued in lily-white stone!
The earth is transfigured; the moon
Has builded the world in a dream
Of silver and silence and soul.
Bosomed in yonder grove
Of live-oaks majestic and old,
Still stands the house that I love.
And the moonlight is streaming down
In splendors that soften the lines
Of time and of sorrow and care.
Old House, old House that I love,
Old Human Heart, thou hast heard
In the far dead night of the Past,
Where the moonlight of memory gleams,
The voices now stilled to the world,
The songs that are hushed and forgot.

A SANTEE SUNRISE

Sweet to the Santee fields
The lovely morning is come;
And in the Santee woods
The light, on awakening trees,
Hallows the fragrant scene.
Those, the pines, that arise
Purple and misty and grand,
That all through the darkness have sung,
To soundings of cymbals and horns,
By triumphs of trumpets and tongues,
The hymns of the human heart,
They are illumined with light,
And sing to the rising sun.
Far on the river, the tide
Sleeps, and the winds are at rest . . .
Soft from the shadowy south,
Still dim in the twilight of dawn,
The roll of the surf-line is heard.
Here where the jasmine flowers,
Tossing her fountains of bloom;
Here where the mockingbird sings,
And the bullgrape blossoms; and here
Where love is born and abides;
Where those who loved me have lived,
And those who love me shall die;
There would I be till the Night
Engulfs me. And if I am borne,
Delivered from dark by a dawn,
Home to as lovely a land,
Home to the hearts that I love,
Verily, death shall be well.

MY COUNTRY

If in my songs the note of grief is heard,
The sound of evening bells and elegies,
Melodies by moonlight of the mockingbird,
The night-wind in the dim and dreaming trees,—
My voice is of my Country. I was born
By sorrowful fair shores, that in the arms
Of visions sleep, far, magical, forlorn,
Mourned by the beauty of pines and oaks and palms

You do not hear me singing. But you hear
The twilight wind through myrtle, bay, and pine;
The mystery of marshes wide and drear;
The golden bells of the lustrous jasmine-vine;
The grieving loveliness that live-oaks wear;
The wildwood where the sad lost moonbeams shine.

TRIBUTE

Whenever I hear the holy hymn
Of the wood-thrush in the pinewood dim,
Or on the dusky dewy hill
Or in the mystic glen apart,
Or by the shadowy fragrant rill,
Music that makes my arid heart
With flowery wildwood beauty brim,
Transmuting into song
All love, all loveliness for which I long,
That can celestial hopes fulfil,
The only praise I can convey,
The only tribute I can pay
Is to be still,
Is to be still!

SUSTAINED

Love is a wild mysterious miracle.
None can explain it.
When all that stands seems trembling to fall,
Love can sustain it.

FUTILITY

Though she let him have her beauty,
He rose famished from that feast.
Giving love as a sad duty,
Of all lovers, she was least.

I CALL YOU

I call you all day long, and in the night;
Make your name known to darkness and to light.
And I shall tell you in death's final sleep,
Whatever it is the deep says to the deep.

THIS IS WHY

This is why I think you Heaven:
By the beauty of the given
I discern and I discover
All the beauty of the giver.

PLANTATION TWILIGHT

In the blue vase that is the sky
The sunset rose is drooping;
From fragrant misty fastnesses
The shadowy deer come trooping;
From glimmering swamps I hear the owls—
Night's phantom huntsmen—whooping.

A stranger in these haunted wilds
Might wander lorn, half-frighted;
But they are home to me . . . That scent
Is jasmine, dew-delighted;
Yon ghostly blossom is a bay,
Sweet as young love requited.

That shimmer on the live-oak leaves?
A moonbeam's deftly slanting;
That lonely and sardonic bark?
A gray fox, idly ranting;
That murmuring of mystic harps ?
The pines their vespers chanting.

I love the home-woods deep and still,
And full of wonder dreaming;
Above their dewy sleep the stars
Like seraphim are streaming;
But best I love the wildwood's end,
And yonder home-light's gleaming !

THE DRUMMER'S DRUM

Do you hear the drumming of the drummer's drum?
Far from their hillside-home the throbbings come:
Dim blue distances a voice have found,
Silent solitudes a speech profound.
Autumn's glamour in that tone is told,
Vocal its mystery and gleaming gold;
Haunting rapture by a rune is caught,
Wildwood beauty by the breezes brought.

Winy fragrances from falling leaves,
Bright dew-drenchings that the wood receives,
Odors from the hickory, the ash, the oak,
Mist-wreaths winding through the trees like smoke,
What is the language that can now express
All this loneliness and loveliness?
All its meaning unto you will come
When you hear the drumming of the drummer's drum.

Life has for every heart a Neverland,
Another country, an unreached strand;
A Face unfound as yet, for all our search;
Some far happiness beyond our reach.
But in the autumntide our hearts are brought
Close to that Luring Land that all have sought,
Close to the capture of its love we come
When we hear the drumming of the drummer's drum.

EARTH

How wonderful is earth!
This soil of precious worth!
Though gold be gold, it has no life to give;
But in the furrow dark
There waits a vital spark
That whispers to the seed, "Awake and live!"

Sunsets and dawns of bloom
Rise from that rayless gloom,
And thence the Oak receives his massive crown;
The timid wilding Flower,
Frail fairy of an hour,
From dust has made her artful, artless gown.

Far in that night profound,
Each tree its fruit has found,
Each season draws from dust its treasures still.
In happy flower and tree
Dust utters joyously
A language of eternal tone and will.

Toiler beneath the sod
O Worker calm with God
In grandeur of a silent, vast design;
In lifting Life to light
Out of an ancient night,
Love's purpose in the human heart is thine!

FLOWER-SONGS

In ballads blithe, in triolets,
In rondels and in carols free,
Pansies and pinks and violets
Sing of their love and liberty,
Their joy to blossom and to be.

With many a startled lovely glance,
For fear some stranger's listening,
Faint elfin songs of wood-romance,
When dewy glades are glimmering,
The wayward little wild-flowers sing.

The daffodils like dancing fays
Their mirth in laughing lyrics tell;
The rose her royal self arrays
In tints of tone that breathe and swell
To melodies majestical.

The stately light-crowned lilies raise
Serenely to celestial tunes,
Their heavenly hymns of holy praise;
While, humbly glad, the clover croons
A hundred simple sunny runes.

If happy be the heart you bear
As 'mong these faces fair you rove,
Their mystic music you will hear,
Their beauty as you bend above,
If you will listen with your love.

A CAROLINA WREN

The virginal white morning comes,
And in her gleaming beauty glows;
Then through the dewy garden roams
All radiant from rose to rose.

The pure morn glorifies the scene;
Ah, what more sweet could morning bring
Than yonder Carolina wren
Just caroling and caroling!

Oh, carol, Carolina Wren!
The gray oaks waken in the gold
Of sunrise, and the river-fen
Is silver-misted as of old.

Upon a cedar post where climbs
A jasmine vine, he sits and sings
Of happy hearts and happy times
Till all the mellow woodland rings.

Oh, carol, Carolina Wren,
And bring the blue in and the bright;
Bring back lost beauty; oh, and then
Sing all the world to love and light!

I am where pain has never been,
And all my joys awake and sing
With yonder Carolina Wren
Just caroling and caroling!

THE TORRENT'S HEART

Beside the foaming wrack of this wild stream,
Through whose torn beauty tawny rainbows gleam,
Rapt at the roaring torrent's brink I pause to dream.

How brawling, senseless, madly rushing by!
Not pausing to embrace the sweetheart sky
Whose gorgeous blue and stars might on that bosom lie.

But here a tiny tinkling rivulet breaks
O'er the low bank; its shining path it takes
Through the lustrous grass that in its running silver shakes.

Barriers in miniature before it stand:
Singing it conquers minute bars of sand,
While lyric elfin seas break on a fairy strand.

Ah, messenger of mercury that steals
Sparkling along, your purity reveals
The troubled torrent's heart,—and Life's true nature seals;

For, from earth's chaos, fierce and rushing wild,
We turn away; till thoughtfully beguiled
By some pure human heart, tranquil and undefiled.

Though sometimes dark and sad existence flows,
Its soul is pure, though grim its tumult goes;
And one fair heart its truth and beauty can disclose;

A heart whose strength was from Life's torrent drawn;
A heart in whom the light of love is born;
And in whose grace Life's griefs and grievances are gone.

THE SEA IN THE SKY

The sea in the cloudless sky,
Blue, blue the waters lie;
And the hours tremble on
After the trembling dawn.

The sea in the stormy sky,
Dark roll the waves and high;
With the far surf heaving white
On the shadowy edge of night.

The sea in the midnight sky,
Light after light on high;
The wide track stretching free,
And the starry ships on the sea.

The sea in the sunset sky,
Where the gorgeous billows die;
In cloudy ranks they come
Plunging to twilight foam.

FIRST AID

Take your pharmacy away!
Only let me smell the bay,
Or the dew upon the pine,
And my strength once more is mine.
All the medicine I crave
Is to watch the myrtles wave
Where the morning flushes wide
O'er the gleaming forest-side.
Like the children of the wild,
I am truly nature's child . . .
Send no doctor to my aid;
Send me to the jasmine-glade,
To the sunlight and the rain;
They will love away my pain.

VAST EMPIRE

Let me not envy those
Who heap their treasures high;
My realm is wide and deep.
Let me but love a rose,
Or a blue reach of sky,
And it is mine to keep.

The mountain and the main,
The shaggy forest old
Are mine for loving them.
And mine the glimmering plain,
The sunset's fount of gold,
The stars, dark's diadem.

The birds' pure wildwood songs
Are of my wealth a part,
Misfortune to beguile.
Beauty to him belongs
Who holds it in his heart,
Worshiping all the while.

WITHHELD

Since all the joy of earth to me
Is what your love can yield,
I think the bliss of Heaven must be
What you withheld.

From wonder to new wonder Adam strayed,
To all the bliss of Eden strange, naïve,
Discovering his superb astonishment
In the incredible mystery of Eve.

61

THE SILENT HILLS

Out of the silent hills
Of God I came to be.
Their breath my being fills,
Mountains that cradled me.
I with their strength am strong,
Whose music is my song.

Deep in earth's silent hills,
From flower and rock and sod,
I drew the peace that stills;
Where never a man had trod,
I found my faith in God,
And joy in the forest old
For which I gave no gold.

Since Heaven takes my part,
And God is fast my friend,
Hope never leaves my heart;
With joy my life I spend.
Faith keeps me to the end—
To sleep, whene'er God wills,
Deep in His silent hills.

HILLCREST PINE

By all comrades long forsaken,
By the storm and thunder shaken,
He a grim deep root has taken.

Him the wintry blasts discover;
But the wild moon is his lover;
Close to him the white stars hover:

Silent, stark, eternal token
Of the anguish kept unspoken,
Of the will that is not broken.

This the stars in heaven divining,
Their tall thrones of light resigning,
For a crown on him are shining.

62

AFTER RAIN

After rain, after rain,
Earth is Eden once again!
Wafted wildrose fragrances
Breathe about the lands and skies.
All the flowers now are leveled,
In delicious grief disheveled,
See the bluet's fairy pain,
Prisoned in a drop of rain;
Elfin woe the violet has,
Bent beneath a blade of grass;
Plumes of herdsgrass waving proud
O'er the simple clover crowd
Are in humble beauty bowed.
These the light shall soon release
Into airy grace and peace.
Flaring through red clouds, the sun
Over high fields seems to run;
Drenchèd flower and misty grass
Upward look to see him pass;
Dewy daisies glint and shine,
Eyes of innocence divine!
Winy colors flush the wold,
Amber, amethyst, and gold;
Softly gleams the jeweled wood.

And my spirit is renewed
Out of dust and heat, to know
Life as sweet as long ago;
Out of weariness to feel
Strength to toil, and grace to kneel
Unto Him who, after rain,
Walks His garden once again.

Just a bubble of Joy,
Just a hinting of Wit,
Just a jot of Delight,
And a Flirting of whit;
Just an elf of a dream,
And of Daring a dash;
Of Fleeting a pause,
And of Fancy a flash;
The shimmer of brilliance
When lightning delays;
A glimpse of the faerie
Far country of fays;
The wildflower's beauty
That dimples and glows;
The sheen of the dewdrop
That glints on the rose;
The whisk of an arrow
Barbed brighter than mirth;
A tiny sweet song
In the music of earth;
The thin flame of Fire,
Of Light the quick beam,
Of Stars the shy sparkle,
Of Rainbows the gleam;
A lingering moment
Of Flight's thrilling pace,
When sudden-caught color
Lends Beauty its grace;
The glimmer of sunrays,
Of moonbeams the glance,
A smile on the face
Of a child of Romance;
Of Laughter a sprinkle,
Of Speed a bright dart;
Nature's tremulous whim
From her coquettish heart!

KNEELING BRIDE

Though I had heard her music wild,
It blended so with sylvan runes
Sung by the forest undefiled,
All sang the selfsame tunes.
Then suddenly on her I came,
Crowned with a coronet of sky;
On either hand the wildflowers wept,
A noble watch the dark pines kept.
Some say she's but a waterfall.
Far through the hills you hear her call,
Where wild and beautiful and white
She sings to God in her delight.
In her I see (such is my feeling)
A bride before the altar kneeling.

THE SECRET

In the heart of the wildwood
Is a secret known to three:
To the heart of the wildwood,
To you, and to me.

My darkness never is of night,
Through loss of sun or moon or star.
The absence to me of all light
Is not in being where you are.

TOILING ROOTS

Groping dimly underground,
They laid hold on nature's veins;
Strength for life they sought and found.
Not the sun or silver rains
Thus could make that life abound.

Yonder slender-shafted pine,
Soaring steep against the sun;
Yonder lissome jessamine,
Rioting where waters run,
Out of dust they are divine.

Yonder powerful oak and old,
Silvered by the morning light,
Wrought by sunset into gold,
Far beneath him in the night,
Toil his makers in the mold.

Locked from light and happy air,
They have never seen a star;
Shut from lovely things and rare,
Dark their habitations are . . .
Yet through them our world is fair.

INDIAN SUMMER PEACE

Strange is this hush of nature. Fast asleep
Are fields and woods. The marshes drowse and dream.
Calm is the shore. Untroubled is the deep.
Wings of the wind fold on the quiet stream.
Both life and time seem resting on their oars.
Love is becalmed upon a halcyon sea,
And anchors there. The mountains and the moors
Are tranquil as in immortality.

Quiescent rests the world in tranced repose,
Existence standing still, as if suspended,
Or gently come to an eternal close.
Fearing is now forgotten; hoping, ended.
All slumbers in enchantment past belief,
Deep as the massive peace of finished grief.

66

THE BELATED BEE

Though the beacon-stars the azure coasts illumine,
As the sunset-fires smoulder into gloom,
Here beside the twilight path
In the chilly aftermath,
There's a bee still honey-buried in a bloom!

See, you burly-bodied, golden-sided rover,
Though the lacy mist is mantling on the clover,
Here unheedingly you drone
Joyous labor's monotone,
Though the day is done and all its toil is over.

Soon, emerging, do you think that you can find
Glimmering pathways, howeward-leading down the wind?
Will you blunder through the dark,
Or is yonder winking spark
Of the firefly for your guidance clear designed?

Ah, adventurer! How blithely did you roam!
From the waves of flowers gathering **fragrant foam**,
Toiling happy till the night . . .
Will a better guide than light
Now across the darkened country lead you home?

—Well, perchance God's Night will find me toiling so:
Rapt, unwilling well-loved labor to forego;
While on life's broad landscape fair
Comes a darkness unaware,
And my pathway lies through shades no man can know.

May I then beneath life's deeply-darkened dome,
Face with singing heart the twilight that has come;
Grasp a Hand, in that great need,
Better than all lights to lead,
That will guide me through the darkness safely Home!

IN APRIL

Beryl-green the cypresses,
And the poplar's shimmering spire;
Even the ancient live-oak trees
Gleam in emerald flame and fire,
Glow in April ecstasies.

In the lonely woods of pine,
Rapt in sunlight of the spring,
Though they never wrote a line,
Lofty pine-tree poets sing
Lyrics human and divine.

And the far-hid jassamines
Feel the mystic summoning;
Over the hollies, myrtles, pines,
Satin stars of saffron cling
To rich tapestries of vines.

And within a garden fair,
Where the flowers are impearled,—
Less of earth than of the air,
Walks the April of my world,
With a red rose in her hair.

NEAREST GOD

We have been taught that God is love,
O Beautiful, Beloved, and True!
And I am always nearest God
When I am nearest you.

THE RED-WINGED BLACKBIRD

Down in the meadow where the blue flags grow,
Down where the reeds stand tall,
There's a woven nest in the marshes green
Where the mallow blossoms fall.
Over it a blackbird floats and sings,
Bubbling his liquid glee;—
There is no voice more blithe to sing
Such meadow-minstrelsy.

For the red-winged blackbird's singing, O-gl-ee, O-gl-ee.
And the oriole is listening from the misty elm tree;
In those rich notes are blended songs of love and liberty,
When the red-winged blackbird carols, O-gl-ee.

Crimson his epaulets, sable his coat,
Martial is his noble mien;
Like a Lord of the Marches he rules the strand,
And happy is his reign.
Now on a lithe reed swaying low,
Now on a green-plumed tree,
This prince in black from the watery bournes
Is calling liquidly:

For the red-winged blackbird's whistling, O-gl-ee, O-gl-ee:
And the locust blooms are falling from the fragrant bridal
        tree;
Across the limpid landscape of the marshlands stretching free
The red-winged blackbird's fluting, O-gl-ee.

Wood thrushes sing in the deep pine copse,
Robins from the trees of the lawn,
And from far fields asleep in mist
A bobwhite's calling dawn.
But ever the red-wing tells his joy
In a lustral music free;
Of all the murmuring watery marsh
He is the voice to me.

For the red-winged blackbird's singing, O-gl-ee, O-gl-ee;
While the landscape sad and beautiful and wonderful to see
Seems built by that sweet music as a Paradise would be,
As the red-winged blackbird carols, O-gl-ee.

RIDING HOME

After scented summer rain,
We are riding home again,
And the flaring shafts of sunset
Light us down the woodland lane;
Here the myrtle and the bay,
Drenched with dewy-tasseling spray,
Gleam a welcome to us riding
At the ending of the day.

Breathes the sea-wind, warm and sweet,
Where the misty marshes meet
With the lowlands, dumb and couchant,
At the listening forest's feet;
Birds and songs with day are fled,
But the heavens overhead
A mild immortal music
From their silver silence shed.

Here the fragrant emerald oak
Trembles into airy smoke,
And the shadowed copse is shimmering
As though its soul awoke;
With her flowery bosom bare,
And the sunset in her hair,
Nature paces through the pinewood
In the azure evening air.

So, at last we're home again,
Riding after summer rain!
Home! the glimmering house expectant
Down the lamp-starred village lane,
Home! the happy, happy sight;
Home! with laughter, love, and light;
Home! to take us and to keep us
From the dim engulfing night.

Nature's lovely,—and to her
Radiant raptures minister;
And her beauty is pure beauty,
There can none be lovelier;
But the charm of Nature's art
Can, with fading light, depart;
But the love of home and kindred
Is eternal in the heart.

LITTLE LINDSAY

When you left your lovely home
In the heavens, to earth to come,
Little Lindsay, pansy-eyed,
Seraphs were dissatisfied,
And the holy angels cried.
For they love you, and have lent you,
And with joyous pride have sent you
To make beautiful our days
With your deep beguiling ways;
To make mystical the night,
Being of our dark the light.
And the angels who are weeping
All for love of one they miss,
On the nightwind pray us this:
"Hold her in your tenderest keeping,
Our cherub, come from Bliss."
And for loneliness God sighed
When you came with us to bide,
Little Lindsay, pansy-eyed.

From out of the secret mountain deeps my yearning soul
    was drawn,
I flow through violet valleys, and by languorous
    leagues of lawn,
In the beauty of the mountains in the dusk and in the
    dawn.

There I saw the far blue mountains in the visionary
    west,
Saw the mist upon the mountains in the opal evening
    west,
Saw the clouds that labor for me o'er the mountains'
    misty crest.

Then I journey through the midland where the cotton's
    in the boll,
Where the stalwart rustling corn-ranks, like an army
    past control,
March down upon my margin where my waters softly
    roll.

(Once I saw my queenly City, when the foe had stormed
    the gate;
Saw my proud, defenceless City, in the brutal hands of
    fate,
And the land cried out for mercy on Columbia, desolate.

But the ocean ever calls me in a solemn undertone,
Past the mountains, past the meadows where the waving
    willows shone,
Past many a pine and cypress standing sentinel alone.

And so I reach the Delta in the quiet closing day;
Through the reaches of the ricefields, stretching
    mistily away,
I go as a grey spirit through a throng of spirits
    grey:

By the sweet plantations old, where the silence seems
    to fold
Forms of Beauty in caresses with a love that is not
    told,
By the faces that are sleeping, by the hearts so dim
    and cold.

O the places that I passed, and the pictures that I
    glassed,
And the loveliness I mirrored ere I came to rest at
    last,
From Waterhon to Wicklow, and from Wicklow to the
    coast.

There was Hampton on the shore, white and stately as
    of yore,
Seen glimmering through a vista as of years long
    gone before;
Then the desolate Montgomery of those who come no
    more.

Then Fairfield on the high bluff where my waters
    gather wide,
With Navarino Island just across the yellow tide,
With the Wedge and Harrietta gazing from the
    southern side.

Then the ruined Eldorado, the monument to those
For whom no longer flame the stars, nor any lily
    blows,
Nor any flower of summer lands, nor any Southern
    rose:

Though the voices of its loved ones the haunted past
    enshrines
With the broken years of childhood and the light that
    dimly shines,
Yet I hear their voices echo in the music of the pines.

By night I reach the coast-line, wih its myriad creeks
    and bays;
Where the dark palmettoes gather, and the blasted
    cedars gaze,
Lone watchers ever by the deep's tremendous thunderways.

And so unto the ending of my journey do I come,
The sea-wind blowing softly o'er the heaving midnight
    foam;
Within those luminous waters far, my spirit finds its
    home.

HOME

As the azure is to the eagle,
As to the ship the sea,
As to the deer the wildwood,
So are you home to me.

MY HEAVEN

This is why I think you Heaven:
By the beauty of the given,
I discern and I discover
All the beauty of the giver.

EAGLE

It was a simple thing, yet memorable,
And had great power to uplift my heart.
To the lone reedland of the Santee Delta
A storm was coming, a West Indian gale,
With lunatic fringe of shaggy clouds of doom;
And I was on the Delta shooting ducks
When this wild tempest from the ocean came.
Green-bosomed, ashen-lipped it landward screamed,
As furious as a comet in his course.
Before it was pale darkness; under it
A sinister night. The marsh fell flat before it,
And ancient trees shuddered and plunged to death.
Now from the terror of its wild approach
Long regiments of mallards, scaup, and teal,
Herons and vultures, and wide panic flights
Of shorebirds up the shrouded river streamed
Incontinently. Even the gross-billed waders
Fled for the forest,—the moss-hung mouldering
    swamps
That mourn in majesty. There they could hide.
Fearful myself, I watched the fugitives
Dismayed and in disorderly retreat.
But at the height of all this rout and ruin
An old bald eagle that all day had cruised
Far up the river, over the river-swamps,
Appeared against the havoc of the sky,
Mightily heading homeward. Home to him
Was a majestic pine on Cedar Island,
At the dim Delta's farthest southern bound.
With all else abject, with the storm itself
Wild-ramping northward, southward and solitary,
Against the ominously deepening danger,
As if a spirit with immortal strength,
The lordly eagle held his splendid course
Into the raging hurricane. I looked on Valor
Till, at the last, far vanished from my vision,
It came to be a glory to my heart
Forever. For a hero I had seen
As he in the hour of trial best performs,
Amid the whirlwinds of annihilation,
The lonely miracle of dauntlessness.

WATCHERS

In the bushes, in the grasses,
In the gleaming marsh-morasses,
There are eyes that glow and glisten;
There are elfin ears that listen;
If the wind be tainted ever,
There are noses all a-quiver;
Little feet are poised for fleeting;
Tiny timid hearts a-beating . . .
Watchers, wary watchers these,
In the broomgrass, in the trees,
In the sky's serenest blue,
From the baybush peering through;
In the waters' silence deep,
Wakeful in the flowers asleep.
Watchers, wary watchers they,
Swift in flight and swift to stay;
In gay blossoms lying gay,
In the green bush crouching green,
In all radiances unseen;
Than the silence e'en more still;
Stealing like the noiseless rill,
Ever vanishing are they,
Swift in flight, and swift to stay . . .
Wary watchers, fear not me;
For I love your liberty.

OUR LAND

We do not love our land because
Her might can mold all human fate.
Her power has its source in us:
It is our love that makes her great.

CAMEO

Here genius gathered universal grace,
Compelling all the ages to be terse,
Bringing into the beauty of one face
The flowering gardens of the universe.

INHERENT

God sleeps in the stone,
And He dreams in the tree;
He stirs in the brute,
And He wakens in me.

Even in light without you I am lost;
And I would know that all my life were **done**
If in the dark I turned to touch your **hand**
And found that you were gone.

A CARDINAL

Gray from the oaks the mosses hung,
Green from the pine the grape;
Between them flashed a crested flame,
A thrilling lyric shape.
It was the happy cardinal
With crystal-ringing voice,
Whose music summoned all the world
To listen and rejoice.

The red-bud trees were leafing out,
The swamps were all a-shimmer
With twinkling gleams of coming green;
Soft did the live-oaks glimmer
With emerald tints that lustrous shone
Like jewels of a dream;—
'Twas then the cardinal would sing
Above the wandering stream.

He used to mount the topmost twig
Of the tallest tupelo tree,
And flushed by dawn to deeper rose
He sang of love to me;
He sang of purity and grace,
Of life and love and light,
Of hours of tender happiness
And innocent delight.

He loved the birchen thicket grey,
The hollies' safe retreat;
But height and spacious skyward views
Lured forth his music sweet.
When blue and gold the east had flushed,
He mounted from the gloom
Where he could breathe the dawn, could watch
The flowers of sunrise bloom.

The cardinal! The cardinal!
How long ago it seems
That joyous music rang,—how dim
Those far-off springtime gleams:—

O yet when I remember them,
Life's wintry cares depart;—
A cardinal, a cardinal
Is singing in my heart!

NOCTURNE

My heart sets with the sun. But, oh, full soon
With tender-tinted mysteries.

Now all the valley in a lilac light
Lies dreaming in quiescent dim delight.

Charmed by the valley's thoughtful peace profound,
The blue hills seem to gather closer round.

All fragrance shy is fainting to the moon;
Delicious dreams toward her broad beauty swoon.

New every bourne in this fair evenfall
Is to immortal magic marginal.

Whence toward the vale has stepped a wooded hill,
Comes the lost cry of the lost whippoorwill.

The moon is maiden in mysterious light,
A virgin glimmering in dewy night.

How close and tender is her sweet caress!
How intimate becomes her loveliness!

With love's own wistful and almighty beams,
Building again the Eden of our dreams!

MIGRANTS

Through the frosty autumn night,
Luminous and lone and bright,
Come the sounds of rushing pinions
And the far soft cries of flight.
Swift beneath the stilly stars,
Wings that sweep like scimitars
Ever speed and ever onward
From the winter's icy bars.

Looming mountains, vast, unknown,
Now are mounted, overflown;
And the misty plains call "Onward!"
Through the starlight watching wan.
Rolling rivers now are crossed,
Rivers rolling to the coast,
And the lordly purple mountains
In vague distances are lost.

Through the windy wild sea-spray,
Where the inlet feeds the bay,
On glimmering bars of tawny sands
Their sweeping course they stay.
There to bask and float at ease,
Or, when flood meets offshore breeze,
To be shrouded in the surf-mist
From the plunging, pounding seas.

And anon, in creek and bay,
Inland they shall find their way
To the gray abandoned ricefields
And the river-reaches gray:
There through waters warm to roam
Till the voice of Love shall come,
And the spring, through azure trumpets,
Calls them northward, calls them home!

Lo, the hour of flight is near,
Beating pinions climb the air,
Through the darkness, through the darkness,
But to them the way is clear:

By the light of knowledge given,
Wide the ancient night is riven:
And no surer guide than Knowing
Is there granted under heaven.

AUTUMN

Where late the wild wood-warblers sang,
The air is silent in these dells;
No more in trembling beauty hang
The fairy chimes of foxglove bells;
In field and forest silence dwells.
And I shall wander forth to see
How Autumn can revealèd be.

Not in the glimmering birches' grace,
Expressing girlhood to my thought;
Not in the rugged hillside's face
Whose strength a thousand seasons wrought;
Nor need she by the streams be sought . . .
She is a sense of joyous rest,
In stately loveliness expressed.

Deep in a dell, suffused and fair
With golden peace,—how calmly sweet,
With scarlet berries in her hair,
Autumn herself at length I meet!
And raying from her far retreat,
I can behold, around, above,
The fruits of all her toil and love.

A duty finished gives her rest;
Her fruitful heart its balm had shed.
Through ponderous portals of the west
With sunset roses garlanded,
In glory she shall soon be led
Divinelier than angel, bright
With dreams fulfilled before the night.

SAVANNA MUSIC

Would you dream that there could be
In this marsh such minstrelsy?
When the dusk with fingers white
Closes curtains of the night,
Veils the faded sunset rose,
Peepers on their piccolos
Start a piping shrill and sweet
Where dim land and water meet;
Tenor, high soprano, alto,
Minor mystical contralto;
From this haunt of hern and loon,
Xylophone and deep bassoon.
On their drums the bullfrogs drum,
And a thousand voices come,
Join in melody to flood
Wild morass and circling wood.

Glimmering bats are now balleting;
All the instruments are playing:
From the lost fen's pale arena,
Concertina, seraphina;
From the occult and unknown
Many a wildwood bugle blown.
Rich harmonicas are humming;
Banjos and guitars are strumming;
Spinet, fife, and basset-horn,
Clarinet and clarion;
Sackbuts sobbing, and the lutes'
Music blending with the flutes';
Universal glad hosannas
Rising from these dark savannas;
And the throbbing shadows bring
Contrabassos bassoing.

Viol, tambourine, and tymbal,
Dulcimer and harp and cymbal,
Trumpet, trombone, tuba blowing,
On the night their songs bestowing;
Clavier and clavichord
With their antique stately word.

This is more than a cantata,
Serenade or love-sonata.
Madrigals from marsh and sedges
Of the minatory edges
Of the misty swamp rejoice
In a transcendental voice,
Praising God in concert moving
For the mighty gift of loving;
Worshipping the Lord of Heaven,
Giving back His music given.

A JESSAMINE

Enshrined in laurel rustlings and perfume
Of myrtle and of pine;
Burning in misty beauty, half concealed,
In odorous dusks that are too sweet for gloom,
Thou, yellow Jessamine,
By thy own fragrance art revealed.

The lustral river knows no loveliness
Like that it takes from thee,
When deeply mirrored in its yearning breast,
Thou liest unconscious in its soft caress,
Unreal and shadowy,
Yet of all love, most holy tenderest.

The longing river bears thy memory far
Through languorous Southern lands:
By cypress shades and billowy leagues of lawn,
All day, all night, until the morning star,
Above the sea-coast sands,
Fades into blue and gold and crimson dawn.

WILDLIFE NOCTURNE

Just when the day and night are meeting
A daytime army is retreating:
Those dusky forms so swift above
The pines are dove on speeding dove.
With elfin step and wary eye,
Roostward the quail go trooping by,
While to their rookery the crows
Follow a course their wisdom knows.
Along the glimmering edge of even
The redwings darken all the heaven.
Clear comes the wood-duck's watery call;
The widgeons' wings are musical
From bracken, marsh, and hedge are heard
The good-night songs of many a bird;
And though the light is dim, their songs
The radiance of the day prolongs.
Long lines of egrets homeward stream
Like angels flying in a dream;
An old wild gobbler takes the air,
Climbing a pine-crest's darksome stair.
An eagle, cruising down the coast,
Is soon in twilight merged and lost.
Save for the veery's astral flute,
The fading, mystic woods are mute.
White ibis pass in snowy flight
Into the dusk . . . And all is night.

Now that the light has been defeated,
And daytime's army has retreated,
Another host, on shadowy wings
On silent steps, the evening brings.
Their ways are all oblivion's,
The tacit, surreptitious ones;
Secret and vanishing, they steal,
Lurking, recondite, and unreal.
Delighting in the occult night,
An owl in swift and muffled flight
Discovers all that's in the dark.
A fox's mordant, rasping bark

Tells that he's ready for a raid
On prey that's followed or waylaid . . .
Still, minatory, silent, grim,
A wildcat crouches on a limb
Above an eerie wildwood trail,
Watching for what he may assail.
Down a wood-path a raccoon rambles;
A wheedling opossum shambles.
One with the thoughtful dark, the deer
Mysteriously disappear.
Veiled and allusive, starlit, wan,
Hour by hour passes on . . .
A heron's calling far away.
Wild bird-songs wake . . . And it is day.

THE MOON AT AJALON

"And the moon stood still at Ajalon"
                    —*The Book of Joshua*

O not more still
Above a hill
Did the moon stand
At God's command
At Ajalon
Than I, when first I saw
Your beauty. Then my awe
Stayed all my motion. And
I still so stand.

THE RETURN

I am on my way at last!
Now the purple pines flit past,
Glimmer now the white road's winding;
And the sweet-bay's fragrant foam;
Beckon now the past and far,
And I journey where they are
Though the ivory April moonlight
On the road that leads me home.

Long the years were, dim and strange;
They have brought us death and change;
Sighing have we seen the red rose
Falling, and the morning fade.
And loved faces, sweet and brave,
Gently gliding toward the grave,
Leaving all our world in darkness,
Leaving Love's own heart afraid.

Here the shadowy tupelo tall
Guards the swamp's menacing wall,
Here the owl whoops, and the nighthawk;
But the night is fair and still,
And the ghastly Scrub Oak Hill
I have passed without a shudder,
Or the hearing of a sigh.

I have hunted in this wood;
There's the black pine where I stood,
And the four-snag buck fell yonder
Where the green gullberries grow;—
Here we gathered evergreens
For the dear lost Christmas scenes,
Hollies red, and pale cold berries
Of the mystic mistletoe.

From the border of the dark
Comes a fox's mordant bark;
Now the pines begin their anthem
With a music manifold.

Now the stars wheel up and by,
And the night's infinity
Vaster grows like some tremendous
Thought the heart can never hold.

Just beyond the pines' blue crest,
Heaves the ocean's old unrest,
Lure the gray coast's gaunt austerities,
Mysterious evermore;
There the ancient cedars gaze
O'er the sea-tide's battle-ways,
When the thunder of his striding
Is reverberant on the shore.

So, I'm on my way at last!
Faithful to the living past,—
Loyal to the love unfailing,
Sacrificial, deep, and pure.
Has dividing land or sea
Wearied one who waits for me?
Lo, this night will take me to her,
By the memories that endure!

SPANISH MOSS

In Spanish moss there's a mystery:
It veils the southern coast;
It shrouds the oaks and cypresses;
In it the little birds are lost.
It makes each wood a haunted place,
And every tree a ghost.

When over all His trees God hung
This gray and grieving moss,
He must have been in a mournful mood,
Or purposed to express love's loss;
Or, as a loving Father, had
Far visions of a Cross.

O it's not the bull moose of New Brunswick,
Or Wyoming's wapiti tall,
Or Canada's caribou tall,
Or the Kodiak bear
That I see and I hear
When I vision the forests of fall:

It's the buck with the wide-branching horns!
My strategems wary he scorns,
My artifice wily he scorns.
He is haunting my dreams
Of the mountains and streams.
My evenings, my nights, and my morns,
The buck with the wide-branching horns!

The dark has no mystery deeper
Than the shadowy stag it conceals,
Than the spectral old stag it conceals.
Like a spirit he roves
The wilds that he loves,
His presence their magic reveals.

His crown is diadem royal,
The stars on it sparkle and shine,
The stars on it twinkle and shine;
Now splendid he'll loom,
Now fade in the gloom
Where glimmer the cypress and pine.

When red is the reedland at sunrise,
And mallard and teal are in flight,
And gray goose and black-duck in flight,
Many men of good breed
Find the sport that they need,
But mine is a different delight:

It's the buck with the wide-branching horns!
His beauty the wildwood adorns,
His wonder the wildwood adorns.
He is haunting my dreams
Of the mountains and streams,
My evenings, my nights, and my morns,
The buck with the wide-branching horns!

THE ROSE AND THE BAY

The rose is in the garden,
    and the sweet-bay under the pine;
Through vistas soft as memory,
    Her far white flowers shine;
Her fragrant flowers tremble
    To the rub of a velvet horn,
For the buck will follow the branch
    Where the buck was born.

The roses under his window
    Are fair to the hunter's eyes,
And fair are the sweet-bay flowers
    Where the red-buck lies;
From the peace of the old plantation
    The hunter would not roam,
Nor the buck from the warm sweet thickets
    Where he has his home.

The holly is on the hill,
    And the white bay in the vale;
Through the dim purple aisles of pine
    Her far sweet blooms are pale;
Her far white flowers glimmer
    In the mist of the early morn,
For the buck starts in the branch
    When he hears the horn.

The holly is red, and the rose,
    Their lover has gone away;
In the deep branch the bay is sweet,
    And she was loved as they:
Ah, the long silence after,
    And the strange years swiftly flown,
And the white bay still so beautiful
    When the buck is gone.

SOUTH OF RICHMOND

South of Richmond roars the train:
Subtly o'er my weary brain
Dread delicious languor steals;
Peace my tired spirit heals.
From the struggle of the mart
Hurrying to the homeland's heart,
Through the deepening night I glide
Into dreamlands sweet and wide.

South of Richmond, fields of sedge
Brimming to a pinewood's edge;
Tides of cotton rolling foam
Toward the planter's lonely home;
Clash and clangor fading, ceasing,
Joyous depths of calm increasing;
Dreaming streams and drowsy shores,
All life resting on its oars.

South of Richmond! Ah, it seems
Hearts have kept the olden dreams
South of Richmond: here life means
More than time to work machines;
For by gentle quiet ways,
By unthrifty sweet delays,
Life has time her feast to spread;
Love has grace her light to shed.

South of Richmond, and I come
To the country I call home;
To the glamour and the gloom
Of the swamps in glimmering bloom;
Jasmine bowers, sweet-bay brakes
Where a silver bay-leaf shakes,
Telling of a buck that listens
Where the dewy bay-branch glistens.

South of Richmond there's a warm
Shelter from life's bullying storm;
Winsome welcome in the staying
Of all hastings,—in the straying

Into shrines where still the sense
Of an antique reverence
For the soul's slow nuturing proves
Here the way of life is love's.

South of Richmond! Down we thunder
Through the land of dreams and wonder;
Where the warmer hearts are willing
Laughing hours to be spilling;
Where, though little gold is hoarded,
Time to live can be afforded:
Of life's weary lane the turning,
Homeland, homeland of my yearning!

FAIREST

"O Singer, what is sweetest in thy song?
O Watcher, what has kept thee watching long?

The foam-white moonlight and the stars' caress
At midnight on high waters motionless?

The cool green blades of darkly-waving corn;
Beneath the morning pines the hunter's horn?

Red sunset shafts across an autumn plain,
Mysterious with falling of soft rain?

Far mountains; silent evening rivers old,
That soon the holy evening stars will hold?"

"These are all fair, but fairer than all these,
Than autumn sunsets and than moonlight seas;

The holiest visions that the eye hath seen;
The noblest thoughts that in the mind have been,

These I behold in all their strength and grace
In sweet communion on a mother's face.

She bears a hope celestial where she goes,
And wears at heart a wild white spirit-rose."

SANGUILLAH

(Seminole Indians called the painted bunting "Sanguillah")

Like a blown blossom
Fluttering on a bough
A wild sanguillah's
Singing now,
Singing in my live-oak from a green tall bough.

Radiant as the sunrise,
Restless as the breeze,
Firebird, firebird,
Burning in the trees,
You are calling lovers. But I am not of these.

Laureate, laureate,
Chanting like a child
Of a gold moonland.
Is my heart beguiled,
Knowing all the nothingness behind love's glamour
    wild?

Mad minstrel burning
On the bough of oak,
Youth is a ruddy flame,
But age is a smoke,
Dying down to darkness that no light ever broke,
Down to a silence that no song ever woke.

Your song like a standard
Down the morning streams,
A blue bright banner
That sunward gleams,
Leading hearts that listen to a land of dreams,
But I have had my dreams.

Sanguillah singing,
How could I sustain
All the blind ecstasy
Of love come again?
How could my heart hold all the joy and pain
Of love come again?

Troubadour, troubadour,
Sparkling is your lyre;
Your hope is a fever,
And your faith is a fire,
A fervid music flaming on the altar of desire.
To peace I would aspire.

Sanguillah, sanguillah,
Heed no word I've said!
He who listens not to love
Dwells among the dead.
Bring me by your music
Where the wine of life is red.
Lead me by your singing as the youngest lover's
    led!

THE FLOWER UNBROKEN

He found a flower in the wood,
Dewy in fragrant solitude.
It had no fear of any harm,
Nor any cunning wish to charm.
It trembled on its slender stem,
Its loveliness its diadem.

O eager Hand that reached to break!
O tender Heart that would not take!

Because he let this beauty be,
He gathers flowers of mystery
That have become of him a part
To bud and blossom in his heart
Deep in the dead of winter cold,
Deep in the years when he is old.

Her lover was a hunter;
But she hoped when they were wed
He would give up his childish ways
And be a man instead.
But when she found his hunting kept
Her man a little boy,
She gave him as a birthday gift
A coat of corduroy.

He wore it in the mountains,
In the marshes, on the shore;
It lost its color in the rain,
Briars its beauty tore,
And yet she wonderingly finds,
The shabbier it grows,
Its tattered charm superior
To that of costlier clothes.

Because it brings her snow and wind,
And hills of lonely height,—
Her hunter setting forth at dawn,
And coming home at night,—
The fragrant wilderness with him,
The wildwood's shine and shade,
It's taken on strange beauty that
Its maker never made.

SPRINGTIME FLIGHT

Though the hillsides harbor snows,
Every heart wild gladness knows
As northward through the misty night
The clanging chorus goes.
Ranging through the vaulted deep,
Gray battalions grandly sweep
Through the fields of stars and azure,
Up the glimmering stairs of sleep.

Fog-mysterious village lights
Turn them from their tingling heights
As over house and garden pass
The dark imperious flights—
Bringing news of glamour-climes,
Roses, myrtles, jessamines,
Southshore springtime, far green glimpses
Of bright bayoux fringed with pines.

Valiantly the streaming wedges
Graze the wild moon's icy edges;
By tomorrow they'll be sporting
In the Athabascan sedges!
Daring trumpeters who bring
Summons to the heart to sing,
For they van the march triumphant
Of the legions of the spring.

IN MINIATURE

I have heard all joy a-carol
In one cardinal's call;
Seen the pride of all the summer
In one red leaf fall;
Felt the universal rapture
In one singing bird;
Known the anguish of creation
In one loveless word.

ABSENT-MINDED HUNTER

In the river-marsh I kneel,
Waiting for a flight of teal.
Now the flocks come glimmering by,
Silhouetted on the sky.
Now they tower, now they reel
With a thrilling wild precision
Equal to their urgent need;
For, though dazzling their speed,
To direction they give heed.
Is there any man would try
Such manouvers . . . could he fly?

Dark has fallen ere I rise.
Stars have taken all the skies.
Suddenly I'm in the night.
Every teal is out of sight—
Though they linger in my eyes.
What a man of indecision!
As I lift each frosted boot,
Ribald owls begin to hoot.
Why did I forget to shoot?
I had had too much delight
Watching green-wings in their flight.

ALWAYS

Always to be sure of love,
Always;
Needing nothing to prove
That the stars keep their place,
Giving Heaven its grace;
That the Song is still sung,
And its music is young.
Never having to wait
In dread at life's gate.
Never to be afraid
That the roses will fade.
Always to be sure
That love will endure
Always.

TO AN OAK

Since I last saw you, I have been
To London, Paris, and Berlin,
Oceans and mountains I have seen;
Strange wondrous ways I've wandered in.
Yet, after years, I seem unchanged—
Or worse . . . for all the world I've ranged.

Here you have stood through calm and storm,
Growing more beautiful and strong;
Have felt the southwind rushing warm;
Have heard your turrets filled with song
Of mating birds. Your world are these
Home fields, home forests, home seabreeze.

Here you abide in beauty lone.
I find you here to welcome me.
Here you will be when I am gone
Past every land and every sea.
You, braver than my heart is brave,
Stand in your cradle and your grave.

DAWN

On a dewy dawn-bough in her heart's deepest woodland
A wild bird is warbling; a fragrant wind moves;
A secret stream's flowing past shy flowers blowing;
The daybreak is coming . . . She is loved, and she
    loves.

TWO LOOKS

Two looked on her—the evil and the good.
One's stare undressed her naked where she
    stood;
The other's gaze, her beauty to revere,
Apparelled her in glimmering garments rare.

Deep River

DEEP RIVER

How like the channel of a stream am I
When all the living waters are withdrawn:
Dry sand, bare rocks beneath the burning sky,
And arid even in the misty dawn.
The wildflowers die; the trees for mercy yearn
When tides of love through me no longer roll . . .
From far and fragrant hills, return, return,
Restore my life, Deep River of my Soul.

Flow through me, Beautiful Waters, once again!
Then will the sands like jewels shine; the shore
Its lustrous shade from foliage regain.
The birds shall sing their melodies once more;
And from the banks bright wildflowers will start
When your wild beauty brims my dusty heart.

NONE OTHER

No mystery have they like yours:
They in life's open sunlight shine.
Never their charm my heart allures,
For love has never made them mine.

But all about you is the fall
Of waters in the lonely wood,
The music of the cardinal's call,
The veery's, lost in solitude.

And all about you is the rush
Of angel wings from Heaven speeding;
And all about you is the hush
Of every care of earth receding.

THE LISTENING NIGHT

Now that the moon has sunk from sight
I listen to the listening night.
The fields are listening and the woods,
And the wild delta's solitudes.
Silence some secrets seems to tell
From the mute land where spirits dwell;
And we can feel but cannot hear
That more than sorcery is near,
Save for the stars, there is no light.
They listen, and like them I hark,
All of us listen to the dark.
We know from whisper, hint, and sigh
That everlasting Beauty's by.
The silences are listening, too.
The darkness is a rendezvous
Of wonderers hoping for the light
Deep in the huge and thoughtful night
Under the stars the river flows,
And listens as it onward goes;—
Over it leans a listening rose.
The river-marsh hears more than we,
The marsh that marches to the sea,
That margins on eternity.
Among the old momentous trees,
The ceremonial cypresses,
Some hear what may have passed us by
Under the hushed mysterious sky.
What do we in the silence fear?
What reassurance long to hear?
If all of us could have a choice,
What we need most is love's dear voice
Nor is hope vain. For dreams abroad
Come from love only, and the Lord.
And everywhere we look and listen,
Bright angels seem to sing and glisten.

YOUTH'S PERMANENCE

'Tis said Time takes our love and joy away;
That roses, rainbows, stars, no more can be
When Youth is gone . . . It is not so with
    me;
For what was best in that blithe far-off day
Returns; whether with dawn's awakening ray,
Or at the laughter, comrade-like and free,
Of dearest friends; or when at eve I see
A wildrose west; or hear the marriage lay

Of mated birds in the glimmering morning
    singing,
Or mark the robes that earth by moonlight
    wears,
Each day some new or old sweet joy is bringing.
But, O most blest, in every hour divine,
One starry face beloved through life is mine,
Hallowed by gathered beauty of the years.

GREAT OF HEART

Give me the great of heart; the mighty winds
That sway the pendant world; the hale glad sea;
The wild moon homing for the haunted west
O'er mountains in their freedom vast and old;
The towering stars; the huge sequestered night;
Ancestral ancient trees; skies, rivers, dawn,
And glimmering evening's long-lashed mysteries.

My friends, though few, let them be great of heart!
Dauntless, yet near to laughter and to tears;
Disdainful of all gain save comradeship;
As elemental as the candid plains
Or intimate deep forests; lovers true
Who have the spirit's fathomless far reach
To the heart of God. O may such friends be mine!

TO ONE COMING OF AGE

A thousand minds for you have thought,
A thousand hearts more kindly grew;
For you a thousand hands have wrought
To make you wise and brave and true.
Within your eyes there shines the light
Of stars that long ago have set;
As, deep within their happy night,
Are splendid stars unrisen yet.

For you the cloudy battle roared
Along the plain of Marathon;
For you the Roman eagles soared
Against the thunder and the sun.
The fealties of every race,
The noble deeds of every age
Are yours to teach you knightly grace,
Are your heroic heritage.

O loyal friend, with eyes so true,
By gentle manhood treasure fast
The trust of those who died for you
Far in the dim and shadowy Past.
In their proud giving, they were glad
To face the desert, dare the foam;
They gave to you the best they had
To make your world a sweeter home.

O friend, the latest and the best
Of Nature's plan and Man's desire,
You too must labor and not rest,
Must pass perchance through flood and fire.
When Honor leads, there boldly charge
Into the vortex of the fight,
And your bright memory shall emerge
To shine in some far future night.

LOVE'S WATCH

Many watch over me, care for my need,—
Constant, to every want giving their heed
By loving wish and thought, by kindly deed.

And not alone the ones who in life's fray
Strive for me, am I in debt day by day,
By others silent now, far, far away.

There was a comrade once. My life to save,
From a wild river's wrath, his life he gave . . .
Now for his valiant sake I must be brave.

There was in time gone by a mother who
Each fear and hope of mine tenderly knew.
Aye to her faith in me I must be true.

There was a sweetheart who, long, long ago,
Gave me a trust to keep . . . Through joy and woe
I must remember it as the years go.

Many watch over me, guarding my days:
Those who walk with me still in earthly ways,
Those whom a beauty immortal arrays.

LILIES

A calla lily, a tiger lily:
One to the holy heavens can aspire,
While one is flamed with gleaming earthly fire.
Since I am but a mortal, and as such
Lilies immaculate I fear to touch,
If ever human love should come to me,
Like a wild tiger lily let it be!

COMRADE

Comrade, Comrade, Comrade true,
Constant all the voyage through;

When our ship by dark shores sails,
Never once your courage fails.

Lies the great deep all uncharted?
Peril finds you higher-hearted.

You, through all the dreadful dark,
Helm with me our driven barque.

On its deck when days are fair,
Sing we in the summer air;

Sharing many a lovely dream,
That like sea-stars rise to gleam.

Toiling happy, we shall come
Safely to the harbor home.

Then to God I'll gladly say,
"We have anchored in the bay.

If I mastered wind and wave,
Praise the pilot whom you gave,

This my loving comrade true,
Constant all the voyage through."

SUMMUM BONUM

The sum of nature's loveliness
From single flowers may be learned;
The splendors of the realms of light
From solitary stars discerned.
So in your love my heart has found
The wide world's myriad offerings,
And in your soul, all that the sky
Has promised of immortal things.

106

THE FACE BELOVED

More than the lingered bloom of youth,
I love these lines of pity and ruth,
Time-written on the cherished face,
A certain pure immortal grace,
Allied to beauty and to truth,
Sorrow can subtly form and trace.

These marks, these silver hairs, are signs
Of struggle 'gainst Fate's fell designs,
Of journeys gray, of hours and miles
Of passage through the dark defiles
Of doubt, storm-driven by life's winds;
Of failure met with faith and smiles.

Upon this face behold a light!
A dawning on the mortal night!
Over no forest, field or foam
This mystic radiance has come;
It is the beam that tells how bright
This human heart has kept its home.

These features speak of sorrow borne
Nobly, of life's white flower worn
Fadeless amid the press and storm.
This beauty to the soul is balm.
Deeply to comfort those who mourn
This presence has celestial charm.

Not that the virgin, flowering face
Of Youth, for me has lost its grace;
But these calm features that I love
My heart to nobler purpose move,
And, ere the ending of life's race,
The triumph of the Spirit prove.

THE LEAST OF THESE

Often I paused by your river's shore;
Often I came to your welcoming door;
Often my shadow was on your floor.
I was the beggar. You gave me bread.
I was the mourner you comforted.
I was the little child you led.
Yet when you were so kind to me,
You never thought that I was He.

I was the wind when the willows waved,
Over the wounded bird you saved.
Mine was the face that was grief-engraved
Until you came in your tender way,
Lighting the darkness of my day
Till all my clouds had passed away.
But all the while you were good to me,
You never guessed that I was He.

I to the bitter storm was bared.
With me your shielding coat you shared.
You were the only one who cared
For me, a mendicant and clown.
And when the rain and wind went down,
You bore me safely to the town.
You who were gracious unto me
Never divined that I was He.

I am the lonely one you blessed,
Your gentle heart kept and caressed.
You are the one who gave me rest.
You bound my many wounds that bled.
Your garments with my blood were red,
Upon my face your tears were shed.
Yet you who deeply pitied me
Never once dreamed that I was He.

THE MOTHER

If mountains for me stood aside,
If seas a pathway through their tide
Made for my feet, if now I stand
Safe in a fair and radiant land,

Ah, not by me the deed was done!
Not by my strength was victory won!
My mother had a faith in me
To move the mountains and the sea.

I heard her voice behind me call
In love; she kept me 'gainst my fall;
I passed the wave, the gloomy wood,
Because her heart believed I could.

O Trust divine, sustaining, true,
I, who achieved because of you,
Now take the garlands and the crown
At your dear feet to lay them down.

BABY'S DEBUT

Life is so very great, and she so small,
Tenderly must I tell her of it all:

For she must learn of life from little things:
Listen to the robin when he softly sings

Amid the dogwood blossoms on the knoll
Before she hears the awful ocean roll;

Not suddenly must she behold the dark,
Or the vast wide-winged tawny daybreak mark;

But see in the pine a tiny twilight looming,
And in the rose a fairy daydawn blooming . . .

O baby hands that clutch and cling their need!
O elfin steps, how gently must I lead!

How loving, wise, and patient I must be
With one who has to learn of God through me.

A SON OF NATURE

(To Arthur T. Wayne)

There's a man by Copahee,
Wisest, kindliest of his race,
To our age a noble grace;
And he knows by land and sea
Every wild wing beating free
In aerial liberty.

He has seen wood-warblers build,
And has stayed his steps to hear
Vireos fluting lyrics clear;
When the wide-winged sunsets gild
Vast sea-marshes, he is thrilled,
And his heart with peace is filled.

He has watched day's beauty fade
Glimmering through Long Island's pines,
And has loved the night's designs
When, with fervor unafraid,
Through the gathering velvet shade
He has paced the cedarn glade.

He has watched from Capers' beach
How the ebb goes ramping out,
Heard the wrathful breakers shout,
Learned what all the seabirds teach,
By that knowledge wide to reach
Nature's soul through nature's speech.

Where white stream and starlight meet
Wildly in the wizard glen,
Ere the waters flood the fen,
Cool bay-flowers, fragrant, sweet,
Brush his forehead, while his feet
Stem the twinkling waters fleet.

He has followed lurings shy
Of the wood and of the wave;
Long ago his heart he gave
To the gladness of the sky;
And by work of ear and eye
Brings to us God's wonders nigh.

He has loved the bronzing wood,
And has stood at dusk alone
Where the dreamy cotton shone;
With its ghostly blossoms dewed,
Into starlight life renewed
By the magic of night's mood.

Well he loves the ray that steals
Glimmering through the mystic nook,
Dancing on the brawling brook;
Home for him each scene reveals;
Where the towering eagle wheels
In far skies, his place he feels.

Like a sentry he discerns
Bivouacs of stars that sleep,
Tented in the midnight deep;
For the True his spirit yearns,
Toward the Lovely ever turns,
And of Truth and Beauty learns.

From the broomsedge and the brake,
From the marsh and from the wood,
Home he brings glad news of God,
Tidings high of power to make
Every heart its sin forsake,
Every life fresh courage take.

In his face are radiances
Born of earth and sky and air,
Born of nature's aspects fair;
Souls of bird-songs, blossoms, trees;
In his eyes are mysteries,
Lingering lights of all he sees.

To his life a tone is brought
Out of song and waters falling,
Out of nature's voices calling,
Young and pure and valiant,—caught
From the field and forest,—wrought
By his mind to noble thought.

111

THE MOTHER

She is gone from whom I learned
All love's meaning; for she yearned
Always to sustain and save.
For the strength I did not have
Safely unto her I turned . . .
Though the world would scorn me, break me,
Never did her love forsake me;
Home into her heart she'd take me.

She is gone to whom I bared
All my life; who would have cared
For this loneliness I feel.
She had sympathy to heal
Every wound,—whose pain she shared.
Watching tenderly above me,
Deeply shaken by what moved me,
Well she understood and loved me.

Always mother to her child,
She convoyed me through the wild
Of life's wasteland . . . All was well
Till the parting-time befell . . .
How shall I be reconciled,
With her now no more beside me,
With no hand like hers to guide me,
With no heart on which to hide me?

She is gone who gave relief
To each weariness and grief,
Spent herself on my poor cares;
For my trouble shed her tears . . .
She made natural, belief
In all noble things . . . She sought me
In my sins, and homeward brought me . . .
All I know of God, she taught me.

She is gone and I remain
Solitary on life's plain . . .
But one joyous thought I know—
Where she's gone, I too shall go.

112

Life without that hope were vain . . .
Though my One Beloved must leave me,
Through it all I will not grieve me;
For at last she shall receive me.

THE FRIEND

He is not like another one
Of all my friends. He stands alone.

Beyond the field and bounding wood,
Beside the seashore's solitude,
A Tree behind a rugged Rock
Has long withstood the breakers' shock.
The Rock is bold and clean and hard;
Its face by tempests old is marred;
It changes not in sun or rain,
In calm or raging hurricane.
It has an aspect nobly grand,
Interpreting for sea and land
The grandeur of the gales that break,
Yet cannot once this Titan shake.
It has a beauty fine and grave,
A beauty wrought by wind and wave.
Sometimes in maelstroms it is drowned;
Sometimes by wild foam-flowers crowned
As if the mad gale understood
The Rock's calm-couraged hardihood,
And gave, the harrying waves among,
A tribute to a champion strong.
No storm this outpost has escaped;
Its strength by hardship has been shaped;
By it, in nights of fear and gloom,
The Terrible was overcome.
It won in conflict, not in ease,
Its power of tremendous peace.

Such shelter as it gives the Tree
My steadfast friend has given me.

113

YOUNG POET

Out of the mists of crowds
On the wild city's ways,
Suddenly his face shines,
A star out of haze;
A woodland fugitive,
A wildflower in the mart,
A woodthrush wandered
With a wildwood heart.

O solitary One, my brother,
Nameless, I know you!
And see life's wild black wave
Reared to o'er throw you.
Early forsaken,
With white sails shaken,
Out of your homeless eyes
Far violet visions shine.
You of the Quest Divine,
That, too, is mine.
I know, I feel, I see,
Your desperate fealty:
Looking for blue flowers
In the grime of life's street;
Listening for music
Where ramping hoofs beat!
Far is the place, Friend,
Faint is the gleam,
O yet I know you
Will follow the Dream,
Its beauty and no other,
Gentle, invincible brother.

MY LITTLE LAD

I leave him now with you, Miss Jones,
My little lad . . . He'll learn
From books and maps and charts and rules . . .
Yet over him I yearn,
For he has loved the tiny flowers
That peep beneath the fern.

His eyes will dance, his heart delight
To see a wild rose flush;
Or if a bird begins to sing
In yonder lilac bush,
He will lay down his book, I fear,
To listen to the thrush.

He's just a little wildwood lad,
A lightfoot lad and free;
He's raced the skimming swallows far,
And the sea gulls by the sea;
He's timid as a startled fawn,
Not brave like you and me.

And yet his heart is not untaught:
In awe, in solitude,
He gained the gift of gentleness;
In silence he has stood,
Aware, because of lovely things,
How close to us is God.

I leave him now with you, Miss Jones.
I'm asking much, I fear.
His little heart will need your love
Its tenderness to share.
But women understand. To them
Lads' wildwood ways are dear.

MAD ROBIN

They were all dancing,
But he did not dance,
Standing there watching
In a shining trance;
His clothes all ragged
And his hair awry,
His great eyes burning
Like stars in the sky.

They were all laughing
And loving so gay;
But Robin kept watching
In his mad still way:
They sang and they jostled
At Life's gaudy fair,
While Robin kept watching
With his strange far air.

Then they were mourners,
But he would not weep;
He counted their tears
With a magic deep.
He stood and he listened,
Poor mad Robin wild:
Was he a magician,
Or a fool, or a child?

Now all their dancing
And loving are done;
The sun keeps looking
But finds not one;
Yet if you will harken
You'll know a miracle—
See their beauty glisten,
Hear their music swell:

Out of the buried past
They throng back again
With all the old laughter
And the old wild pain;

They who so scorned him
With heart, voice, and look
Now are made immortal
In mad Robin's book.

AFAR IN THE FOREST

Afar in the forest I'm longing to rove,
Afar in the forest, the forest I love!
All dewy and fragrant at breaking of morn,
To follow the hounds and the echoing horn.

Afar in the forest, O brother of mine,
Afar in the forest of oak and of pine,
I cherish the hope that with you I may roam
Afar in the forest, the forest of home!

There joyous once more at daybreaking to ride
Through glimmering pinelands with you by my side,
When red is the east, or when gold is the west
Afar in the forest's the place we love best.

Afar in the forest are waiting our joys,
Afar in the forest we loved so as boys;
And still for us now in the woods' wildest ways
Afar in the forest are happiest days.

Afar in the forest, O brother of mine,
Deep, deep in those woodlands of oak and of pine,
I'm longing with you in our gladness to roam
Afar in the forest, the forest of home!

V. D. G.

A road runs down through field and wood
Straight to the deep's eternity.
It ends in beauty's solitude,
Where white-winged waves, wild, glad, and free,
Plunge on the beach with sea-shells strewed.
No farther journey can there be.
It ends in loveliness for me:
I am the road . . . You are the sea.

117

THE STRANGER

I.

She stood within the quiet room,
A lovely flower come to bloom,
Appareled in especial light,
A blossom opening in the night.
Her rich brown hair half-framed a face
Transfigured by an inner grace,
As if to her bright seraphs brought
Dreams that illumined life and thought;
As if all summers would disclose
Their culmination in this Rose.
I did not know that there could be
In Beauty such felicity;
Nor dream that for me there could stand
A vision our of fairyland,
Nor hope that if the vision shone
Its radiance was for me alone.
And yet so gracious was her air,
I lingered and I worshipped there,
Enchanted by her charm no less
Than by her perfect loveliness.

II.

I gazed: a longing over me swept
That she from sorrow might be kept,
That for her my far homage might
A beacon burn in life's long night,
That other hearts would feel as mine,
And worship at this sacred shrine,
Would turn from loveliness that's feigned
To loveliness that is ordained.
For Beauty is a destined thing,
Inevitable as the spring,
Having the bright immortal youth
Of virtue, and the joy of truth;
And like creation she is new,
Yet ancient as the dawning, too.

Who at her altar worships well
Shall with the angel spirits dwell;
Shall to a calmer country come
That is the heart's eternal home,
Where love's the only language heard,
Save music and the singing bird.

III.

Sadly, I turned to go . . . Who knows
If I again shall see this Rose?
Ah, but I hold the memory!
Always she will be fair for me;
Forever and forever stand
A vision out of fairyland;
Always on me her charm will keep
Its spell of moonlit magic deep;
Always she will be gracious . . . Pain
Must pass her guard ere I be slain.
Each morn that spreads her azure wings
A message from her beauty brings;
Each Eve that lifts her glimmering eyes
Reveals her soul's divine surprise.
Always in light I see her gleam,
Fulfilling hope's transcendent dream . . .
Far, far I go, but till life's end
Her glamour shall my steps attend,
Her flower of my life a part,
To blossom fragrant in my heart.

MARIUS

Deep in the night a Roman sentry cried,
"The foemen are upon us! We are lost!"
To whom the valiant Marius replied,
"If they be on us, they indeed are lost."

SEED STORE

This seems a place of darkness and of death;
But in these hopeless whispering arid sheaths
Sleeps all the loveliness of our great earth;
All beauty of the universe here breathes.

Our life is mystery. At God's commands
A royal lily from this husk will soar;
Here in my palm a mighty forest stands,
While glorious gardens through my fingers pour.

And though all seems past longing, and past lust,
Its brave vitality returns again.
These roses will make summer of my dust,
And beauty fashion Paradise from pain.

You think on love and life they have no grasp,
These faded husks, these withered shards of doom;
But if you touch a daisy-seed, you'll clasp
The springtime, and sweet meadows deep in bloom.

And when this little acorn shall awake,
Mounting the heavens, a noble tree shall rise;
A mighty immemorial oak shall shake
His craggy boughs against the stormy skies.

Ghostly it rattles as its cerements cold;
As you lift what seems a dead and withered pod;
But all the beauty of the world you hold,
And you are grasping the great hand of God.

CHARLESTON

The night is fair upon the sister streams;
Softly entranced the far shore-visions shine;
Now sleeps the City, mirrored in her dreams.

Not in the sleep that covers Beauty's swoon
From the chill criticism of the stars,
And moody contemplation of the moon;

But in a deep and mystic sleep serene,
Beautiful as to dying eyes the light
On sorrowful far lands at sunset seen.

A voice is grieving from the grieving sea,
A voice grieves of a farewell long ago,
Of spirit-loneliness and memory.

Here where the nations' commerce used to ride,
From the warm South and from the frozen North,
A dim ship swings upon the misty tide.

An elder darkness than the night comes down,
A music deeper than the anthemed sea's,
That fold the dreamers in the dreaming town.

The day is fair upon the sister streams,
A wind is calling from the calling sea;
Still sleeps the City, mirrored in her dreams.

BABY GARLAND

Out of a mystic starland
That we have never seen,
Out of a flowering far land
I think it must have been
God's love that gave us Garland
To prove what love can mean.

121

ROMAIN LIGHT

'Round the great lantern goes,
　　'Round floats the flashing light;
Over the sea it throws
　　A pathway wide and bright
　　Through the wide pathless night.

Now drones the ebb-tide dim
　　Down to the foaming bar;
Down to the white sea-rim,
　　Down to the ocean far,
　　Where the great voices are.

Here the sweet myrtle trees
　　Murmur in soft delight;
There the grey aching seas,
　　Through the waste breach of night,
　　Plunge in toward the light.

Shoreward the lantern shines,
　　And it beams softly come
To the dark sea of pines,
　　Rolling in purple foam
　　Over the pineland home.

Steadfast as God's own star
　　Through the wild moaning night;
Where death and darkness are,
　　Where fails the mortal sight,
　　There will be found the Light.

UNIVERSAL NAME

Once when I wandered from the crowds apart,
I met an Indian named Wounded Heart.
He sat beside a stream, beneath a tree;
As much of Nature as they were was he.
For no especial glory was he famed
Except that for us all he had been named.

BREACH INLET

From the bosom of the deep
    I draw the dreaming tide,
To flush the weary flats
    And the marshes wide:
Man bars my course, but I am still
Master of men, and they obey my will.

The sailors of the deep
    Fear me, and know my foam;
I am the burial-place
    Of those who come not home;
And from me, glimmering to the shadowy coast,
Dead eyes in anguish peer from faces lost.

The full wild breast of the deep
    I give the marsh and shore,
That they may drink and know
    Of weariness no more:
The magic of the ancient coast is mine
From long blue-rolling wave to lonely pine.

On the face of the deep
    My messengers run,
To lure the toiling tides
    From the setting sun:
Beauty I have, and with it cold unrest,
And the sea-thunder surges through my breast.

THE HARVEST

Ages and ages after,
If there be harvesting
Of the old tears and laughter
Stored in the songs we sing—
Some gleaner in the olden
Wide songfields of the Past
May come upon one golden
Lyric I made to last.

123

I have dreamed of a wonderful region
Thro' the mist of the broken years;
It lies thro' the valley of longing,
 Its verge is of tears.

Only those who are brave to be tender,
Whose wills are true to be strong,
Can come to that marvelous region,
 Whose silence is song.

'Tis a bourne for the faithful; rejected
By men, and sorely oppressed;
And there may be sorrowful-hearted
 By the still waters rest.

Deep, deep is the refuge, the refuge,
The peace, the repose;
There blow the sweet winds of the twilight,
 There the tired eyes close.

But the region,—O where shall one find it?
Is it after the wild journey's end?
It is found with its beautiful solace
 In the heart of a friend.

TWO ROSES

This rose, some sculptor of the long ago,
Carved from Carrara marble, pure, austere,
With touch as true as on a cameo,
A thing immortal, amid mortals here.
It has a beauty far beyond the range
Of death or time or tears or any sorrow;
Having a loveliness remote and strange,
It has no dread of what may come tomorrow.

And yet somehow it never makes me feel
As does this rose that's fading leaf by leaf.
This has a poignant and a wild appeal,
Being the revelation of my grief.
The immortal rose is magic in its art.
The dying rose I clasp close to my heart.

THE BABY ASLEEP

A smile, faint, beautiful, and shy
Upon his fairy features gleams;
Of some bright star or butterfly
Or flower he gently dreams.

Perhaps an angel takes his hand,
An angel loving him as we,
To lead him through a shining land,
Or by a singing sea.

His tiny heart with quickening beat,
In happy innocence beguiled,
Is wandering far 'mid clover sweet,
Or rambling roses wild.

O stay not long in fields afar,
Nor lose Love's hand in sleep or night!
When fades the lustrous morning star,
Return to be our light!

YELLOW ROSE

You gave me once a yellow rose.
I treasured it until
It went the way all roses go,—
And died, as roses will.

And yet, although it is but dust,
With all its beauty shed,
I love all roses for the sake
Of one rose, long since dead.

BEAUTIFUL WINGS

Beautiful Wings, no more, ah, nevermore,
By Copahee, or Capers' wild seashore,
Or in the parish pinelands sweet and old
Shall his clear eyes your radiant grace behold.

Beautiful Sunsets over Cooper River,
His glory shall be given you forever;
Beautiful Dawns that on the sea awake,
Henceforth your light shall of his light partake.

Beautiful Woods and Marshes, he shall roam
Your solitudes no more, that were his home . . .
Hereafter you shall never be the same;
Each path he walked lives brightened by his fame.

A nobler grandeur wears the live-oak dim,
And the momentous pine, remembering him,
A taller splendor; in each birdsong sweet
A melody his life has made complete.

Beautiful Minstrels, he who heard you best,
Listening all his life, now takes his rest.
Sing to him sleeping! He has loved you well.
Now let your love of him your music tell.

And let the sweet bay and the jasmine frail,
And the immaculate magnolia pale,
The tall wood violet on swaying stem
Weave for his fame a fragrant diadem.

Darkness, deal bravely with my gallant friend
Who walked in light and virtue to the end . . .
Land that he honored, honor well your son
Whose life and your own glory now are one.

THE PEAKS OF OTTER

I shall never, never see the Peaks of Otter,
In the Valley of Virginia, far away;
But beautiful beyond all other mountains
They are glorious in my dreaming night and day.

For when I was in trouble came a letter
From a friend who has been faithful all the years:
"Come with me to see the lovely Peaks of Otter;
They will cure you of your weariness and cares."

Though I never shall behold their silent beauty,
Sleeping radiant in that fair Virginia sky,
Yet I love them with a love past understanding,
And their vision I shall cherish till I die.

For they speak of the compassion of my comrade
Who would share with me the loveliness he knew;
And that is why I love the Peaks of Otter,
For they tell me of a friendship that is true.

And now, whenever doubts and fears assail me,
To those mountains like a wild bird I can flee
To the dreamland of the orchid Peaks of Otter
With the friend who in my sorrow thought of me.

TURNING AWAY WITH WONDER

Turning away with wonder
From every wildflower's face,
And from the grass thereunder,
And the maternal grace
Of the good earth that bears them
I worship; for I ween
That the same Hand that rears them
Brings me upon the scene.

A SONG FOR THE SOUTH

O light in Southern women's eyes,
O dawn divine in heavenly skies,
To point the path to honor clear,
Extinguishing all doubt and fear;—
Before this human Holy Grail,
This soul-light of the South, I kneel.

O light in Southern women's eyes,
Life's hope within your radiance lies;
Love's earliest dawn wakes in its beams,
Love's latest fire and sunset dreams;
And, ere the night, in it I see
Promise of immortality.

My South! My land! No flag has she . . .
Henceforth her emblem fair shall be
No banner lost in battle-years,
But what prevailed o'er death and tears:
The light in Southern women's eyes
That shines from Love's eternal skies.

IDLE HEROINE

Behind her Dresden cups she's out of place.
The splendor of that heart needs nobler spending:
To be sung of and died for without ending;
Such loveliness belongs to all the Race.
And all that hope desires is in her face.
The dying brave of war she should be tending,
Who, at that haunting beauty o'er them bending,
Foreknowledge of all heaven well might trace.

I see her not behind the trivial glass
And trifling china. In far hills forlorn,
Fast-spurring deep through that disastrous pass
Where heroes heed the sound of Roland's horn,
With banners streaming wild I see her come
Where the last bugle's sounding the charge home.

HER SILENCE

No word of her sorrow is spoken,
While tenderly listening to mine;
Her grief, with its silence unbroken,
How might I its presence divine?
Because human natures inherit
An insight that Heaven confers:
That only a travailing spirit
Has sympathy like unto hers!

Her sorrow no outward expression
May wear, and no language contain;
She hears my heart-broken confession
That life after grief is in vain.
Her sorrow—and how does she show it,
And grief, that of her is a part?
The depth of her trouble, I know it,
Because of the depth of her heart.

By love it is measured, and ever
In silence its tone can be heard;
But life's darkest hour can never
Bring forth of its passion one word.
O yet in such grief is high glory:
Her heart, to hold love, is made deep;
For herself is her own sorrow's story,
For us, only love will she keep.

In sorrow, life's gladness retaining,
Most noble when suffering most,
The present through her is regaining
The soul of the lovely and lost.
The voices of others are yearning
To tell of the world and its strife,
From her beautiful silence I'm learning
The hymns of the valiant life!

A MEMORY OF HOME

The vast and wandering Night is come
From pines to sea the shadows creep;
A white sail slips in silence home,
And the soft landscape sinks in sleep.

Pure in the west a holy star,
In dewy-silver solitude,
In tender-tinted regions far
Stands white above the solemn wood.

And now a bell across the fields
Peals mellow music, rolling far;
My spirit to the music yields,
And shines with yonder setting star.

And still, though I have gone away,
I see the splendor of the star,
And hear the bell at close of day
Its mellow music rolling far.

ELF SONG

Your ways are not our ways;
Only by love we're bound;
Under spirea-sprays
Secrets of love we've found.
We know all beauty hidden
And take it for our own.
To us naught is forbidden
If it be love's alone.

At midnight in the wildwood
We trip and dance and play,
Each singing as a child would
Until the break of day.
We drink of starlit flowers,
Laughing among ourselves.
Would you had joy like ours!
Would you were elves!

130

THE OLD JUDGE

We loved the Judge, though we would say
That he had long outlived his day.

Upon a southern slope there grows
An orchard: rows on glimmering rows
Of clean-barked apples, strong and young;
And when the trees with fruit are hung,
Or when the bridal mood of spring
Has set their beauty blossoming,
They are the marvel of the vale:
The orchard's crops can never fail.
Each tree is stalwart, trimmed, and taught
Efficiency by modern thought;
Each tree is meant to bear; each tree
A mighty bearer comes to be.

Beyond the orchard, by a stream
Where nature-lovers come to dream
There is a gnarled old apple tree
Worth nothing in efficiency.
Its branches spread a generous shade;
Heaved roots an armchair-seat have made;
It bears sweet blossoms unconstrained,
And sheds its gracious shade untrained
Here the clear stream delays its sweep;
Here winds of summer fall asleep.
Loved by all hearts, this ancient tree,
Offers its welcome, kindly, free.
Full of quaint faults and winsome ways
And gladsome light of other days.

The Judge? In modern men you see
The Orchard; and in him, the Tree.

THE BARD

Today I am lost in the sorrow
And clamorous cries of the crowd;
But mine is eternal Tomorrow;
My moonlight shall conquer this cloud.

The foam of my fount shall be springing
In years that are hidden in haze;
And lovers my songs shall be singing
Beyond the horizon of days.

Of spirits I live in the keeping;
I drink of the Evening's dark wine;
On the breasts of the Night is my sleeping;
The wings of the Morning are mine.

On me is a springtime immortal;
I fade not and never grow old;
I am toward the future a portal,
Where flower the gardens of gold.

All beauty of earth is my mistress;
Like angels all visions attend;
My might is a music resistless,
And God is my intimate friend.

Not here and not now—but forever
I stream like the life of a star;
I flow like a mountainous river . . .
Where I am, eternities are.

Though the shadows about me may darken,
My voice be unheard in this night,
Yet to me the ages shall harken,
And turn to me as to the light.

WHEN YOU ARE GONE

When you are gone, there comes to me
A shadow that I cannot flee,
A trouble that no words can tell,
A deeper meaning in farewell,
A sense of loss in all I see.

The gleams that dawned so beauteously
On human face, on flower and tree,
And love, confirming all is well,
Vanish with you, their source, to dwell.
Life is defeat, not victory,
When you are gone.

I miss your laughter and your free
Blithe comradeship, gay constancy.
The brightest star that ever fell
Gave no such light, shed no such spell,
Left no such dark as comes to be
When you are gone!

A LAD READS HOMER

Now he shall never be a child again!
This ruddy blue-eyed lad with tawny hair,
Too young to know how perilously fair
The world can be; this stranger unto pain
Suddenly finds his boyish pastimes vain.
Behold his glamourous and mortal air,
His poignant surmise and his still despair,
Now the Blind Bard has caught his soul amain!

From Troy's grim walls he views the martial strand,
The warriors, the camps, the swaying ships:
The beauty of the world in Helen stands
Full in his arms, her kiss upon his lips,
Then, as of yonder battle he is part,
Achilles' shouting spear drives through his heart!

133

"Now, Miss Grace, you'll think it strange:
But, when riding on the range,
I feel more than just a cowboy,
For it brings about a change.
At the ranch-house I'm a hand;
And they'd never understand.
In the wilderness I'm certain
Something else for me was planned.

You're a woman; but somehow
You might know, you might allow
That a man can rise much higher
Than he is right here and now.
In the East you folks are wise;
And maybe you might surmise
Why a cowhand of the ranges
Sees *his* rainbow in the skies.

Leave the boys to their guitars;
Let us pass the pasture-bars.
Here you'll know the spell I'm meaning,
In this country full of stars.
Don't you feel now how it seems,
In the starlight by these streams,
With the big night all around us,
And the darkness full of dreams?

Now of course the boys would laugh,
And they'd guy me with their chaff,
If I ever hinted what I saw
And felt—or even half!
With their fingers to their noses
They would call me Holy Moses,
If I told them how the sunset
Was a garden full of roses;

And how somewhere on these plains,
Where the silver moonlight rains,
A princess will be waiting me,
To break a cowboy's chains;
How we'll ride in joy away
To another night and day,
To a strange and far-off country
Full of palms and of ocean spray.

So you do not think it strange
For a rider of the range
To be dreaming like a schoolboy?
And you comprehend my change?
Here's the place I saw those deer . . .
I'm a fool . . . Miss Grace, I swear,
How'd I know *you* were the princess?
That's the dress she used to wear;

And she had your eyes. *Your* hands
Led me to those other lands.
And you have her voice, her stillness;
And your heart, it understands.
Pardon, Ma'am . . . You're crying, too?
Lord, Miss Grace, what shall I do?"

"Did you ever kiss your princess?"
"Then . . . you . . . mean . . . my dream's
        . . . come true?"

THREE BIRDS

A cardinal upon the wing
Is like a radiant flying rose,
Or like a ruby that can sing;
The great-crest's thrilling yellow note
Comes from a wild sweet violin's throat.
The woodthrush, as the evening nears,
Weeps holy love's divinest tears.

THE FAIRIES' DANCE

In the moonlit happy glade,
Where the lights and shadows made
Glimmering shapes of haunting silence,
Forms of mystery and shade,—
There I saw the fairies dancing
With the moonlight softly glancing
On the starry steps entrancing.

White above them swam the moon
In the midnight's purple swoon,
And the hour in glade and thicket
Seemed at golden-cloudy noon:
Then there came a crystal ringing
As, on beams of moonlight swinging,
Soft I heard the fairies singing.

When the pine trees swayed and sighed,
Then I saw the fairies ride,
Floating misty in enchantment,
Dreaming on the night-wind's tide:
Then with dewy laughter sprinkling
All the flowers, and with tinkling
Song, they joined in dances twinkling.

THE SCORE IS EVEN

Though hardly one month old, she brings
Wonder to life that laughs and sings.
She looks at us with innocent eyes
Who are so worldly and so wise.
She never saw a rosered dawn,
A buck, a doe, a spotted fawn,
The dream the evening's builded on.
She never heard a wild bird sing;
She never heard a church-bell ring;
Really, she does not know a thing!
Yet though of life we know so much,
And though her ignorance is such,
Yet, after all, the score is even:
Does she not give us all of Heaven?

136

"AS WILD DOVES FLY"

This is the book that dear Josephine wrote.
These are the songs that she sang from her heart.
Sweet through life's forest the melodies float;
Music and nature are all of her art.
Out of the silences, haunting, remote,
Hear this wild bird in the woodland apart.

Singing in sunlight, with laughter atune,
Tenderly telling the tale of the years;
Now her contralto voice makes for the moon,
Deepening in beauty the deep of her tears;
Strange is the rapture, and mystic the rune,
Hymning of love and of joys and of fears.

This is her book and her heart and her song!
It is pure spirit, all winged and alight . . .
Soon comes our evening, and it will be long.
Tall are the shadows, and endless the night.
Yet for eternity music is strong,
As are the pinions of eagles in flight.

Here are her willows, the river-tide sweeping;
Her fairy fingers these bell-flowers rang.
Blooming forever, unfading, unsleeping,
Here are her roses that tremblingly hang.
Safe are they now in eternity's keeping.
These are the songs that dear Josephine sang.

AUTUMN SONG

In many a land, by many a tongue
I heard it said, I heard it sung,
"As strong as love when love is young."

By that the story's not half told.
That is but silver. Here's the gold:
"As strong as love when love is old."

137

OLD BENBOW, MY BLOODHOUND

With noble resolve on his wrinkled wise face,
With ponderous elegance, massive deep grace,
Old Benbow's my bloodhound, sagacious and true,
Whose pendulous dewlap is sweeping the dew.

Though fading the scent on the vanishing track,
He follows and finds. He will never turn back;
Through strangeness and darkness where men would be blind
Unerring his way to his quarry he'll find.

I remember the child that was wandered and lost,
Lamented by all those who loved him the most . . .
With his nose for a compass, his heart for a light,
Old Benbow recovered him deep in the night.

How gentle his mien, how forebearing his ways,
How far second-sighted his mournful proud gaze!
Relentless he'll bell on the trail without rest.
Life's glory for him is the baffling quest.

PORTRAIT-PAINTER

The beauty of the flesh means nothing to him,
For that is manifest as daisied meadows.
The flagrant lure of bosom, eye, and limb
Charms not his genius. . . . Deep in mortal shadows,
Sequestered in the midnight of the mind,
Veiled in the curtained heart,—there is his goal,
The buried treasure he is pledged to find,
The wonder of the wild mysterious soul.

His task ends not with finding . . . Glorious Lover,
With vision of all limitation free,
That its eternal grace we may discover,
He gives that spirit immortality.
The being God created, yet concealed,
By his unerring magic stands revealed.

NO COMMON MAN

Although I try as best I can,
I cannot find the common man:
Look here, look there, how different all!
And not one common will I call.
To live on earth and to be human
Is always to be most uncommon.

My Negro plowman has a way
Of singing at the break of day;
I know a tramp who's always smiling;
A blacksmith with blue eyes beguiling.
I know a mountaineer who plays
The dulcimer on dreary days.

All these are humble, all diverse;
To call them common is to curse
The varied wonder of each heart.
Eternal law sets us apart.
Each is original and lonely
As if the Lord had made him only.

All human spirits deviate,
Marvelous, whether small or great.
A tiny mountain stream I know,
Whose warbling secret waters flow
With elfin song and fairy motion
Is fascinating as the ocean.

A WISH

To love you in the light;
To be your strength and song
The whole day long;

Ever to hold and shield you in the dark;
To be your music in the night
Between the woodthrush and the lark.

I remember Ephraim, I remember Amos,
Pino, Abel, London, Linus, Lewis,
Always working with the pride of craftsmen;
Gabe, my handyman, hewing out of hickory
All my axe-handles. Wary for perfection,
Choosing patrician ash and straight-grained white oak.
I see Sambo squinting at the sleepers,
Broad-axe four-squared for the sure foundation.

I remember Rollins, amiable giant,
Always called on for the heavy lifting;
Strong as Samson, huge as Goliath,
Gentle as David with a lost lamb rescued.
I see Rollins with the massive shoulders,
Always bowing to receive their burden.
All of these workers, meek yet mighty,
Living out their lives on my far plantation.

It was black Gideon who taught me adoration,
Saying with a half-smile, "*Talk* isn't anything;
You've got to *do* it." And then his face was radiant,
Rapt with his dreaming of created beauty.
I remember Gideon, who once said to me,
"I can't pray well. I can only tell my Lord
That I am trying, always by the way I work
To praise His name. That's how I have to worship."

I remember all these, and would pay a tribute
To these unsung builders of America,
To these obscure unpraised architects,
Lost in the long ago, lost and forgotten
Save by Him who will remember always.
And I often wonder whether I shall find again
Any who will equal in their grace of spirit
These dark humble aristocrats of Africa.

STEELE'S HILL

Always Abner Lane, the engineer of No. 47,
About the time when the first stars
Were set in Heaven,
Would blow for the crossing,
Blow as he was passing
By the dark of Steele's Hill,—
Just where long ago,
If Abner had not blown for the crossing,
Ben Burley might have been killed,
Ben and his wife Lil.
Just when the night was getting still,
Abner would blow:
And we nearly always would know
What time it was; and it gave us a thrill,
A romantic friendly feeling of good-will
To hear Abner blow
By the dark of Steele's Hill.

Now the old engineer has made his last run;
And all his faithful blowing for the crossing
Is done;
And they have even
Taken off No. 47
Yet since nothing for us
The void he left can ever fill,
As long as life lasts we shall hear,
Just as the dusk is getting chill,
About the time of the first whippoorwill,
The wild drumming thunder
Of the train's rolling and tossing,
And Abner blowing for the crossing,—
Until
Like him we shall have found
Another night and day,
Far, far away
From the dark of Steele's Hill.

FRIEND

I have a friend to whom I seem
The coming true of every dream;
Whose eyes see in my every act
The pinnacle of wisdom, tact;
Whose faith's dismayed in me no whit
By all the blunders I commit;
Whose love for me, unselfish, strange,
Endures beyond all time and change.
For all I do seems good and wise
To those large trustful, faithful eyes.
He finds in fate no hard decree
Save in those hours unspent with me.
Hearing the coming of my feet,
He feels that life is passing sweet;
He finds the world gone bleak and gray,
Hearing my footsteps fade away.
Against him, if my anger burn,
He has no malice in return.
How joyous at my side he strays!
His love my every step waylays.
From every ambush, every foe,
He will protect me as I go.
And every day he teaches me
The meaning of fidelity.

High in love's radiant catalog
Of fealty, I place my dog.

IDYL

If you have ever seen
Two lovers in a lane,
Two lovers, gentle, strong,
Hearing a late bird-song,
With honeysuckle by,
And locust blooms above,
And an orchid sky,—
More hope, more love,
Wherever you have been,
You will not see again.

TO JEANIE

The beauty born of quietness
In her heart dwells;
Her stillness is the melody
Of wildflower bells;
Not by her words but by her ways
Her love she tells.

It is as if on mountain-tops
A gleaming row
Of angels just arrived from Heaven
All stood tiptoe,
Lifting their golden trumpets high
Their song to blow.

In all my years she never turned
Her face to me
But in her look I saw her love.
No need has she
For words to make me understand
What love can be.

MY COUNTRY

If in my songs the note of grief is heard,
The sound of evening bells and elegies,
Melodies by moonlight of the mockingbird,
The night-wind in the dim and dreaming trees,—
My voice is of my Country. I was born
By sorrowful fair shores, that in the arms
Of visions sleep, far, magical, forlorn,
Mourned by the beauty of pines and oaks and palms.

You do not hear me singing. But you hear
The twilight wind through myrtle, bay, and pine;
The mystery of marshes wide and drear;
The golden bells of the lustrous jasmine-vine;
The grieving loveliness that live-oaks wear;
The wildwood where the sad lost moonbeams shine.

143

Whenever I consider
What I shall leave behind,
The Cokers of Hartsville
Keep coming to my mind.

Perhaps I'll leave a ballad,
A sonnet, or a story;
But they bequeath the future vast
A heritage of glory.

They took a land forsaken,
Stricken with warfare's woes,
And out of pain and shadow wrought
The wonder of the rose.

Thus, while I sang of Nature
They toiled with her, to bring
Her beauty into blossom sweet,
Her winter into spring.

Loving their Carolina
Too well from her to roam,
They have a message for us all:
Life's Promised Land is Home.

I look, but cannot find it—
A work of equal worth—
Devising for posterity
The empire of the earth.

Charming the world to flower,
Sharing their noble skill,
They give the hearts of coming years
Wealth that no monarch will.

They are the unforgotten,
They are the good and great
Whose courage leaves to all mankind
Its infinite estate.

So when I think of heroes,
And their bequests, I find
The Cokers of Hartsville
Keep coming to my mind.

Let us all be praising God
For the woman with the rod.
She will urge her man till he
Is the man he ought to be.
Other girls their trophies wave,
But she has a soul to save.
Seeing what she is about,
All the heavens with joy will shout.
She will follow and will drive
Just as long as she's alive.
Not by road or dune or cape
From her love can he escape.
He is sullen, he is dense;
His salvation he resents.
Venus with her scented ways
Of allurement, she waylays;
She may be one of the furies,
But detours him round the houris.
To the woman with the flail,
Heavenly angels cry, "All hail!"
For the wife will goad and drive
Just to keep her Man alive;
She is willing to be mean
If her fury keeps him celan.
Lest his soul be driven down
To the harlots of the town.
Risking even love, a wife
Gives her valor and her life
That her Man may perfect stand,
Upright, dauntless. That her rose
Blooms for him, he rarely knows.
Let us all be praising God
For the woman with the rod.

MOUNTAIN MAN

In Danville, by the River Dan,
I met a bronzed old mountain man,
As weather-beaten as a berry
Amid the storms of January.
From Carroll County he had come
To make his daughter's house his home.
But there was in his banished eyes
A longing for the ampler skies
Above the craggy peaks he'd known
So well they had become his own.
As dauntless as the heart's despair
He had a lonely valiant air;
As from the crowd we stood apart,
He spoke to me straight from his heart:

"My children, they are good to me,—
Jane and her man,—good as can be.
But I keep walking in a dream.
I still can hear a panther scream;
I think I see the eagles go
Above the hills I used to know.
I walk these streets, yet I do not;
For all I am is quite forgot
In what I was, and what I'd do
Back in the wilderness I knew.
I'm sure I smell the watery sedge
A-waving by the river's edge;
I know I scent the rainy pines
That hold the swaying muscadines.

I dream so much I never feel
That living in this town is real.
I listen to the birdsongs wake
From every blossom-tasseled brake;
I hear the wild stream warbling
That's always in the mood to sing;

I know I'm here; and yet again
I'm pheasant-hunting in the glen
Where all the rhododendrons are;
And then I see the rising star
Above the Peaks of Otter. So
I guess it's time for me to go
Back to my cabin. Now, would you
Get used to living as I do?"

I met a very homesick man
In Danville, by the River Dan.

BEATRICE

As once I saw her stand, she'll always seem:
With unintended grace, as in a dream,
Leaning upon the western garden-gate,
Waiting, not knowing it is vain to wait—
Looking into the sunset—and at Fate.

She loved a soldier—would you hear her story?
And he had found an early grave—and glory.
Loving with love that never could be less,
She felt this fading eventide express
The passion of her spirit-loneliness.

Radiant for him who cannot come to claim it,
Her unspent beauty—grief could never tame it.
Another heart to hold her wildly wept,
But she that grace immaculately kept
For him who irrecoverably slept.

Forever in my thoughts, by day and night,
Beatrice stands dreaming in that dewy light,
The tall white lily-stars blooming above her;
Her flower of beauty open for her lover,
Who never shall that heavenly rose recover.

147

THE PURITAN

Of steel on steel he knew the ring,
This man who stood at Marston Moor;
Dreadful and spare the arms he bore,
This iron man who killed a king.

O'er him no banner flaunted bright,
For him no bugle proudly blared,
For he in sterner glory shared,
This simple soldier of the Right.

Truth was his banner, Faith his shield;
Terrible strength from God he took;
The Bible was his only book,
His place, the blood-red battlefield.

He fought to set his people free,
By wintry strife to haste the spring
Of Love's pure flowers blossoming,
This champion of liberty.

Banished from paths he fain had trod,
He turned his bleak face toward the West,
To search the wilderness for rest;
Banished from Man, at home with God.

DIESEL ENGINE

Down rushed the Diesel locomotive, bringing
The Crescent Limited out of the North, the night;
Southward she swept like a migrant swiftly winging,
Seeking far shores, enchanting in delight.
Then I saw in their cab the old white engineer,
And the Negro fireman,—good comrades who
Were guardians of lives entrusted to their care.
Coeval honor rested on these two.

And I said, "I see America, the heart, the whole:
The black man and the white are faithful brothers,
Holding the powerful Diesel in control.
Ceaseless the watch they keep for the safety of others,
Caring for them with equal loyalty.
I love a Land where such a thing can be.

148

HEART OF JOY

Beauties of the earth and air
Promise presences more fair;
Ever to divulge they fail
What is lost behind the veil!
Ever luring fields there are
Just beyond horizons far,
Bournes of glamour, whence emerge
Visions beckoning on the verge;
Mystery beneath the grass,
Bringing miracles to pass;
Secret sunset radiances
Undisplayed on mortal skies;
In the red dawn glowing hints
Of unseen celestial tints;
In a child's eyes, light not drawn
From the sunset or the dawn;
Melodies that can withhold
Music more than they have told;
Far eternal language heard
In the veery's mystic word.
Something's under nature's cloak,
Mighty in the massive oak;
Shadowy hands that shape the pine,
And its banding muscadine;
Premonitions of pure grace
In the wilding flower's face;
And the deep majestic sea
Moved by loftier majesty;
In earth's silences a tone
Not yet numbered with her own;
Glimmering messages from God
In the dreams of motherhood;
Spirit trembling forth in art
From its home within the heart.
Everywhere a Source unknown!
Everywhere a shrouded Throne!
Love unveiled for me one shrine,
Love, compassionate, divine,
Showing me the heart of joy
In my little laughing boy!

ADVICE TO A DEBUTANTE

From the tumult turn awhile,
From the street of Smartest Style;
Turn to nature. Innocently
Will her naïvete beguile.
Without strategy the wonder
Of the wilderness will smile.

Unaffected grace to learn,
Heed this rhythmic swaying fern;
Mark the meadow-grasses' moving,
And the gliding cloud discern;
On the wings of loving silence,
To her nest, the bird's return.

Listen to the thrush's tone
That is tenderer than your own;
Harken to the hid stream's warbling,
To her wildwood bugles blown;
Hear the harping from the pinewood
When the moon is on her throne.

Nature's beauty has no pose.
No theatric art she knows;
For there's no pretentious violet;
No designful lily glows;
There's no ostentatious orchid,
And no ceremonious rose.

ABSENCE

I thought the day would never end,
The dark would never come:
Morning had taken you away;
Evening would bring you home.

I thought the night would never pass,
The light would never come:
Evening had taken you away;
Morning would bring you home.

150

ON A BUST OF SIR ISAAC NEWTON

How calm this countenance of long ago,
How joyous and serene this classic face!
Nor faith nor knowledge only made it so.
His was a figure poised with massive grace
On spiritual truth and learning vast.
Genius and reverence his soul possessed.
From him and from his like we learn at last
Life's noblest triumph is a heart at rest.

As the great Angel seen on Patmos' strand
Stood, one foot on the shore, one on the sea,—
So Newton, poised with one foot on the land
Of law and nature and reality,
Leaned also on love's spiritual deep,
An everlasting tryst with God to keep.

CAESAR AND CLEOPATRA

I was a soldier, and a Roman one,
Clanging down martial corridors to fame;
Blazing against the thunder and the sun,
My eagles made far-terrible my name.
In clashing combat, brother to red Mars,
Kingdoms to deep oblivion I hurled;
My legions conquered under Gallic stars.
Mine and the might of Rome dismayed the world.

But suddenly I came on power more vast;
They failed me then, my strength, my legions true;
A conqueror, I trembled at love's charms.
All I had dreamed was triumph faded fast,
All I imagined glory,—when I knew
The mystery of Egypt in my arms.

THE CHILDREN

Their world is not our world,
They are dawn-hearted;
They know a rose-land, whence
We have departed.
Moonlit are all their streams;
Starlit are all their dreams;
They walk where wonder gleams
Through lands love-charted.

Their ways are not our ways:
Their sight ne'er wearies;
They see the nymphs and elves;
They see the fairies.
For them each wildflower glows
More than the regal rose;
Each brook a river flows;
Each song's the veery's.

Their hearts are not our hearts:
From dawn to even
They in a country dwell
Bordering Heaven.
As on another star,
Where once we were, they are
In a near land, yet far,
To children given.

SCULPTOR

There is a vastness in his soul;
We feel his strength like thunder roll,
Or like a tempest treading down
A massive oak-wood's old renown.
Its power is Nature's, and its might
Has all the majesty of night,
Immense and naked, thoughtful, deep,
Where angels for our anguish weep.
It seems all waters: the wild main's
Huge waves, the rivers, and the rains.
It seems all music: like the far
Grand universal orchestra,
Brimming with tears and love and laughter,
With spacious silence following after . . .
With lordlier mountains lost to view,
And violet vales we never knew,
It looms like range on mountain range,
August and beautiful and strange,—
Realms whence solemn stars emerge
Upon eternity's dim verge.

HOUR-GLASS

God set the sands to run,
Now darkened by the shade,
Now lightened by the sun.
As down life's glimmering glade,
Their fall is almost done.

I contemplate the sand:
Now almost all is spent.
I think I understand
God's merciful intent:
The sands that have run through,
At his command,
Still, still are permanent.

PEACHTREE

I want to go to Peachtree;
The river there is wide;
The moon, unmoored from Fanny Meade,
Comes sailing up the tide.

The quiet beach, windbroken
By deer-deep shrubberies
Looks to a far shore sentineled
By brave old cypress trees.

I want to go to Peachtree
To see the Peachtree Oak,
To hear black Gabriel's hunter-talk
About the woodland folk;

Of otter in the old canal
On Navarino wild,
Of bucks he watched by broad moonlight,
Of foxes he beguiled.

I want to go to Peachtree
To mark the sea-tides come
In wonder to dim forest shrines
Far from their tawny home;

River and wood shall friend me,
And over me the skies'
Bright wilderness of loveliness
Whose beauty never dies.

I want to go to Peachtree
To feel upon my face
Wet delta marsh-winds blowing;
To marvel with what grace

Beyond the lonely pinelands,
Austere, remote, sublime,
Up evening's oriel windows tall
The sunset roses climb.

I want to go to Peachtree
To see the ducks deploy
Above the yellowing ricefields old
As when I was a boy;

There as a boy I hunted,
Dreaming by shore and bay
Dreams that the mighty river caught
And carried far away.

Oh, I must go to Peachtree
(Ah, sweet wild questing vain!)
Upon the mightiest hunt of all:
To find my heart again.

OLD DEER HOUND

Old Bugle's hardly ever still.
He, even in siestas, will
Imagine that he's in a chase.
His feet keep running in a race.
His joyous muffled barks proclaim
A shadowy following of game.

He used to make the wildwoods ring,
Old Bugle with his bugling.
And now from dewy pinelands dim
A tangy fragrance comes to him:
I know he winds a buck, and yearns
To race him through the forest-ferns.

His splendid hunting days now done,
Bugle lies drowsing in the sun.
But dreams will never let him be,
For in his slumber he can see
The stags he sped across the river,
Swimming forever and forever.

Authentic as the oak that stands,
The monarch of his native wood,
Who draws his strength from Nature's own,
In modest majesty he stood.

We learned from him, who walked with God,
At peace amid our sin and strife,
The triumph of the great of heart,
The beauty of the blameless life.

His magic was forever old,
Forever new upon the earth:
The mystery of human charm,
The miracle of simple worth.

The elder grace we mourned as dead
Lived in him, clear for all to see;
His quietness was virtue's strength,
His presence, true nobility.

His loving spirit, generous hand,
His mind, that lifted high her light
For others, taught fidelity
To truth and charity and right.

For us a great transition comes
With death. But from our sight he fared
By gentleness and grace of heart
For his eternal home prepared.

For him, in that far other land,
Life should not different be or strange,
For living as he did on earth,
In heaven he has no need to change.

Familiar to him was the course
On which our souls must pioneer;
For the straight path that leads to God
Is the same path he followed here.

Beyond the Veil, we cannot see;
But in that Place where now he is;
If there be honor, he is crowned;
If there be glory, it is his.

THE LAST RED ROSE

The universal sky to chaos thundered;
The moon plunged stricken from her azure throne.
Tall Everest had in the great deep foundered;
Earth's bravest battlements went shuddering down.
In the last land a garden's glimmering grace
Inviolate shone, ringed by the shock and slaughter;
And there, the ultimate hope of all the race,
A lonely woman stood,—Eve's final daughter.

Fearless she faced the burning direful west.
"Eve wore the first one; I shall wear the last;
I am her daughter." In her beauty drest,
While ruin from all quarters gathered fast,
As for a festival with gallant air,
Dauntless she set the last rose in her hair.

GENIUS

Genius, I think, must soar the higher
In one whose gift is to inspire
Than in the one who, touched in heart,
Reveals that glory in his art.
Greater than her memorial,
The visionary Taj Mahal,
Was she whose Love found her the giver
Of all his spirit sought forever.
Greater was grim Horatius strong
Than is Macaulay's martial song;
Than sad Rossetti's lays of rue
The damozel who loved him true;
Than Poe, his Helen's beauty pale;
Than Keats, his haunting nightingale;
Than Shelley wild, his springing lark;
Than Thomson, his far City dark;
Than Robinson, his silent hills;
Than Wordsworth, all his daffodils;
Brighter than Noyes his Marian glows;
Than Millay, her autumnal rose.

157

FATHER TO SON

I battled alone through the night
Till the dawn in the distance grew bright.
I could not win to the mark,
But I would not yield to the dark,
That you might stand in the light.

My vision your eye has scanned:
My sabre is in your hand—
Though I lie with forgotten men
In a country beyond your ken,
By your side in the battle I stand.

And my wounded escaping foe
You shall utterly overthrow.
That Hill where my life I sold
Your courage shall capture and hold.
On its crest shall your banners glow.

O Son,—you who carry my name,
Within sight of the City I came,
Beyond whose defending wall
Towers the Citadel tall
Whose conquest shall be your fame.

BROTHERHOOD

Under the setting moon, the westering stars,
The tide had ebbed, as if earth's end had come;
Forsaking creeks and bays and shining bars,
Unto the mighty deep withdrawing home.
Lonely I stood upon a lonely slope,
Where mournful pines o'erlooked a desolate shore;
And as the tide retreated, so my hope
Ebbed out as if it would return no more.

But God rebuked me. With stupendous might,
After the water-harps a prelude played,
The tide returned like trumpets in the night.
How could I any longer be afraid,
Feeling my gathering strength a native part
Of the awful valve-gates of the ocean's heart?

ALLEGIANCE

By fragrant furrows turning
We know the spring has come;
By dreaming and by yearning
We know the season. Some
Will fall in love this springtime,
Will lead the bridal forth;
'Tis pledge-time and ring-time,
East, west, and south, and north.

But he will never marry,
Spring, summer, winter, fall;
For in his heart he'll carry
Allegiance to recall
A beauty past forgetting,
A rose that's always young,
A star that has no setting,
A song forever sung.

WORSHIP

We listened to the organ's shuddering gold
Of ocean music; to the anthems sung;
To the resplendent psalm in beauty rolled
In eloquence by a sonorous tongue.
Kneeling repentent to the King of heaven,
Sins we confessed, and were absolved of them.
We cast down crowns and diadems. We even
Felt we were healed,—had touched His garment's hem.

'Twas thus we worshiped there. As thence we passed,
We came upon a woman staidly weeping
In anguish by the way. From hope outcast,
A lonely tryst with sorrow she was keeping.
One of us knelt beside her on the sod;
And he alone knew how to worship God.

159

RISE, WEEPING HEART

Rise, weeping Heart, and be rose-crowned. You gave
All that a perfect love can ever give;
And love as great and beautiful and brave
Was given you. As long as you shall live
Triumphant love will lead you like a star
That never sets, but guides you toward the mark
Of virtue and of honor. Though afar,
It will not ever leave you in the dark.

Life's victory is yours: beloved to be,
And so to love that timeless is the spirit
That will sustain you over land and sea;
All beauty of the world you shall inherit;
And strength to master every high endeavor.
Rise, valiant Heart, and be rose-crowned forever.

THE FINGER OF GOD

In the dark, on the deep,
And in vain was the chart;
Vain also our stubborn
High valor of heart.
But then a star shone,
And we knew where we stood,
And we found our way home
By the finger of God.

SAVED

Deeper than any towering pine
Plunges her root beneath the sod
To find a life to save her own,
I will lay hold on God.

160

EVENING

There is no peace so perfect as the Day's
Surrendering to Night. Submissive, grave,
Light listens to the darkness,—and obeys.
Renouncing all her banners bright and brave,
Day abdicates her turquoise throne with grace,
Passing from beauty unto beauty's bourne;
Though of her glory there is left no trace,
Not ever for lost splendor will she mourn.

So when my evening comes, let me be still,
A sharer in the silence of the world,
Subdued as the quite vale, the tranquil hill,
With flags of pride and glory gently furled.
When night and stars arrive, O may I be
Native to their divine serenity.

FAITH

The listener on a little hill alone
Some evening at the coming on of spring
Hears in the heavens many a mystic wing
And converse of a fleeting joyous tone,
Yet can not see the migrants in their flight,
Although into the misty waste he peers,
And from the dim and viewless vastness hears
Sidereal voices haunt the ghostly night.

So are we certain, though we can not see
What we believe, in life's strange darkness deep.
There is in faith a power that sets us free
To vision what the night would from us keep
Clearly as noonday earth shows to the skies'
Cerulean and meditative eyes.

161

ARRIVALS

The child who leaves that mystic cradling
Beneath his mother's heart,—how can he guess
Of waiting true love's welcoming caress?
What knowledge of his new world can he bring?
What knows he of a mother's ministering?
Yet love yearns over his mere helplessness,
With strength to shield, with holy prayers to bless,
With arms to hold, and tenderest voice to sing.

So when his feet upon life's western slope
Are setting toward that other land unknown,
His heart shall be sustained by this sweet hope:
That as to mortal days, naked, alone,
Weeping he came, yet found love's welcome here,
Solace no less than love's shall be his there.

DEEPER NOSTALGIA

I know that you are homesick, far away,
Missing the river and the quiet meadows,
The trout-stream, warbling at the close of day,
The aromatic pines,—and even the shadows
That veil the hills, along whose dusky crest
The stars begin in mystery to move:
You yearn for these, and yearn for all the rest
That makes your home the place you dearly love.

And your repining soon may have an end;
All you have lost, tomorrow may restore;
Home fields and stars may greet you; many a friend
Rejoice that you are with your own once more,—
While I must live with longing that is vain,
Homesick for one who comes not home again.

SURVIVAL

When from your wings life's dust is shed;
Your light alive, your shadow, dead;
When nothing mortal's left to mar
Your spirit; when alone, afar,
To Many Mansions you are led,
You'll take to Heaven's holy star
Only the beauty that you are.

THEN AND NOW

Beauty of earth to me
She used to be, . . .
Darkening the rose and the sun,
And the stars every one.
All loveliness
My heart could capture and might safely keep
She could express:
The breath of the soul's wing,
Sweet virtuous passion of the virgin spring,
Love, rapture, beauty, glimmering innocent sleep.
And now she is away.
Yet she makes fair my day,
And beautiful my night:
Immaculately an hour
Trembling in the wildflower;
The thought of her in darkness brings me light.
She comes and goes
With rainbow and with rose;
In the sad moonlight streaming,
And in the wild star gleaming.
Beauty she was to me
In her mortality:
But now, and ever to be,
Beauty is she.

MY GLORY

I who have sung to you,
Silently clung to you,
Come again singing,
Down the sweet woodland road
Wild flowers bringing.
Of nature's beauty-dress
You are the wearer.
I feel your loveliness
As I come nearer.
Child of all fragrances,
Sweetheart of light,
I'm coming home again
To my delight:
I who have sung to you,
Silently clung to you
Come again singing,
Wild roses bringing.
They, if my speech should fail,
Will tell my story;
You are my Holy Grail,
You are my glory.

TOILERS

Who'll break the tough glebe now?
"I," said the patient plow.

Who'll smoothe the field tomorrow?
"I," said the hardy harrow.

Who'll wet and warm the clod?
"I," said unfailing God.

Who'll gather in the grain?
"I," said strong Farmer Lane.

And gather him, who must?
"I," said the quiet dust.

LONG ARMISTICE

Where they meet no more to part;
Every one lies heart-to-heart;
Every one goes hand-in-hand
In that far mysterious land.
Pride, the Countess, coming down
From the lofty place she had,
There commingles with the Clown,
In one dusty mantle clad.

In those mansions calm of shade,
Universal truce is made;
Hostile hearts, at last benign,
Everlasting treaties sign.
All their cares a twilight's hushing:
There the darkness and the sun,
There the fading and the flushing,
There the rose and thorn are one.

In one sleep they all are dreaming,
Over all one banner streaming
Keeps them safe from every ill;
In one silence all are still.
There no creed or caste or station;
There no boundary holds apart.
All are of one race and nation;
All are of one mind and heart.

By the passionate impure
There the virgin rests secure,
And the black man and the white
Share one blanket for the night.
There eternal Love and Hate,
Joy and Sorrow fast are wed
In the dim, immaculate,
Long armistice of the Dead.

GALATEA

I wonder whether Galatea gained
By her transition? Out of dreaming stone
Pygmalion wrought her with a joy unfeigned,
A perfect statue in her beauty lone.
She knew no hope or fear, no love or hate;
She had no longing, and she had no care;
Passionless, beautiful, immaculate,
Calm as eternity and as austere.

Now furious through her veins and arteries
The wild blood races, for she is alive;
Sentient to love, to pains, to ecstasies,
She learns to wait in silence, and to strive
How to sustain, of joy or grief, the shock,
Who was at peace while sleeping in the rock.

HEART'S CITADEL

I saw one weary, weaponless, alone,
And no retreat, and no advance he found.
And all his hopes by hurricanes were blown
To deepest hell,—yet did he hold his ground,
His heart's high citadel. The foe's arrays,
Discovering him, could not discover fear.
Dauntless upon his doom I saw him gaze,
And heard him challenge fate, "Halt! Who comes her"

"Ah," then I said, "although his life is o'er,
"Fate is defeated, though his victim falls.
Frustrated death from that dark combat bore
No trophy for his dim memorial halls.
Behold, the Citadel stands as before,
With all its banners streaming from its walls."

166

GENTLE MEETING

Men made me dread to meet
God,— but I found it sweet,—

I who had disobeyed
The laws men said He made.

But from Him was no, "You!
You wretch, for mercy sue!

You wicked sinner!" Rather,
Just like a gentle father,

"Son, how your garden grows!
I love that yellow rose.

And that narcissus seems
Come from a land of dreams.

For the fine work you've done,
I'm proud of you, dear son."

SURPRISE

I never remember your beauty without saying,
"Glory to God who brought you into being,
Visioned the miracle of your arraying
The lonely pathway of my pilgrimage.
For me the aspect of all life you change.
My journey with your tender grace waylaying;
And even Paradise you can presage.
You are the mystic, beautiful, and strange
Wildflower I had no dream of ever seeing,
The answered prayer I had no thought of praying."

SOLDIER'S RETURN

To the wilds and the wolves
Went my innocent son;
To the jades and hyenas
My dear guileless one;
By many a perfumed
Rose-gateway to hell;
By many a naked
And fain Jezebel;
By Beauty betraying,
His honor unspent,
His armor still burnished,
He came as he went.

TO A VOYAGEUR

My Love to foreign lands has gone
To see the paintings, glorious, lone,
Out of the centuries that were;
To view the statues wrought in stone,
Beauty on her eternal throne—
Old as the cloudy kings of Ur.
If artists of the Past had known
My Love, how gladly would they own
They learned of loveliness from her.

THE REACH OF VALOR

It well may be that in that battle old
In which Arminius defied the might
Of Rome, magnificent in armor bright,
Led by proud Varus, corsleted in gold;
It well may be that one barbarian bold,
In the war's heart, and at its wavering height
Of fury, stood his ground and fought his fight,—
A hero long forgotten in the mold.

We never know how much we should rejoice
In valor, or how vast its realm will be:
A man unknown made an immortal choice,—
And gave us England, beautiful and free;
He gave us Shakespeare, and the mighty voice
Of Milton, rolling like the Cornish sea.

WHEN THE WINE IS RED

Why, from the banquet, when the wine is red,
And Beauty beckons with surrendering eyes,
When joy and mirth their radiances shed,
Should I in anguish suddenly arise
And into darkness go? The feast is young.
The revelry is gay. It is not late.
And many a friend with praises on his tongue
And grace in his fond heart would bid me wait.

But I renounce the glamour and the light.
The wine of glory on the ground I pour.
Turning my face into the quiet night,
Of fame and triumph will I dream no more.
No more for me be any trumpet blown,
Since she who would have cared to hear is gone.

169

THE TROUT STREAM

Rising in the mountains old,
Young at heart and pure and cold,
Down the laurelled gorges flashing,
Brimming sunlit pools with gold,
Warbling water I have heard,
Water warbling like a bird,
Murmured music of the woodland
On the listening heart conferred.

O at dawn my stream to meet!
My blithe singing-friend to greet
When the dew is on the wildrose
And the mist is on the wheat!
Gurgling waters heard again,
Waters gurgling down the glen,
Flowing through the home of nature,
Far from haunts of weary men.

Bright and clear the noonday stream;
But when moonrays on it beam,
Every pool's a purple jewel,
Every wave's a sparkling dream:
Twinkling silence there is found,
Silence twinkling into sound,
Drifting into music-mist that
Fills the fragrant woods around.

On a sea-beach, far from home,
I have watched the twilight come,
With sunset wildly reddening,
The maned sea-breakers' foam;
Trampling thunder toward me bore,
Thunder trampling on the shore,
Then I longed for my sweet wood-stream
And its gentler love and lore.

Yours is an endearing art,
Charming more as years depart,
Full of glamour, and of golden
Memories that haunt the heart!

Noble rivers, deep and free,
Rivers rushing to the sea,
Wake my wonder; but my wood-stream
Ever holds the love of me.

NOT FLOWN AWAY

Like a singing bird
From a blosssoming bough
Beauty has flown away.
With rapture I had heard
Those lyrics sweet and gay.
But now
My music is no more. No lute
Or far or near
I hear,
For the wildwood song of love is mute.
O Song that was my Hope, a lyric voice
To make my heart rejoice!
Now in what vale, now to what height have you gone?
To leave me in silence alone?
Beyond what towering mountain, spacious river,
Have you vanished, and is it forever?
Yet even as my brow is burning,
My soul in sorrow yearning,
I hear a song returning,—
Over all barriers its lyric art,
From every other music far apart,
Comes home, comes home to my desolate and yearning
        heart!

O NOT FOR ME

O not for me the beach's dolorous thunder.
Take me into the wildwoods, where the songs
Of birds make music out of love and wonder.
With such melodious peace my soul belongs.

MAULFRY

Maulfry, the ancient witch, the old woman wise,
Lived in a lonely wood, and lived all alone;
Too deep for sorrow or for joy or surprise,
She dwelt there like a tree or the earth or a stone.

To her many women brought griefs and troubles old.
Once there came a mother of a loved and only son.
"Maulfry, I would have him treasure Truth above all gold.
"Teach him well to love it, and your task is done."

"Maulfry, I must leave him soon. This is the prayer I pray:
I would have him travel onward straight to God's throne.
How can I have certainty he shall not miss the way?"
"Teach him to love Beauty, and your task is done."

She laid her heart to Nature's in that wildwood place,
Did Maulfry in the moonlight, Maulfry in the sun.
"O I would have my darling lad to wear a heart of grace."
"Teach him to love Honor, and your task is done."

Mothers true of all mankind, you know unrest;
Yet each can make the future for her worshiped one.
Would you leave to your beloved the treasure that is best?
Teach him well to love it, and your task is done.

THE TROUBADOURS OF GOD

Glad is the dawn with gold and silver voices
From mockingbird and thrush and cardinal:
Each with sweet music's ecstasy rejoices,
Since all their hearts are holding festival
For love's return. The Giver of Love they praise,
Caroling to Him their joy in perfect song . . .
And there is this high wisdom in their ways:
Only by yielding all can love be strong.

Wild minstrels of the field and fragrant wood,
In your sweet choir I would have a part,
At one with your adoring joyful mood;
For shame it were if my ungrateful heart
Should be as cold and silent as a clod
When I might join the troubadours of God.

172

BRIDAL BIRCH

On angel wings of light
Past man's devising,
In the misty wood arising
A silver spirit gleams
With silvery dreams—
Her argent body bright,
Shimmering in night—
In the dewy moonlight fair,
With streaming hair,
And cool and lustrous body bare.

So in the dark and dew
When Adam came to woo,
Might Eve have stood
In Eden's odorous solitude,
Bridal and beautiful,
A chalice with love's cordial brimming full—
Trembling all over,
Waiting her lover.

Waiting some sweetheart now
My birch-tree stands,
With delicate stars burning around her brow;
With silvery hands,
And wild still hair alight,
Her argent body bright,
In the sweet wood gleaming,
Her virgin heart a-dreaming,
Its flower opening wide,
A spirit and a bride—
Trembling, joyous, brave,
Submissive, grave,
A sybil yet a child,
Mysterious, wild—
Luring her lover near
With more of hope than fear.

SEA-ISLAND EVENING

Silently now in the set of sun
Paces a stag where the green waves run.

Over the marsh where the tide brims high
Whimpers the willet his human cry.

Beating his passage above the foam,
Cruises the great bald eagle home.

Hushed by the silvery footfalls of night,
Shimmer the woods in a faerie light.

Veeringly fleet in the first stars' glow,
Hurry the teal to the reedy floe.

Over the darkly momentous pines
Far and more fair the sunset shines:

Oriel windows of evening tall,
Radiant with roses that clamber and fall.

Keeping with shadows a dewy tryst,
The wood-thrush (exquisite elegist!)

Breathes from his delicate astral flute
Music that utters all magic mute;

Music like mystical fragrance beguiled
From blossoms of wonder and beauty wild.

LIKE THE DARK EARTH

Like the dark earth I seem:
Your love, the sun.
Joyous I gleam
In its beautiful light.
If that were done,
There would be left to me
Nothing but night.

174

MOCKINGBIRD BY MOONLIGHT

Listening when loved ones no longer are near,
What is the message of hope that I hear?
What is restoring my heart to her throne?
Only a mockingbird singing alone.

Only a minstrel by moonlight rejoicing,
Yet in wild magic his melody's voicing
Beauty that brings back a love that was gone,
Magical mockingbird, singing alone!

Hymner of dreams and of vanished delights,
Singing alone when all else in the night's,
Bringing to me all the years that have flown,
Marvelous mockingbird, singing alone!

Plunged is the world in the silence of sleep;
Mystical out of the dark and the deep.
Telling of love that for death can atone,
Only a mockingbird singing alone!

Hateful to me was the moonlight so fair:
What saved my spirit from death and despair?
Waking my heart to the joy it had known?
Only a mockingbird singing alone!

SONG OF THE QUEST

From mighty minds, in volumes old,
Who, though departed, ne'er depart—
The truth I sought,—from Nature, Art;
But more of Truth in you is told
Who is its beating heart.

On oceans far I held the helm,
Through wondrous seas the course I laid;
Through fairest lands my quest I made;
But nought I found in Beauty's realm
To make your beauty fade.

NOSTALGIA

Is the red-bud glowing,
By the river in the rain?
Is the spirea snowing,
Now I come not again?

Is the Negro singing
Beside his creaking cart,
Because the year is swinging
Her censer through his heart?

Is the night-hawk calling
Down in the pasture dim,
Just when the dusk is falling,
And stars their vespers hymn?

Now through my heart wild-thronging
The sweet old memories come:
And I am sick with longing
For my plantation home.

SECURITY

Unguarded on the hill the orchis lifts
Her saffron spire; by the lonely stream
The rosebay, like a dreamer in a dream
Fearlessly blooms. From vulnerable rifts
In the wild rocks the columbine is flaunting
Her crimson kirtle. In the ancient wood
Exposed to peril of their solitude,
The infant trees their enemies are daunting.

Having a faith that is their sure defense,
Their loveliness unshielded is displayed
Radiant in virgin beauty's innocence,
In armor of the love of God arrayed . . .
There is a Heart that watches over these,
Are we not more than many flowers and trees?

TIME FOR HOME

When the wailing whippoorwill
Wails upon the lonely hill,
Where the locust-blossoms falling
Float the fragrance of his calling,
When the Dusk with fingers white
Closes curtains of the night,
Homeward I my way must take,
Or my heart is like to break!

When I hear the sounding frogs
Sounding from the lusty bogs,
From enchanting dim morasses
Where the waters drown the grasses,
Minstrels of the quaking sod,
Twilight carolers to God,
While the blinking stars awake,
Then my heart is like to break!

When the moon like love is setting
With a glamour of regretting,
Like a doomed and splendid sail
Passing far through portals pale,
When the night's a sorceress,
Yearning, yearning to caress,
Then my wilds I must forsake,
Else my heart is like to break!

Now the evening pines are chanting,
And the sweet-bay glimmers haunting;
Now the oaks in dewy sleep
Tower in dark silence deep;
Now a misty wind comes cold
From the swamp that molders old—
Of these charms if I partake,
Then my heart is like to break!

LOVE IN THE WILDWOODS

Secure within the arms of love he lay,
Though never human heart against his beat,
Or purple vows were breathed in that retreat,
The certain death of passion to withstay.
On the deep bosom of the earth reclined,
He listened to the voices of the wood,
Yielded his soul to fragrant solitude,
And all his coming years to God resigned.

There is a peace the world can never give,
But nature grants it, joyous and profound,
Unto a heart to beauty sensitive . . .
That conquering compassion he has found
Who on the heart of God, in wildwoods lone,
Sustains and stills the beating of his own.

THE USURPER

While walking in the yellow wood,
I heard a song-bird's sweet refrain;
And as I stopped, there came a hush;
Then it began to sing again.

It sang of what my dreams were made,
Of Carolina bay and pine,
Of sunlight gleaming on the grass
Where soft the warm savannas shine.

Then, rising high, the fugitive
From winter sped adown the deep
Of autumn skies, and left me lone,
Feeling as if I wished to weep.

O Lover of my Summer Land,
For you her lustrous beauty gleams:
Unto your breast you'll clasp my bride,
While I shall hold her but in dreams.

FUGITIVE NIGHT

As I came out at daybreak
Into the glimmering dawn,
There was an air of loneliness,
A sense of beauty gone.

Here from the moonlit garden,
Just when the light was gray,
She who had been at revelry
So swiftly sped away.

That I am sure she dropped them—
Though I did not see her pass—
This misty mantle on the lawn,
These jewels on the grass.

TWILIGHT ELEGY

Beautiful singer of the gorgeous rite
Of setting suns, calm elegist of Light!

If purple anthems from the pineland rolled,
Blown by the pines' rich organ-basses bold;

If music of undiscovered oceans tossed
On mystic shores, to all but dreamers lost;

If flowers, rosy with the dawn's caress,
Found utterance for their dewy loveliness;

If twilight, lingering in a fragrant dell,
Were lyric with the thought of life's farewell;

If these were tuned to love by heavenly art,
Divinely penetrative of the heart,—

They would be vocal in thy poignant song,
Floating the holy woodland aisles along,

When, ere the magic star of evening gleams,
Thy mortal music builds immortal dreams.

PLANTATION MORNING

A thousand pines are burning bright,
A thousand warders of the night
Along the gorgeous sunrise line
In red pulsating armor shine.
Far-glowing as a mystic sea,
The sedgefield's rolling goldenly.
All dewy-tender is the blue
Of early skies; while breathing through
The trembling pines a dawn wind seems
Whispering the giants from their dreams,
Until their voices, nobly one,
Go thronging joyful to the sun.

Lyric in their fair morn of spring,
The larks are flying wing and wing;
Through twinkling dews ambrosial
Echoes the bobwhite's ringing call;
Where mistily the woodlots meet,
The cardinals are whistling sweet;
The mock-bird's singing joyous-free,
The bluebird's warbling sunnily;
From glistening elms and laurels tall,
Bright restless blue jays fly and call,
Scattering the shining drops that fall;
High in the dreamful sycamores
That sentinel the river shores
The wild dove suns her rosy breast,
Visioning love, and mate, and nest.

The ancient home comes into view
Far down the shadowy avenue;
Glimmer beneath their live-oak shades
The cool, colonial colonnades,
The porches broad, the pillars white,
The leaded windows twinkling light.
The sunrise shimmeringly discloses
The dreams the garden had of roses.
In bridal bloom the cherry trees
Are fluttering in the fragrant breeze;

Long rows of cotton and of corn
Are gleaming in the gaudy morn,
As far fields swim into the gaze
Beneath the soft mist's sparkling haze.

In beauty, by the dark pine groves,
A mystic radiant spirit moves,
Touching the home, the fields, the trees

THE CONDOR

Red dawn is on the Andes, and the snow has kindled flame;
The flaring splendor wakens, in his aerie on the height,
The lone and lordly condor from his spacious mountain dreams,
And he spreads his mighty pinions in the grandeur of his flight.

Below him, lost to sight of man, his visioning is clear;
His fierce unlidded eye has swept the forests and the plains;
He rides the wind of morning and he soars against the sun;
He plunges through the thunderstorm and distances the rains.

The condor! O the condor! How magnificent he is!
The spirit of the loneliness on far eternal hills,
The voice of solitary space, the wonder and the might
Of earth's primeval splendor his character fulfils.

Superber than the eagle, and expressing more than he
The solitude and vastness of mountain-majesty;
His the remotest fastness now that baffles human strength,
And his heart forever is unconquerably free!

NATURE'S MISTAKE

As his loving ardor burns,
To his bride the bridegroom turns,
Lying listless by his side.
Yet not once life's long night through
Be he tender, be he true,
To the bridegroom turns his bride.

181

THE HEART'S TROUBADOURS

Life still has its choir of those
Who exalt our desires and dreams,
Who sing us the lily and rose,
Who lead us by magical streams.
When earth's other music is mute,
And the voices of heaven are dumb,
With the harp and the viol and lute,
And tidings of glamour they come.

When weary of thundering hooves
Of war and of progress and fame,
When ashamed of ignoble loves,
And of victories sullied by shame,
O hark to the voices that bring
Enchanting brave melodies true;
For only the songs that they sing
Are ever worth listening to.

A realm romantic they make;
They give us the beauty we crave;
An astral far splendor they wake,
As the moon on the western wave.
And love they apparel in light,
In wonder that makes it divine;
They praise its mysterious might,
And build it a glimmering shrine.

They heal us, the heart's troubadours,
As they chant of the golden years.
Their music life's magic restores.
They sing; and a vision appears
Of hearts that are valiant still,
Of grace and of glory to be;
Of strength like the height of a hill,
Of love like the deep of the sea.

SPRING IN THE SOUTH

All in this greenly-shimmering spring,
In dimly-iridescent days,
I hear the mated thrushes sing,
And down the fragrant woodland ways

Shy happy birds with plumage rare
Flash through the glimmering solitudes,
And like sweet censors swung in air,
Perfume with song the dewy woods.

The yellow pine that soars above
The bullgrape-woven thicket dim,
Bears to the blue a song of love,
Bears to the earth his azure's hymn.

The columbine her ruby cup
Uplifts, brimful of honey rare;
The jasmine-fountain tosses up
Her saffron showers, stayed in air.

When, as a raindrop on a rose,
A white star in the red west gleams,
Peace wraps the world in deep repose,
In silence, sleep, and lovely dreams.

More magic's by the night conferred!
While for a sinless world I long,
I hear a midnight mockingbird
Rebuilding Eden with a song.

PLANTATION CHRISTMAS NIGHT

The sun his race superb has almost run,
And now is sinking into tall pine-crests;
Light's glorious service to the world is done,
And on the landscape calm in farewell rests;
Afar on happy fields fall his bequests.
Soft breathes the earth in quiet confidence.
The birds are swaying in their gray moss nests,
Gently the dusk unfolds her misty tents
Against the west remote in red magnificence.

Star-spangled Twilight, diademed and dim,
Hallows the world with her resplendent reign.
The lyric heavens are a noble hymn
To the Creator in His mighty fane,
Unutterable song and glad refrain
In which all hearts must join in pure delight
Of listening love and hope. Now shine serene,
Arriving silently with faces bright,
The wise, companionable stars. And it is night.
A mist had veiled the eastern river-fens,

But beauteously the Christmas moon breaks through;
Hale fragrances are breathed from pinewood glens;
The live-oaks old glimmer in silvering dew,
Shivering sweet 'neath the high tent of blue.
Pale pendulous mosses wave. The dusk-owls sigh
On muffled wings as they their prey pursue.
In marshy ricefields feeding wild-ducks cry
In happy concourse 'neath the wide and moonlit sky.

The great white house is dreaming in its grove
Of laurels and of live-oaks. Overhead,
The Christmas stars in stately marching move,
And on the earth their benediction shed.
For Love is born, and ancient Fear is fled.
Far-off, clear strains of mystic music swell
From Negro hearts whom love has comforted.
Their common faith they sweetly, humbly tell . . .
It is God's Holy Night, and all the earth is well.

Ah, all is well! although a thousand years
Roll into shadow, into dust may roll.
Humanity with all its faith and fears
Is led by one imperishable soul,
The Master. He can make the broken whole,
Heal the sick mind, the wandered steps can lead,
Gladden the heart by making clean the scroll
Written against it. He is love indeed,
The only power of which life stands in constant need.

For love and for her Lord of Light arrayed,
From mist emerges fair the roseate earth;
Night's glories deepen as they nobly fade
In grave obeisance to the Master's birth . . .
Until His Day, all days were little worth.
But by God's gift, each day love's gift can bring.
Let every heart proclaim its Christmas mirth!
Love, love alone is conqueror and king;
And mortal hearts at peace their Christmas songs may sing.

A SOUTHERN WIND

Hear the sound of the wind on the desolate sand-dunes,
The whispering sea-wind that cautiously moans,
Up in the green hummocks of myrtle and cedar,
Down o'er the dells of wild oats and wampee,
Up to the pine woods, low-laden with fragrance,
Deep to the grey old swamp, home of the cypress.
Then the fair laurel leaves laugh as it lingers,
Turning their gleaming sides bright in the sun's glow,
Now to the shrubbery, dark with its verdure,
Cool in its darkness, sweet in its quietness—
Then from the low-lands the wind fast up-springing,
Flies in an ecstacy up to the mountain tops,
Tosses the fronded oaks, sways the dark, tranquil pines,
Then wanders once more adown to the seashore,
Weeps o'er the sand hills and sobs with the surf,
And then, with a faint and a farewelling murmur,
Loses itself on the glimmering ocean.

185

SOUTHERN PINES

O the Southern Pineland free
Breathes immortal melody,
Like the immemorial music of the old melodious sea:
Purer than the live-oak shrines,
Sweeter than the jessamines,
Is the wild and lonely liberty beneath the windy pines.

Nor is any land diviner
Than the one whose sons enshrine her
In their hearts of hearts, though exilted, as their Mother
Carolina,
And she holds their love in keep,
And when shadows gather deep,
To her fragrant sanctuary they will come home to sleep.

From the sea-coast and the hill,
They go forth against their will,
Yet they shall return at evening when the weary heart is s
When the eyes are dark with tears,
And the fainting spirit hears,
From a bourne exceeding beautiful, the voice of other years

They will gather from afar,
As at evening star on star,
Fills the ancient courts of heaven where God's peace and
silence are.
On their tired brows no bays,
Nor around them shouts of praise,
As they gather in the sunset after many, many days.

They will gather in the gloaming,
In the twilight that is coming,
They will gather, they will gather when the time is done
for roaming.
When their sun is in the west,
And the air is tenderest,
Then their Mother Carolina will enfold them on her breast.

Under that sweet Southern sky,
   All untroubled they will lie,
They will dream and see beloved faces of the days gone by;
   While the mystic pine-wind blows,
   And the quiet river flows,
Bearing hearts upon its bosom to the Lily and the Rose.

   Southern Pines, still hold for us
   Magic sweet and perilous,
Dreams that linger longest and make darkness luminous.
   Though on alien shore and foam,
   We can hear you call us home,
And we answer you in spirit as in truth we soon shall come.

   While thine altar fires burn,
   While the heart of man may yearn,
O my Mother Carolina, unto thee we turn, we turn;
   Bearing thee as love's own token,
   Love, with dying accents spoken,
Hearts, that by their coming, give the gift of faith unbroken.

THE STAG

Today in the wild pinelands a stag I saw,
A noble buck in the lone pinelands today.
I was walking upwind. At the end of a swampy draw,
Bounding from his bed of ferns, he fled away.
It was not for long I saw him, but long enough
To see his lithe and powerful grace, to mark
His craggy antlers, beaded and brown and rough,
And his flag that glimmered white through the forest
   dark.

It was more than a deer I saw in the wildwood green,
And the presence of him filled me with awe; for I,
In that shaggy, proud, primeval stag had seen
America under a prehistoric sky;
A tawny sleeping empire, boundless, blest,
Before Columbus dreamed there was a West.

187

YOU'LL WEAR MY LOVE

Some carry love as if a cross
They dutifully bear;
And some sustain it like a yoke,
A harness, or a gear.
But you will wear this love of mine
As a wildflower is worn,—
Transfiguring your loveliness,
And by your beauty borne
As lightly, as eternally,
As intimately yours
As any star to Evening's breast
That sparkles and endures;
As if beside a meadow-stream
A wild rose you had found,
And in your hair for joy of love
Its fairy hope had bound;
As if you, as a radiant cloud,
Above Time's sea and shore,
Forever iridescently
A glorious rainbow wore.

LOVE IS A LITTLE THING

"Love is a little thing," I heard it said;
"A childish dream, a tremulous rainbow hung
In vanishing beauty; a confection, fed
To visionary women and the young.
But we are made for sterner tasks; for those
That clamor for an iron conquering:
Let weaklings sip the dew upon the rose;
Life calls for valor . . . Love's little thing."

A little thing? Then naught at all are these:
Glory, with all her solemn flags unfurled;
God, and our drams divine that toward Him roam;
The music of all the birds in all the trees;
The might of all the waters of the world
As one vast tidal wave deep-thundering home.

TRIBUTE

Others had praised her. It remained for me
To be the perfect tribute. When I came
Within the circle of her mystery,
I lost my memory, my place, my name.
All that I once had been I was no more;
For now I was a symbol and a sign
Of her own loveliness. The air I wore
Was the effect her spirit had on mine.

Other acclaimed her. Mute I stood and still.
Not alabaster or the marble cold
To beauty wrought by the sculptor's passionate will,
Or emblem fashioned from the ruddy gold
More of the artist's deathless dream could tell
Than I, who stood a statue to her spell.

MY CITY

I know a lady veiled beside the sea;
A spirit beautiful with mystery;
From sin and death she sets her lovers free.

But those who pass across the darkness far,
Seeking for darkness, nor for any star,
And find themselves, beholding what they are—

Barbaric wanderers,—never unto these
Will she reveal her beauty and her peace,
Sweet by the dreaming of her purple seas.

He who would pass behind her veil must die;
He must renounce his earth to reach her sky;
And he must lose himself in chivalry.

She is not desolate: love has sufficed.
No scarlet flowers have her heart enticed;
And still she gazes on the face of Christ.

The veil that guards her features trembles, stirs;
She smiles upon her transient worshipers,—
Knowing her Own, and love that still is hers.

NO OTHER LIGHT

There is no other light
Like the love-light;
For it alone illumines life.
The source of its mystical beauty,
Its might,
No one knows.
Flaring away from the victor,
On the vanquished it sometimes glows.
On husband and wife
It sometimes shines—
But oftener not.
To men by men forgot
It gives its gleams,
Turning defeat into glory,
And dust to celestial dreams.
I once heard a story
Of a pearl of great price.
But even if one were a king or an earl
And had such a gem to possess,
And covetously to caress,
A pearl can be only a pearl,
Perfect and beautiful and cold,
To be bought and sold.
But the love-light,
If it should deign to shine on you,
Will transfigure all that you are,
Even your failure and shame;
Your spirit will blossom tall
Under its radiant star,
Flowering fragrant forever
By the banks of eternity's river.
Its flame
Alone confers rapture and grace.
O pray to all gods
That to you may be turned
The light of love's face.
Then will you be stronger than sorrow
However cruel tomorrow,
You will to no anguish surrender;
Having known ultimate splendor.

A SONG IN ABSENCE

For the Girl that I love I grieve:
All the beauty of life I leave
When I must be far from her;
For she alone can confer
The wonder none other can give,
By her love alone can I live;
By her glamour like moonlight glowing,
By the power that comes from knowing
That she will forever care.
I grieve; but wherever I fare,
Her love will not ever forget,—
My crown and my coronet;
My peace amid anguish and strife,
My Resurrection and Life!
Although I am far, far away,
Her love is my strength and my stay.
The source of my joy is her heart;
And though we are sundered apart,
So fast in deep love are we,
No nearer we ever could be.

OUR SONG'S RETURN

To our need is brought the beauty
That we feared had gone away,
Long ago and far away;
And the music of that singing
Says the things we cannot say.
True love cannot be defeated;
For the tide that has retreated
Turns again to flood the shore
With more rapture than before.
All the glory that seemed going
Gleams on us and lights our way;
For the spirit has a reach
Far beyond all mortal speech;
Has the power to divine
All the love that's yours and mine.
And is so divinely strong,
It can bring us back our song, . . .
Lovely, though still far away;
And the music of that singing
Says the things we cannot say.

191

WELCOME HOME

If I have a home
On the sand or the rock,
Should you come there,
You need not knock.
Be my gates made fast,
And my windows barred,
Against your love
I have no guard.
Though my doors be locked
Impregnably,
To all I am
You are the key.

HEART'S SANCTUARY

I who was restless found
In you my rest;
I who was homeless lay
On your sweet breast.
I who had need of song
Heard in your singing
Music the wild bird makes
To his love winging.
I whose deep anguish seemed
Never to cease
Found in the gift you gave
Peace, perfect peace.

LOST LITTLE CHILDREN

Caroline, Garland, Lindsay, and Sue,
What in the world could have happened to you?
You were all here only yesterday.
You were all merry, at innocent play.
Roger and Johnny and Tommy and Sam,
Where are you now? For right here I am.
Where have you gone, you little lost children
Just when we all were so joyous and gay?
Why have you left us and all gone away
Taking with you all the flowers of May?
With those who love you, O could you not stay?
Is life a fairyland, were you all fey?
Bright was the world when of it you were part.
Bright were the hopes in my laughing glad heart,
But with your going the sky has turned gray.

Why, little fairies, belovèd and loving,
Why from the springtime of life should you stray?
See, we are left in a lonely dismay.
Caroline, Lindsay, Garland, and Sue,
Though from our lives you have wandered away,
May all the flowers to each one convey
How much we love you by night and by day.
It seems too early for children to be
In the stern Land of Maturity.

THE LOOK

The solemnest sight that I have seen
Upon this earth, beneath our skies,
Beyond all other looks has been
The heaven-lost look in a baby's eyes.
Where bluebells rod, and drowsy roses clamber,

MEMORY

Out of the past
That cannot die,
From a great evening
I descry
Two hawks to a hill
Through a red, red sky,
Two wild doves homing,
As wild mates fly,
A bright tear brimming
In a beautiful eye,
One of us saying
We must not cry—
Long, long ago
As we said good-bye.

HOW WILD THEIR LOVE

"Strangers until the accident, they were married three days later."

News Item

Remember that they did not come to this
By moonlight and by meadowy waters gleaming.
They were not idlers, happening on bliss
In quiet gardens full of dreams and dreaming.
Think not of them as dalliers, who stroll
Where bluebells nod, and drowsy roses clamber,
Or saunter where the beach's anthems roll . . .
If there be wildness in their love, remember

How suddenly, upon the brink of death,
In terror, and in anguish and alarms,
Facing eternity with broken breath,
They found themselves fast in each other's arms.
Nor life nor death shall ever shake or sever
The tie by which love made them one forever.

194

DEDICATION

My ship of song is coming home.
The voyage is o'er, the peril past.
The twilight harbor, glimmering, vast,
Is tranquil, without sound or foam.

Is this the hour I dreamed would be?
No crowds are waiting on the shores.
No music peals, no rocket soars
To greet my ship come home from sea.

The beacons blazing in the night
Are set for nobler crafts than mine;
Yet in my heart I can divine
That One will lift for me a light.

For, ere the voyage, the chart she gave;
In darkness on the distant sea
Her loyal love, remembering me,
Was like a star above the wave.

And she will meet me on the strand,
Who for my joy and safety yearned,
And love my ship of song returned,
And all its story understand.

BIRTHDAY PIECE

Our love was ever of the skies;
It came to us with mystic flight;
It came to us with starry eyes,
On wings of light.

Its hands of hope, toward every dream
Of Beauty leads us without fear;
Its presence is our heart's supreme
Great answered prayer.

All things of earth to dust depart;
Descending to forgotten urns;
But nothing of our love, Sweetheart,
To earth returns.

VEILED EROS

I

O let there be
Between us never any land or sea,
Or wall of wood or stone,
O vigil kept alone,
No friend for one the other may not greet,
No victory that for one shall mean defeat,
No bliss we shall not bare,
No sorrow, share,
No solitary star
That one may love afar
Without the other.
Ah, closer let us live than are
Sister and brother!

II

Yet, dreadful, sweet, and strong,
Let love divide us thus:
In marvel glorious,
And lyric, incommunicable song.
Intangible as air,
Let something terrible and fair,
And powerful as fate
Still keep us separate and great;
Love beautiful and whole
Demands supreme integrity of soul;
Thus even with her giving, she denies
Completeness that her wisdom may devise
Glad premonitions of divine surprise;
Behind reality, a magic deep,
Remote as lonely winds that starward sweep,
As fathomless as orchid skies asleep
Beyond the burning west—
Haunted with glamours of the Unpossessed.
O never wholly intimate
Should lovers be, but veiled,
Each one a land unknown, a sea unsailed,
An ocean spectral and a shadowy shore,
A far sad sea-horizon, promising more
Than the Hesperides could hold in store,

A perilous, impassable divide
With Paradise upon the farther side,
Dim vales delicious, valleys undescried,
That purple slumbers of the mountain hide:
Each hold from each a shrine inviolate,
Beautiful in a sunlight never guessed,
For all their vows confessed,
A high-walled wondrous garden with no gate,
A visionary dwelling,
A legend with no language for its telling . . .
O guard it well,
The secret and the spell!
The mightier music, keep inaudible.
This meaning past the momentary bring:
A phantom's at the heart of everything,
And all that is not fey,
Long ere the break of day
Shall vanish utterly, utterly vanish away.

III

The broad, apparent Day,
Barbaric, gay,
That would divulge the ultimate worst and best
Can lovers slay.
Be not the accessible blossom, bold and bright,
Too shrill and obvious for long delight;
But be, by moonbeams made more magical,
The witching wildflower by the waterfall,
That now is seen, and now is lost from sight.
For modesty and delicate reserve
The gods implacable of the future serve.
Learn not too late
Surrender to abate;
Let enigmatic reticence withhold
More fragrance than the flower does unfold;
Let even love's most affluent excess
Still promise more than passion can express.

Let rapture even,
While yielding earth, suggest approaching heaven:
The enchantment of an Eden never trod,
The immortal lure of Beauty and of God.

IV

Far-glimmering in the dews of wonder shine
With sorcery no searching can divine—
That even love's fulfilment shall but seem
Of joy to come, the hinting and the gleam;
Be every flower that your beauty yields
An intimation of Elysian Fields—
So keep, my Darling, ever keep for me
Your strangeness and your mystery,
Your sense, not of what is, but is to be.

SONG

Your love was always like the moon—
How fair to rise, to cloud how soon!
Then cold above me far to ride,
Her face behind the clouds to hide.

Your love was ever like the sea
In mystery, in mystery:
It flooded bright and full and warm,
But ebbed in darkness and in storm.

And now has set that sailing moon;
And now that joyous tide is gone;
How dark the world without her light;
Without that tide, how still the night!

O shall that moon e'er rise again,
And shall that tide once more be seen?
In yonder east there is a gleaming
As of the moon on waters beaming!

AT THE LAST

In your hour of need,
In your hour of dread,
When your foes crowd in,
And your friends have fled,
In those shadows wild
That have no end,
My love for you
Will be your friend.

When the waters rise,
And the towers sink,
And I stand alone
On the caving brink,
In the night, in the storm,
That shall not cease,
Your love for me
Shall be my peace.

But past the shadows,
The storm, the fear,
With hope retreated
And death drawn near,
Out of the ruin
And out of the night
Our love shall be
The morning light.

FLOWER AND VASE

A blue flower
To a blue vase
Brings beauty,
Brings grace
And modesty
And purpose new:
The vase, my heart,
The flower, you.

O it would be
A vase forlorn
With the flower gone!

THE TWILIGHT

He saw the sunrise on the hill,
But was not comforted:
His heart longed to be still;
"Would God the day were dead,"
He said.

His heart longed to be still;
Longed for the deep shadow-waves,
The sweet fields growing dark,
The late bird-voices, and the bells,
The evening's dim farewells,
In the distance dying;
For the light on far pale streams
After the sunset, and the silent trees;
The quiet west,
Tranquil with gorgeous dreams;
The tall white lily stars,
As God's watch over these,
And these lying
On the bosom of Rest.
She, in that weary hour,
Turned to him with a mystic grace
The Twilight of her Face.

SONG OF MARY MAGDALENE

The hills are folded in a mist
By Galilee; on Galilee
A silence comes, and it is night.
The stars awaken tranquilly.
Night's beauty, mirrored in her dreams,
In Galilee, in Galilee,
Sleeps, and the stars like spirit barques
Where bluebells nod, and drowsy roses clamb
Move softly on a spirit-sea.
The winds sigh with immortal grief
O'er Galilee; and Galilee
Seems mortal, and remembers all
That cannot be, that cannot be.
The shores are hushed; the winds are still
On Galilee; o'er Galilee
The stars are setting far away,
And One has died for you and me.

HOW WIDE THE WINGS

If now to the eastward
You'll fly swiftly, without any rest,
Even to the gates of the royal palace
Of the burning sunrise;
Then speed to the glimmering limits
Of the deep haunting west,
Where the blue lyric Day
In tawny beauty dies
(Those being the far bournes
Where Morning and Evening abide),
You will be hinting how spacious,
How heavenly wide
Are the mighty wings
Of even a mortal love that is strong,—
That is all of life's meaning and spirit,
Its music and song.

HOMECOMING

When you come home to me you bring
    Refuge and rest;
The music that love, listening,
    Learns to love best;
Peace, and the after silencing
    Upon love's breast.

What home was there for me, when you
    Were far away?
What joy for me, when joy with you
    Had flown away?
What help save my own thought of you
    From day to day?

How shall I answer for doubt's past
    Delirium?
When you come home at last, at last,
    Dear, when you come?
I shall be strong to hold you fast
    When you come home.

L'ENVOI

My life is numbered by your days,
    My sorrows are the tears you shed;
For we are one in thoughts and ways,
    And what you speak my heart has said:
Can you recall and I forget,
Or suffer and I not regret?

Let other hearts and other hands
    Their tributes bring, but still will mine,
In other times, in other lands
    A star upon your forehead shine;
For love is strong, though love's alone,
And even in darkness knows its own.

You may not give this gift away,
    Not even to the one who gave;
It goes with you the long, long way,
    And you will bear it to the grave.
The best I have to you is given
As treasure laid away in Heaven.

May the same light waken us,
    And the same darkness close our eyes;
For the same fears have shaken us,
    And the same dreams' sublimities:
And the same future hopes are ours,
The blooming and the dying flowers.

Year after year the spring will call,
    And the deep summer hoard her sheaves;
For us will flame, will fade, will fall
    The crimson and the golden leaves:
And for the glory that departs,
We clasp love closer to our hearts.

AS A STAR

Lo, your face that led me far,
Still will lead me, as a star
Leads the darkly-wandering night,
Till both vanish into light.

You are of the silent hours,
Of the strange and mystic flowers;
Beautiful, and true, and tender,
Unto you the stars surrender.

Depths of quietness will come
In the day's delirium;
Thoughts of mountains, rivers, seas,
Dreams of you in all of these.

Fair your memory will remain
When all else will seem in vain;
When all else is faded, broken,
When the lips' last words are spoken.

For your face led me far,
Still will lead me, as a star
Leads the darkly-wandering night,
Till both vanish into light.

ANGEL KNEELING

Over me
Suddenly
Rapture and awe came stealing;
Hushed rapture, sacred awe;
For, beautiful as an angel kneeling
In holy prayer,
I saw my Loved One there,
Bending, bending above
Me with her love.
All hallowed be His name
Who gave this beauty wild
To me, His longing and His lonely child.

203

A DREAMER

Between the stars and desert sand
    Move clouds of faith, and clouds of fire;
I follow through the desert land
    The pale dream and the dream's desire:
Still let me strive, yet feel you move
Within the cloud and fire, Love.

I fall with all the fallen brave,
    And rise to many a starry height;
Yet unto me the Father gave
    Not strength, as those who, flaming white
With joy and song press to the mark,
But deeper music, and the dark.

To me are vanished faces sweet,
    The veiled future's mystic spell;
With dreams forgotten let me meet,
    Still let me fear to say farewell:
But turn not from me if I fear
Lest dream and memory disappear.

O if, with darker mold of mind
    I feel hearts tremble, heave, and break
With every cry upon the wind,
    Be near, be near me then and make
Thy day the fairer for my night,
My darkness nobler for they light.

ATTAR-OF-ROSES

In the Carpathian Mountains, in the Bulgars' land,
It takes twelve wagonloads of perfect roses
To make one vial of the precious attar.
Though it is hard for me to understand
The magic that your fragrant heart discloses,
The wonder of my silence does not matter.
For I know your source; there starry mountains tower
Above a valley's roses, all in flower.

RECOMPENSE

I love all little leaves,
All gentle native things;
From them my heart receives
The lonely grace of wings.
The wildflowers turn their eyes
On me. They so resemble
Angels from Paradise,
I worship and I tremble.

But if for me no star,
No wildflower would shine;
If all the things that are
Wonders, could not be mine;
If I no song could hear
Amid life's shadows tall,
O yet, if you were near,
You would suffice for all.

DISTILLATION

All the far thrill in the capture
Of a song's remotest rapture;

All the beauty and the wonder
Of the beaching billow's thunder;

All the mystical divining
Of the hill-stars in their shining;

All the glamour and regretting
Of the sea-moon in her setting;

All the dewiness adorning
Roses in the bridal morning;

These are from thy spirit thronging,
Beauteous bourne of all my longing.

NOT EVER FOREVER

He sought her as haven, home, harbor, as a welcoming river
Into which as a gale-driven ship he to safety could glide,
On whose tranquil and starry deep stream he could restfully r
Finding anchorage, refuge, repose, finding fastness and rescu
From the tempests outside.

O Beautiful Covert and Shelter and deep Sanctuary,
O lovely Retreat out of storm,—not for him, not for him!
Not for him all her songs like the songs of divine Seraphim;
Now for him, all alone, all forsaken, the dark winds are risin;
The black waters brim.

And yet for her only were all his true dreams and desires;
And for her alone were his longings, the foes that he felled;
By her beauty alone were his valorous darings impelled.
But her stilling of storms and her cooling of fell mortal feve
From him are withheld.

Forever, not ever for him her deep mystery joyous,
That gathers all wonders of love that are and that were,
Her jacinth and frankincense, ivory, attar, and myrrh;
Not ever forever for him her wild music in darkness, her
    moolight,
Not ever from her.

MIRACLE

The miracle most merciful,
When all is done and said,
Is that incomparable love
Is never merited.

So daring and irrational,
So wild a plan and odd,
Naïve, fantastic, beautiful,
Must have been dreamed by God.

WHAT FLOWERS GIVE

Upon my garden's sheltered slope,
This heliotrope!
Fragrant as it is fair,
It might be Hope,
Thwarting this dead pine's tall despair.
See how this royal yellow rose
Beside my monumental white oak grows.
The black-eyed Susans sway in golden glory;
The daisies tell their alabaster story.
The fringed petunias have enchanting grace,
As if each flower were a fairy's face.
This elfin stargrass opens amethyst eyes
To the azure skies . . .
All have their loveliness, 'tis true, 'tis true;
And yet they give me,—not themselves,—but you!

STILL SABBATH

To you my life belongs,—
Its lyric, joyous hours,
Its music and its songs,
Its fragrance and its flowers.

All yesterdays, tomorrows,
All that this hour brings,
All my dark storms and sorrows
You cover with love's wings.

Yours is my innocence,
Beautiful bourne and goal;
Yours is my reverence,
Still Sabbath of my Soul.

LOVE IS LIKE THAT

She thought love was a holiday,
With joybells ringing all the way,
With bliss beyond all dreams of knowing,
With only orange blossoms blowing,
With glamour only shed.
"Love is like that,"
She said.

But then an angel took her hand
And led her far through life's stern land,
And showed her one who, strong and still,
Stood steadfast on a battle-hill
Whence a great host had fled.
"Love is like that,"
He said.

And then she saw one giving glad.
All treasures that he ever had,
All wealth that he had ever earned,
Nor wished for aught to be returned,
Living on scanty bread.
"Love is like that,"
He said.

And then she heard no cry from one
Over whom closed oblivion
As valiantly he strove to save
Another from a wild sea-wave,
Yielding his life instead.
"Love is like that,"
He said.

Then she beheld with pitying awe
Life's field of conflict. But she saw,
Above the carnage and the doom,
The triumph of a floating plume
That ever onward led.
"'Love is like that,"
He said.

Now when to her young lovers throng
Idly with laughter, jest and song,
Remembering glory she has learned,
How love is not with dust concerned,
How splendid are its ways,
"Learn what love means,"
She says.

ELF QUEEN

She is a woman very fair,
With fascinations sweet and rare;
With power to reach the heart's far deeps;
And yet another charm she keeps
For me: for often she'll appear
A little girl with golden hair.

She has an everlasting air
Such as all angel spirits wear;
And, full of naive witchery,
The Queen of Elfland she might be;
And though of mysteries aware,
A little girl with golden hair!

MY LONGING

Behold all my longings:
Upon the white sand
To wander beside you
And hold your brown hand;
To know that you love me,
Nor wish me to go;
To feel that you trust me
Through life's ebb and flow;
With stars on the sea-rim,
The wind in the south,
The moon on the waters,
Your mouth on my mouth.

WERE I BY SHADOWS BOUNDED

Were I by shadows bounded,
Among lost souls that were,
By dread and death surrounded,
Still would I worship her
Who splendid made my story
By minding not my dust;
Who gave me of her glory,
Her mercy and her trust;
Who led me through a portal
Of Paradise a part,
Opening on the immortal
Deep Heaven of her heart.

HERE STANDS A SERAPH

Do not discuss it,
For words would be in vain;
Never examine
Or try to explain.
Who can investigate
Mystical song?
Who can interrogate
A seraph strong?
Who can arrest it,
The storm in the night,
Or stay the comet,
Ablaze in his flight?
Argue not, reason not,
Do not explore:
Love's sea is rolling high
Wild on your shore.
Do not consider,
And do not debate:
There's an archangel tall
At your life's gate.
There stands your royal guest
From Heaven come.
Welcome him, welcome him,
Welcome him home!

CHALICE ETERNAL

Over the dim mountain pines,
Across the glimmering meadowland
There comes, as a fragrant night-wind comes,
The voice of one who loves me vainly:
We are betrothed by bereavement
And wedded by separation.

He has never wished me anything but joy,
Nor even asked that I should love him;
For he knows that love is a wild free spirit,
That may give itself away completely
But none other may rein it or direct it.
It is a god; and its celestial ways
Are not the ways of men.

In the still darkness I hear his voice,
And it means to me nothing but peace,
Peace of his homage and his honor,
The music of his faithful love.
This is a spirit voice,
Coming to say to my spirit,
"Glory to you forever,
Who gave me a dream and fulfilled it,
Whose tender compassion I wear
As a garment of rainbows fashioned."

THE VOICE I LOVE

I hear a music in the night;
I think it is my heart that hears
The voice I love that comes to me
Across the broken years;

Across the years that are no more,
Through shadows veiling land and sea,
The wonder of the voice I love
Makes music still for me.

ROSE OF MY DREAMING

Red roses of all roses, and rose of the wide world
    for me,
All beauty your beauty discloses that was and that
    ever can be.
You bloom in my shadows; my dark is illuminated by you;
From you are my valleys emblazoned, my skies take their
    blue.
Wild rose of my wonder, awaking my love with delight,
Your music I hear in my silence, your song in my night.

Your love is my strength, deep inflowing as flows in
    the tide
That the shore will embrace as a bridegroom his life-giving
    bride.
Far away in that land that I long for, the mystical
    bourne
Of your beauty, you burn. For that beauty I murmur and
    mourn,
O Rose of my Dreaming, O Flower by hope's magic
    foretold
Till all that in vision I clasp, to my heart I shall
    hold!

SOMETHING THERE IS

Something there is that never dies:
Not glory of the evening skies,
Or song by golden voices sung,
Or blossom when the year is young.
All these are fated from their birth
To fade and perish from the earth.
All music into silence goes;
To dust departs the regal rose;
The lily that you wonder on
Is wedded to oblivion.
Yet on one thing the heart relies:
Something there is that never dies—
The love that blesses you and me
Lays hold on immortality.

212

SUCH IS HIS LOVE

When from that magic hour we must emerge,
With parting near, with the future vast and
     dim,
With never a light upon its lonely verge,
Perhaps her heart will hold one thought of
      him
Tender and dear: the memory that he never
Asked for the boon that might her spirit
      mar.
Now not a wave upon her lovely river
Mirrors less silverly each quiet star.

She never knew how wild and strong and deep
Was his desire. No heart but his could
      know.
Yet he had made a promise he must keep:
That for love's precious sake he must forego
Her final wonder, longed for, but unknown;
The beauty of her ultimate rose unblown.

PALM, PINE AND RIVER

As solitary as a single tree
Upon a lonely hill, that looks forever
Down on the journey of a joyous river
That through a land of dreams and mystery
Flows toward the distant and desired sea:
But as the day and night cannot deliver
The tree from loneliness; so no endeavor
Can change the fate that has befallen me.

So great his longing and his need, until
Far, far away from that tall grieving pine,
A palm tree dreams of that sad lonely hill.
Their beauty deepening as on her they shine,
The stars look down, and tremble, and are still.
Ah, River, if your joy fulfilled were mine!

PEACE AFTER STORM

Where now are the trembling,
The tumult, the wonder?
O where have they vanished,
The lightning and thunder?
The torrent, the tempest,
The rainbow, the rain—
Were they but illusions
That come not again?

Love's always a mingling
Of tears and of laughter;
Tempestuous music
With calm coming after;
And none should be saying,
When hurricanes cease,
Their glory was greater
Than silence and peace.

THAT LITTLE SONG

Of all the men she had ever known
One always stood unique, alone—
The only one who held apart
A mystic shrine, deep in her heart.
In life he played no royal role;
Yet he was strangely great of soul
And would live on, though he were dead.
This she discovered when he said
A little thing that kept her young.
Out of his heart this song he sung.
It was a tiny thing, and yet
Never will she that song forget:
"If we will wander up this lane,
Delicious after summer rain,
A host of wildflowers we shall see:
Compassed by beauty you will be.
I want you to see them; and, too,
I want the wildflowers to see you."

DEEP IN YOUR BEING

Deep in your garden
You let my love go.
There by the roses
The founts overflow.
There wild azaleas
Are softly aflame;
And all your violets
Call me by name.
Into your wildwoods
In rapture I roam,
Where all is beauty
To welcome me home.
Into your blue sky
My being takes wing;
In lyric concert
We soar and we sing.
Then by your white waves
I dream, and am blest,
Your spirit hushing
My longing to rest.
Far on your waters
I sail with delight;
Into your harbor
I come for the night.

CARING COMPLETELY

To sorrow are they faring,
In dusty raiment clad,
The hearts whose futile caring
Is less than wildly glad.

O, Love, with wisdom stranger
Than that of elf or child,
Protect us from the danger
Of caring less than wild.

MOTHERS

Just as a mother when the day is done,
Shepherds her precious children off to bed,
Wondering why some lag, and why some run,
While with her kisses each is comforted;
Then turns her to the task of gathering
The scattered trinkets littering all the floor.
Some order out of chaos will she bring.
Today they will not need them any more.

So Nature, when our night is coming on,
Knows that our childish frolics here have passed;
As pleasures of the hour, and one by one,
She, gathering up the joys that cannot last,
Since they were merely playthings of the day,
Tenderly lays our little toys away.

THE FEW

The songs that poets sing are mortal, too;
But most miraculously in a few
The granite of eternity lies hid.
The great song builds its own proud pyramid.

GARDEN GATE

To walk with your beauty
My spirit is free;
And, deep in your wildwood,
Your thrush in your tree,
Enthroned in dim fragrance,
Makes music for me.
For all that we are,
Have been, and shall be,
My path's on your shore,
And my ship's on your sea.
The gate of your garden
Is open to me.

THE PAST

Here where the twilight trees
Gather strange darknesses,
One lies low;
And to her I must go,
Even as today glides into yesterday,
Not dead, but passed away.

Mysterious Past! how like a face I knew.
Long dreaming now:
The shadows of thy silent years
Sleep, as the tall dark firs
Over that dream of hers.

The warm hand and heart,
The loveliness of days,
Must needs depart,
Must go their ways;
God wills it so,
That they should go.

But in the Future's eyes
I read the unsurprise
Of wondrous things concealed
She holds to be revealed,—
The face that I have seen,
The land where I have been.

Mysterious Past! how like a face I loved,
Long sleeping now;
O'er thee thy grey and shadowy years
Dream, as the high dim firs
Over that sleep of hers.

THE HERITAGE

We gathered about her
To speak of the days
Her love had illumined . . .
(We spoke as in praise).

But deep in divine eyes
Her soul in light moved:
"My children, my children,
You were born to be loved."

This heritage, Mother,
All else is above:
To be brought to life's bourne
By that beautiful Love

For which every true heart
Foregoes earth's renown,
And all other glory,
And each other crown.

ROSE AND SONG

Soft flamed the rose,—but it is cold,
And chill as are the dead.
When telling of the tale is told,
No more may then be said.

The roses flame, the roses fall;
Pale are the dying roses:
Pale is the silent interval
When all the story closes.

A flower and a book have we,
A story and a rose:
The flower cannot withered be,
Nor shall the story close.

Because the trembling story flows
Like heaven's crystal flood,
Because the fadeless flower grows
In gardens of our God.

218

THE PLEDGE

The eyes, when faithful lovers part,
Utter the language of the heart.

She does not tell him to be true
Save with deep eyes of tenderest blue.

That radiant, silent, sweet appeal
All hope, all trust, all love reveal.

He does not tell her to be brave
But with his gray eyes valiant, grave.

No promise made by him or her;
For in that look their hearts confer.

And he shall know, 'neath alien skies,
The sill embrace of those calm eyes;

And she, through lonely days and long,
Shall feel him like a shelter strong.

The heralds of the heart have spoken
A pledge that never shall be broken.

COMPLEMENTS

There's something of the forest,
And something of the sea;
And something of the sky's deep blue,
Holy, immaculate, and true,
In you.

There's something of the hunter,
And the sailor rough and free,
And much of mortal yearning dust
That to your sky looks up in trust,
In me.

219

FAR AWAY

O how is it with me when fabulous moonlight is futile,
And stars have no music or meaning for me any more?
From what was heart-breaking in beauty is gone all the glory
And there is no song in the waves as they weep on the shore.

The pathways that led me, delighted, now lead into darkness;
And all that was fragrant, alluring, now seems empty, inane.
O how is it with me when grace most enchanting but mocks me
With skies unavailing, the earth and the ocean superfluous,
    vain?

The light has gone out on the hills. From the valleys is
    missing
The radiance more fair than the wildroses heralding day.
And nothing forever has import, or can be momentous,
Or lifts my lone spirit: my loved One is far, far away.

17

A SONG OF HOME

I dream not of the far lands
Where wondrous waters flow;
I long not for the star-lands
Brighter than these I know;
Nor look for lovelier garlands
That in my garden grow.

More than all scenes can render
Home yields to my glad sight;
Where the old true hearts and tender
Beat radiant round with light;
Where joys serene surrender
To me in safe delight.

Here have I many a token
That Love o'er life is king;
By his sweet language spoken
To calm hearts listening;
By his great bonds unbroken,
Whate'er the years may bring.

220

NOT OTHERWISE

Ah, not alone the lily,
Not of her strength alone
Is born that glimmering beauty tall,
That frozen waterfall
Of wonder's magic tone.
Some splendid deep conspiracy gives birth
To loveliness on earth:
From dim and occult sources it is drawn,
From angel evening and from seraph dawn;
By miracle on miracle it grows.
Not otherwise the violet,
Not otherwise the rose.

Not of itself the pine
Into the azure soars.
Her symmetry's shaped by a shadowy **Hand**,
Whose power no mind can understand,
But the heart adores.
This tree makes mystic matings dark
With the soil's vital spark;
The sunlight lifts her might amain
And the silver rain.
Astral her song, sidereal her story;
Not otherwise her mystery,
Not otherwise her glory.

Not of itself our love,
Not of its mortal part:
From realms of wonder, and the strange
Dominions of the spirit's range
Comes splendor to the heart;
From bournes of beauty, and the place
Where dwells eternal grace;
From music out of unknown oceans old,
On unimagined shores in anthems rolled.
Valor is hers from far celestial things:
Not otherwise her golden harp,
Not otherwise her wings.

THE REAL MYSTERY

Her mystery makes orchids seem
Common as daisy-flocks that teem
The obvious sunny meadow through,
Eclipsing all I ever knew
Of beauty and of glamour's dream,
    Her mystery.

The bloom of wonder in the beam
Of moonlight on the secret stream,
The magic of the rose in dew,
The marvel of the sky's far blue,
They yield to sorcery supreme,
    Her mystery.

That fearie charm,—how can a ream
Of words express her spirit's gleam?
Yet the enchantment that is she
Miraculously cares for me . . .
This of all wonders I must deem
    The mystery.

HER FLOWER

"O what is love,—who knows? who knows?"
" 'Tis the first lily, and the last rose."

"O how arrives it, and how goes?"
"Like the first lily, like the last rose."

"Whence rises it, and whither flows?"
"From the first lily and the last rose."

"When will it dawn? When will it close?"
"With the first lily, with the last rose."
"But my love shall not be like those—
Like the first lily and the last rose:

Mine is a love that shall not close,
Eternal lily, immortal rose."

222

EVEN THEN

When a little dust encloses
All our rain and all our roses;

When a tiny hush expresses
All our joys and our distresses;

To a narrow stillness bringing
All our sighs and all our singing;

To the silence and the mold
All the glamour and the gold;

Even then, there would be glory
In the telling of our story.

NEAREST GOD

We have been taught that God is love,
My Beautiful, Beloved, and True!
And I am always nearest God
When I am nearest you.

FAIRY SHORE

I am a mortal barque;
You are a fairy shore.
Whether I reach anchorage
I could not love you more.

WHEN THE LIGHT IS LOW

If I could see your face, I would be glad
If it could be the last of all I saw
Upon the earth,—such perfect joy I had
In you, Beloved! O when I must withdraw
From mortal sight, and view no more the graces
Attending beauty; when I shall no more be,
Of all the glances from all starry faces,
Most Pitying Eyes, be yours my last to see!

And as the myriad sounds of life are stilled,
Though all but one are mute I shall rejoice.
My heart with wild sweet music will be filled
If I can hear the violins of your voice;
If, as I turn into the Silent Land,
Life's farewell touch comes from your loving hand!

THE CYCLE OF DESIRE

There is a cosmic cycle of desire
That makes the magic of the universe:
One feels it in a master's mighty verse,
Whose exaltations sink, and then aspire;
Now the flame rises, and now fails the fire.
The stars and roses gather, then disperse.
As if a rhythmic ritual to rehearse,
Love's dreams draw near, and then love's dreams
        retire.

Such is life's mystery divine and true.
Longing is variant, and afar it roams:
Love, passion, and desire flush and fade,—
Inconstant yet recurrent . . . Fortunate you
If even once another's cycle comes,
And on your orbit perfectly be laid.

AFTERWHILE

With his book in your hands
Some trancèd quiet hour,
Some day, long after,
In reading all that he wrote
To you who meant
The beauty of life to him,—
The words will blossom for you
Into many a flower,
Into many a scarlet leaf like a fairy boat
On a memoried stream afloat;
Into many a thought mysterious,
Sacred and dim;
Sacred with thoughts of him.
Then will you say,
"I know he loves me forever.
He could not ever have written like this
Unless
Love were his will and his Lord,
His purpose and high endeavor.
And to me he gave
The strength of his gentleness.
Should not a woman be proud
In her heart to know
That another spirit
Could worship and love hers so?"

WHEN TO THE WOODS

When to the woods I wander,
With springtime in the air,
I hear you in the bird-songs,
See you in all that's fair.
But O that I might find you
In fragrant wildwoods deep,—
Might meet you as I know you,
A loving tryst to keep;
There, under stars and silence,
And safe from all alarms,
I'd tell you all my story
As you lay in my arms;
Under a dusky oak tree,
Beneath a shadowy pine,
I'd hold you warm and vibrant,—
All woman,—and all mine!

WHERE I AM YOU ARE

Under many a dim sea-star
You are all about me,
Closer than life's breath.
I am where you are.
In love's celestial calm
You are where I am.
Lovely and final as death,
Your proud head and pale brow
Are over me now.
Your beauty upholds me;
Your fragrance enfolds me.
It is not surrender.
It is just that all that I am
With all that you are
You cover
With tender
Compassion,
O Lover, my Lover!

TOGETHER

Tiptoe together we can stand
Upon the verge of elfinland.
I am the sleep; you are the dream;
I am the bank; you are the stream;
I am the oak that stands forever
Upon the margin of your river.
I am your yellow longleaf pine,
And you my clinging jessamine.
A fairy wildrose you resemble,
Whose mystic beauty makes me tremble.
The sea and shore of you and me
Are close as love can ever be.
One melody to us belong.
I am the voice, and you the song.
Always illumined where you are,
I am the night, and you its star.
The magic of our love is such
We would make music should we touch.

SURPRISE

I never remember your beauty without saying,
"Glory to God who brought you into being,
Who dreamed the miracle of your arraying
The pathway of my lonely pilgrimage.
For me the aspect of all life you change,
My journey with your tender grace waylaying;
And even Paradise you can presage.
You are the mystic, beautiful, and strange
Wildflower I had no dream of ever seeing,
The answered prayer I had no thought of praying."

SEASONS

We wait for springtime hours
To see the flowers,
Whose beauty comes to birth
Here on our mortal earth
Only by joy's bright powers.

But in the spirit's land,
Amid the snows
Of wintry grief and care,
From anguish will appear
Love's lily and her rose.

APPEAL

"Absent thee from felicity awhile"
　　　　　　　　—HAMLET

Dearest of friends God ever gave to me,
Beloved and beautiful, who bore my cross
Of anguish, and from sorrow set me free,—
I know I never could abide the loss
If you should leave me. In the world apart
I'd wander, calling you. None else I know
To whom I'd trust all that is in my heart.
For Jesus' sake, from me you must not go.

I know a glory is prepared for you,
And that for you angels have always yearned,
But my dear comrade, wise, and sweet, and true
All that I know of love from you I learned.
While I am in life's lonely last defile,
"Absent thee from felicity awhile."

THE WONDER OF IT

I rise in wonder from your kiss;
And I must ask from sun to sun,
"God, what is it that I have done
That I deserve a love like this?"

For I forget it is not merit
That love repays. It comes to bless,
And counts not my unworthiness,
Such is the glory of its spirit.

ATTAR

God had so loved, and had so given,
How could I vision more?
Mine were the valleys and the hills,
The forest, sea, and shore.
How could I dream His mercy had
A miracle in store?

On me, of all earth's loveliness,
An attar He bestows;
For the wild beauty of your love
All beauties wild enclose;
Gathers all waters in one wave,
All blossoms in one rose.

MIRACLE MINE

As the stream finds the river,
The river, the sea,
All I need forever
Your love gives to me.
Life's storms wild and olden
You hush and you still,
Love's promises golden
In beauty fulfil.
Strong saviour from starkness,
Bright star through my pine,
Dear rose of my darkness,
O miracle mine!

MY PRAYER

I pray that peace and joy may be
Comrades to keep you company;
That love alone in you may reign
With everlasting beauty. Then,
That you may have no pain or fear,
I pray a strange and tragic prayer,
A wild appeal, yet true and deep,
For the dear one my heart adores:
I pray that God will safely keep
You from a longing for my love
As I have always longed for yours.

THE SUMMONS

Now I walk with you alone,
Every fear I had is gone.
Blithe this idle day of summer;
Yet I hear a distant drummer,
Drumming for me far away.
I must go. I cannot stay,—
Leaving joy and love behind me,
Going through shadows that may blind me

HOME

In a strange night, from dreams of sorrow deep
There came a voice, and from beyond the foam
Of darkened seas that held me in their keep,
From perilous shores where I was wont to roam,
    It called me home.

Life's weariness, the misty hours of tears,
The desolate sea on which my spirit tossed,
Doubts, hesitancies, trouble, scornings, fears,
The darkness of the River to be crossed,
    In thee are lost.

All that had vanished with the early light,
Dead with my heart, and buried in the ground,
Far mystic flowers of faith, and pure delight,
All that I lost, passed beyond sight and sound,
    In thee is found.

No longer need I look to earth and skies
For veils of loveliness to be withdrawn,
For all the night is gathered in thine eyes,
And in thy face the stars,—when night is gone,
    Thou art the dawn.

THE CLOCK

The clock that has no bell
Speaks not at all;
And yet it is within your power
To tell the hour:
Look and behold,—
And the time is told!

I seem to have no words
Commensurate
To tell my heart's wild love for you,
Its depths how true;
But you may see
If you look at me!

231

ANSWERED

From gladness and safety
You turned at my cry;
And you sped like a dove
Through the darkening sky.
The night could not stay you,
Or danger delay you,
Whose far bourne was I.
O greater than glory,
And nobler than fame,—
The thought that you heard me,
And loved me, and came!

O VIOLET EYES

Forget-me-nots from fairy skies
Are your deep dewy violet eyes.
Their beauty, come from God alone,
He mercifully makes my own.
What loveliness He can devise!
The lone lobelia in the wood,
The azure queen of solitude,
Has not your magical surprise,
O Violet Eyes!

Beneath their blue I recognize
Your depth of heart, how sweet and wise!
Through you all mystery is known,—
The shrine, the altar, and the throne.
Each moment you immortalize.
If Heaven by me be understood,
You love me as an angel would,—
Who loves, and lives, and never dies,—
O Violet Eyes!

IF

If I lay dying,
And you were by,
Mine would be earth
And sea and sky;
The land below,
The sky above,
The level sea,—
All that I love:
For you have always
Been to me
Beauty of land,
Of sky and sea;
Beauty of heaven
That angels wing,
Beauty of shores
Where sirens sing;
Beauty of mountain,
Vale and hill;
Beauty of song,
Of all that's still.
To life and death
Love holds the key,
And I shall live
If you love me.
If I lay dying,
And you were by,
Loving and true,
I could not die.

YOUR DAY AND NIGHT

O well I love the Day of you,
The radiant sunlit way of you,
The laughter lithe and gay of you,
The morning and the May of you,
Your azure with its lark.

But O the glimmering Night of you,
The stealing wild starlight of you,
The mystery and sleep of you,
The shadows and the deep of you,
The secrecy and hush of you,
The hidden bloom and blush of you,
The fragrance in the dark!

SAFE CONVOY

If in defeat he wandered
Through darkness deep and wide,
From light and gladness sundered
How swiftly to his side
Her love would come to guide,
Safe convoy to provide!
With shadows wild behind him,
With night before to blind him,
He knows whose love would find him,
And with him would abide.
He knows whose arms would hold him,
Whose wings with joy would fold him,
Whose loyal love be told him,
Whatever may betide.
Whatever can betide,
Wherever he may fare,
There will be one to care.
Whatever be his lot,
One will forget him not.
O if he fall or stand,
Her love, forever nigh,
Refuge and rest shall be
Upon whatever land,
Beneath whatever sky
Beside whatever sea.

234

HILDA'S HARP

Hilda, play on! You lead me to the fountain
Of nature's mystic music. The dark pines
That mourn melodiously upon the mountain
Sing in your harp their grave and splendid lines.
I hear the wild birds warbling where the wood
Is magic, and of streams the silver speech,
Far fairy chorals out of solitude,
And rolling anthems of the lonely beach.

Hilda, play on! You lead me to the place
Where darkness dawns into a world of light,
Singing me home to beauty and to grace,
The immortal glimmering to my mortal sight.
O magic harp, O golden voice that sings,
To intimate unutterable things.

SPIRIT DAWN

When the shielding night was young
Heart to raptured heart we clung,
Wildly, intimately glad
In the bridal that we had.

Ah, but closer far were we,
Spirits mated sacredly,
Soul to soul as we lay
In the dawning of the day.

235

SWIMMING DEER

As day's last lights grew dimmer,
I watched the waters gleam
As a dark and tawny swimmer
Stemmed the mysterious stream.
It was a wild deer swimming,
At home in that faint light,
With the sunset's opals dimming,
With the coming of the night.
Out of his reedland hiding-place
Beauty he brought, and strength, and grace.

Beneath the shadowy treeline
The tide in silver broke
As the old buck made a beeline
For a landing by an oak.
I saw his haunting antlers shine
Above the waters dim:
Although the bright day had been mine,
The dark belonged to him.
This cameo I have forever:
A deer that swims a glimmering river.

A CARDINAL IN SNOWFALL

A cardinal in falling snow
Pictures to me life's joy and woe:
For he is radiance in the gray
And stifling dusk that shrouds the day;
And ruddy warmth amid the chill
Lost flakes that whisper and are still;
He's color, merriment, and song
In a dead frozen world of wrong;
He's hope amid our shadowy fears,
And love's compassion through life's tears.

THE LEGACY

How little can we leave who go
On life's last journey long!
No gold have I to give, no fame,
No jewels, and no song.
While still I am, who soon must be
Among those who are not,
For hearts beloved, and other hearts,
Unknown and unbegot,
Now will I plant a flowering shrub
That will go blossoming on
That they may have compassionate
Beauty when I am gone.

THE COMPASS

Regard this compass:
How veeringly the needle turns,
Yet ever northward yearns,
And at the last will come
Fatefully home.
Even so my love
Resembles
The needle; for it turns to you
And trembles.

MAGIC HOUR

As the first stars begin to shine,
The forest to festoon,
As the whole world goes argentine,
All sound's a silver rune.

'Tis now or never for romance!
The earth has wed the moon;
And the dim bats begin to dance
Their dusky rigadoon.

Deep in the mediative night
With wisdom we commune;
But in the evening's elfin light
Life is with love attune.

It is the hour of faerie chance,
An hour that passes soon,—
When the dim bats begin to dance
Their dusky rigadoon.

WHITE IBIS

Nothing I saw with you can fade;
Each moment is immortal made.
Wherever we have stood, we stand.
Love's is an everlasting land.
Because with you I saw them fly
Under an amethystine sky
Of evening, by the river-bend,
That magic flight can never end.
The ibis in their snowy streams
Still wing through my far heaven of dreams;
And I shall watch with you forever
White ibis flying down the river.

LIFE IS A FLIGHT

Life is a flight, and love its wings;
Across the land and o'er the sea,
Above the dust of mortal things
From dawn to sundown beating free
In light and thrilling liberty.

Life is a flight, and love its wings,
Superb, sustaining, of the sky;
I trust this strength that soars and sings . . .
Life's source and bourne are veiled; but I
With love, fear not to live—and die.

TRANSFIGURED

A deeper blue have sky and sea,
A rarer radiance the rose;
More splendid meaning comes to me
From beauty that the stars disclose.

A lovelier music from the thrush
That can the spirit's pain relieve;
And in my heart a deeper hush
That song celestial to receive.

Strange glory now the wildwoods wear;
A lyric light is on the river.
All this has come because I bear
Your beauty in my heart forever.

AS A WILD WAVE

As a wild wave upon the distant deep
Longs for no goal but the desired shore,
Alluring far away beyond the sweep
Of many waters; so, not less but more
He strives until her magic strand is reached,
Where love, come home, is like a breaker beached.

LONG REMEMBRANCE

I shall remember longest
The twilight of your hair;
The moonrise of your jasmine breasts,
The starlight of your air.

These will I always treasure
All memories above:
The sunrise of your beauty lone,
The blue sky of your love.

The floodtide of your magic
I shall forever keep;
The ocean of your mystery—
Wild, wonderful, and deep.

O I may be forgetting
All other things but this:
The violets of your glad embrace,
The wildrose of your kiss.

THE WAY

Dear, as our love is true,
So shall our lives be, too.

And as our hearts are brave,
Shall we be strong to save.

"Live, live," let others cry,
"For after life we die."

"Love, love," my spirit saith,
"For love lives after death."

NOT THE RED ROSE

O not the red rose of the garden,
Or the wildflowers faerie and free;
Nor the daisies that gleam
By the meadowy stream;
Nor the lupin that grows
Where the dark river flows;
Nor the violet that shines
Under murmuring pines:
No flower of the forest,
Of valley or lea;
No bloom on the mountain
Or by the blue sea
Can mean what your spirit
Forever shall be,—
My wild and mysterious
Night-blooming cereus
That flowers in life's darkness
For me.

LOVE AS SENTRY

Sentinel upon your round,
Far more faithful am I found;
Guardian with the falcon eyes,
I see first our enemies;
Watcher by the bed of pain,
Should you go, I shall remain;
Keeper of the vigil long,
If you faint, I shall be strong;
Warder of the inviolate portal,
You are mortal; I, immortal.
Of the treasure you would guard,
Let me be the watch and ward.
Scanning mountain, valley, knoll,
Vedette, picket, and patrol,
I am arm and sword and shield.
Listening for the foeman's coming,
I will slay him far afield,—
Being Love. . . . To none I yield.

VAIN BURIAL

In the snowy hollow
Of the frozen hill,
Deeply, darkly,
When the eve was chill,
Sadly, gently,
By an icy rill,
Sternly, tenderly,
Past good or ill,
Love's dream I buried,
Beautiful, still.

Long, long after,
As I came by,
A sudden gleaming
Did I spy,
A glamour radiant,
Bright and shy:
It was a violet's
Amethyst eye,
Laughing and singing,
"Dreams never die!"

HER EYES

Brimmed and beautiful her eyes,
Brimmed with joy are they;
And their trembling laughter-light
Spills like wine away.

Brimmed and beautiful her eyes,
Brimmed with grief are they;
Glory deepens with the tears
That they shed or stay.

Brimmed and beautiful her eyes,
Brimmed with love. Shall they
Be the shrines of joy or grief?
Lover, you shall say.

LOVER, TO YOUR LOVE RETURNING

Lover, to your Love returning,
Bring no triumphings to prove
You are worthy of her wonder.
Bring not anything but love.

All the wealth of conquest offered
Has no meaning in that land
Where she waits you, dream-enchanted;
And she would not understand.

Why you brought her all the riches
Of the fabled seas and shore.
In her heart is pure devotion.
You need give her nothing more.

Fashioned by her heart, your glory
Is a splendor she has made;
She has wrought a golden hero . . .
Tarnished will that image fade

If the beauty of her vision
Cannot in your spirit trace
Kindred virtue . . . For her longing
Love alone has answering grace.

LAST LONGING

To dream and to discover
More than the dream foretold,
Finding your heart the giver
Of more than mine can hold.

O Love, my longing stilling,
I have one yearning higher:
That I may be fulfilling
Your dream and your desire.

243

MY LIFE

Unless for you, my life I live,
    It is not high, it is not true;
My life is lost, unless I give
    My life, and live for you.

Unless like you I may become,
    I am not true, I am not brave;
I turn me, weary, to my home,
    I turn to you, and you will save.

It is not lost, the life we give;
    The life we lose, it is not flown;
And I, who have an hour to live,
    I offer it unto mine own.

The end of this brief hour I live,
    However high, however true,
Is lost, unless at last I give
    My life, and die for you.

A LIFE

Thy life, my life, or gold or dust,
    Or flower or sod;
In one alike we put our trust,
    Thy God, my God.

Thy grief, my grief; the journey wild
    Is thine and mine;
Hands clasped to find the Way, dear child,
    Thy way and mine.

The evening gathers over us,
    And fades our light;
Yet we are glad to have it thus,
    Thy night, my night.

BALLAD OF TRUE LOVE

Now, touching my true love; her heart is a place
Where grasses grow bright, and the beautiful face
Of heaven shines mirrored in a delicate lake
All fringed with blue lupins—where columbines
    shake
Their carillons crimson—where tiny birds swing
From blossomy tassels and shy carols sing.

My true love has showed me a heart like a rose
That blooms by a river that fragrantly flows,
A deep rose, a red rose, a dark-glowing flower
That makes of my desert a radiant bower:
And whether in darkness or whether in sun,
My Rose and the beauty of nature are one.

A true love have I; and her heart's like a fane
Where oriels brighten the shadow called Pain,
Where vespers are sung, when the roseate gloom
Of the west makes the shrine like a magical bloom,
Where silence and singing and prayers that arise
Draw God down to earth, and lift me to the skies.

LASTING SONG

I will sing of you until
Twilight veils the field and hill;
In the night, however long,
Of my love shall be my song.

When the day begins again,
In the sunlight or the rain,
Love, you shall remembered be
By the songs you hear from me.

In the immortal day and night
When we stand in God's own sight,
With the angels all in view,
I shall still be praising you.

THE DOVE

O the wild wood dove on the yellow pine,
Where the sprays of the yellow jasmine twine,
Has more wisdom than yours or mine
About the things I am thinking of—
Song and sunshine and happy love;
Has more fullness of life's delight
In a little day between dawn and night
Than we with our years of joy uncertain,
With eyes a-stare at death's dark curtain,
Wondering, dreading, doubting all,
Till sudden for us that curtain fall . . .
On the pine-tree bough the shimmering dove
Lives in the joy he is dreaming of,
Lives in the rapture of song and love . . .
O wild wood dove on the wild pine-tree,
As you are joyous and wise and free,
Your spirit lend to my love and me!

THE HOLY GRAIL

Within your eyes are deeps of peace;
The sleeping stars above the trees,
The white moon dreaming in the skies
Are of your eyes.

The mystery of the night is theirs,
And all the yearning of the years,
A farewell and a sacrifice
Within your eyes.

Far deeds of valor shine through them,
The Knights before Jerusalem;
A dying martyr's glorious spirit
Your eyes inherit.

The constant followers love has had,
Love-led, and by Sir Galahad,
Find in your face, when wanderings fail,
The Holy Grail.

THE WOMAN IN THE WEST

There is a Woman in the West
Who robs my spirit of its rest.
Her hair in tawny glory shines
Above the mystic mountain pines.
She wakens when the daylight sleeps;
A tryst with night and stars she keeps;
Her face has all the luring light
Of beauty on a summer's night;
Her fathomless and orchid eyes
Waylay me with delight's surmise.

Hers is the love that I shall miss,
And hers the lips I shall not kiss;
Far from a land I cannot reach
I catch the music of her speech.
I see her glimmering and fair,
With fragrant flowery bosom bare;
I see the waving of her hands
Far-beckoning to fairylands:
The haunting Woman in the West
At sundown on the mountain crest.

STAR AND TIDE

The silver stars were burning
Above the quiet sea
As, toward your beauty turning,
I met your mystery.

The stars in Heaven gleaming,
They will not there abide:
Of love their beauty's dreaming,
Fulfilled deep in the tide.

A star told all my story:
How could such splendor be!
A star, I sank in glory
In your mysterious sea.

247

THOU AND I

So live, so love, that each day ends
    The work God gives, or low or high;
Not lovers only, but as faithful friends,
    So live we, Thou and I.

So trust, so pray, that loss nor gain
    Changes the faith years sanctify.
May we be stronger for each pain
    And braver, Thou and I.

So wake, so toil, that evening brings
    Unbroken peace upon our hearts to lie,
Then shall we speak of happy things
    Together, Thou and I.

So rest, so sleep, that o'er our home
    Sweet will the stars be in the sky,
Even when silent voices come
    To call us, Thou and I.

THE LAD OF LONG AGO

To jilt him her father besought her,—
The lad who had stolen away
The heart of his loved only daughter . . .
Her mother had nothing to say.

For, far in the hills of her childhood,
Long ago, of her dreaming a part,
A lad like this one woke the wildwood
And wonder of love in her heart.

And so, while the father was fuming
(A man without vision was he),
The mother, indifference assuming,
Was praying to God it would be.

TO RECALL

What is it to recall?
To dream a forgotten dream?
To hear, by Memory's stream,
    A voice at evenfall?

What is it to forget?
Dimness that veils the eyes?
Stars that no more arise?
    A face no longer met?

Recalling thee, I come
To the deep silent hours;
To a lost land of flowers
    My heart returneth home.

Forgetting thee, I still
Am as the world has known,
Fugitive, fearful, alone,
    And as the wind's my will.

I will no more forget,
But look unto those skies
Whence the old stars arise,
    And the lost face is met.

WINGS OF LIFE

Life is a flight, and Love its wings;
Across the land and o'er the sea,
Above the dust of mortal things,
From dawn to sundown beating free
In light and thrilling liberty.

Life is a flight, and Love its wings,—
Superb, sustaining, of the sky:
I trust this strength that soars and sings,
Life's source and bourne are veiled; but I
With Love, fear not to live—and die.

LONELY HARP

O lonely Harp,
Mute are your strings.
Music is in you
That never sings.
Where are your melodies?
Your lyric words?
Why sleeps your wonder,
O mystical chords?

"Only one hand
Can my music awake.
If you but touch me,
I tremble, I break
Into wild songs
Of such joy that they prove
Yours is the spirit
Alone that I love."

PREMONITION

Beyond the mountains and the town
I dare not watch this sun go down;
I dread to see this day depart
That takes from me your loving heart,
Not knowing when, or if again,
My head shall lie where it has lain;
Or if the voice that I adore
Shall make me music any more;
Or if the eyes that are my light
Will close for me tonight, tonight;
Whether the hand whose tenderness
Of touch was always a caress,—
O beautiful, beloved, and true,
Be lost to me, as mine to you.
This sunset for our hearts may bring
For us the close of everything.
This bright day's death I dare not see,
That may end all for you and me.
—Yet for our love no end can be.

FINAL PROOF

I do not have to watch
The wild waves rolling;
To consider the sea,
When on its far fabulous beach
In awe I am strolling;
Nor require the glory
Of the pageant of stars,
Marching in such great beauty
Up heaven's blue hill,
Telling their story
Stately and still.
I do not need some tremendous miracle
To give me faith in God:
A violet would do,
Or a spire of goldenrod,
Or a daisy or two.

But if I had to have
A magic and a wonder
To rend my doubts asunder,
To prove God true,—
That would be you!

VICTOR

He, on her love relying,
Has sword and shield to fend;
Armored for death-defying,
Will conquer to the end.
In every noble quarrel
He will stand up and fight.
But, O lay not the laurel
Upon his brow at night,
Though he comes plumed and splendid
With glory round him shed;
With the long battle ended,
And his grim foeman dead.
Remembering all that moved him,
And brought him to renown,
Remembering one who loved him,
Give her the victor's crown.

CERTAINTY

Others will laugh with you,
Love you for being
All that I know you are;
They will be seeing
How dear my Darling is,
How wise and strong:
Your love a chalice tall,
Your life a song.

Others more lovable
Tributes may pay;
Others more eloquent
Say what they say;
Yet though divided by
Mountains and moors,
I know your love is mine,
My love is yours.

LYRIC LOVE

A radiance is about her
Untouched by time and pain;
We think of life without her,
And know life would be vain.

We have not her decision,
Yet with her dreams confer;
We still can share her vision,
And be beloved of her.

Ideals we vainly cherish
Perfect in her we see;
In her our failings perish
To all we long to be.

Though light and strength forsake us,
And fate his goblet fill,
No fear shall ever shake us
If she will love us still.

We cannot live without her
While in the world we live,
For there's a peace about her
The world can never give.

A SONG

Dear, as our love is true,
So shall our lives be, too.

And as our hearts are brave,
Shall we be strong to save.

"Live, live," let others cry;
"For after life we die."

"Love, love," my spirit saith;
"For love lives after death."

EVENING STAR

You are
My Morning Star.
I waken to your gleaming
After my dreaming;
But then you fade.
Although you lead me,
Although you need me,
I cannot see you, hear you,
Though I am near you.
O that you were,
What in God's sight you are,
My Evening Star—
Unsetting,
Unforgetting,
Giving to me your love and light
All night, all night.

OUT OF DARKNESS

Out of the night of my loneliness,
Of my ceaseless longing for you,
In the dark, the harp of my love will sound,
And with music your courage renew,
Singing wild songs to quiet your heart,
To give you mysterious hiding,
A shelter of joy, and the knowledge
That love is abiding.
Out of the shadows, my voice,
Singing to you of delight,
Out of the distance and silence,
Out of the dream-deep night;
Out of the haunted mist
Fashioning valiant and fair
Hymns like wine for your spirit,
Victory out of despair.
Hold fast to me, Love, in the darkness;
For all that keeps us apart
Is never so strong and so changeless
As the love in my heart.

A SONG OF LOVE

Guard it ever faithful,
Hold it ever fast;
'Tis the only treasure
That will ever last.

Be your heart its garden,
Your care its sun and shade;
'Tis the only flower
That will never fade.

Keep its rapture singing,
Let all else go by;
'Tis the only music
That will never die.

Follow it, though rugged
Be the path and strange;
'Tis the only beauty
That will never change.

Follow, follow after
Over land and foam;
'Tis the only comrade
That will bring you home.

CRY IN THE NIGHT

Deep through the dark I heard
A far cry in the night;
Across the world to me it came,
Like some wild flashing of a light,
My name! My name!

It was your voice, Beloved;
Its loveliness I heard.
You must have waked and loved me so,
I could but send this answering word,
"I know! I know!"

TRIUMPH

Where through the meadow-mist,
Stealing on silver feet,
A lithe brook's running fleet,
There a fair wildrose gave
Her image to a wave.

Swift through its moorland wild
Hurried the wave away:
Died the bloom of a day.
Yet their love seems to live,
Fleeting and fugitive.

Heart, O that you may say
Ere to death's gulf you go,
"Though it was long ago,
Let this life's glory be:
Beauty once leaned to me."

SACRAMENT

No holy water on my head,
And not the wine and not the bread
Shall lead me to the blest abode
Of peace, of beauty, and of God.

Not any prayer, or penance done;
Or vigil in the moon or sun;
Not even valor has the key
To that still place where I would be.

When shall we learn it, you and I?
And not to learn it is to die—
Ah, let us, ere it is too late,
Our wanton spirits consecrate

By coming deeply to divine
Love is God's holy bread and wine;
The only Saviour to us sent,
Love is life's only sacrament.

ONE WAY OF LOVE

We cannot think alike, and this
Is grief to you;
O yet, so thinking, may our hearts
Remain more true
Than if they acted as one heart,
Less wise than two.

For by that difference, the foe
Is sore beset;
Divided we, yet in true love
Forever met;
One looks, one listens, you recall
What I forget.

Two comrades traversing the world,
Loving and true,
Each by a way and thought distinct,
A varied view,
Protect and guide and counsel best
The journey through.

WAS IT NOT STRANGE?

Was it not strange
There was no strangeness in it?
But only beauty
And the dream's fulfilling?
All was as if
We'd found the end of searching,
Reached the goal of longing,
Found the precious treasure;
Come, after wandering,
Surely, joyously
To the visioned Homeland,
To the magic country
Of our heart's desire.

PARTING

Over the hills where night her vesture weaves
A dust-wind grieves;

Now in the violet valley lying still,
A whipporwill;

Then the weird dark so strangely rushing on
After the sun.

Tears come resurgent, filling faithful eyes
With voiceless cries;

The quivering lip, yet the brave clasp of hands
God understands.

For we must part. There was so much to tell
Ere this farewell.

But now let silence all our troubles keep
Lest words should weep.

The daylight disappears in crimson fire;
Thus dies desire;

Starlike there dawns what has been and shall be:
My love for thee.

WILDROSE LOVE

I meant to bring you roses,
But sometimes I brought rue:
I beg for your forgiveness,
For pardon would I sue,
Since, through life's changes, chances
You'll have a gleaming air
Of love that never failed you,—
A wildrose for your hair.

INADEQUATE

Were every mountain mine,
Each valley, wildwood, sea;
And all the stars that shine,
And all the flowers that be;
Were every gem the hills
Deep in their bosom hold,
Beneath the rocks and rills,
The silver and the gold;
The wildflowers in the glen
That look with elfin eyes;
The ferns that fringe the fen
With fairylike surprise;
Could Music's heart-blood bleed
And to my realm belong,
To intimate my need
In everlasting song?

And I assigned to you
This splendor of the world,
The sky's savannas blue,
Like banners broad unfurled,—
Not all earth's beauty given
Could my devotion prove;
And all the stars of Heaven
Could but suggest my love.

LOVE IS

Love is the step for which a woman's whole life listens;
The lily that in Time's sweet wildwood glistens.
Love's are the tears the heart has wept alone;
It is the star deep in the jeweled stone,
The sapphire's light, the ruby's secret rose.
It is the stream that through wild meadows flows.
It is life's mystery, its beauty, and wonder;
Its flashing lightning and its rolling thunder.
And though he knows it not, nor gives it heed
Love is a man's supremest joy and need

259

LOVE WILL SUSTAIN IT

Mysterious as a little child
Who can despair dispel,
Love is an elfin, wild
Immortal miracle;
A fairy sentinel,
Who in the deepest dark
Can lilac dawn foretell;
And to a storming sea
Bring peace to be . . .
None can explain it.
For any other hope
It is in vain to call;
But when all strength that stands
Seems swiftly sure to fall,
Love will sustain it.

I SEE HIM NOT

I see him not as others see,
For he's my own true man to me.
Their eyes behold him. I, his friend,
Have deeper ways to comprehend;
Visioning them with love's own art,
I see him only with my heart.

I hear him not as others hear.
For me his life makes music clear.
They harken for the voice of dust;
I hear his song of faith and trust.
They hear his tones of street and mart.
I listen only with my heart.

So seeing and so hearing, I
The beauty of his soul descry,
Marking amid life's shrouding storm
His spirit's tall illustrious form.
—Nor do we love in ways apart:
He sees and hears me with his heart.

COMPENSATION

I love all little leaves,
All gentle lovely things;
From them my heart receives
The lovely grace of wings.
The wildflowers turn their eyes
On me. They so resemble
Angels from Paradise.
I worship and I tremble.

But if for me no star,
No wildflower would shine;
If all the things that are
Wonders, could not be mine;
If I no song could hear
Amid life's shadows tall,
O, yet, if you were near,
You'd compensate for all.

TAKE THIS ALONE

God grant that you may ever be
From all my pain and fear apart;
And that your eyes may never see
The dagger rigid in my heart;
That from my shadowy sky you'll hear
Only the glad rejoicing lark,
Only the mockingbird be near
For you in all my grievous dark.
For you may innocent glories gleam,
And love-delighted quiet scenes;
And may you never know of dreams
What not to have you to me means.
O let me give you only grace,
Your spirit by my own be stilled;
Take from me only love's tall vase
With ferns and fairy wildflowers filled.

TIMING

April's a wild glad day,
Promising May.
With the glitter of freed streams flowing,
With frolic and fairy winds blowing;
With all this beauty about,
And life like a joyous shout,
O do not tell me how
You love me now!
It might not mean a thing
But spring.

But if you have not changed
By dark November,
Remember
To tell me of your need
When all the world's a faded rose,
A withered weed;
With the earth gray below,
And the sky gray above,
O if you tell me then,
It might mean love!

SONG OF CHANGELESSNESS

'Tis here, the moment golden,
The thrilling wonder strange;
The timeless magic olden
For us will never change;
To love we are beholden
Wherever we may range.

Into the land of dreaming
Love led us long ago;
Not less but more the gleaming,
More beautiful the glow,
With lovelier starlight streaming
Where deeper waters flow.

THE MAGIC OF LOVE

I know not whence such color comes!
Blooms from life's barren field upstart,
Giving it glory, beauty, grace,
Waking wild wonder in my heart.
Perchance love's magic is akin
To that the artless flowers disclose,—
The vision in the violet,
The dream that reddens in the rose.

YOU MAKE THEM MINE

The bird on the blossoming bough,
The flowers that perfume the fen,
The stars in the crested pine,
The song of the stream in the glen,—
Your loving me makes them all mine.

Through you have I learned of life's peace,
By your tranquil wild gladness I live;
You are refuge and solace and rest;
I am, through the love that you give,
Of Beauty immortal the guest.

And when the dread dark is most deep,
When all other guidances fade,
I have not a fear of the night;
For, holding my hands in the shade,
You are to my life all my light.

The billows that break on the beach,
The curlews that call by the sea,
The wildflowers blooming alone,—
Your love has conferred them on me:
You make all earth's beauty my own.

THE VEILED ROSE

Your heart alone, Beloved, can see
Most magical and deep in me
The great rose,
The wild rose,
The veiled rose,
The miracle of all flowers:
Your rose and my rose,
The love that is ours.

LIFE'S ONLY SONG

In all the world there's but one song,
True, beautiful, and wise.
It will outsoar all suffering.
When all else fades and dies,
It falters not, but will endure,
Though dynasties may pass:
A song about a wildheart lad
Who loves a wildheart lass.

LOOK TO THE BATTLELINE

If you would know how deeply loved you are,
Look not for light amid the rioting roses,
Or to the beauty of the evening star.
No answer for your heart the dawn discloses;
Song will not tell you how the matter stands,
And music will conceal what you would see.
The rainbows gleaming over seas and lands
Will veil your glory or Gethsemane.

If you would know how greatly you are loved,
Look to the battleline, the blood, the dust;
Look to the stormy van where valor's proved, ...
The place where heroes are. For you can trust
Your Dear One's love if with the brave he's found.
. . . See how he stretched your foes dead on the ground

264

BEAUTY ETERNAL

When I begin to feel that I am not
All that I was, nor cannot be again,
I know I have what shall not be forgot:
Treasures of long ago unchanged have lain
In memory's keeping. These I look upon,
Love them, and lay them in their beauty by.
They are a part of me; and were I gone,
They would speak for me, saying, "Here am I."

Among these glimmering jewels of the past,
Unchanged as any precious stones, there gleams
One loveliest, that shall the longest last,
Eternal as far visions and great dreams:
Our love and longing shall immortal be
While mountains stand, while rolls the restless sea.

YOU COULD

If my heart were a jewel
Lost deep in life's night,
Your coming could prove
All the triumph of light;
For I know that you could,
And I dream that you would
The dawn in my diamond,
In my topaz the sunset,
The sky in my turquoise,
In my emerald the sea;
The moon in my opal,
The rose in my ruby,
The star in my sapphire—be!

WONDER SUSTAINED

Last night he lingered
Upon a dark hill
Under dim hemlocks, all
Spicy and still,
Hearing the mystical
Wild whippoorwill.

Far in the valley-mist
Faded day's lights,
Migrants deep in the dark
Fluted their flights;
Fairies were near him when
All was the night's.

Now in this office where
He earns his pelf,
He had forgot that world
Of sprite and elf
Had not a girl here been
Wonder herself—

Being the beauty that
Shadows imply,
Fragrance of hemlocks,
Night's violet sky,
Mystery, starlight,
The whippoorwill's cry!

SAFE FOREVER

The perfect hour vanished,
That left us long ago
Is safer in its beauty
Than anything we know;
It gleams with changeless glory,
Eternal through the years,
Beyond the reach of darkness,
Beyond the touch of tears.

266

GOD'S DAUGHTER

God loves her; for in sun and shade
She loves all beauty He had made,
And gladly worships, without words,
The poetry of His wildwood birds.

The heron on the lonely shore
In silence will her heart adore,
And bless her Maker, without speech,
Where breaks the blue wave on the beach.

In deep still rapture she has stood,
A wildflower of God's wildflowered wood;
And He has seen her lean to bless
Hearts longing for her loveliness.

And how she goes to them in grief;
Her beauty brings their pangs relief;
And how all little children prove
Her tenderheartedness by love.

And how in mercy she will be
Beside one in his agony;
An artist in her selfless grace.
A heroine of all our Race.

God holds her hand; with her He goes,
His daughter lovelier than His rose;
In glad approval He avers,
"Of all I made, the glory's hers."

BLAME NOT

In aromatic dells,
In meadows, fields, or fells
Blame not the bee
That loves the wildflower's bells.
—And blame not me.

Sonnets

REGRET

Safe in her castle on life's wild seacoast,
She heard a fateful crying in the night,
Yet feared to answer that despairing, lost,
Imploring voice, or lift a rescuing light.
She dreaded; for she did not understand,
In her young beauty, in those days that were,
How all his hope was but to grasp her hand
In friendship, and in spirit worship her.

'Twas long ago he cried to her in vain. . . .
Now, in the night, when all is very still,
She dreams she hears that longing voice again;
And though in pity, from her castled hill,
She hastens, even to the perilous shore,
There's no one there to need her any more.

GLADNESS OF THE DUST

When from the South the warbling minstrels come,
And emerald mists the woodlands sweetly dim;
When by the earliest blooms the wild bees hum,
And silence is a prelude to a hymn
Of joy, that death and winter now are gone;
Then, though the heart be hidden, and no voice
Has it for utterance, yet it has its own
Still adoration whereby to rejoice.

Under the mold, the faded leaves and sere,
Tremendous visions take their shape and form.
Spring is not only of the upper air:
Through soul and soil her virgin passions storm
Till all life feels the triumph of long trust—
The sure and terrible gladness of the dust.

271

THEIR FINEST HOUR

Loving her always with a deepening sense
Of wonder, as the wild sea loves the coast,
Yearning to reach her with desire immense,
He often questions when he loves her most.
What is the perfect hour his heart remembers
With purest joy? The one of tears and flame,
Of fire and of fervor and of embers,
When love a passionate hurricane became?

Rather he must believe it was the hour,
Tranquil and gracious, that in talk they spent,
Love reassured by gentle, quiet power;
Untouching, yet so wed they were, it meant
That if Time took the passion from their story,
Of love there would remain the nobler glory.

ENCHANTED HOURS

Remember the enchanted lyric hours
Love gave us with its gracious and divine
Seraphic insight. We had need of flowers
Unknown to mortal meadows. They were mine
And yours, most beautiful and perfect girl!
By Heaven's mercy we were led by those
Immortal spirits, whose wide wings would furl
About us, guarding love's mysterious rose.

What lies before me know not, but we know
Our love can never in the years grow strange.
Steadfast it stands, whatever tempest blow;
Changeless, although all else should suffer change
It is God's gift, most beautiful and tender.
Our rapture and enchantment, O remember!

272

MOST PERFECT LOVE

Most perfect love is that which is in vain;
For in it is no jealousy or fear,
No dread of disillusion, mirage, pain.
While love attained is doomed to be aware
That transitory joy can have no hold
On immortality: the glorious rose,
Destined to dust, to darkness and the mold,
Proves human beauty comes to such a close.

But spirit-beauty to his heart belongs
To whom the love he yearns for is denied.
For him alone are fragrant wildflower songs
That have not faded, and that have not died.
Mysterious is a spiritual thing,
That even in defeat can soar and sing.

LOVE'S BOUNTY

All that I was I gave you, never dreaming
Of a return, for it was love I gave,
As a wild star her sumptuous beauty streaming
In deep of night to a dark western wave.
It was my spirit that I yielded to you,
Surrendering body and soul; and asked no more
Than that my mystery none other knew
Should be the secret diadem you wore.

But love is richer than we ever know:
We lavish it, and love comes back to us
A thousandfold. Why should I think it so?
How else? Our little child proclaims it thus;
For in him love returns in flower and light
More than I gave you in the glimmering night.

ROYAL GUEST

He will not stay forever anywhere,
This princely guest. Once he was in our home.
I think his name is Rapture. He was here.
But no one knows when this fair god will come,
And none can tell the hour he shall depart.
He is a seraph. On his wings of song
He visits many a loving, faithful heart,
But is not pledged to stay with any long.

Yet since he came, we are not what we were,
We have inherited a proud estate.
His beauty lingers in our hearts, that stir
With everlasting joy. Not desolate
Are we who learned of him how love is tender,
Who gave us glory, and who left us splendor.

LIKE ONE WHO ON A PEAK

Like one who on a peak at twilight stands,
Surveying boundless country, lying lone;
And sees above the spacious sleeping lands
Star after star ascend her silver throne:
Yet turns from too much amplitude, to love
A swaying violet in a rock-cleft dreaming,
Here, at his hand, with delicate ferns above,—
A modest fairy in her beauty gleaming:

So from life's prospect vast and fair and wide,
Bewildered by allurements brave and bright,
Of wealth and loveliness and fame and pride,
Long, long ago I turned for my delight
To one who to me mystically meant
More than the world, more than the firmament.

HEREAFTER

I wait and hope that there shall come a day
When we shall meet, and never again shall part;
That dawn will come, and shadows flee away;
And we shall be as one, and heart-to-heart,
With longing all fulfilled. There is a tide
That sets in from the ocean; it will come
Out of the multitudinous seaways wide
Until it finds a river that is home.

O that your faithful tide might find my river.
The coming of your love will make all change.
I watch and wait, although it seems forever.
For your arrival beautiful, and strange;
And yet I know your waters, wild and sweet,
Will mingle with my own, when we shall meet.

ONCE TO HIS LOVE

Once to his Love a conqueror returned
From battles far away and perils drear,
Imagining that for his spoils she yearned,
And would his triumphs and his trophies wear;
Yet found her but an artless faerie child,
Amid her blossoming garden well content,
By all his clanging glory unbeguiled,
And too naïve to be magnificent.

So to my Soul I brought the splendid dust
Of victory. But wistfully she said:
"O Lover, even now the moth and rust
Consume your gifts. Immortal things I need:
That for eternity I may be strong,
Give me a dream, a sacrifice, a song."

275

KINGDOMS PASSED AWAY

Long had he, as a soldier, known the shock
Of battle, and the brazen voice of death,
Whose merest whisper rives the granite rock
Of valor. Well he knew the rancid breath
Of bellowing guns. And often had he knelt
By dying comrades; in a maddened flood
Had seen tall thrones swept headlong, and had felt
The crash of falling kingdoms in his blood.

But all these seemed as naught when he descried
The end of Beauty's heavenly estate:
He, gazing on the glory as it died
In one adored, by grief made desolate,
Saw, like the doom in splendid sunset skies,
Love's noble empire fading from her eyes.

I HAVE SEEN GLORY FADE

I have seen glory fade, and I have heard
A silence after trumpets. Fortune wanes,
And triumph falters. The resplendent sword
Of valor rusts. Of grandeur, what remains?
Fame's music sounds, and then the music ends.
Even sweet hope herself declines and dies.
Despite all courage, strength to weakness tends.
There's but one thing that every change defies.

From year to year its beauty and its power
Ascend amid defeats and fading prides.
With all else dying, it will come to flower;
With all else failing, nobly it abides.
Its virtue 'gainst all enemies avails:
If love be truly love, it never fails.

MATED

"Now shall we have our joy," the lover said;
The waitings and the partings all are done.
Now shall our hearts by bliss be comforted,
By joy alone, and so shall we be one.
Love is the happiness that smiles at fate,—
Being life's blossom of immortal birth:
Some angel, dallying at the heavenly gate,
Let fall this dewy rose to dusty earth."

"Not joy alone," she said, "shall make our song;
Nor rapture, nor the stars of bliss that shine;
Nor beauty, nor release from waiting long;
For 'tis ordained we never shall divine
How deep love is, how true, how passing strong
Until my grief be yours, your sorrow mine."

FREEDOM

I cannot liken love to prison bars
That hold the captive fast; love that reveals
The unconjectured glory of the stars;
Unlocks the occult and eternal seals
Of Beauty; gives the heart that final power,
Deep incommunicable grace to share;
And makes the humblest dusty wayside flower
A dawning of divinity to wear.

Your love has led me to a lordlier land,
Mountains more mystic by a vaster sea,
Where ampler skies the Infinite unfold;
As if a magic and immortal Hand
Threw wide a casement on eternity,
And gave me boundless vision to behold.

THE GIFT SUPREME

All things were beautiful in virgin Eden;
And to the First Man everything was new;
And all was his except one Tree Forbidden.
All life created formed his retinue,
And he was lord. Yet for him was to be
The last and loveliest gift God could conceive;
To still his spirit with love's mystery,
With wonder sweet and wild,—God gave him Eve.

Not less than he who first looked on such wine
Of all delight in beauty trembling;
Not less in awe I gaze at what is mine,
The Garden's final bloom resembling.
God made so many of my dreams come true;
Then gave me the undreamed-of,—gave me you.

SUPREME ASTONISHMENT

Still am I startled when I hear it thunder;
And lightning makes me shiver with surprise.
A wildflower never fails to make me wonder.
Why the tide turns, I only half surmise.
I marvel how the mist the mountain veils;
All unexpected wonder makes me start,
As when the moon through dusky pine-trees sails.
Spellbound I watch the rose reveal her heart.

As one of altars and of shrines aware,
At your mysterious loveliness in, awe,
Miraculous Nature, I bewildered stare,
Joyful and breathless. Yet never I foresaw
Completeness of your beauty, half-concealed,
Until my Love was radiantly revealed.

BUT ONE

I

In all the gardens of the earth,
Of all the flowers come to birth,
That any human eye can see,
There's but one Rose—
One Rose for me.

II

Of all the dreams by day and night,
However fair, however bright,
However great their glamour be,
There's but one Dream—
One Dream for me.

III

Life is a forest where are heard
Voice after voice of singing bird—
Music in every bush and tree . . .
There's but one Voice —
One Voice for me.

IV

Innumerable hearts are full
Of love that's high and beautiful,
Of love that sets life's prisoners free;
There's but one Heart—
One Heart for me.

V

One Rose, one Dream, one Voice, one Heart—
One hope that we shall never part
By any land or any sea . . .
There's but one Love—
One Love for me.

LIFE AND LOVE

Fair, infinite with ancient memories,
Gather the stars. What have their hearts not seen,
All that I am, all that I might have been;
They gaze upon me with imperial eyes,
Calling my spirit straightway to arise:
Ah, pitying God, the woeful gulf between
Their steadfast beauty, changelessly serene,
Their glory and my heart's best sacrifice.

Life still must have its anguish and its dust,
Its barren sorrow when self's will is done,
Its mortal dimness and its fear that mars;
Love lights her spirit-flame of changeless trust;
When the rain falls, fear not for yonder sun,
Nor in the tempest tremble for the stars.

SINGING FRIENDS

If I depended on my voice to tell
All that is singing in my heart for you,
You would not know my love. O, it is well
For me that singers wild and sweet and true
Express the otherwise unknown. . . .It seems
Divine conspiracy to aid me. All
Beauty that sleeps or wakes or gently dreams
For your dear sake and mine is lyrical.

O listen to the azure song the sky
Hymns of my love; and how along the river
The river-marsh is whispering what I
Would tell you now, and tell your heart forever.
And in the dawning's and the evening's hush
My love sings to you in the hermit thrush.

WHEN FROM HIS TOWER

When from his tower the watcher of the skies
Thrills to the planet and the asteroid,
And in the dim and nether deep descries
Far realms of light where he imagined void;
When, rapt with awe from gazing, back he turns
To tell what glimmering country he has trod,
So great has been the loveliness he learns,
His silence speaks the miracles of God.

So when into your eyes I gaze, I see
Beauty that brings a hush about my heart,
With wonder of more wonders yet to be,
Far mysteries, of which I know in part:
Marvels of love that to my hope respond,
Deep after deep, with starry deeps beyond.

RECOVERY

For beauty lost and loved my spirit grieved,
For music muted, for romance long sped;
For lone Isoult, and for Cordelia dead
In her sweet bloom; for all whose hearts believed
In lyric love, yet early were received
Into death's hushed and holy halls of dread . . .
Over my youth was Farewell's glamour shed . . .
Yet suddenly all losses seem retrieved;

For you are come; and by your coming brought
Streaming wild starlights of the long ago,
More magic than Mage Merlin ever taught,
Leading to all I love and long to know,
Bringing me home, and bringing home to me
Of all things fair and lost, recovery.

DAYBREAK

Like one who, blinded from his birth, has known
No sight of star or human face or flower;
But wanders in oblivion alone;
And only of great darkness feels the power:
So rode the earth in night original,
With ebon clouds investing land and air,
Stemming the deep abyss through shadows tall,
Of all Light's coming glory unaware.

And in life's orbit darkly was I whirled
Until you came. In shades of doubt entombed,
I had not known a comrade save the night,
Until your beauty gleamed, as to the world
That first far dawn, when dim creation bloomed
At those tremendous words, "Let there be light!"

CONSUMMATION

Joy did not join us or the golden air
Of peace upon the limpid landscape spread.
Though all our world was jubilant and fair,
Into love's inner shrine we were not led.
Dallying in the sweetness of the summer bowers,
To keep refreshed our drooping rose we strove;
But the sad task was far beyond our powers:
In idle happiness we found not love.

Then after calm came tempest and wild weather,
Sorrow and peril and the grievous blast;
Yet we found love in facing loss together
And by bereavement were betrothed fast . . .
Love's bosom never is so deep and warm
As when it is a shelter from life's storm.

282

GLORY TO HER

Glory to her forever and forever!
For not as others' was her love for me.
Theirs was the rivulet, and hers was the river;
Theirs was the wave, and hers the boundless sea.
Not mine, not mine can ever be repayment
To one who with compassionate tender grace
Clothed me in beauty like celestial raiment,
Gave me her angel spirit to embrace.

And stranger, sweeter ever is the knowing
That all she gave was not in mere surrender:
She longed to bathe me in her wonder, flowing
Like starlight and like singing and like splendor.
Her mercy, that my heart could hardly bear,
Gave me her own wild mystic rose to wear.

EYES OF LOVE

The depth and beauty of your love for me,
In spite of all the glory you had given,
I did not comprehend, I could not see:
Although I knew that I was in God's heaven;
And felt your strength, and that it could not fail;
Saw stars more splendid in more lovely skies
The mystery divine behind the veil
I knew not till you loved me with your eyes.

For then our spirits mated and I saw
Your soul look into mine, revealing all
Love's perfect beauty and its secret awe;
I felt your spirit answer my life's call . . .
O, Eyes of Love, look into mine, and see
How we are one for all eternity.

EVERLASTING ROSE

I

One thing has haunted me through all my years:
Why is it that a woman loves not less
Her man for all his sins? Her tender tears
Wash quite away his wanton wickedness.
Nor will she ever love him any more
For all the good he does. Her soul's offended
By piousness; for in life's forest dim
They are alone; and nothing there is splendid
Except his love for her, her love for him.

Too long I dreamed that virtue is repaid
By joy and constant love. It is not so.
Love is a wildflower that will never fade,
Though tempests may assail it. It will grow
In grief and sorrow. No one knows its source;
And reason has no power to chart its course.

II

O could it be that love is not of earth,
Immutable as are the heavenly hosts?
Than mortal hearts, had it another birth?
And is its bourne on far celestial coasts?
It may be that it burns with other light
Than what we take for sparkling vagaries.
So distant and divine has been its flight
A radiance from other lands and seas

Round it effulgent gleam. We cannot tell
By human standards what love's nature is:
If it be true and deep, we know full well
That it will never change, that all life's bliss
In it abides. Perchance each woman knows
The wonder of her everlasting Rose.

LOVE'S WORLD

With all the rivers of the world in flood
I thought the End would come; with planets reeling;
With shuddering thunder and with wounds past healing;
With a sky darkened, and a moon of blood;
With wailing from each perishing sea and wood;
Then a deep silence over chaos stealing;
With all lights quenched,—save a last light revealing
A firmament fallen where a firmament stood.

Yet quietly and now the end of all
For me may come; for am I not your world?
Your little hands cradle my destiny.
One loveless touch makes all my stars to fall.
My universe to ruin can be hurdled
By one chill word or glance from you to me.

"WE BROUGHT NOTHING . . ."

Though naked to the world I came, and brought
No gold or silver and no precious gem;
No power and no music and no thought,—
Yet had a dream about a diadem
Of jewels made, that came not from the earth:
I brought this yearning, here to be fulfilled,—
Immortal longing, with me from my birth,
And destined by God's mercy to be stilled.

Out of the world, whenever I must go,
I shall take treasures with me manifold,
Nobler than other riches that I know,
More precious than all jewels and all gold:
Because the beauty of your love I found,
Here and Hereafter I am glory-crowned.

285

THE MYSTIC ROSE

As in the ruby burns a mystic rose
That is, yet is not, of herself a part,
But is a vision's glory to disclose
The meaning and the magic of her heart;
And as that loveliness, beyond all capture,
Beyond the touch of time and tears and change,
Beyond all anguish and beyond all rapture,
Remotely radiant is, splendidly strange;

So, Love, there is within you such a light,
A glimmering bloom within the jewel rare,
A starry deep beneath the starry height,
A region past the realm of mortal care.
A mystice rose within the ruby burns;
Toward that alone in you my spirit yearns.

YOU CAME OUT IN THE RAIN

You came out in the rain to say goodbye,
And stood beside the car. I did not know
You lingered there beneath that weeping sky
Because you did not want to see me go,
Or wanted to be with me one more minute.
I did not guess that gracious gesture's worth,
The quiet beauty and the wonder in it,
Hinting of all the glory on the earth.

So much I have forgotten! So much goes!
The loving things that many lips have said;
Triumph and sorrow, ashes and the rose . . .
Yet by one memory I'm comforted:
It sings to me again and yet again:
To say goodbye, you came out in the rain.

286

IMMORTAL

The hero fallen on the battlefield,
Or any one at home who sinks to sleep
Amid his friends, who love him as they weep,
Each, each and all to death's dread power yield.
Gathered to him, the flower of the field,
The leaf in the forest's powerful vain keep
Pass into nothingness with wounds so deep
That nevermore shall one of them be healed.

But I have seen Love through the heart clear riven
Rise with a beauty greater than before,
And stronger, and to greater glory given,
Her splendor deepening as she suffers more,
Emerge triumphant from death's sombre portal,
To prove that one thing's in the world immortal.

REMEMBER ME

Remember me beyond this darkened hour.
Remember me as one who loves you well.
For you to love me was not in your power;
Love's was a story that you could not tell.
Yet when your face from me was turned away,
Still did I love and honor you. You gave
All that you could, said all that you could say;
And in denying me were just and brave.

Remember me as one who to the end
Found all life's glory in your heart alone.
You gave me exaltation, and the power
To worship what could never be my own.
Remember I shall love you all the more.
When life's last wave breaks on its final shore.

LOVE TRANSFIGURES ALL

I cannot see the ocean ever again
As once I did—since we together strolled
By the blue waves that on the white beach rolled,
Feeling together all the joy and pain
Of wild love surging like the surging main,
By God alone created and controlled;
Hearing the dee-toned bells the breakers tolled;
Watching the yearning sea the shore attain.

Immortal beauty has your love conferred:
Always I seem to be where we have been,
Hearing forever all that we have heard,
Becoming one with all that we have seen:
I am the shore . . . Your love, the eternal sea,
In everlasting music breaks on me.

ROSES IN THE DARK

A traveler told me, who had seen it done,
That in the Carpathian valleys, in the Bulgars' land,
Where fields of roses flower in the sun,
To make the precious attar,—not one hand
Will touch them in the daytime. It is known
That only in the deep and glimmering night,
Amid the dewy shadows,—then alone
Will the floodtide of their fragrance reach its height.

We, too, can gather roses in life's dark,
Guided to them by hope's unfailing star,
And love the nightingale more than the lark.
In grief we can be one with them who are
Harvesting roses ere the break of day
In the Carpathian valleys far away.

FORGIVE ME

Forgive me for the times I tried to tell
My love in words; for all the songs I sang
To make you understand I loved you well.
All through those years my empty music rang:
Beauty of thought in language sweet I wove,
Building you palaces of glimmering dreams;
Yet vain were all the protests of my love,
Its visions vain. How poor such tribute seems!

For how much more than music have you given!
A tender vigilance that never sleeps;
A counsel wise; a gentleness; the heaven
Your quiet spirit always for me keeps.
Forgive my words, and teach me to return
Such love as from you every hour I learn.

WHEN OTHER EYES

When other eyes than mine the spring behold
In warbling woodlands with white dogwood bright,
When flower by flower the mysteries unfold,
And all the world is one of song and light;
And you, O lovers of the years to come,
Through whom the beauty and the awe shall sweep,
I too once found the heart of love my home,
And longed and strove and joyed and fell asleep.

O lovers of the future, when the bells
Of yellow jasmine tassel all the woods,
And in your hearts the mystic music swells
That wakes for lovers in spring's solitudes,
My hope is that your hearts may there discover—
He, his one sweetheart; she, her destined lover.

THE LIGHT

The light goes out with you; it reappears
When you return. I do not ask to know
Why it has been like this through all the years.
You bring me victory. Life's overthrow
Is in your absence. Is it weakness, Love,
So to acknowledge your high mastery?
Who would deny what days and moments prove?
Conquest and loss alike you mean to me.

There is a pine tree in the forest old,
So overtowered by far greater trees,
Only at times it flushes in the gold
Of sunlight, or to moonlight's mysteries,
Now tinged, and now transfigured from its shade;
So all my light is by your shining made.

THE FORETELLING

I saw the dawn on hills of amethyst.
In the dim glen the kalmia blushed for me.
Beauty there was on everyside to see.
In mountain meadows mantled in a mist
With rose on pale wildrose I kept a tryst,
Hearing the mated birds make melody.
But promise of a splendor yet to be
Made my heart feel some marvel it had missed:

Beyond all fragrances, a last perfume;
Beyond all other raptures, one most blest,
Beyond all other flowers, an ultimate bloom;
Beyond all little loves, the loveliest;
Yours being the beauty they but intimate,
Their wonders on your final wonder wait.

THE MIRACLE

Only her memory can now be mine,
Yet it means more than anything I hold
Finite and real; for it is all divine . . .
The heart alone can make a dream of gold.
I was by her beloved, O miracle!
An angel stooped to me her loveliness.
Ah, I was nothing! nothing! She was all,
Whose beauty was a heavenly caress.

See, I am nothing—something to be scorned,
To be passed by forgotten . . . Yet if you turn,
Discerningly, you'll see me fair adorned—
Fair as a god. You'll for my splendor yearn;
For by her deathless love adored, I gleam
In the eternal glory of her dream.

IF ANY KINGS

If any kings I see,
I have no jealousy,
I envy not them.
Your royal diadem
Of perfect love and trust
Makes all their glory dust.
Your gift, that is my royal crown,
Is more than their renown.

Their splendor is a tarnished thing
To the glory that you bring;
Their might is but a feeble wraith
To the handclasp of your faith.
If any kings I see,
How they should envy me!

PEACE

There is a peace of river and of lake,
And mountains, silent in the afterglow;
Yet transient is the quiet dream they know:
Some tempest their serenity shall break.
But there's peace of heart that shall not wake
To fear or anger or to any woe;
A joyous strength that through all griefs may go,
And naught from storms except their valor take.

There is a peace too deep and true for change;
When all the world is riot, it is rest,
Stilling the spirit with its beauty strange.
When life is darkness, it is radiance blest;
From every care sure refuge and release,
Eternal in the heart, Love's lyric peace.

BRIMMING CHALICE

A roamer of the wilds, he loved rock-roses,
Swamp honeysuckle, star anemones;
The cardinalis that in flame discloses
Her presence, yet conceals her mysteries;
Like sleeping beauties, ladyslippers lone,
Valerian, spikenard, star-grass, meadow-rue;
Patrician rosebays, with contralto tone
Of color, and the darling speedwell blue.

So when he offered love, with it he gave
Fringed gentians, cool lobelias, columbines;
Forests and fields with tranquil beauty grave;
Rose-mallows, yellow daisies, jessamines . . .
All nature's grace was of his love a part,
And wildwood wonder brimming in his heart.

FRAGRANCES

Not nard or cassia out of Samarcand,
Or aloes of Arabia,—not these;
Nor attar from the high Carpathian land,
Or essences and eastern spiceries
With heavy perfume made as merchandise
For passion's market, and the weary whirl
Of love for gain . . . O native-sweet and wise,
Not one of these suggests you, Darling Girl.

You make me think of evening, and you bring
The breath of woodlands wild and delicate;
The mint upon the meadow's dewy slope;
The dusky pines where mystic thrushes sing;
Myrtles and muscadines where warblers mate,
A fairy garden dim with heliotrope.

ROYAL STAR

The heart that's greatly loved must never grieve.
Honor and glory and the splendor wild
Of starry wonder does that soul receive.
To all life's ills it should be reconciled.
For what are they to love's estate supreme,
The immortal dawning on the mortal sight,
The vision and the gladness and the dream,
The triumph of the spirit's pure delight?

Within that heart a beauty lives forever;
Time's fading touch can have no power there:
As if a star, deep in a magic river,
Eternal, tranquil, shines so bright and fair
That all the waters wide illumined are
By the strange radiance of that royal star.

REASSURANCE

There are no words to tell you how I love you.
Look in my eyes. Read there my honest story.
It tells there can be no one else above you,
And that for me your love is all of glory.
Read deeply, and to mystery be brought,
With wild harps choiring on a starlit shore;
Read on; and if you find a single thought
Or word that is not true, then read no more.

Look in my eyes. There love and trust abide;
Deep after starry deep is all for you:
See there the wings beneath which you can hide,
The strength of soul forever to you true.
And more than any comrade, friend, or lover,
If you will read aright, you shall discover.

WHY

O searcher of the records of the past,
Recorder of the years of long ago,
Among the singers you will come at last
Upon my name. Then would I have you know
That of all those who ever touched the lute,
And from the harp melodious music drew
So that all listeners with joy were mute,
Mine was felicity none other knew.

Then will you say: "There was a cause for this:
Though others sang, yet in him was a song
That only those can sing who drink of bliss.
Her love sustained him when the way was long.
With splendor let her starry brow be bound:
She was the glory that he sought and found."

LOVELIEST BOOK

Once in a lonely night, for company,
I sought some of the books I love the best:
Poor Enoch Arden's tragedy of the sea;
Shakespeare's Cordelia, truest, tenderest;
Jane Austen, wisest of the novelists;
My Browning, Keats and Shelley, Poe and Scott;
The Brontes wild; Blake glimmering in his mists,—
All, all are friends, beloved and unforgot.

Then I remembered You, to whom I owe
All joy, all wisdom. O divinest Star
That the long night of my dark life can show!
And when I thought of you, and all you are,
Laying my other treasures by, I said,
"You are the loveliest book I ever read."

GLORY OF THE VISION

In this dark world it is radiance to have known
About your wonder. Mine it could not be.
But the deliverance of your beauty comes to me
Outside your garden, loving and alone.
Merely the vision of you can atone
For life's long shadows and its cruelty.
Inland, I hear the music of your sea,
Exalted by what cannot be my own.

In this dark world it is splendor to have found
In a mortal heart all things that are divine;
To have felt that where you are is Holy Ground;
To have heard the chorals in your mystic shrine;
To have seen, from Nebo's solitary height,
Of my Promised Land, the glory of the sight.

BEAUTIFUL ANSWER

Darkly life's questions come. I know not why
I cannot answer them, or why I feel
They must be answered. Wherefore should we die?
Who made it sin to love? How shall we deal
With jealousy, that hydra-headed snake?
How wildly love, and yet be ice, not fire?
How to bear parting, when the soul must break?
How not to weep, denied the heart's desire?

Beautiful Answer, you are love's reply
To anguish, and to all that troubles me.
In you my spirit finds hope's azure sky,
And hears the music of faith's boundless sea.
Darkly life's questions come, and all is night.
And then I turn to you,— and all is light.

WILD HEART OF CONSTANCY

Wild heart of constancy,
How far you follow me!
If I should lose my way,
You would be break of day.
Should I lose sight of you,
You could my course pursue
Clear to another star.
Whither I go, you are.
In parting's cruel night
Your love's my only light.
No mountain is so steep,
No valley is so deep,
No water is so wide
But you are by my isde.
How far you follow me,
Wild heart of constancy!

296

BRIMMING TIDE

Love is the only thing beneath the sun
That of itself takes no account at all;
And though with generous giving never done,
Its stature grows more splendid and more tall.
Seek it above all else. Not in the mart
Will it be found, or any marketplace,
Being a spirit of glory in the heart;
Seek it where honor dwells, and truth, and grace.

Though bartering not, love magically buys,
By sacrifice, this world and heaven beside;
As if of every age the argosies
Of all the multitudinous oceans wide,
Laden with spoil from earth and sea and skies,
Rode safely home upon one brimming tide.

ULTIMATE BEAUTY

There is a beauty hidden in the hills,
A beauty that the sea will not reveal;
Nor does the wood divulge it to your gaze.
Although it is the peace that tumult stills,
It may escape you, though to it you kneel,
And may go undiscovered all your days.

O I had known the magic of the wood,
And I had watched the wonder of the skies,
And to all song a listening ear had lent.
But ultimate Beauty kept her solitude
Until I saw in your confessing eyes
Love's calm and beautiful acknowledgement.

LOVE'S PRESENCE

Say not that we have parted: nevermore
Can we alone upon this planet tread;
For now the World, by love interpreted,
Has not a lonely wood or wild seashore
Where we cannot as comrades meet once more . . .
Love's influence upon existence shed
Is life's true resurrection from the dead
Into a glory never dreamed before.

We know love's mystic language,—you and I;
And in love's land no power can part us far;
The beauty of communion there abides . . .
In chantings of the seasons and the tides
We shall converse, or when some lyric star
Breathes unimagined music through the sky.

WITH EVERLASTING GLORY JUST BEGUN

He who has known love's final joy has passed
Destruction's reach,—beyond oblivion.
He and eternity are now as one.
Forever will his radiant rapture last;
For he belongs to love's patrician caste.
With everlasting glory just begun,
His immortality already won,
Strong is each sail, immutable each mast.

When I consider how gross hordes are fed
In sodden troughs that swine might well abhor,
On wine contemptible and paltry bread,
In humble holy gratitude and awe
I lift my eyes, adoring the Divine,
Who made my own Beloved, and made her mine.

HER VOICE

I have heard mountain streams, deep in the dark,
Singing primeval song; and by the shore
On starry evenings I have paused to hark
The darkened music of the deep. Before
The coming of the dawn, in pinewoods dim
I've listened to the fluting of the thrush,
Of morning's dewy music the first hymn,
Amid the sleeping forest's fragrant hush.

O Voices of wild nature, you who make
Melodious all the world—one Voice I know
Whose tones can all my ecstasies awake:
There is no other voice delights me so.
For me to listen to that lovely song,
I would not find Eternity too long.

REMEMBER

If love has not the same delicious glory
That once it had: the incandescent dawn;
The night felicitous; the joyous story;
The Eden to enchant and wonder on;
The silver harps, the viols, the golden bells;
The flights of spirit now no longer flown;
The sweet wild meetings, wild and sweet farewells;
Hushes too deep for any but love's tone—

Remember, O remember, all that's ours
Begins in dreams, and in the dust has ending;
Yet if love rears but vulnerable towers,
Adventurous, too mortal for defending,
Still always like a miracle it seems
Such beauty can be built by dust and dreams.

"Now I will go where we have never been
Together; and it may be if I do,
If I behold what we have never seen,
Amid strange faces that we never knew;
If with new friends my heart I will
    beguile,
With other beauty, amid other scenes,
I may forget your presence for awhile,
And lose the anguish that our parting
    means."

So said he, and to alien lands departed,
Heard other voices, songs before unknown;
Saw many a scene of grandeur and of grace.
But all was vanity; for, broken-hearted,
'Mid myriads, he longed for one alone,
Hearing her voice, seeing her haunting face.

ALL IS WELL

There is a lovely red Rose that I know
Which blooms in darkness and in bitter cold;
Against the dreary North will it unfold
Its beauty, blossoming amid the snow . . .
There is a Music mastering every woe . . .
There is a happy story to be told,
Dearer for every telling . . . Every foe
Of joy this champion can overthrow.

It is the only Voice which sings when all
The world beside with grief is stricken still:
It is the only Hand that can be laid
Upon the pulse of grief. Whate'er befall,
Its magic power matches its sweet will:
Love, Love it is . . . O wherefore be afraid?

THE PLACE

Incredible it seems that one so sweet,
So gentle and effacing in her ways,
Should be the place where the great waters meet,
Tumults and tempests, meteors ablaze
From life's deep sources. There wild spirit calls
To spirit, and the mighty chorus swells
Of purple forests and white waterfalls,
Viols and cymbals, harps and choiring bells.

I look on you with wonder, mystic Place!
In you abide my rapture and my peace.
Dwelling upon the beauty of your face,
I marvel how, when all the whirlwinds cease,
You are like evening, cool, and all alight
With stars, and fragrant as the violet night.

BLUE GATHERED FLOWER

"The flower gathered is the flower lost,"
So sang the poet. But I disagree;
For the blue flower I love and honor most
Is one that gave her loveliness to me.
How could I know her sweetness and her deeps
If she were alien, distant, and aloof?
Love always loses everything it keeps.
Love's final giving is love's final proof.

To Beauty inaccessible, remote,
I can pay tribute; but it would be pale
Beside the honors that to you belong.
Should I my life to you alone devote,
To recompense you, all could not avail
Who gave me flame and glory, flower and song.

301

HOW WOULD IT BE?

Since we, when for a little while we part,
Lose the felicity that we have known
Together, and feel frustrate and alone,
Unsatisfied by any human art,
With souls that cry, with tears that swiftly start;
With music mute, and all life's glory gone—
Sure that for parting nothing can atone,
Since each one's home is in the other's heart:

How would it be, O Love, if you should say,
"We must not ever, ever meet again"?
Then would all splendor fade from land and sea;
All beauty suddenly would pass away.
Without your love, Tomorrow would be vain,
And death alone be merciful for me.

FALLING STAR

Like them who view that splendor of the sky,
The streaming beauty of a falling star,
Forgetting where they are and who they are,
See nothing else except this mystery,
Transfiguring creation—so did I,
Lost in a flaming loveliness afar,
With no mortality its grace to mar,
See a resplendent vision passing by.

Across my heavens swept love's mighty dream,
Illumining life's hills, its plains, its sea,
Its wonder giving me a natural gleam
Of all the magic that can really be.
Since long ago this blinding beauty came,
Nothing at all has ever looked the same.

302

MY FORTUNE

Rare are the precious jewels that I own,
Beyond all others of the world in worth;
Yet they are not of any fabulous stone;
No sea or hill or valley gave them birth.
They are the constellations of my night.
Their lyric beauty sings my heart to rest.
I listen to their song for my delight,
Clasping them close and closer to my breast.

The jewels of my fortune are but three:
Brave gems are they, each flashing like a star.
They are not pearls out of some jacinth sea,
Or moonstones from some mystic mountain far,
Or rubies red as crimson roses be . . .
Your words, "I love you,"—these treasures
    are.

WONDER

That one who all her life has walked the heights
Of Beauty, and has held the hand of Grace;
Has known of Art its mystical delights;
Has nobly loved,—that she should turn her face
To me; should listen to my cry; should yearn
Over my wounds; should be compassionate
To grieve for me; should of my longing learn
With pity; that her starry steps should wait

Even for me,—how wild that miracle!
I feel as does a traveler, wandering lost
To find a way, yet has no chart to tell;
Who knows not how this desert should be crossed;
Who, having dread and blinding dark to try him,
Suddenly finds a loving Angel by him.

303

THE REFUGE

There is an end of all things: Beauty dies
Beauty of earth we see not any more.
The sea upon the happy summer shore
Holds the deep voice of death and sacrifice.
Beneath the flowers, how many a fair face lies;
The roses white and red the garden bore
Pass, as their lovely sisters passed before,
Yet still we pray, and still we lift our eyes.

There is an end of all beneath the ground,
And death were King of Kings had not God sent
One refuge;—for in the dark world I found
A beautiful light like Faith in this, in this,
A woman's lips pure from her mother's kiss,
A woman's heart thro' wisdom innocent.

THERE IS NO HEART

There is no heart that yearneth after glory
But glory it shall have, of its own kind:
Some seek it in the sanguine song and story
Of battle-strife. Some search it with the mind
That dares the riddle of the universe.
Some gather power. Some, as glory's goal,
Will make the mighty music of their verse
Down the long years like funeral thunders roll.

Giver of glory, if my heart can claim
From your compassionate grace a single token,
I ask not wealth or power or pride or fame;
Let this my glory be: to keep unbroken
The faith of love, its beauty aye to see
Under the aspect of eternity.

WAITING

One day you waited for me where the ways
Deep in the woods divide. For you had gone
Ahead—yet waited. Love only so delays.
You did not want me to be left alone.
I never would have known which path you took—
Yet could not make you wait. I could not bind you.
But for my sake your purpose you forsook—
Since being lost means that I cannot find you.

O tenderest Heart, forever for me wait!
I will be coming, and you are my Way.
To fairyland you are the orchid gate.
To my long night, the rose of breaking day.
Merely by waiting you can intimate
More than all music and all words can say.

CONTRIBUTORS

God brought me into being; and my Mother
Gave, as a mother will, her life for me,
And down life's pathway, many and many another
Offered their gifts: the forest and the sea
Of their wild strength and beauty freely gave;
The mountains all my dreaming skyward drew;
The rivers with their sea-tides deep and grave,
Conferred tranquility. But it is you

Who brings the joy of life, the laughing light,
The magic and the music and the dreams.
You are the one who leads me out of night,
And, singing all the way by starlit streams,
Gives me a love to keep my whole life long;
Gives me a heart that cannot sleep for song.

LOVE'S BLINDNESS

They told me love is blind, and I believed it.
They said, "Love cannot see life's dross and tears."
This was their story, and my heart received it,
For they had learned of life for many years.
Smiling at love in tolerant derision,
They went a bitter way, and thought it true.
I followed,—till I found a starry vision,
That they, for all their wisdom, never knew.

Heaven has some flowers to earth's gaze forbidden;
The eyes of love alone their grace can see.
From mortal sight there is a beauty hidden.
If love is blind, such blindness give to me,
Divine far insight that alone discloses
All the heart's hanging rainbows, climbing roses.

STORM AT SEA

Once, when there was a storm at sea, they saw
A noble vessel, with her flags all flying,
Shudder and sink . . . It blanched their hearts with
    awe.
Long afterwards, he came upon her crying,
And tried to comfort her . . . "Ah, foolish me!"
She sobbed upon his shoulder; "for I thought
Our love a vessel, and our life a sea;
And I remembered what that tempest wrought."

Faithless he proved . . . And his tremendous doom
Was seeing in her deathstruck loving eyes
An ocean, once alight, now plunged in gloom,
Where sunless, moonless, starless were the skies;
Beholding love, their ship, with havoc round her,
With white sails wild, in an immense deep founder.

GRACIOUS GUEST

When you must go, your spirit you will leave;
For you have magic to transform a place:
Nothing but gladness to the world you give,
Lending to beauty wild a wilder grace.
There's nothing here will ever be the same
Since you have touched it with your radiant light.
All loveliness is lovlier since you came,
As when the moon arrives unto the night.

The ancient oaks, transfigured by the glow
Of beauty that their years have never seen
Stand grateful; and the towering laurels know
That Love their gentle dazzling guest has been.
Near you, camellias feel their beauty fail,
Yet love you, crying, "Sister, Hail! All Hail!"

BRIMMING SILENCE

Oft in the wildwoods, on the wild seashore
A brimming silence I have heard, that seemed
About to overflow in song. No more
Mysterious fairy music could be dreamed,
With love and laughter as its theme. Inthralled
Have I been held by this strange stillness. What
Could it portend? Of love it offered all. I do not.
Yet who deserves such beauty?

And yet this miracle I understand:
You are so far from me, and yet so near;
Your love, a silent song, is close at hand.
The magic of its meaning I can hear.
Its music choirs to the stars, and I
Weep for the bliss that brings your beauty by.

307

GRIEVE NOT

For little faded things of earth you grieve,
The wildflowers that you treasured for an hour,
As brief as beautiful. They felt the power
Of time; and in their passing you perceive
A loss and change . . . In something else believe:
Though roses are rejoicing in their bower,
Gleaming in radiant sun and silver shower,
Their beauty shall the dust ere long receive,

Yet ever blooms, unchanged by light or shade,
Though suns and systems into wrack may roll,
Your loveliness;—not as the rose you wore,
Now withered; for you have what cannot fade:
Virtue, that is the beauty of the soul,
And this in you I love forever more.

NO IDLE WORDS

He longed to tell her of his journey wild
Through perilous life. Deep in his heart he felt
That their strong love, so true and undefiled,
Should know all things; and if his spirit knelt
Before hers in confession, there would be
A final blessing on their troth and pledge,
A valiant proof of his own constancy.
To keep aught from her seemed a sacrilege.

"Ah," said she, "after anguish we've reached home
On this green island with its singing birds;
Since to this joy we've mercifully come,
Let us not mar our peace with idle words.
I know the demons against which you strove.
Tell me not of them; tell me of your love."

FORSAKE ME NOT

Forsake me not, whatever comes to be!
Well as I know you, still to me you seem
To have strange magic like a secret stream,
Flowing through wildflowers to a mystic sea.
Those ardent minds that make discovery
Their goal, could never of your beauty dream,
Whose mysteries are miracles that gleam,
But God revealed your tender heart to me.

There is one grief for which there is no
        cure.
Beyond that sorrow is no promise bright.
Who knows that bitter anguish can be sure
Never again to love the morning light.
Forsake me not! God's pity would divine
The wound was mortal, and the wound was
        mine.

FOOTSTEPS

As one who listens for a friend to come,
And waits for welcome footsteps; and then
        hears
Footsteps retreating, and his lonely home
Is lonelier when no loved one's face appears.
And as he looks through darkness to discover
If by mischance his guest has lost his way,
And may turn back, his bearings to recover,
Yet only hears far footfalls fade away:

To light my night of life with tender gleams,
So once I thought that you were coming to me;
But all my joyous hopes were futile dreams,
For that which might have been shall never be.
I hear retreating, while dim starlight streams,
Far solemn footfalls of eternity.

THE RUINOUS FACE

Beautiful girl, why should you ever long
For glamourous power, that can often be
To mortals fatal? Rather, to be strong,
Generous, and sweet of heart, and brave and free,—
These are the gifts for which your soul should pray,
For they alone have power your life to bless.
Since too enchanting beauty can betray,
Care only for your spirit's loveliness.

Helen and Cleopatra, Guinevere,
Brought nothing but disaster to the men
Who loved them most. Death, jealousy, despair,
Go hand-in-hand with fatal charm. O then,
Beware of beauty! 'Twas Eve's naked grace
Allured the serpent's flat and venomous face.

THEN

And then no more the parting and the aching.
The empty arms that find not you to hold;
The longing, the frustration, the heart-breaking;
The solitary daybreaks, and the gold
Of lonely, futile sunsets, far from you.
No more the envying of wild birds' singing,
Joyously mated; nor, across the blue,
The beauty of doves at evening homeward winging.

O Love, dear Love, so brief a time is ours,
And all is lost if we must be apart!
In every field you would be fragrant flowers,
Of all felicity the beating heart.
And never any more the sad, vain dreams,
The desolation that your absence means.

TIDAL RIVER

Of changeless strength some streams are
    never sure.
When through hot skies the burning sunrays
    strike.
Their beauty has no power to endure,
And ends in dust. O Love, let me be like
The faithful tide of some remembering
    river
That can be trusted, though it often goes
So far it seems it would be gone forever,
Yet its true course, its home beloved, it
    knows.

And to that place unerringly returning
It brings far tributes from the foreign
    shores
It visited, but for its homeland yearning;
Though it be midnight, and the tempest roars,
Through storm and darkness will the river
    find it,
With all the might of all the main behind
    it.

THE CHANGE

Your having been there changes every place.
It cannot ever be the same; for there
Your beauty lingers and your beauty's grace.
Because of you, a seashore is more fair;
Skies lower lean to love and to caress;
A garden with transfiguration glows;
More radiant is a wildwood's loveliness,
And with a deeper ruby burns the rose.

You in my heart abide, where'er you go.
And I can always tell where you have been;
Ever I am beside you, though unseen;
And all the glory that you are, I know.
Where you have been, no place can be the same:
My world was wonderless . . . And then you came.

311

NOT ISIS AND OSIRIS

Not Isis and Osiris worship we,
Nor Aphrodite rising from the wave,
Selene in the starlight by the sea,
Bare in her beauty in the Latmian cave.
Not all the deities whose temples were
Where ruins now are reigning: Memphis old,
Persepolis and Babylon and Ur,
Tyre and Sidon with their domes of gold.

Great Cybele has but a cyprian face;
Not to Apollo look we for the light;
Rimmon, Bubastis give to life no grace.
Our beauty gleams beyond Diana's night:
Love is our only god, and Love alone;
His the high altar, the eternal throne.

BRIGHT ANGEL

Bright Angel of my soul! To you I kneel,—
Beautiful spirit who above me bent,
My anguish to assuage, my wounds to heal,
Who to my dark your heavenly radiance lent.
Upon your flowering beauty moonlight streams,
Sweet wildwood source and secret of delight,
Haunting as starlit music heard in dreams,
Mysterious as the deep and meadowy night.

Whatever charms there are, may be, or were,
The beauty of the world you are to me.
Of song the enchanting joyous chorister,
Your love means all that love can ever be,
Giving life grace; and for me you confer
Upon each moment, immortality.

MUSIC AND SILENCE

Let there be music in our hearts forever!
If there be silence, let it be like song;
Or like the muted hymn of a mighty river,
For earthly melodies too deep and strong.
For over us have starry angels hovered;
And we have been appareled in the light
Of glory, —though our human need was covered
Under the dusky wings of love and night.

Let there be silence in our souls,—the thrilling
Quiet that comes with peace, when heart on heart,
Love's sweet wild storm mysterious love is stilling,
While we are mated, never more to part.
Music and silence, blending to express
My longing, answered by your loveliness!

REQUEST DENIED

Ask me to sail into the storm; to roam
The trackless wilderness, the shaggy wood;
The desert where death only is at home,
The mountains, lonely in wild solitude.
Ask of me some great task: it is completed;
Ask some deep sacrifice, and it is done.
No wish of yours need ever be repeated;
Ask of me anything at all—save one:

For there is one thing I can never do,
One sacrifice that I can never make
Even for my Beloved,—even for you.
I cannot grant it—even for your sake.
Pray not that I from loving you abstain;
For such a prayer shall be forever vain.

313

BLUE SKY

I never see the blue sky any more
Without remembering: so was it blue
That magic day I roamed the wilds with you,
And learned your trembling spirit to adore.
The woods a promise of the springtime wore;
And like that promise you were sweet and true,
Teaching me sacred things I never knew . . .
Now turquoise sky that magic can restore.

When wide and high above us gentian skies
Looked down in loveliness; when by a stream
A wild bird sang a passionate refrain,
I could not see the heavens for your eyes.
Now when the sky is amethyst, I dream
Your beauty's bending over me again.

O TURN NOT FROM ME!

O turn not from me! If we walk alone,
We go into the dark. Too long the light
Of love has led us. If the light were gone,
Neither could find a way through such a night.
Still hold my hand a little while; still keep
The faith we pledged. It is too late to part.
Before us lie the mystic fields of sleep.
If there we rest, let it be heart-to-heart.

There is no other who can know what roses
Bloom in your spirit's garden. I have tended
Their beauty, that to me alone discloses
Your mystery. Love's story's never ended.
I, in life's dusk, without you would be lost.
O turn not from me when I need you most.

314

THE ENDURING

Say not that nothing constant is but change;
That nothing in existence can endure.
Behold that monumental mountain-range.
It has not moved. Forever it stands sure.
Although this rose tells but a transient story,
It is continued on another page.
The loveliness of earth repeats its glory,
Renews itself by magic, age to age.

Hear the sea-music shores have always known,
The trampling thunder of eternal tides.
No oriole has from life's orchard flown.
Immortal spring's apparel is a bride's.
The marching stars that down on Eden shone
Still shine on us with beauty that abides.

INCONSTANT

She turned her face to him; then turned away
Lightly, as if his love were but a toy,
That she in a wilful moment might destroy.
She had delight in it when she was gay,
Yet took it as the plaything of a day.
But he had found in her his spirit's joy,
His wonder, and his gold without allow . . .
And why she changed, he cannot ever say.

She left him suddenly and long ago
Nor told him aught. A little hour she gave
Her love, her caring. He shall never know,
Unless such knowledge lie within the grave,
Why she love's wildflower seeds in him could sow,
Nor care to watch their blooms in beauty wave.

315

BEYOND YOUR VALLEYS

Beyond your valleys lie no vales for me;
No mountains rise above your mystic hills;
No ocean rolls beyond your azure sea;
Your love for me life's final hope fulfils.
After your blooms there are no flowers
    forever;
No heavens past your eyes my eyes to meet;
No waters flow for me beyond your river;
No forests lure beyond your wildwoods sweet.

Strange was the way I came, and long and far,
O End of all my world, all beauty's verge!
My harbor, haven, terminal you are.
For me no lights beyond your light emerge.
I see one star above life's lonely hill.
I see no other and I never will.

MIDSEA WONDER

When from the deck you view the midsea sun
That sparkles on the boundless waters deep,
And watch the waves forever rolling on,
As if some everlasting tryst to keep;
When in the night you see the stars arise
In ancient beauty, ageless and unchanged,
Marking how sentinelled are all the skies,
How far the watchmen on the walls are ranged—

Know, were they sentient, they would be aware
Of all your wonder, deeper than their own;
While of their glimmering mystery you share,
In sweetness of the heart you stand alone.
I know, as at the very first I knew,
All beauty God imagined meets in you.

316

IDENTITY

Long had I heard of love, as one may hear
A story from a land, far-off and strange;
A land to which I never could be near,
A valley over life's high mountain-range;
Or as a flower inaccessible,
Mysterious, of radiant heavenly birth,
Of which I heard some lonely traveler tell,
Who saw it gleam beyond the bounds of earth.

How different is your love that holds me fast!
And yet not different: wonderful and sweet,
Most intimate and precious—mine at last!
My life, upon your coming, was complete.
I heard of love. Till now I never knew
That for my heart forever—love is you.

THE REASON

Not for the mystic starlight in your eyes,
Nor for the orient tresses of your hair;
Not for the body's beauty, like the sky's
Glory of dawn or sunset; nor the air
Of immortality in which you move;
Not even for your laughter in life's night,
Carolling your blithe spirit—These I love.
But not for these are you my heart's delight.

It is not for the way you turn your head,
As if love turned to comfort and to bless.
It is not for life's wine and for life's bread,
Graciously given to my loneliness.
It is the glad surmise that, wild and free,
The tenderest heart now beating beats for me.

317

SENTINEL

By what last test shall constancy be proved?
By parting's anguish? I have felt that sword.
By joy to meet again my own beloved?
By gratitude because my heart has heard
The music of your deep melodious mind?
To stand between you and the world? To care
In every way with tenderest love? To find
Your face alone in beauty everywhere?

I know not if I fail you. But I know
I stand as one who, faithful to a trust,
Seemed Faithfulness to me. For, long ago
(My memory of him shall be august),
I saw a sentry guard an inviolate gate,
Strong, tacit, valiant, proud to watch and wait.

TRAVELER

When from the deck you view the midsea sun,
That sparkles on the boundless waters deep,
And watch the waves forever rolling on
As if some everlasting tryst to keep;
When in the night you see the stars arise
In ancient beauty, ageless and unchanged,
Marking how sentineled are all the skies,
How far the watchmen on the walls are ranged,—

Know, were they sentient, they would be aware
Of all your wonder, deeper than their own;
While of their glimmering mystery you share,
In sweetness of the heart you stand alone.
I know, as at the very first I knew,
All beauty God imagined meets in you.

IF I RETURNED

You who have waited loyally and long,
Whose love I cannot, as I would, requite,
I come to tell you that mine is more strong
As day by day goes by, and night by night
And, oh, be sure we have not ever lost,
The dream abides. Our love immortal steals
Like starlight down life's solitary coast.
It saves us, for our wounded hearts it heals.

The world would end for me, and life, and all
Your love made beautiful: our spirits' mating;
Th music of your voice—a wild bird's call;
The floodtide of our love with no abating.
All I had built, and hoped to build, would fall
If I returned and would not find you waiting.

YOUR SILENCE

There's soundless wonder in a sea asleep;
And of the mountains in the tranquil night.
There is a stillness, everlasting, deep,
About the Dead, whose last and long delight
Is quietness. They never speak again.
Mute is the music when the hand resigns
Its magic touch; silence, when, after rain,
Hushed are the harps high in the dusky pines.

But there's a reticence more dread than these:
The song unheard—for which the soul has yearned;
The vain appeal; the star one never sees
In darkness; and the longing unreturned.
O God, what have I done against Thy will
That I have made one matchless heart so still?

319

THE CARDINAL WILL COME

The cardinal will come when I am gone;
The quail will troop along the wildwood's brink;
The titmouse and the towhee that have known
Your love, will visit you to eat and drink.
For you, the nuthatch, upside-down, will peer
Into your window, or will spread his wings
In mock defiance if a thrush comes near.
They sing not, but their quiet beauty sings.

With you I watched them. Now I never see
A bird we saw together but I dream
That you and I are one; that I am we!
We watch the birds; we hear the rocky stream.
As they come to you, let them always be
Love's messengers,—far more than what they seem!

YOUR MATE

Somewhere upon a thronged chaotic street,
Or on a lonely beach with billows loud,
Your mate you may, or may not chance to, meet;
She may be all alone, or in a crowd.
Walk warily. For if you miss her, all
The fame you win, the wealth and power you gain
Shall be but ashes in your mouth, and gall.
Missing her love, your triumphs will be vain.

If not today, perhaps tonight may bring
Her thrilling presence. You will never need
A guide to her. Your heart will wildly sing;
Then to its strange sweet song alone give heed.
Until you find her, you will never live.
Discovering her means all that life can give.

ONE RIVER

There might have been a time when you and I
Could, like mere friends, have said goodbye. That hour
Is gone forever. Love is destiny.
Nothing can part us. Nothing has that power.
Too deeply have we loved, in glory burning;
Too fast together to each other clung;
Too splendid is love's way—and has no turning;
Too wild the music that our souls have sung.

We are not streams that near each other flow,
Close but untouching, and that gently part;
Mingled, our waters now one channel know,
Each giving to the other all its heart,
Our tides have merged, and we are now one river,
Having one song, one joy, one strength forever.

FIRST AND LAST

Remember how I loved you at the first—
Strange yet not strange, and beautiful and sweet;
How your first kiss then quenched my lifelong thirst,
Making my yearning and my rapture meet.
It was a sacrament all hope fulfilling,
And rich with joy as only love can be;
The trembling starlight of your beauty stilling
My spirit, as the Master stilled the sea.

Remember I will love you to the last.
We know not what for us may be in store.
Safe in our hearts we hold the precious Past,
Wearing love's rainbow raiment that we wore
When first we met. Whatever comes, O Friend,
Remember I will love you to the end.

COAT-OF-ARMS

The mystical insignia that we wear,
The royal symbols that our spirits own,
Are theirs alone who greatly love. We share
The honor that earth's noblest have known.
Such love's a gift all life to glorify,
In worth beyond all gold, all precious gems.
In the deep Past were men who loved as I,
Women who wore their loves like diadems.

The blazons on our coat-of-arms are these:
A flashing sword protecting the Beloved;
A star unsetting, robed in silver fire;
A cloud that curtains sacred mysteries;
A rock that from its place shall not be moved;
A wildrose; and a tall enchanted lyre.

PATTERN ALTERED

I think that when God made you, He conspired
To bring into the world a beauty strange
And new and magical; for He had tired
Of what was merely lovely. He would range—
And, gathering all that on His flowering earth
Was delicate and most fragrant and most wild
In wonder, He then brought your soul to birth,
Bright Angel Spirit, joyous human child!

You are the wildflowers we had never found,
The starry music we had never heard;
About your brow an aureole He bound,
And to your heart He spoke the mystic word
That gave you power to love and to be loved.
And His own miracle God has approved.

GREATER LOVE

Some in the battle have laid down their lives
For all of us. We honor them. Their names
Are wrought in bronze, whose hardihood survives
All victories, all glories, and all fames.
They are humanity's great heritage
Most precious ; and like setting stars they loom
Larger as they recede, from age to age.
No hero ever sleeps within the tomb.

Before the silence comes, I lift a song
For one who has laid down her life for me:
When I was weak, her courage kept me strong;
Her only care was evermore to be
Beside me in each battle that I fought,
Hers being my valor, though I knew it not.

YOUR BEAUTY

Your beauty breaks my heart. In it I see
All that I ever longed for on this earth,
All that my yearning thought could never be . . .
Through you all blossoms have another birth,
Mystic and wonderful. In you I hear
All music that before I never knew;
You are the peace that is the end of fear.
And love itself has its wild source in you.

Your beauty stills me as the heart is stilled
By moonlight on wide waters, when the waves
Caress the beach, and all the air is filled
With murmuring songs. How tenderly it saves
My soul that else upon life's shore alone
No beauty, calm, or rapture could have known!

TIDE AND MARSH

Male and immovable the sea-marsh lies
Between the mainland and the female sea.
Now she has yielded him felicity,
In beauty she recedes, for she is wise,
She's gone into the deep, where fountains rise
From fabulous sources, occult, primal, free.
There she renews her immortality—
Returning to him with divine surprise.

Even so my Love goes where I cannot follow:
She is the tide, with mystic ebb and flow;
Hers are the wings of sea-gull or of swallow;
Hers, secret places that I cannot know.
But like the marsh with joy I can discern
Her love will flood me with its wild return.

THE MASTERY OF SORROW

Since all I longed for is denied me quite,
Let your great love sustain me in this hour.
If you come to me with your mystic power,
I will not turn my face into the night.
Your love can be my music, and my might
To conquer clouds, however they may lower;
Could be the banner of my life's dark tower,
A dauntless symbol of eternal light.

What right have I your mercy to implore?
Though there are myriad reasons, these are some:
I only know I could not love you more;
That when grief calls, it is like love to come;
That could I dream that you might care for me,
The master of my sorrow I could be.

CONJECTURE

When she is sewing, of me unaware,
I never understand her; for she seems
Now but a little child. Upon her hair
The sunlight writes its scattered golden **dreams;**
Now like a mother with a brooding **heart;**
Now like a heroine about to be;
Now like an angel in a shrine apart;
Now like a Sybil deeper than the sea.

I never know the meaning of her then,
What her far earnest manner signifies:
A heavenly vision deep beyond my ken?
Voices that come to her from Paradise?
Imagined jewels on her bosom glowing?
Or some wild tryst with wonder and **foreknowing?**

THE SHELL

Frail on the beach it lies, a shining shell,
By monstrous seas and gloomy tides obscure
Brought past abysmal places to the shore
Immaculate, a fairy citadel,
In rainbow-raiment gleamingly arrayed.
Fair through its vales and down its blushing snows
Flare into violet, deepen into rose
Wan beams that brighten, radiant beams that **fade.**

Such is the magic that its beauty wields,
By spiritual grace that conquers ill,
That this wild flower of the ocean-fields
Has loveliness to sway the human will;
At sight of it, where late an atheist trod,
A worshipper lifts up his heart to God.

WOUNDS AND WATERS

There is a healing for your wounds of war
Where wildflowers in their timid beauty weep
By quiet waters; in the awful sweep
Of ocean's orchestration rolled afar.
The silvery bells of streams will set ajar
Windows to your recovery. The deep
Silence of lakes will bring white sails of sleep,
Bearing the racked to where the rescued are.

But if the wounds be love's, they go unhealed
By rain on scented pines, or the laughing run
Of rivulets through forest, glen, or field,
Or mystic mountain lakes in the setting sun,
Or ocean's wild old melody. They yield
Only to Lethe and Oblivion.

BRIGHT FACADE

As one who comes upon a wildwood deep,
Not seeing what may be within, but only
The beauty and peace that on its margin sleep,
Will marvel at the loveliness, the lonely
Spirit of song and light that here abides;
Yet cannot tell what is beyond: what shrines,
May moulder where the fitful moonbeam glides;
What gardens fade where wan the starlight shines.

Behind your valor's bright facade, none knows
What longings may lie ruinous, what dreams
Are fallen on the sleep that has no waking;
What withered violet, and what perished rose.
You are most gallant outwardly, it seems,
Most beautiful, whenever your heart is breaking.

THE INLAND TIDE

Like a grave seatide, inland drawn afar,
Is our existence: out of cosmic sleep
Awakening, we forsake the epic deep;
And under pendant moon and trembling star
Enter life's river-mouth . . . Like a stranger goes
The tide, past bowers of jasmine and of rose,
An alien always; conscious evermore
Of kindred with the deep, the distant shore.

Then down the reaches of the deepening river
Like the ebb we glide, with mightier movements
     flowing,—
A part of power whose kingdom is forever;
Austerely summoned to the ancient bourne,
From life withdrawing, what have we to mourn
Whose hearts, long exiled, home at last are going?

IMPOSTER

In some dark hour you may have your way,
But you are doomed, O Doubt! You stand alone.
And none shall grieve when you are dead and gone.
Though you have power to menace and to slay,
Yet leagued against you is the rose of May,
A thousand daffodils against your thorn;
And love and laughter 'gainst your lonely scorn.
You are outnumbered by a great array.

The stars are for us, and the marching sun,
The order that the farthest planet knows.
And love, Imposter, makes your strength forlorn.
Behold our allies gathering one by one:
Out of the dust, the summer, rose by rose;
Under the night, the trumpets of the dawn.

327

SAGACITY

The stern and steel-clad march of time, that goes
Clanging down highways, lovers never heed;
But into haunts of violet and wildrose
They wander,—Beauty being all their need;
Now listen to a bird's wild caroling;
Now marvel at the sky's lobelia-blue;
Now laugh for joy, and to each other cling . . .
Only the lovers are the wise and true!

Oblivious to the march of time are they:
Like happy children in a field of home,
A little boy and girl who sing and play,
Where o'er the waves of grass the wilflowers foam;
Nor heed grim warring hosts that thunder by,—
Lingering to live, while fools rush on to die.

EVE

What could a motherless maiden know of love?
Eve in her naked beauty, sweet and free,
Under the tower and temple of a tree
That stood where Eden's rivers met. Above
Her glimmering grace there mourned a joyous dove.
The mother of the Race she was to be,
For so God willed. But how, unerringly,
Was this first girl her womanhood to prove?

Of bliss alone the song-birds sang that hour,
When Adam came. And Eve was not afraid.
To love is not to feel another's power;
To mate is only to be wildly made
One with another's beauty. There they were:
And all there is of love he learned from her.

BROTHERS OF GREAT DEFEAT

With failure we are friends. The gallant oak
That crashes in his strength falls not alone,
For we plunge with him from his azure throne,
Aware that we ourselves shall thus be broke
In some far storm, even by such a stroke . . .
Or if a star fall, we that fate have known
In one beloved whose beauty briefly shone—
The transiency of each, the other spoke.

Brothers of great defeat, our hearts are welling
With cosmic pity for all lives frustrate,
Whose doom our common destiny's foretelling:
Fair Joan unto the faggots dedicate;
Scotland's proud queen of beauty on the block;
The Corsican upon his lonely rock.

OTHER BEAUTY

We speak of Beauty, and we seem to mean
An outward charm of loveliness and grace;
But there's a deeper beauty that's unseen;
That is not manifest in form or face:
It is the love that ever is the same;
It never wavers, and it never breaks.
Sorrow and death it conquers. I acclaim
It stands forever perfect. And it takes

All storms upon its wide eternal wings,
Knowing a course, knowing an ancient portal
Opening on fair and everlasting things.
O mortal tenderness, with strength immortal,—
Beauty of Spirit, from life's darkening slope,
Still hold to us white hands of heavenly hope!

329

POETRY

A little child who runs along the shore,
Coming upon an opalescent shell,
Cries, "See what I have found! A mermaid wore
This for a brooch!" And who could better tell
What poetry is? Come from mysterious deeps,
Seraphic wonder from the gross concealed,
Where life's wild wave upon love's sea-strand weeps
To the innocent heart divinely is revealed.

Forever to the soul its voice is singing
Like sea-wind of a song of long ago;
Always to us in beauty it is bringing
The magic we forever yearn to know.
It is a miracle by the spirit made,
A glimmering wildflower that shall never fade.

WONDERS

"Across the continent at cyclone speed,
A glimmering shuttle between coast and coast,—"
So of man's latest triumphing I read,
Yet am unmoved by all this mortal boast.
For I am asked to make of this my joy,
My wonder, and a thing to awe my soul;
To marvel at this brief mechanic toy,
While ancient stars march under God's control.

See how Capella dips below the verge
On mighty wings of light. O little Man,
Mark how lone Vega, o'er the pale sea-surge,
Rides radiant, though her speed no eye can scan;
And where the Known and Unknown dimly merge,
How constant in his course, Aldebaran!

FAR COUNTRY

As one who has returned from Egypt far
She comes from Grief. But nothing shall restore
The rapture of the heart she had before.
Who bears the brunt of battle, shows the scar.
Nor homeland fields, nor well beloved star
Avail her, alien on her native shore,
Whose silence, telling nothing, tells the more
Of days that have been that no longer are.

She has brought back the mystery of that land;
Her heart the music of its Memnon hears;
Gorgeous insignia and regalia grand
Are hers, whose brow the cobra-chaplet wears;
The lotus of the Nile is in her hand,
While from her eyes the Sphinx of Sorrow stares.

HOME

As the azure is to the eagle,
As to the ship the sea,
As to the deer the wildwood,
So are you home to me.

PITY ME

If in the dusk I stumble, pity me!
I am a little child who wanderingly
Listens for music that it cannot hear,
Looks for a guiding star it cannot see.

DAUNTLESS EAGLE

Stupendous on his wide and swarthy wings,
With massive power and grace, his mighty form
Shoulders the gale, through the green tempest swings,
And plunges ponderous through the thunderstorm.
Dawn he patrols like some archangel tall,
The glimmering camp of evening sentinels;
In splendor paces noon's wide azure hall,
And wheresoever goes, in glory dwells.

Not the wild speed, like a fledged spearhead flying,
Not the broad pinions, sensitive and strong,
Not all the valor and grace, the gale defying,
Not all that rhythm like creation's song:
Not any of these I envy or would have,—
But that proud dauntless heart, serene and brave!

WHAT THOUGH WE FAIN WOULD LINGER

What though we fain would linger for awhile
With the loved visions, Youth and Memory,
Yet with the world of toil such cannot be.
Each hath his journey of a mortal mile
Thro' woods and fields and many a dark defile
With now and then a sight of open sea,
Blue-rolling in the distance beauteously,
And edged by dewy forelands that beguile.

Oh, that we aye might linger, thou and I,
In this dear valley with the scented wind
Sweet from the Southern roses that unbind
Their fragrant tresses, or, Oh, fair and free,
The mountain laurel in the glens enshrined
Breathes beauty that is immortality.

332

IN A NEW DAY

Behind us is a noise importunate,
A gathering mighty, whose oncoming proud
And stormful high advancing, sunrise-browed,
Is the Future bold, with wilful youth elate.
Another generation cannot wait.
This tide tremendous thunders on our bowed
And humble heads. The right of way's allowed.
If we are far from home now, we are late.

What then remains for us? Merely to stand
Aside, to watch with kindly eyes the throng
And listen to new laughters through the land,
Nor mourn our triumphs o'er, our faded flowers;
For if the strife and crown to them belong,
The finished race, the promised rest are ours.

ETERNAL SEA

Before they came, the sea talked to itself.
Then for a little while this ancient beach
Welcomed glad children, each a seaside elf;
And wearied hearts beyond the breakers' reach
Found what the fetid city would deny.
By the melodious anthems of the shore
Some plighted pledges. Some would yearn and sigh
For the lost lovers who were theirs no more.

Multitudes on the beaches play and rest;
So many voices make the air resound,
One with wild wave, and with its snowy crest,
It seems that here all earthly joy is found.
But when all these have vanished quite away,
Still shall the sea have endless words to say.

FULFILMENT

Being a poet, Nature meant to me
All glamour of the vital gracious
    earth;
Love had in her a fabulous bright
    birth,
And wonder dawned, and pure felicity.
My bliss was in the wildwoods and the
    sea;
In fields and mountains were my joy
    and mirth,
Little beyond her realm seemed of
    worth.
In her glad beauty I was glad and
    free.

But then you came! And your arrival meant
A magic more mysterious and more true.
You to Creation a new glory leant.
I learned of beauty that I never knew.
Though I still love the wildflowers,
    stars and trees,
Your love fulfils what nature promises.

NOT LUCIFER ALONE

Not Lucifer alone! I saw today
A spirit of light that had his bounds forgot,
Who strove his puny passions to array
Against Eternal Will, that alters not.
Forgetting that he was but feverish dust,
He moved against the majesty of Law,
While keepers of the covenants august
Waked far away upon the bournes of Awe.

They woke, the warders of the Will Divine,
Champions of doom and mighty overthrows;
And as he neared Truth's white inviolate shrine,
To his advance their power to oppose,
Solemn, in an unbroken battleline,
The legions of the universe uprose.

334

GREAT WATERS

As one who knows but little streams and rivers,
Far inland, and of waters knows no more—
All unaware of how the main delivers
Its mighty anthems to the vast seashore;
Yet comes mysteriously at last to face
The splendor of the ocean, and the sweep
Of lordly sea-winds, and the silver grace
Of sea-stars blazing on the ancient deep—

And the blue expanse of boundless waters rolling:
So, little loves were mine. And then I came
On a great flood, the tides of life controlling;
On glory without limit, without name;
And heard, out of love's heart, wild as the sea,
Majestic music of eternity.

MOUNTAIN MEADOWS

All through this flowering fragrant land
Let lovers dance and sing and laugh.
They know not I am close at hand:
This wildrose is my epitaph.

These mountain meadows that they see
Might by their beauty represent
To all who follow after me
By loving will and testament.

Still shall this sandy creek flow on, . . .
Another boy, another girl,
Long after you and I are gone
Will hear these gentle waters purl.

These hills that tower in the blue
Will tower on through all the years,
Will look in vain for me and you;
Yet, Darling, have no doubts or fears.

For He who reared the mountains' height
And set the stream to course this field,
Has all there is of heavenly might,
And to no other power need yield.

We have His love,—we know not why,
But know it is of mercy made.
He is the Lord of earth and sky,
The Sovereign of the light and shade.

He knows love's high mysterious art;
And though our joys and hopes grow dim,
He's master of the human heart,
And we can trust our years to Him.

On earth He gives us love and peace,
And gives us grace all grief to bear;
Nor shall His caring for us cease
At any time, or anywhere.

Our faith knows well His love will care
For us, wherever we may go;
And in His glory we may share
For all we know, for all we know.

336

REJOICE

I

The trumpet has sounded,
The bugle has blown;
The limits are bounded;
The promise is known.
Of one mind, creation
Swings onward in rune;
Each man and each nation
Should join in the tune.

II

Though rocking and reeling,
The earth travels on.
Her way she is feeling
Around the great sun.
She takes up the slack,
And she bends to her task;
Low-bowed is her back,
But no question she'll ask.

III

To the last star that sleeps
On the frontiers of Heaven,
To the heights, to the deeps
Is one command given.
And to man comes the order
In duty to move
In grace to life's border,
And guided by love.

IV

Orion's aware
That his Maker is nigh;
And Vega the fair
Feels her Lord passing by.
Capella and Rigel
Are trembling fast;
One law rules the atom,
The same law, the Vast.

V

O Man, King of all things
Except the high God,
You even have wings
To sweep the sky's sward,
Be humble and contrite;
In the trumpet rejoice,
And find your delight
In the bugle's wild voice.

SIGNATURE

Before we were, who through this country came?
Whose are these flares and signals in the night?
Whose seal is on the darkness and the light?
Whose symbol on the shadow and the flame?
The constellations in their song proclaim
Illustrious authorship. On depth and height
His proud armorial bearings are in sight:
Royal insignia reveal His name.

All Beauty bears His signet and His crest.
Upon the mountains and the sunrise shore
His sign is set, and on the wildrose west.
The evening star is His bright semaphore.
All glories to His glory must attest,
Acknowledging His sovereign signature.

FAITH CONFIRMED

"There is no God," the unbeliever said.
"I cannot find Him in the light or dark.
Of all life's paths, no path to Him has led.
I cannot hear Him, howsoe'er I hark.
He must have been, yet now seems gone away.
He heard me not although I cry and call.
Still unrevealed He is, by night or day,
Lost in the light, or hid in shadows tall."

Love, if there were no beauty but your own,
No other music than your golden voice,
Yet should I know that God Himself alone
Could bring to be what makes my heart rejoice.
So magical you are, so wise, so true,
No one but God could ever have made you.

LIGHTS IN JEWELS

'Tis not the jewel that arrests the gaze,
But in the jewel Light's eternal rays.

Gazing on jewels, varying lights I saw
To charm, to thrill, to startle, and to awe:

Autumnal suns in rubies risen red,
And setting moons through opals sadly shed;

Far premonitions of a faerie spring
In dewy beryls greenly glistening;

Lost purple pageants of the long ago
Throbbed in the amethyst's depths of beauty and woe;

And glittered in their crystal heavens bright
Stars of the diamond's snow-enamelled night;

Down many a glimmering and rose-misted whorl,
Dawned the pure ivory twilight of the pearl;

Deep in the topaz did mine eyes behold
Romantic sunsets gorgeous in their gold.

Cold crystals, what rare radiance in you burns!
Light into splendor all your darkness turns.

And hearts no less with ardency divine
Shall glow, if God's great light shall thro' them shine.

SURVIVAL

When from your wings life's dust is shed,
Your light alive, your shadow, dead;
When nothing mortal's left to mar
Your spirit; when alone, afar,
To Many Mansions you are led,
You'll take to Heaven's holy star
Only the beauty that you are.

TO HALLEY'S COMET

Far-rushing as a lordly storm
Of fire through the mighty skies,
We feel thy mute, majestic charm
With rapture, awe, and wild surmise.

With rapture: through tremendous space
Thy form has raced with star-flashed light;
And proudly kept the awful pace
Of Neptune plunging through the night.

With awe: beyond our mortal sight,
Profounder systems, star and sun,
Have gazed upon thy wondrous flight,
And of their glories named thee one.

Perchance beyond thy boundary lone,
We might surmise, there wait for us
Our Loved, our Lost, our very Own,
And He, their Master glorious.

DARK HILLS OF TIME

Dark hills of time, dark hills of time,
As up your shaggy steeps I climb,
The pathway for my feet is worn
By them who, ere I came, are gone.
They knew the fear, the pain, the night;
Yet they kept climbing for the light.
O if the way is dark and long,
Their spirit serves to keep me strong.
Not knowing where the path may end,
I must not falter, but ascend:
The farther upward that I go,
The higher hope to them below,
Behind me on the shrouded slope.
If I fail not, I give them hope
That they your bastions may climb,
Dark hills of time, dark hills of time.

341

LOVE'S LARK

When the tide turns,
And we must embark,
Will there be violets
In that deep dark?
Red roses and music
Under the dark?
Faces adored,
And voices beloved,
Or the long silence stark
Where darkness abides,
Where ramp the sea-tides,
And the savage white shark?
No one discloses
If music and roses
Abide in the dark;
Or if there shall perish
All beauty we cherish
In the deep dark.
All that one knows is
How tender the promises
Sung by love's lark.

BLESS YOU

Bless you for being in my sky
So bright a star, so bright a star.
Bless you for being to my heart
All that you mean, all that you are.
My radiance arrives with you.
With you it goes, with you it goes.
Bless you for being to my life
So sweet a rose, so sweet a rose.

SIBYL-ROSE

Wonder still haunts our common world;
And I would say, ere I go hence,
A wife is not so much a wife
As a divine experience.

There's mystery moving on the earth,
And magic winging through the sky;
The ruby in the rose is blown
When she comes in her beauty by.

From her of secrecy I learn;
She keeps the keys of magic hidden;
She opens wide the sacred gates
To walk in gardens long forbidden.

I now have faith in miracles.
Before, I could not ever see one.
Yet without effort my dear wife
Shows beautifully how to be one.

She is the music that was mute,
The loveliness I never saw,
The liberty I had not known
Beyond the boundaries of law.

She makes me a believer in
All that I felt could never be;
I hear the harp in Tara's halls,
And Sappho singing by the sea.

I see the things I had not seen.
I hear what all the wildflowers say.
I go where I have never been.
If there's no path, she knows a way.

At Delphi was an oracle.
I have one in my home. She knows
The answers I have always sought,—
My strange, sweet, secret Sibyl-Rose.

"NOTHING IS LOST"

I would that in your eyes I might be mirrored
Always, for they transform unworthiness,
Making me great of heart. How I have sorrowed
That I had little that could nobly bless
Your beauty! Is it not passing strange
That your great love has power to refine
Dross into gold? My nature you can change,
So that I gleam with lights that are not mine.

Though I am mortal, dusty, grimed, and dim,
Your love exalts me into what I'm not, . . .
Akin to seraphs and to seraphim.
Your dream me Tristram, Roland, Lancelot, . . .
God to the one goddess that I ever knew,
Lord to my Lady, beautiful and true.

THREE MYSTERIES

You ask me how this frail sea-shell
Treasures the ocean's thundering songs,
Repeating every fall and swell:
All this to mystery belongs; . . .

As much as true love, driven down
To dust, to dwell with worthless things,
Will rise with rubies in her crown,
And take the sky on rainbow wings;

As much as in my cloistered heart
I hear the songs that are no more;
And, from all other sounds apart,
Loved voices from some distant shore.

CHRISTMAS SONG

No conquest gained, no glory won,
No honor bought by sword or pen
Has half the beauty or the worth
Of peace on earth, goodwill to men.

Goodwill toward men, and peace on earth:
O there was One who brought this word!
This triumph, down the centuries,
Alone can joyously be heard.

Still golden in the gloom about
This message saves us now, as when
It first arrived; this gentle charge
Of peace on earth, goodwill toward men.

What other message brings us hope?
A master race? Some order new?
Older and nobler is the faith
Men have found beautiful and true.

Of peace life's Caesars give us naught
But ashes . . . Love's unerring ken
Follows the everlasting light
Of peace on earth, goodwill to men.

SUNSET CUP

With clamors hushed, with glarings dimmed,
There is a drink to heal your heart,—
A chalice with wild beauty brimmed,
Held by the far hills, ruby-rimmed.

By wonder magically made,
No boon is asked for all its bliss
Of fading light and dawning shade;
For all its joy no price is paid.

To feel the rest of tranced things,
The wine of sunset drink! For then
The heart's wild harp no longer sings,
And folded are life's beating wings.

PRELUDE

I will sing of the sun, and of all that expresses
    his power divine;
Of all lights of the world; of the love that has
    power in darkness to shine;
Of the soul within light, that, penetrant, silent
    and pure,
Awakes in the seed the new life, and to glory that
    life can allure.
I will sing of the changes of light; of the red
    dawn resplendent and bold,
Of its ardency splendid of youth, its fulfilment
    at noon, and the rest
Of the falling hours of day, when the light is all
    in the west . . .
I will sing of the sun; for ever in awe my heart
    has believed
That from One greater than he, the sun has his
    glory received.

Of life I sing, and of death; of the purposeful
    stately transition,
Of the summoning forth of the soul on a far and
    celestial mission;
Of the lyrical silences after, thrilled with God's
    design in the change,
With mighty survivals made grand, and with mystery
    shrouded and strange.
I will sing of the greatness of life; of the power
    and glory thereof;
Of the lordly high stayings of Law, and the beautiful
    leadings of Love;
Though life's pathway be fearful with pitfalls, with
    ambushes deep as the grave,
Then more is the need that we face them with hearts
    that are steadfast and brave.
I will sing of this valor of spirit; that listeners,
    hearing my voice,
Shall look upward, see stars and sun; remember love,
    and rejoice.

Angels walk in the moonlight,
Angel spirits of sleep,
Angel bringers of dreams;
Out of the dark and the deep
Their beauty like moonrise gleams;
Like silver music they move,
Angel spirits of love.

Angels walk in the moonlight
From bournes of mysteries,
Across the fields in flower,
Beneath the glimmering trees,
Coming with beauty's power;
With voices of sweetest strain,
Like bird-songs in the rain.

Angels walk in the moonlight,
Tender, compassionate, wise;
Love is the song that they sing
Under night's violet skies;
Rest is the gift that they bring,
And reconcilement serene
For joy that might have been.

Angels walk in the moonlight,
Closing the eyes that weep;
They soothe the brow of care
And calm the pulse's leap;
Hushing the heart's despair,
They sing to the thwarted will:
"Peace, be still, be still."

THERE IS ONE THING

There is one thing I never must forget
Amid the chaos of the passing days:
Beauty's the seal of God on virtue set.
I must be guided by this light always.
For out of it come flowering peace of heart,
And steadfast joy, and hope that never falters;
It is of faith the everlasting part;
The gift supreme for love's eternal altars.

The venal loveliness men follow after
Is never ultimate in form or face;
The nymph and fawn, for all their mirth and laught
Have not the regal spirit's heart of grace.
He has all truth if he this knowledge knows;
Beauty's the garden where God plants His rose.

NIGHT AND GOD

All day we turn the wheel;
All day we plow the sod;
But when we lay us down to rest,
We leave the night to God.

We yield us to His care,
Forget our joy and pain,
Knowing that He will keep the watch
Until we wake again.

When ends life's little Day,
With all our journeys trod,
In perfect trust we'll turn to sleep,
Leaving the Night to God.

THE FIRST RED ROSE

Like the gold stillness of an afterglow
The Past gleams radiant. "They were better days,
With gentleness and grace of long ago,
Like childhood's gladness and its innocent ways."
So dream we of the haunting times of yore,
When life seemed lovelier and the heart more warm,
Thinking that Beauty's sun will rise no more,
Now that we face the darkness and the storm.

Yet all the joy that earth has ever known
Is with us now to make existence sweet:
The nightingale of Keats has never flown,
And Shelley's lark still sings above the wheat.
When Eve in Eden wore it in her hair—
That first red rose—than ours 'twas not more fair!

KAHMA

God does not always pay the score
This Saturday night.
Perhaps
After a lapse
Of days and months and years,
In the dark or the light,
He makes up all arrears.
No yesterday
Ever by Him shall be forgot
Who faileth not.
As surely as rock stands,
Or water runs,
The Ruler of the suns,
The Master of all lands,
Some day
Shall turn this way,
Mightily to repay.

TESTIMONY

I. The Centurion

Of them that did Rome's bidding, I was one,
Far in a foreign land. An alien, I
Saw that the will of Herod aye was done.
I lived for Caesar, and for him would die;
Nor trouble knew until my servant dear
Fell sick almost to death. And then I thought
Of the strange rumors that had made us fear,
Of the Messiah and the deeds He wrought.

I would have gone to Herod, face to face,
Or even to Great Caesar. But I knew
Myself unworthy of this Being's grace.
All faith I had, and all my trust came true.
Who healed my servant with a little word
Had power none can ever have save God.

II. The Woman of Samaria

Taking my precious pitcher, I had gone
To jacob's well, to draw my water there,
As is my wont. And I was all alone.
But there I met Messias. Unaware,
I took him for a stranger, and we fell
To talking. As he told me wondrous things,
Another world waked for me. On the well
I left my pitcher. Homeward, as on wings,

I sped to tell my friends to hear and see . . .
Beautiful was the pitcher that I left,
A vase of Sidon with blue lilies rimmed.
But O the living water born in me!
Over my loss I could not be bereft
Now that my heart a golden chalice brimmed.

III. The Maniac of Gadara

I prowled the midnight as a lone wolf prowls,
Dwelling among the mountains, in the tombs,
Beneath those cliffs whose shaggy thunder scowls
Over the sea. In caves as dark as wombs
I had my home. A maniac, I dwelt
An outcast, and no man could bind me sure.
With jagged rocks I gashed myself. I felt
Not any hope, or love to make me pure

Until He came. Far off I knew 'twas He.
I ran; I fell before Him, worshiping.
"Son of the most high God!" I cried aloud,—
My voice proclaiming I at last was free.
For the first time I felt my heart to sing
As His immortal light dispersed my cloud.

IV. Lazarus

Lost, lost to life I lay, and lost to light,
Couched for the centuries in that lone cave,
As cold and silent as my granite grave,
At one with solitude and death and night,
Then came that dreadful summons of delight,
"Lazarus, come forth!" O Master, strong to save!
Great Death himself is but a willing slave
Before Thy conquering love's resistless might.

No other human heart since time began
Heard such a far compassionate command,
Music that joyous through my being ran
Like spring and laughter through a wintry land.
When I came forth, there stood awaiting me
My sisters, and my friends amazed, and He.

351

VISION ETERNAL

Abandon the mountain, the wildwood
The field, and the meadow,
The sea-beach, the stream;
Relinquish the dawn and the sunset,
The light and the shadow,
The sea-stars a-gleam;
Renounce all the wildflowers of wonder
In life's El Dorado
That beckon and beam:
But never the Vision Eternal,
Belovèd and loving,
O never the Dream!

Say farewell to pride and to power!
Their end is but sorrow,
Though splendid they seem.
Deserting all mortal dominion
Of crest and of furrow,
Ambitions extreme,
Forget every song but the one
That can hallow tomorrow;
Immortal its theme.
Hold fast to the Vision Eternal,
Belovèd and loving,
Cling close to the Dream!

Resign fame and glory,
Their orchids, and roses;
Their worth disesteem.
No longer pursue after fortune,
That never discloses
Life's beauty supreme;
Lose all other hope save the hope
In which power reposes
All loss to redeem:
For that is the Vision Eternal,
Belovèd and loving,
O that is the Dream!

THE STARS AND MAN

The stars their duty understand;
The Voice Eternal they have heard:
Capella burns at His command;
Orion rises at His word.

God set the course. He gave the chart.
They hear the Word. They know the Way.
Each constellation has a heart
Attuned to honor and obey.

The Message comes. They are elate;
One song ascends through all the sky.
Antares feels her splendid fate,
And Riga knows her Lord is nigh.

Far Vega, corsleted in light,
Moves to His wand with mystic grace.
The glimmering legions of the night
Stand in their own appointed place.

To space profound the order goes;
It comes to earth to guide and bless:
The wind, the tide, the oak, the rose
Tremble and turn and acquiesce.

How true is deep Aldebaran!
How leal is Lyra! What can save
The wild and wayward heart of Man
That leaves the orbit that Love gave?

DELAY

Pilgrims who haste and falter
Along life's toilsome way
To reach some shrine and altar
To worship and to pray,—
Why not with Beauty tarry,
Where wildflowers glint and shine?
Then in your hearts you'd carry
The altar and the shrine.

MASTER OF MIRACLES

Out of the lonely meditative night,
The thoughtful vast of mystery and darkness,
Guided by God's great gift, the mind of man,
The radio's delicate apprehensive fingers,
Detect and capture far immortal melodies,
Bringing their music intimately to us,
Conveying voices we have longed to hear;
And songs like fairy wildflowers dancing
At hide-and-seek in the aromatic breeze,
Most lyrically enter our lonely, silent homes,
Becoming sidereally our very own,
To have and to hold in our hearts forevermore.

All this is faerie, fey, incredible,
Yet hauntingly real and beautiful and true,
And out of the deep and the primeval wood,
As virginal as odorous, misty Eden,
Enchanting fragrance breathes delightfully
From wild azaleas and the balmy bay,
From dusky pines and long-tressed cypress trees,
Exhaling in perfume their secretness,
Their strength and beauty and their reticence.
And as night deepens, all the faithful stars,
With the queenly moon, controlling wandering tides,
Assume their argentine eternal guard,
Suggesting that great love remembers us.

Who can ignore the Hand that scepters all
The host of Heaven, yet with tender grace
Uplifts the violet's fragile loveliness,
Its humble beauty, to divine compassion,
Momentous as the rising of Orion?
Whether of wildflower or by womanhood,
A magic intimates the grace and glory
Of One who, while creating firmaments,
Is mindful of our trembling little longings.

And yet, and yet, some dare to question whether
God is not master of all miracles—
Like answering prayer, like making us immortal.

354

GOOD FRIDAY NIGHT

The hills are folded in a mist
    By Galilee: on Galilee
A silence comes, and it is night—
    The stars awaken tranquilly.

Night's beauty, mirrored in her dreams
    In Galilee, in Galilee
Sleeps, and the stars like spirit barks
    Move softly on a spirit sea.

The winds sigh with immortal grief
    O'er Galilee; and Galilee
Seems mortal and remembers all
    That cannot be, that cannot be.

The palms are moving in dim waves
    By Galilee: on Galilee
The starlight falls on motionless
    Blue waters of a quiet sea.

The shores are hushed, the winds are still
    On Galilee; o'er Galilee
The stars are setting far away—
    And One has died for thee and me.

AFTER

After the sunset
A white star to rise;
After its shining,
More stars in the skies;
After their setting,
The daybreak to glow . . .
For all our knowing,
How little we know!
After the parting
Of death, it may be
Shall come a meeting
For you and for me.

THE GREAT KINSHIP

My God is to me
As the sun to the tree,
To the leaf as the root;
As the player to the lute
(Else the music were mute);
As the rain to the flower;
To weakness as power;
As the air to the bird;
As the sower to the seed;
When the storm would o'erwhelm,
As the hand to the helm;
As the source to the stream;
As the heart to its dream;
To the plant as the soil;
And as rest is to toil;
As the word to the wire;
As the kindler to fire;
As peace is to strife,
And as love is to life,
To the ship as the sea:
To time as eternity
God is to me.

HEART'S EAGLE

Though twilight falls, and night assumes her reign;
Though all the lights you love the best seem lost,
Yet never dream that love can be in vain,
Yielding to doubt what you should treasure most.
The glory of the heart ends not in shade,
In silence, like the fading of a flower.
One said, "Let there be light!" His mercy made
All trials that love's strength could prove its power.

Always there is an end to every night.
Love's floodtide to life's dim forsaken shores
Returns in beauty; and the morning light
Her ruby to love's darkened rose restores.
Song follows silence; shadows take their flight;
And the heart's eagle in his azure soars.

THE TRAIN

The silent summer country woke
To roarings soft. The glimmering rails
Hummed, and afar a burst of smoke
Blackened the gorge between the hills.

The queenly train lay on her side
And took the curve at cyclone speed.
God, that a Hand that force should guide,
And that Man's mind conceived the deed!

With hot tumultuous clangors wild
The impetuous giant thunders past.
Bright thoughtful human faces mild
Fleet onward with the monster vast.

A far thrill trembles on the cliffs;
The silences resume their reign;
A distant smoke-tuft slowly drifts
Beneath the evening star serene.

O lyric Star! How tawdry seem
The rocking engine, rushing cars,
Children of Man's frail frantic dream,
When one considers God,—and stars.

As on the heavens I meditate
And sense their far majestic law,
Fades every deed that men call great,
Sinks every feeling but my awe.

Yet God is maker of all things:
Though systems vast be in His plan,
Flowers are His imaginings,
And He has made the mind of Man.

So when a splendid deed there be,
I honor Man's great mind the more;
For I, when Man's great mind I see,
More deeply can my God adore.

By gazing on the dusty clod
If you can plot the course of God;
And in the mud and slime can trace
The waterlily's coming grace;
Feel in the bare and lonely tree
The slumbering spring's divinity;
Beneath the seal that winter sets,
The breathing of the violets;
See in the little acorn brown
The massive live-oak's old renown;
Can feel the love of God beneath
The mailed and mighty stroke of death;
If you can find the undefiled
In yonder sad corrupted child;
If through abhorrences you can
See a dim Christ in Caliban,
And by the promise in a soul
Vision it beautiful and whole—
I'd say you had a gift to give,
And should a little longer live.

SHRINES

Tremendous Vision hewn to solemn stone,
Thy Cross among the stars, towering in night!
Shall God in thy tall splendor take delight,
Letting thy beauty for our sins atone?
Shall He who reared the firmament alone,
Whose mansion is the dwelling-place of light,
Marvel at Man's magnificence and might?
God has a sanctuary of His own.

Aye, in each heart God made Himself a shrine,
A secret place to which He might repair,
Fashioning it with love's own art divine . . .
And still it has His tender wistful care,
Whether the lights upon the altar shine,
If sweet the music, and unfeigned the prayer.

THE KEEPER OF THE QUIET HEART

I listened how the wintry wind
Raved through the bare trees' barren boughs;
Wildly he stormed about the house,
Tempestuous, fruitless, cold, unkind.

With blustering fury hurrying hence
The bitter blast went shouting by;
Silence alone was earth's reply
To all his savage violence.

But came a night of peaceful rain,
Of gentle southwind warm and sweet;
It soothed the chill and patient wheat;
It waked the world to life again;

To life and song and leafy limb,
To beauty and to old delight:
The wrathful wind raved in his might,
But love made no response to him.

For not the storm upon the wold,
With brutal wind and whirling snow,
Can bring one tiny bud unfold.

When in thy soul the storm would lower,
Remember spring's persuasive rain:
The way of violence is vain;
The way of gentleness is power:

The way of gentleness! The part
Of sunny mind, of voice serene,
Of silent strength that aye has been
The keeper of the quiet heart.

THE VOICE AT EVENING

Over the marshland now a curlew's crying;
Along the beach the dusky doves are flying;
Seaward the ebbtide dredges with its foam;
Evening is calling all her wanderers home.

From the far sea the fishermen return;
Gladly the laborer sees his home-light burn;
From strident marts of trade, half-mad with might,
Myriads escape before the fall of night.

"Come home!" a Voice is calling to them all;
A tender voice that thrills the evenfall . . .
To many a lonely heart, where'er it roam,
The Voice of Love is calling, "Home, come home!"

O Life, what richer gift is in thy power,
Than wide to set home-doors at twilight's hour?
God pity them for whom no home-voice calls,
Whose hearts are homeless as the evening falls.

But if to Him they turn, His peace shall save;
Calm shall they be, because of hearts made brave.
They in His love eternal light shall see,
Whose home the loving heart of God shall be.

THE TRINITY OF JOY

There is a trinity of joy;
For thrice its beauty comes to be:
In hope, in consummation deep;
Then in mysterious memory.
And of these three I think I know
Which one eternally allures:
Hope and fulfilment pass away;
Immortal memory endures.

PINELAND HYMN

By their tall beauty beckoned,
Under the pines I rove,
Whose meaning can be reckoned
Only by mystic love.

With starlit tresses streaming,
Majestical they stand,
Sidereally gleaming,
A lofty seraph band.

I know not in creation
Profounder peace than theirs:
In silent adoration
Watching above the years.

To me they're always bringing
Wonder of valiant will;
For always they are singing,
Or always they are still.

How beautiful and lowly,
Rapt, nobly awed, they sing,
"O holy, holy, holy,
Lord God, Eternal King."

RESCUE

In the dark, on the deep,
And in vain was the chart;
Even vain was our stubborn
High valor of heart.
But then a star shone,
And we knew where it stood;
And we found where we were
By the finger of God.

HOPE IN THE HEAVENS

Almost disdainfully they burn,
The sun and moon and stars in turn,
Austere in their vast unconcern.
Though they quite unresponsive are,
Proud moon and sun and haughty star,
As for their sympathy I yearn,
Changeless and beautiful they ride;
With all else failing, they abide,
Giving me cause my God to bless
For symbolizing Steadfastness
By bright eternal loveliness.

THE SILENT HILLS

Out of the silent hills
Of God I came to be.
Their breath my being fills,—
Mountains that cradled me.
And in their freedom free
I with their strength am strong,
Whose music is my song.

Deep in earth's silent hills,
From flower and rock and sod,
I drew the peace that stills;
Where never a man had trod,
I found my faith in God,
And joy in the forest old
For which I gave no gold.

Since heaven takes my part,
And God is fast my friend,
Hope never leaves my heart,
With joy my life I spend.
Faith keeps me to the end;—
To sleep, whene'er God wills,
Deep in His silent hills.

DUST

Of dust our mighty world
Was made by Thee, dear God;
Yet out of dust arise
Rose, lily, goldenrod.

The massive mountain-pine,
The wildflower by the ford,
These are of thee, O Dust,
But also of the Lord.

And dust of dust are we,
Dim motes; but in God's beam
Of love we'll turn to gold,
And in His glory gleam.

Nor shall we sleep in dust
Forever: all we see
Of beauty slept in dust
Till wakened, Lord, by Thee.

Therefore we will not fear.
God drew us out of dust.
This He can do again
As He loves, and we trust.

IF YOU HAD LOVED ME

If you had loved me, I had never lost
The bloom of wonder by that grace conferred.
My strength would be the strength of a great host,
My wings as eagles' if my heart had heard
Your wild heart calling mine. But all was still.
There was no music. Had you loved me, I
Would sing forever from my spirit's hill,
Feeling the mountains mine, the sea, the sky.
A spring upon a crested height divides:
One stream into a sinister desert flows.
The other in gladness and in beauty glides
By many a rhododendron, many a rose.
I am the stream the desert sand-dunes smother.
If you had loved me, I had been the other.

363

SECOND COMING

I saw my Master, Jesus Christ;
Not come in glory's clouds had He,
Illustrious by the sumptuous shore,
Resplendent by the gorgeous sea,—
But humbly He returned to earth
As at His stable-manger's birth.
Although from Heaven I knew He came,
I found Him busy in our hell;
He stilled the racing pulse; he even
Made music of death's mournful bell.
Not regal or in royal state
Was He, but ministering to woe,
Healing the stabbed and laboring heart
As once He did, long, long ago.
By no pretensions heralded,
His advent unmagnificent,
Unostentatious,—to our sins,
Longings, and griefs His aid He lent.
I saw this miracle befall:
Christ came to visit earth again
Just as He came in ages past
To conquer doubt and death and pain;
To give to them whose rest was gone,
To bring to weary eyes that weep
A bourne deep as a mother's breast,
The sacred sorcery of sleep.
I saw my great compassionate God
To His frustrated world return,—
Not to disdain, denounce, accuse,
Not to rebuke, condemn, and spurn;
Rather to bind each bleeding wound,
To yearn His sad loved sinners o'er;
To bless, to praise, and to forgive
As His wild mercy did of yore.
He came to loose our cankering chains
With tender care's companionship;
Only to lift love's golden cup
To mortal fever's flaming lip.

OUTLAW

The stars their duty understand.
The Voice Eternal they have heard.
Capella burns at His command;
Orion rises at His word.

God set the course. He gave the chart.
They hear the word. They know the **way.**
Each constellation has a heart
Attuned to honor and obey.

The Message comes. They are elate.
One song ascends through all the sky.
Antares feels her splendid fate;
And Riga knows her Lord is nigh.

Far Vega, corsleted in light,
Moves to His wand with mystic grace.
The glimmering legions of the night
Stand in their own appointed place.

To space profound the order goes;
It comes to earth to guide and bless;
The wind, the tide, the oak, the rose
Tremble, and turn, and acquiesce.

How true is deep Aldebaran!
How leal is Lyra! What can save
The wild and wayward heart of Man
That leaves the orbit that Love gave?

BEAUTY AND THE BLOW

Since the rock shows no fire forever
Till a blow strikes a flame from the stone—
If you are deep wounded, remember
The stroke that Fate deals you may give **you**
A beauty you never had shown,
A glory you never had known.

THE NEW SOUTH

Sing with me, for my heart is at song,
    Sing for the night is past;
Cry with a sweet voice, brave and strong,
    The day has come at last.

Weary I was with sighing and tears,
    Weary were my children's hearts;
Let us forget the sorrow of the years,
    For grief forgot departs.

I have arisen; I see a light,
    Risen from ashes gray;
Sing for the passing of the night,
    Sing for the golden day.

Let us forget the places of the tombs,
    And turn from pain away,
To see the white cotton whirling on the looms,
    And the glimmering spindles gay.

To see the great rivers rushing down alone,
    Past beauty that gives increase.
O children mine, my beauty is your own,
    My joy, my strength, my peace.

I have renounced the shadows and mist,
    The dust, and memories gray;
My heart is glad, for the rod I kissed
    Is made my staff today.

Let us forget the mourning pines,
    In a more triumphant song;
Come let us build on our ruined shrines
    A temple bright and strong.

So may we toil, and as we labor, sing,
    Uplifted, glorified;
Brave must we live, remembering
    The Brave who for us died.

THE TWO HOMES

The glory of the star that shines
Above the misty morning pines,—
The sunset-colors, glowing, still,
On wide salt creek and cedared hill;—

The willet whistling from the edge
Of beaches brown, where dry sea-sedge
Lies tumbled, and the curlew's call
Along the marsh at evenfall;—

These haunted me from boyhood days.
I said, "I will return once more,
Renewing happy days of youth
In fragrant woods, on friendly shore."

And I returned. It was the same,—
Yet not the same: where'er I ranged,
I saw the old beloved scenes,
But somehow sadly I had changed.

For to these places of delight
No longer could I bring a heart
Of boyish rapture brimmed with mirth,—
Of every joyous scene a part,—

But touched with grave humanity,
And mindful of the trembling lease
Of life and love; and seeing clear
The one dark path that leads to peace;—

Remembering comrades of old days,
Now fallen asleep; who now no more,
(Although they loved then even as I)
May pace these woods, may walk this shore.

Ah, then, I said: "There is a Place
That changes not; and thither come
Our well beloved. And there, O there
Shall be no parting in that Home."

RESTORATION

When my heart's like an empty cup,
I go to God to fill it up.

Into my arid spirit flows
The rainy fragrance of the rose,

The wide-winged sunset's glamour far,
The hyacinthine evening star.

The rosebay's chalices divine
Brim with wild beauty and are mine.

All nature's loveliness is free:
God fashioned it for you and me;

And gave to us, to make us wise,
The soul's invincible surmise

That Beauty is no accident,
But is Love's forethought and intent
To be the heart's replenishment.

PILGRIM

In two worlds I walk;
With two tongues I talk;
My one hand holds my brother;
Angel spirits, the other.
I feel with senses ten.
I stride with men
By mountains, by the sea;
But spirits also pace with me.
And in the silences from life apart
I tell them all the secrets of my heart.
And when of grievous things I tell,
They kiss me, and they whisper, "All is well:
Earth and her thrones are dust.
In our bright realm trust,
Where comes nor moth nor rust."

From world to world I move,
Pilgrim of pain and love.

TRANSFERENCE

Light that for me must die,
Dawn to the blind man's eye!
Shine where no path. is seen;
Show where brave deeds have been.

Youth that must leave me,
May they receive thee
Who in good works are strong,
That they may labor long.

Joy that from me must part,
Enter the broken heart,
And to the vanquished give
Hope, that they still may live.

Love that from me must go,
Ah, that it must be so!
Speed, speed from coast to coast.
Help him who needs you most.

Love, Youth, and Joy, and Light,
Pass not into the night!
Unto some other come;
Enter his heart and home.

GIFT OF WONDER

If only gold were wealth, how poor were I!
But riches are the heart's fulfilled desire:
The miser piles his dusty hoardings high;
The hill man loves his cabin and his fire;
For all are lovers. Here the conqueror clangs,
Enamored of his might. The poet dreams,
Rapt where the blue lobelia lustrous hangs,
And lyric where the blushing rosebay gleams.

To some Golconda's glittering spoils belong;
Beauty to Helen; valor to the Maid;
To Caesar, conquest; and to Milton, song.
And He, by whom the universe is swayed,
Giving me power to wonder, gives to me
Royal Orion rising from the sea.

THE SOUL

Imperial, illustrious, alone,
Unshackled by the bonds that shackle me,
She journeys safely over land and sea,
Rides in the whirlwind, to the moon is blown
Like a rose-leaf. But all her way is known.
And presently she comes once more to me,
Through wisdom perfect and by beauty free,
Joy in her step and music in her tone.

How shall this spirit that from star to star
Wanders secure, celestial rapture feeling,
Return to naught? She voyages afar,
And to the heart immortal hope's revealing
When she returns. Her message I will trust,
For I cannot believe that she is dust.

I OF THE SPIRIT SING

I of the spirit sing,
Of the soul and the wing,
Of the vision and gleam;
I of the unseen tell,
Touch the intangible
Hand of the holy dream.

The astral flame forever
Will from the night deliver;
Always I hear,
Far through the clouds and rain,
Far through the grief and pain,
Love singing clear.

Calling my heart to be
Made by their beauty free,
Calm though in strife,
I to the voices hark
In light beyond our dark,
In life beyond life.

IN HIS HAND

Though life's thunders may appall,
I shall never, never fall
If I stand in His hand
In the hollow of His hand.
I shall fear me not at all
In the vale or on the crest
Of life's ocean-heaving breast.
And with darkness on the land,
In His strength my strength shall stand,
By His might to work His will,
In His stillness to be still.
Though my strength cannot avail,
Yet His power cannot fail.
He who guides the heavenly host
Will not let me wander lost.
He who does the stars command
Comforts and remembers me,
Holds my life by shore and sea
As I stand in His hand,
In the hollow of His hand.

THE HOMEWARD ROAD

The Wisemen Three who journeyed from afar
To find their King, adored Him as He lay
A helpless babe, cradled in humble hay,
While over His birthplace blazed the signal Star.
Then after they had made their gifts, the Sages,
In secret, by a way they had not come,
Passed in glad triumph to their distant home,
Having beheld the hope of all the ages.

Homeward they took another road, for they
Had seen the Christ . . . And it is always so.
We travel darkling on life's broad highway,
Careless, in jostling crowds. Sinful we go
Until we meet the Master. From that day
Another path our hearts redeemed shall know.

BEAUTIFUL HOME

I saw a home so beautiful, it seemed
That of its loveliness I merely dreamed:
Glimmering in a flowering fairy wood,
Stupendous mystic trees about it stood . . .
Safe from the world, here was enchanted ground,
Where there was only melody for sound,
Where for emotion there was love alone,
And gentleness the one prevailing tone.

Then to a shining sentinel I said,
"Whose home is here?" I questioned half-afraid,
As if I trespassed into fairy land.
But with a radiant grace he took my hand.
"I'll be your guide. Will you not come and see?"
The calmness of his beauty troubled me,
Who often in the wood and on the mere
Had learned of false enchantment to beware.

Wondering, I went with him . . . We found each r
Fragrant and like a flower in joyous bloom.
So wide the windows were that heaven was near;
And there was nothing hidden, naught to fear.
And happy folk who perfect freedom knew
Were singing, and I felt their hearts were true.
"This is the home of Virtue," said my guide;
"Will you not with us in this place abide?"

THE HAND

Though I cannot understand,
Yet I trust and I believe
From the same Almighty Hand
All the stars their law receive,
Giving sun and moon their rounds,
And the flaming comet bounds.
Where the ponderous planets roll
Is the same Divine control
That I feel within my soul.
To that dim resistless wand
Multitudinous worlds respond;
And the Love that sways Arcturus
And the mightier stars beyond
Makes the shore the wild sea's yoke,
From the acorn rears the oak,
Lifts the wildflower's fragile grace,
Holds the thunder in his place,
Moors the darkly massive mountain
To his granite-tenoned base.
And the Master over these
For my heart a mandate holds
As for burning Betelguese.
All the ancient music golden,
All the august silence olden
Of the far primeval rhythm
In deep harmony's upholden
By the Will that never alters,
By the Hand that never falters.

I TRUST MY HEART

Sometimes in darkness and in doubt,
When life to charm me has no art,
When one by one my lights go out,
I trust a light within my heart;

A sentinel beside the sea,
A star above the rolling foam,
This pilot sees and shows to me
The perils and the channel home.

When dearest hopes have met defeat,
And sadly all my dreams depart,
I still can find that life is sweet
If I will only trust my heart.

That inner light I reverence,
Divine, and yet of me a part;
For when at last I journey hence,
If anything, I take my heart;

My heart that visions happier things
In some far land by some far sea,
Beyond all Reason's reckonings,
In life more beautiful to be.

ALL THINGS

My foemen throng before with purpose grim.
But trusting in the Lord of Life I go.
All things for me are possible with Him.

I see no path; but His clear light I see.
I have no strength. He makes His strength my own.
It is my faith in Him that foemen flee.

Through sorrow's wilds, deep-veiled with shadows dim
I go sustained; my heart, rejoicing, sings,
"All things for me are possible with Him."

So following faith unto life's last far rim,
My lost and loved to me shall be restored.
Even this for me is possible with Him.

IMMORTALITY

A crystal when suspended bright
Arrests the viewless heavenly light,
And into human colors fair
Translates the angel of the air.

But now the crystal falls; the glass
Lies shattered. Vanished, too, alas,
The rainbow colors and the gleam . . .
Then have they merely been a dream?

Ah, no! The light, though now unseen,
Is radiant-strong as it has been;—
Horizons mortal now are gone;
To life divine it passes on.

The crystal's fate is not the heart's;
For as the shattered life departs,
The heavenly spirit hath its will,
The light eternal shineth still.

MT. PISGAH

One hero-wave of flaming heliotrope
Among the mountain-breakers rushes high,
Its thrilling crest a challenge to the sky,
And to my heart! No more I bleakly grope
In sombre valleys. Clad in gorgeous hope,
My spirit rises, and my doubtings die.
Ready I seem for glad eternity,
Dawning tremendous o'er this mountain-slope.

Beyond the silver of the Swannanoa,
In a maned sea of mountains, rolling blue
Into the haunting west, one peak I view,
A tidal wave portentous. And the shore
On which it breaks in Beauty's magic dreams
Like to God's Land Eternal to me seems.

RITUALS

If by the rituals that men have made,
Adoring God, I find myself unmoved;
And if I cannot pray as they have prayed,
It is because I have more deeply loved
A lordlier ceremonial than the psalms
Of choirs choiring in cathedrals dim . . .
Hearing the sea-wind through the pines and palms,
I worship; for it seems the voice of Him

Who made this earth and all the heavens a shrine,
Fashioned the only beauty that abides
Age after age; made mortal love divine . . .
The chantings of the seasons and the tides
Proclaim Him, from this rose's rare design,
To where in solemn light lone Riga rides.

THANKSGIVING

Now God be praised that I can share
The grief of them for whom I care,
That not alone the Cross they bear!

For love more loyally will go
Through sorrow's storm of driving snow
Than where the summer roses blow.

There is no gulf but I will be
Beside them in their agony:
What comes to them must come to me.

We pass together through the night,
And come together toward the light,
To stand together in God's sight.

THE MASTER'S PLEA

I have no hands save your own hands
To lift the burdens, loose the bands
Of Pain; to bear My banner on . . .
Only by you My work is done.

I have no feet save your own feet
To carry far My message sweet;
If they should fail, to every coast
My steps are halt, My way is lost.

I have no voice save your own voice;
Through it alone shall hearts rejoice
To know My tidings. If your tongue
Be silent, all My Truth's unsung.

I have no heart save your own heart
To beat for Me; to act love's part . . .
O Child, though I am throned above,
I have no power save your love.

Your feet alone My race can run;
By your own hands My deeds are done.
Your voice must speak, or Mine is still;
My heart's great task yours must fulfil.

SECURITY

Unguarded on the hill the orchis lifts
Her saffron spire; by the lonely stream
The rosebay, like a dreamer in a dream,
Fearlessly blooms. From vulnerable rifts
In the wild rocks the columbine is flaunting
Her crimson kirtle. In the ancient wood
Exposed to perils of their solitude,
The infant trees their enemies are daunting.

Having a faith that is their sure defense,
Their loveliness unshielded is displayed
Radiant in virgin beauty's innocence,
In armor of the love of God arrayed . . .
There is a Heart that watches over these.
Are we not more than many flowers and trees?

377

MY FAITH

To an end of the road,
The last mile of the way,
To the final dim ford
At the close of the day,—
Leaving life's hoarded store,
And arriving alone,
To the last stream's last shore,—
Where the journey is done,—

But beyond, each shall find
Of his portion a part,
The hopes he resigned
With hid tears of the heart:
Recover the cherished
On God's gracious coast,—
The dreams he thought perished,
The love counted lost.

Though vision be darkened
And hearing be dimmed,
Yet high faith has harkened,
And trusting has limned
What the heart shall inherit
(If but it endure)
By Love's living spirit
Whose promise is sure.

THAT EASTER MORN

Through the chill dawn that Easter Morn
Three women hurried fast;
With love and fear they hastened There,
Shawls held against the blast.
And then one said with anxious dread
(O faithless fears that loom!)
"Now who, I pray, will roll away
The stone that seals the tomb?"

They hasten on. The rainbow dawn
Breaks over the silent hills.
They run apace. Upon each face
Shines love that doubting stills.
And when they come, beside the tomb
A splendid seraph stands:
And he that stone has moved alone
With strength of heavenly hands.

O Life, how dark is faith's faint spark,
Our hearts to fear, how prone!
No strength we have at any grave
To roll away the stone.
Yet when we ask of some great task,
"How can we win the day?"
While we despair, some angel fair
Has rolled the rock away.

QUESTION FOR A CYNIC

O vain, incredulous Man,
Mercy's receiver,
One thing should make of you
A deep believer:

How from the heat and dust,
In occult dark and dews,
Diurnally the earth
Her youth renews:

Revolving in the night,
Her dim way knowing,
Turning into the shade,
Yet lightward going.

Though knowing law is much,
This wisdom is far more:
To know the Lawgiver,
And Him adore.

If any cynic smile
As such a faith he spurns,
I'll ask him, "Who conceived
A world that turns?"

FOREWORD

Of joy and of love, of hope and of far-seeing faith
To you, fellow pilgrims, I sing.
My trust in our God, in the life that's immortal
To you, fellow pilgrims, I bring.
I sing of the wildwood, the seashore,
Of the rivers that roll,
I worship in wonder our Maker
With a song in my soul.
I sing of vision and of valor high,
Of native beauty's art;
I sing of all loveliness that can and will
Exalt the heart.
Of heroes and of heroines is my song,
Of those who hearts are strong;
To the dauntless ones who can my spirit inspire
My ballads belong.
In the lonely dark a light I will lift
For those who are blind
That out of the deep of grief's night
Their way they shall find.
My music shall be of all gladness,
All charm and all grace;
For life is a mighty cathedral
Where hymns are in place
Of praise to the author, the Giver
Of love and of peace:
In my songs I will praise Him, will praise Him
Until my songs cease.

MOUNTAIN EAGLE

I, in a time of trouble
To the wild woodland went.
The paltriness of love and life
Had all my valor spent.
The blossoms of the rosebay
No longer gave delight.
The mountain's massive grandeur
To me no more seemed might.
I wandered through a meadow,
With naught but heaven above,
But still earth's care was with me,
And lost to me was love.
Then in the lonely beauty
Of azure and of wings
I saw an eagle soaring
Like a great voice that sings.
And something of the splendor
Of that illustrious one
Restored life's vanished wonder.
And all the glory gone.

HINGES OF FATE

Fate's mighty hinges often rest upon
Mere agate points. Yet, as those hinges turn,
Our world for centuries may change; the sun
On other life than what we know may burn.
Doom has her children, who are rarely wise:
They may thwart gladness for a thousand years;
In one bewildered moment may devise
The future's anguish and the ages' tears.

'Twas thus when Jackson in the twilight rode!
Disaster fell; when Tristram met Isoult;
When Varus ventured in the German wood.
Often it really does not seem man's fault,—
As when von Spee sped toward the Falklands gray,—
As when von Kluck from Paris veered away.

WHERE WATERS REST

Beneath the pines' heroic crest,
Below the rapids in the glen,
Deep in a fragrant fern-fringed fen
Is a still place where waters rest.

Torrents, once tawny, lose their zest;
Here sound and motion drowse and cease,
Far in this haunt of ancient peace,
To wildbirds known, by wildflowers blest.

When daybreak comes, or when the west
Makes radiance for all to see,
Glimmers the stream's felicity
In silence where these waters rest.

Peace can by beauty be expressed:
An oriole in his glory glows;
The cardinal becomes a rose
By this calm place where waters rest.

A meadow-lark with golden breast
Broods on her young above the pool;
A vireo warbles soft and cool
And joyously where waters rest.

Where ferns a fairy home have blest,
A little while to cease their flowing,
Between their coming and their going
The waters find this place to rest.

Deep in basaltic rock recessed,
Where glimmering hummingbirds can dart,
This is a place to heal the heart,
This halcyon place where waters rest.

With royal mien and lifted crest
A maharaja father quail,
A maharani mother quail
Lead their brown elves where waters rest.

An angel voice says, "Love is Best";
As I approach this tranquil place,
I think of beauty and of grace
Serenely where the water rest.

Here all dissension is repressed.
Under the chestnut oak, the shade
Is deep as is this mountain glade
This gentle place where waters rest.

May you be always love-possessed;
And with your spirit, heart, and mind
God grant that you may always find
A still sweet place where waters rest.

GUIDED

Whether I go by sea or land,
Something there is that holds my hand.
If in a crowd, or if apart,
I feel this power in my heart.
I see it in the wildwoods green,
And in the beauty never seen,
Constantly giving light to guide
Like some dear comrade by my side.
How much integrity we see
In every storm-defying tree!
Even from the little leaves' caress
We feel love's towering quietness.
What brings the flood-tide's snowy shout,
What rolls the ramping ebbtide out?
Whose guidance leads our step aright
Through the doom-haunted, ghostly night?
Some power, as the planets roll,
Exerts supreme divine control.
As through the darkness I go on,
A Hand of Love is on my own.

CHANT A LA MORT

I

It matters not what land or sea we roam,
How deeply love, how passionately hate,
With what immortal visions are elate—
Our paths coverage—to the same place we come.
Sadly do some lament, and proudly some,
Arriving at that frontier, bleakly wait
The passage of the ultimate grim gate . . .
—Or might it be a door opening on Home?

Children and potent kings and maids that weep,
In countless myriads that no mind can number,
Each heart with Death its rendezvous shall keep—
Whose coming's shadowy, whose wake is umber,
Whose mystic voice holds all the runes of sleep,
Whose eyes are darkness, and whose touch is slumber.

II

Hast thou no comfort for us, kingly Death?
We question pleadingly. But all we hear
Is silence and the stillness of our fear.
"Hope and believe," the Spirit whispereth.
"All shall be well," rejoiceth happy Faith.
But thou are very terrible and near,
And so apparent doth thy power appear,
'Tis hard to heed what any angel saith.

What might is thine! The massy earth is shaken;
The heavens tremble at thy silent tread.
What dreadful charm! The bridegroom has forsaken
The bride, and to thy dark embrace is fled.
What pitying love! The tiredest heart is taken,
And like a little child to sleep is led.

III

To know thee, there are many ways to tell:
We feel thee in the drooping of a flower,
In hope's departure, in the waning hour,
By faltering wings; by yonder star that fell
We know thee near, but nearest when a bell,
Deep in the heart, as in some cloistered tower,
Tolls for Love's passing, as it chants thy power:
"Farewell! Farewell! Farewell! Farewell! Farewell

Against thy strength in vain, in vain to strive!
They shadowy sceptre thou shalt ever wield,
And the last living thing thou shalt survive;
Life's latest struggle unto thee shall yield.
All else shall perish; thou shalt be alive
When the last flower fades in the last field.

IV

Eternal King of Fading and Decay,
Thy power too poignant is for mortal bloom:
All life that looks on thee beholds its doom.
In lyric fields the flowers blossom gay,
In maidenly immaculate array,
Rejoicing the long landscape to illume . . .
Tall Harvester, whose storehouse is the tomb,
At thy arrival they are swept away.

And yet no peace is there so sure as thine,
In rapture of a fathomless repose;
Calm rest inviolate, innocent sleep divine,
In a place where with all mortal cares we close,
Where stars upon the Fields of Silence shine
And dreams fold fast the river and the rose.

V

Who sings thee, sings of Dust . . . But we confess
Thou canst be pitiful. And then thy head
A halo wears, for thou hast visited
Mercy on him none other would caress,
Healing on him none other paused to bless.
The brokenhearted unto thee are led
And deeply in the Dust are comforted,
Refuge of all that else were refugeless!

Mysterious Dust! From thee our love upwells;
Beauty's the astral dream of thy delight;
From thy dark harp divine all music swells,
All radiance, from thy deep tremendous night:
Thy darkness is of Death; but it foretells,
Like Death, the dawning of eternal light.

VI

We call thee Sorrow-bringer, and we trace
Grievings to thee, and tears, and shadows wild.
Gardens of joy are by thy step defiled,
O dark Destroyer! Yet the clarivoyant grace
To image God as Love, and face-to-face,
The power with anguish to be reconciled,
The faith like that of any joyous child—
These benedictions come with thy embrace.

By thee the spirit's vision is unbound,
And cloudy Error at thy coming dies . . .
A path celestial through thy shade is found;
What life cannot afford, thy heart supplies:
Immortal anthems through thy silence sound,
Upon thy night eternal stars arise.

VII

Thy solemn secret never has been told,
Although to thee each questioning life is led.
Shall souls that were by love immortal wed
Once more their own beloved ones enfold?
That covenant august—if it will hold—
That there shall be reunion with the Dead,
We'd hail thee as an angel worshippèd
And deck thee like a god with burning gold.

Hast thou for us who live no tender token,
O mighty Death, from dread to set us free?
Since to the ages thou hast never spoken,
Art thou but silence and the whelming sea?
Yet if that awful promise be not broken,
Thou art Love, to lead us homeward quietly.

THE UNATTAINED

Lament not for the longing unfulfilled,
The height unreached, the promised land unwon;
Rejoice in yearning that is never stilled—
If you have not arrived when day is done.
There's glory in the quest. Desire gained
Can mean the end of ardor and of dreams.
Always upon the summit unattained
Life's luring light most magically streams.

Though lordlier anthems choir on that beach
To which in vision only shall you come,
Still is it yours, the goal you may not reach,
For aspiration is love's heart and home.
No journey's end your valor could renew
As will the dream that never may come true.

I NEVER KNEW THE MOONLIGHT

I never knew the moonlight
Until the fair day failed;
I never saw a shining star
Until the dark prevailed.

I never saw the country
Beyond our mortal years
Until I caught its vision
Far-glimmering through tears.

I never heard the music
Sung by the spirit host
Until my heart beat stillest
Because it sorrowed most.

I never felt the beauty
Of pine and rose and rue
Until that bitter moment
That took me far from you.

RENOWN

He planned to bring her treasures won
From many a ruined town.
For her he'd fashion from the spoils
A gold and ruby crown.
But home he came all clad in shame,
His armor rusted brown.
She smiled at him, upon her face
No shadow of a frown.
And when she said with merry grace,
"All else save love is nothingness;
My love your grief can drown;
I need your love my life to bless.
For me that is renown," . . .
He laid his head between her breasts
And let his tears run down.

389

STRANGER, STRANGER

Stranger, stranger, would you see
Her who was the world to me?
She lies not beneath this loam,
But has found another home . . .
I am in the dust—not she.

Unto life she gladly gave
Beauty . . . Ah, not in the grave
Dwells she now . . . My love can trace
In all loveliness her grace,
In all strength, her power to save.

By the harebell gleaming shy,
By the little brimming eye
Of the stargrass you might guess
Something of her gentleness,
And her tender bloom descry.

Stranger, in your radiant quest,
Seek her in the wild-rose west;
See, her modesty is set
On the virgin violet—
And the dews her charm suggest.

If life holds for me one shrine,
If I trust in love divine,
If my dust with dust confers
Rarely, all the virtue's hers,
As the heart redeemed is mine.

TOO DEEP

For song, too deep the quiet
Where darkly she is laid;
For joy, too stilled life's riot;
For dawn, too deep the shade;
For stars, too wide the umber
Beneath earth's solemn breast;
For dreams, too deep the slumber;
For love, too deep the rest.

MEMORIES

She wandered in the garden close
At dewy morning. Glowing there
She found a red resplendent rose,
And took the blossom for her hair.
She wore it through a happy day,—
'Twas when her heart was young and gay.

She in the silent evening stood
Entrancèd by a lustrous star
That burned above the dark pinewood
Effulgent in the dusk afar.
She watched it kindle in the crest
Of pines majestic in the west.

The rose in dust is blown afar;
The pine-trees long ago were felled .
She lives in distant lands; the star
She sees no more that she beheld.
But in her heart the home-stars glow,
And there the sweet home-roses blow.

For she has found that what the heart
Accepts and loves, forevermore
Remains in beauty. Years depart
As waves retreating from the shore;
But beautiful and bright still gleams
The memory of olden dreams.

SAFETY

By her faint words of farewell,
By her touch intangible,
By his dreams of her defended,
He is safe till life be ended:

Hears her voice in song, in light
Sees her beautiful and bright,
Till the wide world dims and darkens,
And the heart no longer harkens.

THE STRUGGLE

Upon birth's battlefield
Death unto Love did yield
That I, thro' struggle born, should take my part
Nobly in strife. For me,
Whatever peace there be
Shall come as I can prove a valiant heart.

Nor should I wish to wait
Until life's western gate
Unfolds, to feel that I have fought my fight;
But as light fades away
Each evening, let me say,
"Today, I've battled; I can rest tonight."

Not if I won or lost
Shall ever matter most,
But rather how I bore the battle through;
Not if my might prevailed,
But that my heart ne'er failed;
Not that I triumphed, but that I was true.

WILDFLOWER MAIDEN

Wildflower, wildflower, blowing shy
In the deep woods' quiet keeping.
Shall I bring you home—to die?
Shall I sleep if you are sleeping?

Where the pine whose ponderous shade
Holds the dew his shadows under,
In the twilight he has made,
I will leave you in your wonder.

Wildwood Heart, I would not capture
For my own your mystery.
I would feel no other rapture
Than to love and let you be.

COMRADES

The blue and rosy light from Parnell dies;
Evening the valley stills;
Silent and tender comes the holy night
From dewy hills.

The Tuscaroras tall are fading fast;
The valley's shadow-crossed.
The world I knew is vanished into shade
With her I lost.

Down from the dewy and the darkening hills
The night has come to me;
But neither light nor day comes to that land
Where lieth she.

My dark is full of dews and very fair;
Radiance comes soon;
Mournful but beautiful into the night
Rises the moon.

When her pale reign is past, and stars are set,
When night is done,—
Dawn's fragrant light is mine, and bird-songs
    sweet,
And the great sun.

My night is very fair; my day is blithe
With sunlight, roses, swallows:
Her night no moon or star nor night-wind brings;
And no dawn follows.

But we are comrades still. A grief we share:
She lost life's radiant light;
And I, in losing her, must evermore
Share her long night.

HOPE

When yonder sycamore
Rustled most liquidly,
And the stream softly bore
Down to the distant sea,—
There once the bright world wore
Light it shall wear no more.

One the world no more knows
Tenderly held me then:
Now the wind o'er her blows
Grieving through field and fen,
And where the river flows
By a sweet fallen rose.

"Love is such living, Sweet:"
Thus I dreamed in my dream;
"Each unto each complete,
Stars in a lustral stream,
That the waves move to meet,
Love is such living, Sweet."

Earth was a languorous bourne,
Folded in violet mist:
Valleys where grew no thorn,
Vales the wind waked and kissed—
There not a voice might mourn
Save doves o'er waving corn.

But on an autumn night
Came winds out of the east,
Bore to the west thy flight,
And all the wonder ceased:
Dimmed was my star of light;
Leaving me night in night.

But shadows manifold
Brought me a light that burned,
(Strange as a love untold,
Or true love unreturned)
Blown on by breath of mould,
Coming from gardens old.

So thus I cry to thee,
In my night thou wilt hear:
In thy dawn thou wilt see
Thy lilies that I wear:
Death is Love's victory
O'er sad mortality.

Wistful the river flows,
Tenderly murmuring:
Unto the deep it goes,
Dimly remembering
Sweet days that sadly close,
And a sweet buried rose.

THE LAST NIGHT

Her western windows front the seas;
Below them sigh the cedar trees;
And the sweet myrtles gather there
The Coast's mysterious silences.

The house is still; no voice is heard,
No silent song of love, no word
Echoes for her in all the world,
Save the low wind that waked and stirred.

Her eyes the Southern coast-line seek;
She hears the mist to the marshes speak,
The wind to the water whispering
Far down the long and glimmering creek.

She sees a shadowy spirit-sail;
Her brow is feverish and pale;
The wind has turned the misty tide;—
No wind or tide will now avail.

From that strange western casement shone
Sweet eyes at evening,—they are gone
Forever, for when night is past,
I shall be here in the dark alone.

MEMORIAL DAY

Out of the grave have come,
From dateless time,
Hopes and uplifts sublime.
Glorious structures out of ashes climb,
From the low earth an everlasting home;
And from death's deep and silent night
Stars of eternal light!
So, from these graves that lie
Patient beneath the sky,
Accepting rain and sun
As benediction,
Come powers to rule the soul;
Great thoughts that cannot die
Rise from them; and they cry
For the stern joy of self-control,
For valor and the life of honor high.
Such memories on this Memorial Day
Rise from these dead, in reverence we say,
The Resurrection and the Life are they.

In lonely homes the silent bugles hang.
From their bright lips the martial challenge
     rang!
Bugles that sounded nobly to the charge,
Thrilling upon the crimson battle marge.
Then into line they sprang,
These ranks that never broke,
These dauntless soldiers, though they were the
     targe
Of savage shrapnel, or that subtler foe,
The whining bullet searching through the smoke
For bosom to be buried in! . . . Ah, no,
These bugles are not silent! We have caught,
In lonely bivouacs by dreaming wrought,
High summons to advance and not retreat,
In open fight the craftiest foe to meet,
Fearing dishonor rather than defeat!

O still for us are splendid challenges,
Even in calmer times, in days of peace.
We hear the trumpets of the spirit sound,
We hear the bugles for the battle blow.
Wherever strength and courage can be found,
There is, for strength and courage, foe on foe.
Far through the conflict of our time are heard
Life's silver bugles and their golden word.

THE TRYST

A dawn-wind wakens in the fields;
Calmly to day my spirit yields:
All dawns save one will flush and burn,
And that the dawn of your return.

I know your spirit passes on
From beauty unto beauty's bourne;
But sooner will the silent urn
Whisper of life, than you return.

When on my face the midnight streams,
And I have lost my life in dreams,
Your glamour from the stars may yearn,
But you can nevermore return.

I know your radiant soul will press
From earth's to heaven's loveliness;
Your gleaming farewell I discern,
But not the light of your return.

Though you cannot return to me,
A mortal, immortality
(Winged by a love that has been true)
Shall wear, and I will come to you.

REQUIEM

Under the ancient pine,
Deep in the ferny glade,
Where the wild jasmine vine
Showers a fragrant shade,
Let me be laid.

Here will the moon and star
Watch with their silver light;
Here woodland winds from far
Haunt the deep purple night
With dim delight.

Here for my watch and ward,
In place of shaft and stone,
Great oaks shall be my guard,
And the tall cypress lone.
Loving his own.

Here let the dreamer rest,
Now that the dream is o'er;
Safe on the wildwood's breast,
Calm by the river's shore,
Waking no more.

THE EXCHANGE

'Tis well to roam on rivers bright,
By winsome shores to stray;
In happy fields to find delight,
To walk the woodland way;
And when is felt the needed rest,
To sleep upon earth's breast.

'Tis well; for in that other home
Of night and loneliness
Blithe rivers over us shall roam,
Fair shores our hearts shall press;
Forests and fields from us shall gleam,
Earth on our bosoms dream.

398

GHOST POINT

Eagle Hummock lies behind
 And the broad bay lies before:
Between the bay and the open sea
Are sunken reefs of treachery
 And ships that sail no more.

Eagle Hummock, where always
 The storm-bent cedars sigh:
Gazing out over the foaming tracts
To the surf-line's glimmering cataracts
 Where wrecks and perils lie.

Eagle Hummock lies behind
 And Harbor Creek before:
Beyond is the bay and the Light House far,
Where the brave and lonely keepers are
 At watch on the lonely shore.

Eagle Hummock—there at night
 When stars with storms are red,
With the dim sea moaning far away,
With a sound unheard by men, the bay
 Gives up her wandering dead.

Eagle Hummock lies behind
 Where the drowned men come on shore:
And save for the obscure laughter heard,
Silently—save for the grey mist stirred
 By them who sail no more.

SOURCE OF RADIANCE

If all things I have known and seen
Are less of worth than they have been,
It is because they've lost the glow
Of one they used to see and know.

Since 'twas from him they had their light,
Their beauty needs must be less bright;
How can I blame their being dim,
Who took their radiance from him?

MOTHER AND SON

She wonders what her boy will be,
And of his future wonders he.
The world allures him, wide and bright;
She seems to see him in its light,
Advancing with the brave and free.

Toiling with heart and hands and will,
The forces of the field and hill
He means to master; or will pit
His mind against the world's shrewd wit,
In subtler games to prove his skill.

Hope like a sun before him shines.
His days are filled with high designs
Of mighty tasks he is to do;
And though she sees this future, too,
Breathless she waits the Sign of Signs.

The lights that in his heart arise
Alone are glory to her eyes;
Not from his triumphs but from him
She longs to hear a noble hymn
Of life ascending to the skies.

Life's deepest values she divines,
And watches for the Sign of Signs—
Honor, to keep him brave and true;
For, lacking this, whate'er he do,
Defeated are her love's designs.

VIGIL

Quiet upon the couch he lies;
Closed is his book; closed are his eyes.
Or be it death or be it sleep,
Love's constant vigil will I keep,
Lest, waking, he should need me near
To be his triumph over fear;
Lest, sleeping, I begin the ward
Of memory's eternal guard.

400

BLONDE DEATH

Because her heart in shadows loved to range,
For Dolores to die seemed nothing strange.
So deep a mystery of night was hers
That her translation was not truly change.

But Constance had no kinship with the dark.
As much of day as laughter, sun and lark,
With orient Saxon radiance glittering
On a blue sea, she was a snowy barque.

Now that past sight of eye and reach of hand
Each one has traveled to the invisible strand,
It seems while Dolores has journeyed home,
Constance has wandered to an alien land.

THE DEAD OF YESTERNIGHT

Ah, me! The Dead of yesternight
Seem wrapt from us as far
As if they'd died when Pharoah lived,
Or blazed the Bethlehem Star.

O tender are my thoughts of them;
So utterly they're gone
That all their monument is now
My grieving heart forlorn.

And when that heart shall cease to grieve,
They will be quite forgot:
O luckless Dead that shall not live
On earth, when I do not!

Forgive, forgive, O mighty Dead!
For in life's deepening night
Brief is my candle, but you shine
In far eternal light.

REUNION

On a shore remote and fair
Gleam those well beloved forms
In the glory spirits wear;
Beautiful beside the sea,
From all care and sorrow free
As that shore is free from storms.

O to join that radiant band,—
That were joy no tongue could tell!
O that I with them might stand,
Free at last from mortal chains,
From life's fevers and its stains,
With the hearts that love me well.

Ah, to meet them I am fain;
And the marvel yet may be:
I shall know them once again;
They shall meet me as of yore
On that far and shining shore,
By that blue celestial sea.

THE TIDINGS

When first the tiding came that she was dead,
Loud were the lamentations that we made
That her young beauty suddenly should fade.
"She was a bride a year ago," we said.
"Her little firstborn son she never knew."
"Her husband dear, how shall he be consoled?"
"Alas for love's rich story, not half told—
So beautiful she was, so brave, so true!"

Yet, on afterthought, happy is she!
Her heart unwearied, and her joy unspent,
A flower of the Maytime yet to be,
In all her dewy loveliness she went . . .
Perfect the life that leaves us at its close
Only the fragrance of the morning rose.

FLIGHT SONG

O Sister, Sister, now the night is closing,
And no stars shine;
The pine-crests blue are misty in the rain . . .
What light is on your face, or joy, or pain,
Sweet Sister mine?

O Sister, Sister, softly the night cometh,
Deep and divine.
What is the mystic garment that you wear?
And that—that strange white flower in your hair?
Sweet Sister mine?

No voice will answer and no hand touch mine
Through all the lonely years;
For, far across the dim and ancient night,
A Spirit speeds with the celestial flight
She had in other spheres.

FAREWELL

When the rose fails, or when I see the form
O Beauty fading, with no help to stay;
Or days of azure darkening into storm,
Or glory into gloom swept far away;
When what was tender grace is grace no more,
And what was swiftness can no longer run,
Or be appareled in the gleams it wore,
O then, rejoicing, I rember One

Who left me in her loveliness and light,
Fair on that frontier where all radiance fails,
Her beauty sovereign as she sank from sight;
As on a sumptuous summer night, when sails
The white-winged moon adown the hyacinth deep,
A tryst with God in other lands to keep.

403

ELEGY McCLELLANVILLE CEMETERY

I

The village faces on the wide
Green-waving marsh that fronts the sea;
There in the coastline's curving side
It nestles white and tenderly.

Behind it are the pine woods dim,
Whose fragrance through the night is borne
To where the salt sea-waters brim
Long beaches with dark sedges strewn.

I see the long white street that runs
From east to west, from morn to night,
A pathway for the splendid suns,
That ends in yonder vista bright.

I see the cedars dwarfed and dim,
The locusts smelling of the seas,
The red moon on the marsh's rim,
The purple night above the trees.

By day the shell-road dazzles bright,
By dark it glimmers softly down
To where the warm high-water light
Is gleaming just beyond the town.

II

The salt creek runs into the woods,
There where the dark swamp-water flows;
Through silvery sweet-bay solitudes,
And under many a wild wood rose.

Far up where tide and wood-stream meet,
And under pure, serener skies,
In dreadful dreamless slumbers sweet
The village Cemetery lies;

Black waters rim that mystic land;
And groups of thoughtful pines emerge
From the long, lonely pinewood strand,
To loom and listen on the verge.

The flood and ebb are passing by,
The live-oaks dip them in the stream;
Here joy, and love, and living lie,—
And there,—that ancient, ancient dream!

The little child is sleeping there,
With many a heart we loved and knew;
The Village Beauty tall and fair,
At last beside her lover true.

The chaste white hearts of innocence,
And they whose lives bore many scars,
Alike await their bearing thence
Beyond the sunset and the stars.

III

When through the cedar-trees the sun
Above the marsh was hanging red,
When labor for the day was done,
And hearts by home were comforted;

Then watched we by the cedar-trees
The birds in homeward happy flight,
And heard the far soft surf of seas
Break on the borders of the night.

Above the faint horizon-rim,
We watched the twilight shadows creep,
Or on the high-tide's opal brim
We sang the summer moon to sleep.

We felt the strong tide drawing full,
And saw the stranded sedges start;
'Twas high tide, bright and beautiful,
And love's high tide within the heart.

IV

If only now upon this coast
The dear dimmed faces that we love
Might tell of living love unlost,
And as of old beside us move;

405

Then we should walk in Paradise,
Through golden light the happy day;
For they were heaven to our eyes . . .
But God has taken them away.

Ah, what to them is love's spring cry,
Or birdsong in the time of bloom?
What memories mount toward that still sky
From that dim land beneath the tomb?

On that still place the sunlight sleeps,
The grasses wave, the pine-cones fall;
The heavy-tasseled woodbine weeps,
And silence stretches over all.

V

In God's own time we pass away:
The weak, the strong, the false, the brave:
Life's morning gives; life's twilight gray
Shall gather what the morning gave.

Yet Love, the holy and divine,
Shall perish not with mortal breath;
Pure love, strong love, all life is thine,
And thou art not fulfilled in death!

For in life's dusk there shall be light;
Not sunset's only, or the vast
Starry magnificence of night,
But all our earthly darkness passed.

MYSTIC FANE

Afar in longing's shadowy domain
Glimmers the beauty of a mighty fane
To the elect of sorrow dedicate:
Lovers who part too soon—or meet too late.

THE BUILDER

When I was young and strong,
Of joy I made a song.
It did not live for long;
It could not last.
It took mysterious flight,
Or died of its delight,
Was silenced in that night
We call the Past.

In after, graver years
I make a song of tears.
The music of the spheres
Took up its tone.
Struck from the harp of woe,
It has not lost its glow,
And it shall never know
Oblivion.

Blooms out of bliss I brought,
Flowers of joy I wrought,
Have never come to aught.
They all depart.
But, red from rayless shade,
A rose that cannot fade
Out of my grief I made,
My broken heart.

A king lived, ages gone,
Whom sorrow left forlorn:
He found in losing one
He lost his all.
Yet out of anguish cold,
Beauty that grows not old,
Beauty he built,—behold
The Taj Mahal!

PRISONERS

In silvery loneliness
Like the first star;
In the vast quietness
Where spirits are,
She's in the twilight
On life's last hill,
Among lilies lying,—
More lovely and still
Than they are even;
For they are dying,
And she, in Heaven;
Or where peace is
On that last border,
Where beauty shines serene
Where tumult has been
All through life's long disorder.

To see her for the last,
Tearful come we,—
Prisoners yet!
(Death has not set us free)
Grimed and unpardoned,
Still wearing chains,
Hoof-hearted, heart-hardened,
Condemned to strife,
Sentenced to life . . .
With poignant joy we see
Her gleaming liberty.
Her prison she's fled.
Wherever she's gone
Glory will be.
Clanking come we,—
Who are the Dead,
Not she!

IN AFTER YEARS

In the warm woods a whippoorwill
Is mourning deeply, far away;
Beyond the woods the house is still,
Folded in evening mists of gray.

Beyond the lonely woods it stands,
Beautiful even in decay;
About it lie the summer lands,
As fair as when they went away.

I cannot look for love's own fear,
Knowing it all how it must be:
Dear voices I would no more hear,
Loved faces I could no more see.

Perhaps the ghostly mists would stir
Against my face in mortal pain
For the brave eyes and heart of Her,
For hands that clasp not hands again.

In the dim vista of old years
I see the day when parting fell,
I feel again the parting tears,
I hear the voices of farewell.

They are asleep and shall not wake,
Yet of their dream I am a part,
And thoughts of them forever make
A sanctuary in my heart.

Seeking a face it shall not find,
In fields or on the river-shores,
The melancholy river-wind
Breathes through the rustling sycamores

Of loveliness that cannot last:
The roses bloom, the river flows;
Ah, but the hearts we loved are passed
Beyond the River and the Rose.

Sweet are the pines and sweet the bay;
The glimmering jasmines softly burn
In vain, in vain for them; for they
Come not, nor ever shall return.

MY VILLAGE

Deep shadows on the marshes fall.
The far-off night-birds sadly call;
The sea-winds move in murmuring waves
That break against the dark coast-wall.

Now the fair moon begins to rise
Silent upon the silent skies;
And in its silver, streaming far,
How beautiful my village lies!

Such light is here as lingers o'er
A dear face to be seen no more,
Or lover's farewells, long ago,
Upon a sweet and dreadful shore.

The moonlight on my village gleams.
Filling the land with glowing dreams.
It floods the marshes like a tide.
Seaward the glory of its streams.

Impartially this light is shed:
Here where the blood of life is red;
And fair on yonder hallowed place,
The lonely hill where sleep the Dead.

O Village, dreaming through the night,
So lovely in a land of light!
Soon, soon your hearts, now deep in rest,
Shall waken to the morning bright.

But when, O Master whom we trust,
Shall waken yonder sleeping dust?
For Thou, as everlasting love,
Must come, the Morning of the Just.

JOURNEYS

The sudden journey to a strange far land
Filled her with dread. She loved her little home
Among the hills, and could not understand
Why into alien mountains she must roam.
A deep nostalgia, ere she had to go,
Tortured her heart, and made her wildly yearn
To stay,— the thought of parting hurt her so:
No light in all her dark could she discern.

But when she came into the country feared,
Beautiful were the hills, the flowers, the streams.
On every hand new faithful friends appeared,
Brothers and sisters of her thoughts and dreams.
Ah, Life, we love you. From you we must part;
Nor else shall find the Homeland of the Heart.

DARK GATEWAY

Think not you are the first to enter here.
Than this there is no other way so worn
By myriads. The cruel cross you bear
Unnumbered multitudes have bravely borne.
You shall not lack for many a friend and guide,—
Being not first or last,—and not alone.
For in this mystic country there abide
The hosts of grief,—of which you are but one.

Fear not to enter even a gate so dark;
You'll find yourself in noble company:
Dante and Heloise and Joan of Arc,
And Enoch Arden by his lonely sea.
Their valiant comradeship your heart can have
If, even as they, you will be very brave.

411

THE LONG NIGHT

Night falls upon the Southern coast;
To far shores silence stretches pale;
The grey mist rises like a ghost.

By twilight waters red and lone,
Gaunt vultures plume themselves for rest
Upon bald trees bleached white as bone.

The sighing shore-waves slowly curl,
And by the dim creek's shadowy bends,
Softly the ebb-tide eddies whirl.

The tide is out, the moon is low,
The pines are black against the sky;
I never saw them tower so.

I mark the pines, the mist I mark,
But not the holy face of one
Whom night bore to a deeper dark.

AN ELEGY

A wind blew over the river by night;
　　(O the night wind, and the river-mist!)
A wind blew through the fields at night,
　　And the sleeping flowers kissed.

The wind passed through a garden sweet;
　　(O garden sweet and wistful-wild!)
The night was fair, the wind was sweet;
　　And it kissed a dreaming child.

O wind that passed, O river-mist,
　　O garden sweet and wistful-wild;
O flowers that the night wind kissed;
　　O child, O sleeping child!

412

NIRVANA

My little silver locket
You may have to keep.
I wore it waking,
But now I sleep.

The ring I was wedded with,
The gown I wore,—
I shall never, never
Need them more.

My amethyst pendant,
The brooch I loved best,—
You may have them all:
I have rest.

I have no care now
For any of these:
I have all things,—
Having peace.

My pretty blue taffeta,
My shawl so gay,
That were so dear to me
Yesterday;

My rock crystal necklace,
And Mother's cameo,
That were my treasures
From the long ago;

And my gold bracelet,
And my tall comb;
My bright flower-garden,
My children, my home:—

There's not anything
For which I pine;
I have everything:
Nirvana is mine.

Even my true lover
You may take from me:
I am the bride of
Eternity.

If in the twilight of far time
A love survives the rolling years,
Whose star in darkness is sublime,
That love is theirs.

If there be art that can express
The beauty of divine desire,
That art, in fadeless loveliness,
They can inspire.

Love's immortality serene
In art abides. And those who fell
Are all that mortal love can mean,
Or art can tell.

EBB-TIDE

The moonlight lay along the floor,
Cold on the floor the moonlight lay;
The sleeper's face was in the dark,
Chill crept the moonlight, pale and stark,
To touch his features grey.

The ebb-tide flowed beneath the moon
With floating sedge and cloudy foam;
How deep the midnight shadows lie,
The coast-line pines, how dark and high
About the sleeper's home!

The moonlight slept along the floor,
The moonlight slanted to the bed;
The sleeper stirs not any more,
The moonlight glided from the floor
To gaze upon the dead.

How far beneath the setting moon
Will yonder ebb-tide's bearing be?
How far beyond us is the light
Of faces lost in some strange night,
Beyond what land and sea?

VAIN ARROW

What is it Death stills?
Not one note from the lute
(Making music that thrills)
Of this minstrel is mute.
What brings the soul joy
Time can never destroy.

And how noble to know,
Though a singer may die,
That vainly Death's bow
Made Fate's arrow to fly.
For the lyric lives on
Though the lyrist be gone.

And the beauty of song
That we love and we trust
Shall be young and be strong
When Death's arrow is dust.
Of the gift the heart gives
All the loveliness lives.

O LYRA!

O Lyra, who watches above,
O Lyra, O saw you my Love?
Her flight that my heart only follows?
Her wings would be swift as the swallow's.
Capella, Arcturus, what range
Has her spirit in spaces so strange?
O heard you her coming? There would
Be a hush in your white solitude;
Or music most beautiful there,
To welcome the good and the fair;
And awe that a being so bright
Should come from mortality's night;
And wonder that any who shone
So lovely should venture alone.
O Lyra, who watches above,
O Lyra, O saw you my Love?

NIGHT ON THE COAST

The wind is in the pines,
And a voice in the wind
Grieving of ruined shrines;
Yet what it cannot find
On earth, is in my mind.

A storm moans on the bar,
And will not cease to be;
A lonely western star
Looks on the lonely sea;
Yet love is here with me.

No more the red dawn foams;
No more the pulses start;
The spirit-evening comes,
Yet all that must depart
From life, lives in my heart.

The sea-wind brings the mist,
That shrouds the silent coast;
A dead face I have kissed,
And loved, of all things most,
Is mine, though all be lost.

LYDIA

Than the white peace of the moon,
Than the green calm of the trees,
Than the ancient rest of night,
Than the depth of deepest seas:

More silent than the air,
More quiet than the ground
Is the place that she sought,
Is the peace that she found.

BELOVED

Yes, there is sone one
Waiting at the door;
But it is some one
Who will come no more.

There is his footfall
As it was before,
Echoing forever
Since he comes no more.

Always listening,
Knowing it is vain,
I hear a voice that
Will not sound again.

Yes, there is some one
Always at the door;
For it is some one
Who will come no more.

HER PIANO

We have not heard its music since she went
Who drew from it sidereal melody.
Silent it stands, its quiet eloquent
Of all her lyrics beautiful and free.
A visionary Grace about it fair,
A Presence and a Voice are lingering;
And there's a mystic stillness in the air
As if an angel were about to sing.

Though 'tis no longer played, and stands apart,
There is no instrument more musical:
Its melodies keep choiring in my heart
From silent evenfall to evenfall.
From radiant Mays to snowy wild Decembers
The music that love played true love remembers.

417

ROSALIE

Forth from life's' forest gloom
She faltered like the delicate perfume
Of a wild jasmine bloom.
Her beauty in this world suggested doom:
Sister of all that's fairest and most frail,
Spirit of all that's frangible and pale,
Sure in all strife to fail.
So fragile was she and so fugitive,
Merely in mellow sunshine could she live.
Sweet as the troubled wonder of innocent love,
Only to be alive she meekly strove.
From musky winds with passion dank,
Exhaling from exotic thickets lush,
She shrank,
Timidly amorous
For the Puritan pine-scents and the shining hush
Of dewhung blossom and bush;
Tranced isolation of the windless places,
The leeward beaches of life's summer sea,
The illumined calm of quiet happy faces,
And stilling beauty's grave tranquility.

For her my heart was wary,
Searching for sanctuary;
To keep her from inexorable truth,
From that most bitter ruth
Of the world's rape of beauty, strength, and youth.
How could I shield her, set her free
From Time, love's enemy?
From Death, my rival, dark and masterly?
O was it just
That beauty such as hers should be
Addressed to dim explorings of the dust?
All challenges to me, all grievings were
That life beleaguered her.

Tremendous piers I sank
Windward and northward;
Rank on shielding rank
Ramparts arose to give my love repose;

Barriers with hasty hands fashioning fast,
Grim bulwarks to the blast;
Tall bastions bold,
In ancient quietude of marble cold,
Placid in solemn strength of stone,
To meet the whirlwind's stress
With blank and tacit courage of their own.
Within, sweet winsome trees had made
With the proud sun armistices of shade;
High-walled the gardens were, coverted deep,
Cloistering my Love in radiant loneliness.
There the whole world seemed roses, roses burning,
Beautiful white and red;

Or this way, at her turning,
Gleamed lilies, with star-lilies overhead.
Here fragrances a poignant tryst would keep.
She drank of dreams. I sang her runes of sleep.
The silent living sunlight's long sweet kiss
Was her extremest bliss;
And, shyest soul-recesses to illume,
She had the moonlight's vast and solemn silver bloom.

Jewels she loved; and oft our fancy told
Tales of the starry twilight years of old,
Till Sappho from the sapphire's shore would yearn,
Dark Cleopatra in the ruby burn;
Lost purple tides of old in the amethyst run,
With triremes plunging toward the setting sun.
The sea-moon through the opal's casement shed
Showed Isoult holding valiant Tristram,—dead.
Through the glimmering Sherwood in the beryl hung,
Maid Marian went wandering fair and young.
But my Rosalie,
Turning from them to me
Eyes that behind my love saw not my fear
Believed that all was well if I were near.
And her deep trust's delight
Undid me quite.

Beyond this halcyon pale
I used to see a peasant woman hale,
Ruddy, and muscled like the knotty oak,
A bearer of men children. By the smoke
Of flaring brush-piles I could see her stride,
Powerful in her mighty body's pride;
By the red fireglow primeval shine.
Within warm walls a lily-love was mine.
Always my eager hands
Strove to unloose all bands
That bind the spirit up to pain and care.
I bivouacked with dreads she might not share;
Beyond our threshold slew grim enemies
Obscurely; bargained fast with Fate,
Black challenger importunate!
Crushing with fealty lone a fatal cry,
I fought with beasts she never knew were nigh.
My spirit oft
Become a watcher by still treacherous doors,
A listener for footfalls fell and soft,
A warder on the tranquil perilous walls,
A sentry with eyes sweeping the far moors,
A guard of beauty in fair desolate halls;
Fathoming the blue day with danger bright,
Patrolling deep the phantom-haunted night.

But God,—
Discerning all my tottering castle fair,
My impotent gardens rare,
My mortal serving of immortal need
Gave heed:
With mercy swift, relentless, sweet,
Almighty, meet,
Terribly toward my jasmine blossom strode.
He could foresee the fall
Of ramparts ineffectual,
And powerful vain piers.
Aware
Of all her care;

Aware not less
Of all my helplessness,
He suddenly wrought
What my imagination all the years
Had never dreamed or thought:
An isolation vast and shining brought,—
Peace,
Which was release
From the inexorable chains I could not sever,
Making her free forever.

God's dark Deliverer
Has taken her;
And on the shadowy tender vale
Where beat her timid heart and frail,
Darkness is set, and rest.
O it is best
That she
Should be
A rose of the darkness no dreaming
Dawn-wind shall shake,
A lily of slumber no streaming
Dawn-gleam awake!

She's of the night;
Of the dark mysteries;
Of vanished delight;
Of twilight and of tears;
Of the Nirvana-years;
Of perished lips and hands;
Of the long-ago;
Of buried bliss and woe;
Of far forsaken lands;
Of old forgotten seas;
Of stars and silences;
But bride of love to be
In my heart's eternity
Is she,
My Rosalie.

HER RETURN

If ever a garden discloses
A red rose more red
Than a red rose should be,—
A rose of all roses,
That might be she.
Or if deep in the wildwood
You happen to see
Wild fragrant azaleas
In flaunting array,
A beautiful throng,—
But one loveliest of all,
Making their beauty a silence,
Her beauty a song,
That would be she:
She would return that way,
Looking for me,
Long, long before
Her Resurrection Day.

LONGING

Deep in the swamp an owlish light is gleaming;
Gray loneliness here makes her sombre throne.
Faintly the star-beams through the trees are
    streaming.
Silence is here, and silence is alone.
Upon the waters dead a stillness broods,
And centuries of dead leaves strew the ground.
If there's a soul here, it is Solitude's;
What here is lost shall nevermore be found.

Most desolate to me had been this place;
But now, on crowded streets, in happy throngs,
I am as lonely for a vanished face
For which my heart with deathless fervor longs
As on this last land of life's last lone shore,
Weeping for one whom I will see no more.

THE HATCHMENT

Lover of sky and of star and of tree,
Lover of pinewood, of seabeach and sea,
Lover of freedom, and all that is free.

With every bird will his spirit take flight;
With every flower expand into light;
With every star will illumine the night.

Beauty's his love; and his longing foregoes
Power and glory, and wealth with its woes,
For gladness of starshine, or river and rose.

Wildwoods and waters lone his feet discover;
Loveliness luring him, holding him ever
Close to her dewy breast, close as a lover.

Ever the flesh for the spirit forsaking,
Ever of beauty's wild wonder partaking,
Life has for him been a joyous awaking.

Over my sleeping what hatchmen shall be?
Only the loveliness dearest to me:
Only the sky and the star and the tree.

BABY JEAN

Bring not to her white roses,
Though she was fair as they;
Nor lay the lily in her hand,
Nor any blossoming spray—
Unless its flower opens
And closes in a day.

Of what shall come tomorrow
She never knew the pain.
Bring her the briefest blossoms:
Like her an hour they reign,
And then their beauty tires
And turns to sleep again.

423

LAST BIVOUAC

The army tented here will march no more.
These soldiers have lain down to dreamless rest.
Oblivion has veiled each tired breast,
Nor shall Tomorrow their array restore.
Heedless of further ventures to explore,
They have abandoned every mortal quest;
By Sleep's compassion they are dispossessed
Of all the banners and the arms they bore.

They are in love with stillness. Captains lie
Mindless at last of martial sight or sound.
This host is covered by quiescence deep.
There is no bugle and there is no cry
Can wake them from the slumber they have found.
—Even the sentinels are fast asleep.

THE FADING

Again, the occult Night, the delphic Dawn;
Like lofty veils their bridal rainbows hang.
But what had been my wonder is withdrawn;
They cannot sing to me what once they sang.
They flame; they fade . . . Once all my heart they had
Their flowery lips caressed; a child I lay
Upon their blossomy bosoms and was glad,
As into fairylands I dreamed away.

Ah, splendors that for me no longer shine!
Your hand, O Love, drawing the curtain by
Of loveliness mysterious, made it mine;
I was an intimate of eternity . . .
But Beauty's banners, flushing all the world,
At one far trumpet suddenly were furled.

MARY ELLIOTT SEABROOK

She waited; but she waits no more;
A prisoner long, she has release;
For death conferred what life denied
Of perfect peace.

That she who knew pain's wakefulness
Should now have sleep in certain bliss;
And that her brave and tired heart
Quiescent is.

With Love we thought to guard her well;
But cruel fellowships she knew
With Sorrow and with Suffering
The long years through.

What mortal hope or faith or joy
Can never on our lives bestow,
The peace we long for,—it is hers
At last, we know.

Beyond the touch of time and tears,
Beyond the grasp of grief she's gone,
To be attended evermore
By Love alone.

VALE

Here lies a hunter,
Whose last hunt ended in rest;
A singer, whose last song
Is silence blest.
Nor ever again
Shall he be seen or heard,—
Unless some word
He sang, shall in the years to be
Make some heart yearn;
Not otherwise shall he return
From the far lands of sleep,
And their dim stillness deep.

COME HOME

The ship to her haven,
The sun to her west,
The bird to her mountain,
My love to her rest.

The white dawn shall waken
In beauty for her;
The dew shall be gleaming,
But she shall not stir.

The wild bird shall warble,
The stream carol clear,
The wind wave the willow,
But she shall not hear.

The deer will go trooping
Through the glimmering brake—
The whole world shall waken,
But she shall not wake.

THE GREAT COMPASSION

Not as the rose of dawn, her heart revealing,
Arrives the future. Occult and unknown,
On shadowy steps through shadows she comes stealing;
Darkness she is, and silence is her tone.
Inviolate, invisible, approaching
As incommunicable mystery,
She has no prelude to her joys to sing,
She hints no glimmer of her tears to be.

Ah, pitying veil that hides from us our fate!
Tomorrow in tremendous night reposes.
We see not death till he is at the gate.
Which kiss is last, O Love, no fear discloses.
We never know which star is ultimate,
Or recognize the rose that ends our roses.

TIDINGS

The Land of Trouble is an ancient land,
Familiar to all hearts. Its vales and hills
Are worn by travelers, who understand
The music of its wailing whippoorwills,
The depth of its dim rivers, and the sweep
Of lonely starlit ranges. Naught remains
Unknown to all: its dark defiles and deep,
The silence of its stark satiric plains.

Breathe not to others of your journey far
Into a country that they know too well;
But if, as from some tremulous mystic star,
You come from Joy, its wonder to them tell!
Beyond all hills of sorrow, vales of fear,
Lies that lost land of which they long to hear.

SONG OF THE NIGHT

In the deep of night,
From the double darkness of a shadowy pine,
A mockingbird awoke and sang
And slept again.
Like a lone light,
Or joy after pain,
Or a star when no others shine,
Or a voice of love that lonely music rang.

I once had dreams of fame,
And an immortal name,
Yet that was not to be.
Now it would make all plain
If you but said of me,
"To darkness, fear, and pain,
From life's deep-shadowed tree,
He woke, and sang, and slept again."

THE FLOWERING

As a wild day that's drawing toward its close,
A day of wind and rain and stormy sun,
Will, at its ending, blossom like the rose,
Serene and beautiful, its anguish done;
And we who marvel at such majesty,
Resplendent in its silence and its sleep,
Now that its warfare's over, only see
Triumphant peace, far-flowering vast and deep.

So one we knew was always danger's mark:
He was forever into peril going,
With thunder and with lightning and the dark,
The horns of lifelong battle for him blowing.
Yet ere the night his glory flowered in view,—
A spirit more illustrious than we knew.

WESTERN WAY

Yes, O my Dear, this is the Western Way:
No more for us the Orient shall glow
Rosy with dawn and flushed with coming day,
For we descend and into darkness go
With withered dreams and thoughts grown gently gr
With autumn and with sunset. Hither flow,
Deep through this valley where the night-winds blow
Proud silent streams to Silence borne away.

Yes, O my Dear, and though our tears must start
In piteous anguish at the nearing end,
God gives us one brave handclasp ere we part,
(O silent separation, friend from friend!)
And quiets longing ere the shades descend,
And we are taken, faithful, heart from heart.

THOUGH I AM FORSAKEN

Though I am forsaken as a bridegroom is forsaken
Who has lost his own beloved upon their wedding day;
Though my heart of sorrow as of venom has partaken;
Though the ramparts of my life be to their bases shaken,
Yet one thought has peace enough my anguish to allay:

Long may be my waiting, and the thought of it be longer;
Deep may be the darkness; very far and wild the way;
Though life's desert I must cross, and know its thirst and
    hunger,
You are safe with One who says (this is what makes me
    stronger),
"A thousand years within My sight are but as yesterday."

THE NATURE OF LOVE

True love is never variable or vain.
Its arias have an everlasting strain.
It is mysterious and very wise.
It opens Delphic doors and windows wide
On other lands, on other angel skies.

What is so very different that is ours?
Strange music makes melodious the hours.
Ours is the home of virtue's beauty vernal;
We walk with stars, and stroll through heaven's wildflowers,
While all about us everything's eternal.

WEDDING RING

Though it is thin and pale and old,
Once did this ring my world enfold;
Worn by a hand I cannot hold
Until my years, like hers, are told.
See, it is worn, as you behold,
Yet it is still a ring of gold.

EVELYN'S BIRTHDAY

Here from the hill serene
I gaze on the valley below;
Sweet o'er the quiet scene
The south winds come and go.
Far in the valley there stands
A tree clothed white as a bride,
Tremulous in the spring lands,
Spiritual, glorified.

What is thy message to me,
Beautiful child of the sun?
Why should I look on thee,
Seeing not one who is gone?
Thy misty halo of bloom
Seems a celestial light,
A glory out of the tomb,
A radiance out of the night.

Thou art the answer I sought
Over the land and the sea!
Love, by thy beauty taught,
Shall rise, a spirit like thee;
Rise in the light of the faith,
Ever in light to abide,
Stronger than life and than death,
Spiritual, glorified.

Aye, we will trust to the end,
Praying for patience and grace.
Father, Saviour, and Friend,
Thou wilt show us her face.
Though all about us we hear
Voices ceasing to sing,
Accents fainting in air,
Perishing, perishing;
Yet will we trust Thee, for Thou
Hast never forsaken Thine own,
Wilt not forsake us now.

This is the day of her birth—
(Lord how Thy years go by
With sorrow and change on the earth!)
Let faith not fail and die.
Master, teach us to bear
Parting this little while,
Parting of hands;
Not of light or of love,
Only of seas and of lands;
Only earth's flowers and foam,
Not of heart and of home!
And her beauty seems ever the same:
Faith has visioned her grace,
Hope has called her by name,
Love has remembered her face.

BRIDE OF THE NIGHT

In a glimmering harbor
Anchored she lies:
Under her, deep waters;
Over her, deep skies.

Mirrored and mystical,
Snowy sails furled,—
Happy, quiescent, tall,—
Not of this world.

Now beyond time and tide,
Oceans and bars,
She's of eternity,
Twilight and stars.

Sister of silences,
Sweetheart of light,
Beautiful Spirit,
Bride of the Night.

431

THE DIFFERENCE

That may be a break
In the old rail fence
Down in the daisied meadow.
Or it may be just a shadow.
You know,
By the cool brook
Where the big blackberries grow.
Anyway, I think I ought to go
Down to the fence and take a look.

I see a kingbird circling
Over the wild cherry tree
Close by the stream down there.
I guess he has somewhere
In that tall tree a nest.
—But who cares about an old rail fence?
You come with me for a rest,
For comradeship is always best.
Save love, all is pretense.
Love makes life's difference.

THE MASTER OF HAMPTON

He, beneath the strewn leaves lying,
Heeds no more the season's call;
Sees no more the green leaf growing,
Or the red leaf fall.

Hears no more the valiant Morning
Challenge him to conflict brave;
Is content with some immortal
Gift that Evening gave.

Looks no more to stream and blossom,
Hears the mockingbird no more;
Now, beyond the rose and river,
And earth's fartherest shore.

And so calmly he is sleeping
Under leaf-strewn quiet loam
That I know his heart is dreaming
Of its Hampton home.

And of him his home seems dreaming;
Yet its beauty cannot be
As it was before he left it
Whose brave heart was home to me.

THE FLOWER

Fairest she was, and first to pass away,
A flower folded in God's twilight peace;
She is beyond the trouble of the world.

A lily of the valleys, yet she knew
The fair immortal grief of setting stars,
The desperate courage on the desperate way.

For her our sun and stars shall rise no more;
The flower of her face a far land knows,
And other fields the lily of her brow.

CARLYLE McKINLEY

(In Lucem Transitus, August 24, 1904.)

I.

An autumn shore, with white waves rolling far
    In silent foam; the failing of the light;
Blue league on misty league to dusk's first star,
    Beyond a sad sea-sunset and the night.

These scenes were dear to him who loved the heart,
    The fragrant rose and alabaster dawn,
Life's frail, dim sweetness, early to depart,
    The thought of days that are forever gone.

II.

Alas for them who in the twilight harken
    For some stilled voice; ah, no, it cannot be;
The winds will moan, the heavens slowly darken,
    And the deep music sound out of the sea—

Yet those who oft remember in the night,
    After day's tumult with its feverish plans,
Oh, well for them!—God's stars shed down the light
    Of some diviner sympathy than man's.

III.

The solemn live-oaks watch above the Dead
    Whose spirit dies not, but a sacred flame,
Burns fair as when it first interpreted
    The fearful beauty of forgotten fame.

Where then is sorrow's strength, and where death's power
    Life's soldiers fall where riddled standards wave;
A soldier fell, free from our fears, from our
    Imaginary anguish of the grave.

IV.

Our passionate regrets he wove in song,
    The pangs of loss for "Swift, sweet yesterday,"
On the night's margin where life's echoes throng,
    And where the sound of singing dies away.

.434

The thought of those o'er whom the shadows close
    The heart's deep evening sanctuary stills,
As a wild river hushes when it flows
    Through immemorial silence in the hills.

V.

We feel his strength when mortal nobleness
    Approaches us as mystery or truth;
His music luring us to tears no less
    Then when we saw, with dimming eyes, in youth,

An autumn shore, with white waves rolling far
    In spirit foam; the dying of the light;
Pale league on azure league to dusk's first star,
    Beyond a sad sea-sunset and the night.

O, STRANGER!

O, Stranger, you have come from her!
How wonderful you seem
Just to have known my Darling!
Now with her light you gleam.
As one who brings from travel
An air of beauty seen,
Reflecting far the glory
Of lands where he has been—
So, Stranger, you are tinted
With wonder not your own:
You wear a trembling beauty
Because of one you've known—
Transfigured by the magic
Of one who is to me
The meaning of the starlight
On an enchanted sea.

THE OLD SOUTH

Far silent country where the white stars shine
On slumbrous river and on dreaming pine,
Art thou the land my heart has loved and known,
    Even my own
    Sweet silent country?

Sweet land, sweet land, I see the grey years creep
Shadow on shadow; and for deeper sleep
Thy dark eyes close. And I am left alone,
    My lost, my own
    Far silent country.

With faint, cold lilies has thy hair been crowned;
Thy pale brow with the purple nightshade bound;
Soft over thee the winds of sleep have blown,
    Over my own
    Sweet silent country.

THE MUSIC OF TOMORROW

The lovers who have lived in song and story,
Sorrow have known. Proud Lancelot, Guinivere,
The Queen who is the everlasting glory
Of ancient Nile,—unhappy though they were
Are now immortal. They who knew the dark,—
Lucia, Dante, Juliet, Abelard,
Isoult, tall consort of the cruel Mark,
Are the beloved of minstrel and of bard.

To others, joy can never join us fast:
By immemorial anguish are we wed;
Now in this moment as deep in the past,
From their eternal wounds we, too, have bled.
Grieve not for lovers who are marred by sorrow.
Of them shall be the music of tomorrow.

THE WESTERN WAY

Down the declivity into glimmering lands,
With quiet songs and tender farewell air;
Down with autumn of our little year,
With hearts subdued, and worn and weary hands;
On to life's margin with its moaning sands,
All doubt behind; it is too late to fear;
We are too tired now to know or care,
Yet the still soul at evening understands.

Behind us, twilight gathers, dim and gray,
And darkness deepens on the path before.
Love leads us through the night as through the day,
As we press on, whatever is in store.
There's light upon the mountains far away,
And Faith stands sentry by the Shadowy Door.

ARLINGTON

The army tented here will march no more.
These soldiers have lain down to dreamless rest.
Oblivion has veiled each tired breast,
Nor shall Tomorrow their array restore.
Heedless of further ventures to explore,
They have abandoned every mortal quest;
By Sleep's compassion they are dispossessed
Of all the banners and the arms they bore.

They are in love with stillness. Captains lie
Mindless at last of martial sight or sound.
This host is covered by quiescence deep.
There is no bugle and there is no cry
To wake them from the slumber they have found.
—Even the sentinels are fast asleep.

LISTENERS

I saw one listening to a mystic strain
Of music . . . And her spirit, long concealed,
Not ever manifest in joy or pain,
Stole to her face, and was in light revealed.
For all the secret beauty of her heart,
And all she might have been, and longed to be
Transfigured her into a soul apart,
Radiant at last, and beautiful, and free.

Again I saw her, when earth's melodies
She heard no more; when to her trancèd face
Death bade the glimmering spirit to arise
In all the beauty of eternal grace . . .
Hearing great music from the gates of Heaven
Alone could give the majesty thus given.

REQUIESCAT

The long and liquid rustling of the corn,
May touch thine ear, attuned to waving lines:
The mortal sighing of the perfumed pines
May reach thy heart in some red autumn dawn:
But kindred earthly longings will be gone.
And each day's sun, and every star that shines,
Discerning Silence and the breathless signs
Of Quiet, singing softly, will pass on.

Naught will thy spirit feel to break repose,
It is so sweet to lie at length in peace!
No sound, though tremulous of the mating dove,
Will bring a yearning for thy sleep to cease:
No sight to lure, not even yonder rose,
Thorn-throned in mystic ecstacy of love.

SLEEP SONG

The live-oak holds his leaves till spring.
About the time when they are falling,
I hear the tawny woodthrush sing.
For aught to die when love is calling,
And every heart is on the wing,
Is a most contradictory thing.

Yet when they earthward drift, to keep
With night a dim eternal tryst,
They dream to music strange and deep
From the grave woodland elegist.
And for their fate I cannot weep
Since Love is singing them to sleep.

ABIDING ROSE

If the foundation had not been of stone,
There had remained no vestige of the place
Where stood the house. The stones supplied a trace,
In that wild wood by thickets overgrown.
Yet there was more to make a memory known,
Giving it fragrance and the color of grace,
Almost a voice,—almost a joyous face,—
Such is the power of loveliness alone.

For close beside the ruin, a red rose
Burned in the wilderness, as if to prove
How beautiful remains, when all else goes,
The sacred and eternal flame of love.
I had not dreamed there could be, till that hour,
Such revelation by a lonely flower.

439

A MOUNTAIN GRAVE

I came upon a cabin in the hills
Long since deserted, and was passing by
When a rude headstone caught my vagrant eye.
And stilled me as all sudden pathos stills.
A standstone mountain-boulder marks the grave
And on it had been painted with red paint,
OUR DARLING . . .
Weather-worn and sprawled and faint,
The letters still their radiant message gave.

Then over me, the sleeping hills around,
And this child sleeping near me as I stood,
There came a sense of peace and joy profound
To find love's altar in dim solitude . . .
Nor is there a memorial that affords
A tribute deeper than those poignant words.

TO ONE ASLEEP

Just as a star blooms out above the deep,
Deep lustral silence of a holy hour;
Just as the dream of some immaculate flower,
    Beside still waters in the fields of sleep.

Just as a star that disappears at dawn,
Leaving a mystic halo where it burned
Passed to the bourne of Beauty Undiscerned,
    Passed from earth's sight yet not forever
        gone.

Just as a star sinks in the sweet excess
Of rose-and-silver dawn within the sky;
Just as a thought that is too fair to die,
    Lives in the heart as Unseen Loveliness.

HER SLEEP

Now she at least is sleeping; let her be,
For who would wake her from her perfect rest?
Who would imprison her, now she is free?
Let her sleep on in beauty. It is best.
What would we have to offer, should she wake,
To make amends for all the peace she yields?
Now she lies happy; let us, for love's sake,
Turn for her to our lonely mortal fields.

And she has joy supernal in this sleep:
The hand of fear shall never touch her more
Hope cannot reach her past those waters deep;
And should Love follow to that glimmering shore,
All his compassion has not one caress
To make her long to leave this quietness.

THE CHILD NEVA

God had decided on her hour:
He took her just before her flower
Had opened. She, her life to keep,
Did give it Him, and fell asleep;
Nor murmured she, nor understood. . . .
So fades from off the lips a smile;
So dies, nor leaves a trace the while,
The song of birds in yonder wood.

THE NUN

To God alone austerely she's addressed,
An awful Lily on her futile breast;
While to her icy mount she gladly goes,
Fades in the valley her forsaken Rose.

441

THE MINGLING

The pines begin their sighing once again.
Their tremulous harps by unseen fingers swept
Give utterance to ancient human pain.
Now may you feel the tears that Jesus wept;
Now hear the loud lamentings of old Lear;
Now dauntless David by his grief dismayed;
Now Edith wailing Harold. And I hear,
Amid loud flames, the silence of the Maid.

Melted and merged in universal woe,
A part of all humanity has borne,
My sorrow, like those griefs of long ago,
The loving pines compassionately mourn.
My infelicity in Man's is lost
Amid the sighing of the pine-tree host.

GUARDIAN SPIRITS

Here they laid the Pharaoh deep,
Sleeping his eternal sleep,
In his dusky splendor hid
Far beneath his pyramid.
Round his quartz sarcophagus
Stand four figures beauteous,
Carved in bas relief. Their wings,
Far extended, touch. This brings
Safety to the soul they ward.
Goddesses are they who guard
In that World this world beneath,
Nepthys, Selkit, Isis, Neith.

Guardian Spirits, we would plead
For your aid in our own need.
Let your mystic beauty hold us,
With your shielding wings enfold us;
For the fate the Pharaohs met,
Unallayed, is with us yet.
There are grievous shades to blind us,
Paths where never a friend can find us.
Spirits of the long ago,
Your compassion we would know
In that World this world beneath,
Isis, Selkit, Nepthys, Neith.

442

The Valiant

MOUNTAIN MEADOWS

All through this flowering fragrant land
Let lovers dance and sing and laugh.
They know not I am close at hand:
This wildrose is my epitaph.

These mountain meadows that they see
Might by their beauty represent
To all who follow after me
By loving will and testament.

Still shall this sandy creek flow on, . . .
Another boy, another girl,
Long after you and I are gone
Will hear these gentle waters purl.

These hills that tower in the blue
Will tower on through all the years,
Will look in vain for me and you;
Yet, Darling, have no doubts or fears.

For He who reared the mountains' height
And set the stream to course this field,
Has all there is of heavenly might,
And to no other power need yield.

We have His love,—we know not why,
But know it is of mercy made.
He is the Lord of earth and sky,
The Sovereign of the light and shade.

He knows love's high mysterious art;
And though our joys and hopes grow dim,
He's master of the human heart,
And we can trust our years to Him.

On earth He gives us love and peace,
And gives us grace all grief to bear;
Nor shall His caring for us cease
At any time, or anywhere.

Our faith knows well His love will care
For us, wherever we may go;
And in His glory we may share
For all we know, for all we know.

CHRISTMAS EVE ON THE RAPIDAN
(1863)

Hal looked to the left, and he looked to the right,
And he looked where the sycamore glimmered white.
The night was asleep, and his regiment slept,
While over his comrades a watch he kept.

The Rapidan smiled when, clear of cloud,
The moon poured her orchid love-light proud.
Hal thought of Bess . . . "I believe I can see
To read the little Book she gave to me."

From his grimy knapsack by his side he took
His love-gift copy of the Sacred Book.
"Bess begged me to carry it over my heart,
But it's been in my knapsack from the start."

It was Christmas Eve on the Rapidan,
And Hal stood reading of the Perfect Man;
Of Bethlehem's Star, and of Mary mild;
Of shepherds and angels and the little Christ Child.

From the glimmering tree by the river's shore
A rifle's sight on the sentry bore.
By the selfsame light that let Hal read
A sharpshooter steadied him for his deed.

A dry branch cracked on the ghostly tree,
And a shot rang wildly and instantly.
At the crack of the branch, Hal the Story thrust
Into his bosom,—then writhed to the dust.

The surgeon was musing: "A woman, they say,
Can keep safe her loved one far away . . .
Hal will come around . . . Now, who but a lover
Would sew steel stays in a Bible's cover?"

THE OLD GUNNER

Cap'n, he's took the bridge . . . Lay the gun
    true!
That's what a sea-fight calls on us to do.
We are their target,—see?
Cap'n the bullseye be.
Where's danger, there is he.
Lay the gun true!

God, there's a matey gone! Lay the gun true!
Slam this one howling home over the blue!
Make matey's answer shout:
That's all to think about;
Give them a cordite clout,
Lay the gun true!

Brave lads! . . . They've done for me . . .
    Lay the gun true!
That's what the Service expects us to do.
And though I miss on the fun,
Now that they are on the run,
Thank God, my part I've done:
Laid a gun true!

SAY NOT THERE IS NO MORNING

Say not there is no morning and no lark;
That all about us is no prospect save
The deep and incommunicable dark.
What makes a heaven of hell is being brave.
Unworthy of him is our least repining;
To teach us how to bear, he nobly bore.
He is a Glory; and on us is shining
A light that never shone on us before.

Nor on us only: any one believing
In honor will his story vindicate.
Every true heart's his heritage receiving,
For he is more than ours: with the great
Of sacrifice he stands,—his valor leaving
To all mankind its infinite estate.

WE ARE THERE

I

Glory can never fade into the Past;
Because of its own splendor it will last:
Still stands the sun above Mt. Gibeon,
And motionless the moon o'er Ajalon.
Even now Leonidas his foes defies,
And now Columbus our New World descries.

II

We to oblivion the Nile might give,
But Cleopatra's beauty makes it live.
This day, this hour the maid of Orleans gleams
Celestial vision of our noblest dreams.
Still Agincourt is being fought: the fight
Won by a touch of Harry in the night.

III

And Spain's Armada, formidably great
Meets, at this moment, brave Sir Francis Drake.
Across the Delaware to Trenton's shore.
Our Washington keeps crossing evermore.

IV

Still Pocahontas saves her lover true.
Still Wellington stands calm at Waterloo.

V

As glorious in the sky as any star
Nelson transfigures for us Trafalgar.
Fame flames forever on life's valiant hill;
For glory that has been is glory still.
And we who think that what we are is lost
May memorable make the Future's coast.

TO A THRUSH

(Heard singing on the Princeton campus—June, 1917)

I.

Delicious-throated bird,
With dewy tones suggesting fragrant fens
And ferny glimmering wildwoods. I have heard
Thy song like waters far cascading down deep glens
But in this crisis it must be
Silent, or else a bugle blowing for Liberty!
This is the hour for the trumpet, not the lute;
Therefore be mute.
In solemn skies our martial banner gleams;
Great armies now are tenting in our dreams;
For we have drawn the blade Damascan, bright,
That shall his hammer huge from Woden smite,
Restoring to a blackened world the sovereignty of Lig
Under no festal arch with glowing flowers dight
To melodies like thine we go.
Ah, no!
In sternest grandeur of the Right,
Stark, epic, mighty is our going,
Past all your thought of knowing,
Delicate lyrist of the throbbing note;
Sweet elegist of Evening and the deep
Places of peace that fringe the realm of Sleep.

II.

Thine is a song for lovers who have grieved,
For hearts and minds bereaved;
For those whom too much joy makes strangely sad;
For those whom grief divine makes strangely glad.
These by thy music made serene and free
Have gleaned in life their immortality,
Visioning through the gates of song that other life to
But in this hour,—desist!
The moonlight and the mist,
Thy song whose twilight glamour once allured,
Vanish in clear sun.
Our time of dreaming's done.
Our song is in the sword!

III.

What, by my hard words undismayed?
Still singing in thy dewy dim retreat,
Sweet with wild fragrance and with music sweet?
Of my cool censure unafraid?
Still with resplendent song, in death's despite,
Brimming life's lustral chalice of delight?
—How radiantly thy certain spirit runs,
Through glooms titanic wrought by setting suns,
Or in rapt splendor fares
Up shimmering sapphire stairs,
Starlike to the loftiest throne of thought?
—Shy Minstrel, have I heard thy song aright?
That melting note, its meaning have I caught?
Some everlasting theme I can divine:
Thine seems the language of eternal light;
The music of immortal love is thine.
No sordid grief or joy is in that tone,
Whose song is of triumphant strength alone!

IV.

Ah, let us hear thy song,
Its triumph still prolong!
For in it sounds that clear victorious tone,
Terrible to every tyrant's trembling throne:
The music by our soldiers' heart-song made,
Music of beautiful manhood unafraid!
—O Singer, hid, serene,
This is thy joy, I ween,
This is thy lyric peace: the calm of Right,
That in the fevered battle's height
Alone can mean
Resistless might!

VISION IN THE VALLEY

Condemned to encounter sorrow's sword of flame,
Into the Valley all alone I came
(Into the Valley one must come alone),
A solitary place of sand and stone,
Had no one been in this wild place before?
Had no one borne the burden that I bore?

But there were mortal tracks in the waste sand
Of this incredibly grim and lonely land.
It was as if, even from the long ago,
Here battles must have wavered to and fro.
All, all humanity before my day,
Predestined to meet grief, had passed this way.

And then the meaning of it dawned to me:
Life is a land of old catastrophe.
Not an alien I, but only come at last
Where all who have preceded me have passed.
And here and there, and round and round about
Valor had challenged Grief, and fought it out.

By grim old relics I became aware
That many a heart, grief-stricken, had been here.
Here lay abandoned, by tall peaks of doom,
Hacked lordly helms, sword, shield, and lance, and plume
Hung on a thorn by a mournful mountain-side
Was a withered rose that had been worldly pride.

Sorrow was the wild foe they had to slay;
And, having triumphed, they have gone away
Into a land where peace is lord forever;
Where, for this desert, they have found a river;
For conflict, calm,—serene and glad and strong;
And for grief's stillness, love's triumphant song.

HOW SOME THEIR GRIEF ADORE

When I behold how some their grief adore,
And to it rear their vain barbaric shrines,
And worship there, and find their sorrow more
Than living friends and love, my heart divines
Corruption in their spirits. For the Dead
Need us no more, since they have reached a state
Beyond the mortal. O let it be said
Loss is life's challenge to us to be great.

Aye, mourn I may, but none shall ever know;
And all the might of sorrow will I bend
To high endeavor. Forward will I go,
Making grief's strength my power to ascend . . .
If I surrender not unto my woe,
Anguish shall be my ally and my friend.

AUTUMN ROSE

There's beauty of the spring and of beginning;
Of innocence, all alien to pain;
A burgeoning of youth and love; a winning
Felicity unfought for to attain;
Artless Arcadian loveliness and joy,
Ingenuous, and aweless of the years;
The laughter and the light of girl and boy,
Naive of life, and guileless of her tears.

But beauty's crown is valor. When I see
A rose in autumn, in a dying world,
I say in tribute: "Though the enemy
Is hard at hand, with fateful flags unfurled,
There stands a soldier on a lonely hill,
Intelligent of death, yet dauntless still."

451

THE BALLAD OF JIMMY VANCE

By the foaming Linville fountains
In the shaggy Blue Ridge Mountains,
Jimmy Vance, a mountain lad,
Did a thing that made me glad;
Ragged little Jimmy Vance
Had and took a fearful chance,
And he's nothing but a child.
High on old Black Mountain wild
He was herding in the sheep
That it was his task to keep.
Creeping through the twilight dim,
Slinking up to them and him,
Came a mountain lioness.
In that lonely wilderness
Jimmy faced her all alone.
"I got me a great big stone;
I just got a rock and hit her.
My Pa never raised no quitter.
There and then we had it out.
'Twarn't no use for me to shout.
All the folks were out of hearin'
Of that pasture in the clearin'.
Sure she clawed me; and yet still
I kept after her until
I had knocked her down the hill;
Kilt her by a big oak tree
With a rock as big as me.
That's her hide right there you see.
It warn't nothin'. Pa says, "Son,
If it's fightin', never run.'
Did she scare me? Well, she tore
All my clothes off, sartain, sure;
But I couldn't let no critter
Say my Pa had raised a quitter."

Somewhere in our mountains sleeping,
Somewhere in our cities' keeping,
Lives the valor that created
Here the home all hearts awaited.

Even as Jimmy dauntless stood
On that dreadful hill alone,
Even so stood Washington;
Morgan, Sumter, Marion
Such a fight would carry on.
Modern hearts of granite augur
Other rocks of Chickamauga.
Jimmy, on that bloody heath,
Face-to-face with snarling death,
Showed us once again the breed
That shall save us in our need.
Perry's ship that would not yield
Was the vessel Jimmy sailed;
In that place of blood and pain
Bedford Forrest fought again.
From the shops, the woods, the farms,
At the sound of war's alarms,
From the hill and from the shore
Come our Alvin Yorks once more;
Many a David Crockett grim;
Stranger, take no chance with him!
To our battleline arriving,
Many a Daniel Boone now living.
From our sidewalks and our thickets
Throng our Custers and our Picketts,
Stonewall Jacksons sweeping up!

Let us raise the brimming cup
To the ones who will not fail us
When the trumps of doom assail us.
I, by doubt and fear half-blinded,
Of our heritage reminded,
Find in rest my Country's lance,
Thanks to little Jimmy Vance!

RICHARD

All men by some peculiar strength are known,
Or mastering weakness; and if they survive
In mankind's fading memory, they live
By that which gave them color and a tone.
If one is great, he always stands alone,
And he is crowned, whoever else may strive.
A tall criterion to the race they give,
As each ascends his solitary throne.

Jesus the heart of love shall always be;
And Caesar for the Roman genius gleams;
A sleeping star above a quiet sea
Guatama shines, a light half-lost in dreams;
And mighty even among the great departed
Is one remembered as the Lionhearted.

LEE

As Arthur is to England,
As Roland is to France,
Beyond the range of time and change,
Immortal as Romance,
America, whose heritage
Of heroes is your crown,
Forever shall the fame of Lee
Be one with your renown.

O Land, his chivalry of heart
In all your glory gleams;
And from afar his spirit's star
Dawns through your noblest dreams,
Who through eternal years shall mean
In your superb advance,
What Arthur is to England,
What Roland is to France.

HELMET

Somewhere in Korea
A helmet you'll find;
A hole's in the helmet
Before and behind.
The head that it covered
Went deaf, dumb, and blind.

His station you'll know not,
His name never learn,
Who left his loved homeland
And shall not return.
His heart that was homesick
No longer can yearn.

For now he is sleeping
And shall not awake;
He's deep in a nightland
Where day does not break.
He's just a good soldier
Who died for your sake.

HERO STILL

We did not dream that he would ever falter,
However hard the road or high the hill;
We thought he'd lay at last upon life's altar
His valor and the triumph of his skill.

But in the dusk of that last day he stumbled,
And he went down to darkness and defeat;
And yet our pride in him was never humbled,
And we will hail him hero when we meet.

For to the end his course was always vanward;
He never turned; he never called for aid;
And even in falling he was fighting onward.
He strove. He failed. But he was not afraid.

455

This is the ballad of
The King's Mountain riflemen:
Frontier fighters
From the Old Dominion;
Men from the Blue Ridge
Of the Carolinas;
Men from the Smokies,
Tennesseans rugged;
Men from the wild glens
In the north of Georgia,—
Rabun Gap bear-hunters,—
Tawny pioneer patriots
From Talullah's gorges.

Faintly to them
With hardly any meaning
Had come far rumors
Of the Revolution.
Distant it was
As was the alien ocean
Far from their homeland
In the shaggy mountains.
They had heard stories
Of fighting on the coastline;
But as yet no war-cries
Had waked their wild high country,
Sleeping in the heavens.

But then came Ferguson,
Ferguson the redcoat.
Colonel Pat Ferguson
Threatened them with hanging
If at his summons
They would not all surrender.
Ferguson mistook
The men he was addressing.
Fatal it is
A mountain man to threaten.
If you really want to fight,
Try to intimidate
The free men of the mountains.

Ferguson, a fighter,
With his dangerous army,
Two thousand strong,
Had word of coming trouble
Gathering against him
In the misty mountains;
Wherefore warily
He and all his followers
Climbed King's Mountain
To its rocky summit,—
That strange lonely peak
High-looming in the valley,
Far-sundered from the Blue Ridge.

Williams and Cleveland
And John Sevier and Shelby,
Patriot commanders,
As the evening deepened,
Drew in towards the mountain
All their wildwood fighters:
Coonskin-capped
And jacketed in deerhide.
Terrible marksmen,
King's Mountain they surrounded,
Stealing like deer
In furtiveness, like panthers
In their vengeful purpose.

And ere the midnight
The patriots were posted.
Then John Sevier,
A backwoods Indian fighter,
From man to man
A simple message carried,
Stark and grim:
"These people who have threatened us
Fight in the open.
We'll kill them out of ambush,
Indian fashion. If you can bark a squirrel,
You can kill a redcoat,
And make tomorrow ours."

Ferguson was brave,
A tried and skilled commander;
And when the battle broke,
On his white charger mounted,
He led his men,
His silver whistle shrilling.
But their elevation,
Chosen for its safety,
All their equipment,
Discipline and training,
Availed them nothing
Against American hunters,
Woodsmen all,
And angered by a threatening.

Creeping up the mountain,
Dusky in its duskiness,
Pouring deadly fire
Into ranks of redcoats;
Hidden by dim boulders,
By trunks of oak and chestnut,
Upward they climbed
Toward victory and freedom.
Ferguson fell,
And all his men fell with him
On wild King's Mountain,
To whose immortal captured crest
The victors thronged rejoicing.

And now King's Mountain
Is far more than a mountain;
For where there has been
A sacrifice, forever
Shall be a shrine.
This is the place where
Our loved and Wounded Country
Trusted her salvation
To her mountain children,
To her wild strong sons,
Her dauntless and her daring sons,
The King's Mountain riflemen!

THAT EAGLE LOOK

He always had an eagle look.
Lithe-limbed and glad and swift was he.
He was a bow forever bent,
Clean as a slender white-oak tree.
He was a sword that had no sheath,—
Dauntless, confronting destiny.

That eagle look! That eagle look!
It meant a flag not to be felled;
Valor's unconquerable spirit;
It meant a helmsman who held
Safe on her course his gallant ship
Though wild the breakers round her belled.

Brief was his life but beautiful
Because grim challenges he took;
For the mountain crags, the pinnacles
Life's sheltered meadows he forsook.
He always was a lance in rest,
And he never lost that eagle look.

CONTAGION OF VALOR

Though I could not see his face,
Though I could not hold his pace,
Yet the runner on before me
Kept me running in the race.
Over hill and over hollow
He was swift as any swallow;
And as long as he kept running,
I had strength of heart to follow.
Who he was and why he sped,
With what love his steps were red
I was never to discover
As I followed where he fled.
Radiant valor winged his flight;
Faith alone gave him his might
As his dauntless spirit led me
Out of darkness into light.

THE SHRINE OF THE MOUNTAIN MEN

(King's Mountain, October 7, 1930)

Proud at King's Mountain America's keeping
Memory's vigil above the great dead . . .
Heroes of old, in your mystical sleeping,
Beauty devoted above you is weeping;
Over your slumber love's glory is shed.

Here is the hill where your hearts did not falter:
Where there's a sacrifice, there is a shrine!
Heroes, immortally here to exalt her,
Made you this summit white Liberty's altar,
Made of King's Mountain a temple divine.

Riflemen, Riflemen, far had you ridden;
Out of Virginia and Georgia you came;
From Carolina, from dim valleys hidden
Deep in hill-country, by passes forbidden,
Searching the pathway to freedom—not fame.

Down past Roan Mountain and by the Toe River,
Over Gillespie's Gap southward you rode;
Linville and Cherokee's Fording forever
Gleam with a radiance none can dissever
From your allegiance to chivalry's code.

Then in bold manhood—but now in our dreaming—
With Williams and Hambright and Clarke and Sevier
Out of the wild hills you Hotspurs came streaming;
And in these deep wildwoods your rifles were gleaming
Campbell and Cleveland and Shelby were here.

Found you a noble foe, gallant, sagacious,
Here on this hill where brave Ferguson fell,
Dying a soldier of memory gracious . . .
Men of King's Mountain, intrepid, audacious,
You won from a hero this grim citadel!

Riflemen, you made the wide world awaken
When your long rifles this wilderness woke,
Empires you took when this mountain was taken,
Shook the whole earth when this fortress was shaken;
For through your conflict humanity spoke.

Pioneer patriots, how can we render
Praise that is meet for immortals like you,
Who are the soul of America's splendor?
Safe is our Country if we shall defend her
With your stout fortitude, dauntless and true.

Heroes of old, from war's red conflagration
Yours was the valor that saved us that day:
Sons of our morning of high consecration,
Yours was the spirit that made us a nation,
Up this eternal slope leading the way!

Wounded, your Country in anguish titanic
Leaned on your strength 'gainst the ultimate stroke.
On that dread day when this mount was volcanic,
Yours were the great hearts that never knew panic,
Yours were the ranks that the foe never broke.

Now in these dark pines your high ardor clambers;
Now in these white oaks your chivalry climbs:
Spirit like yours never rests, never slumbers;
And a deep love that reveres and remembers
We shall bestow till the twilight of time.

Towering forever, King's Mountain resplendent,
Stand while the stars o'er your dark summit shine!
Holding the fame of your heroes ascendent,
Teaching America's latest descendant
Where there's a sacrifice, there is a shrine!

461

DESTROYER

Breathless, impetuous,
Dauntless One, proud and strong,
Sudden and glorious,
Bold as a battle-song,—
Shrewdly, at cyclone speed,
Serving the Nation's need!

Death's on the deep you ride;
Fearful the odds you face.
Valor is in your stride;
Rescue is in your pace,
While the foe's submarines
Learn what intrepid means.

Black as a thunderstorm
Your sombre smoke-clouds roll,
While your sea-shouldering form,
Like the mad tempest's soul,
Flashes with deadly might
Through the foam's tossing light.

Brave in your perilous place,
Shielding the battle-fleet;
Rushing like doom apace,
Danger's grim van to meet,—
Swift your delivering saves,
Wild Hotspur of the waves!

BODY AND SPIRIT

Disdain the rusty scabbard;
But by the living Lord
Scorn not the ever-dauntless,
The bright eternal sword.
For though the sheath be tarnished,
And all its colors fade,
Beware the fateful lightning
Of the immortal blade.

462

SOLDIER

I

As a wild day that's drawing toward its close,
A day of wind and rain and stormy sun,
Will, at its ending, blossom like the rose,
Serene and beautiful, its anguish done;
And we who marvel at such majesty,
Resplendent in its silence and its sleep,
Now that its warfare's over, only see
Triumphant peace, far-flowering vast and deep.

So one we knew was always danger's mark:
He was forever into peril going,
With thunder and with lightning and the dark,
The bugles of lifelong battle for him blowing.
Yet ere the night his glory flowered in view,—
A spirit more illustrious than we knew.

II

Now he is gone, we see him much more clearly
Than when life's clouds were round him; and we are
More justly moved to love and hold him dearly
Now that he stands revealed . . . Of a noble star
That all night long, obscured by mists, at last,
Nearing the radiant west, his journey ended,
Nothing is seen, the lonely struggle passed,
But what is beautiful and true and splendid.

Death seems to end in us all that is mortal,
Purging away the dross, leaving the gold,
Destroying all except the living spirit;
And he, emerging from that mystic portal,
Suddenly shines in light, and we behold
The Glory that he is,—and we inherit.

MEMORABLE MAID

Out of Domremy, humble and obscure
There came the Maid; by beauty unadorned,
Nor given what the world acclaims as charm;
But being what she was brought forth her bloom.
Though young, she heard the Voices, and her eyes
Looked upon Life and Virtue lovingly.
Although a peasant, she was nobly born,
And lived and fought and died a heroine.
She awed the English archers, fighting men,
Who never before had quailed until she came.
Upon her mused the chivalry of France,
But none could comprehend her mystery.
All, friend and foe, would wonderingly say,
"Something there is about her." They could feel
Her mystery, for she drew them near to God.
"Something there is about her." Nothing else
Save wonder makes a woman memorable;
And Beauty never should deserve renown
Unless, like Joan's, its charm is character,
Valor and grace and greatness of the heart,
Loyal to others even unto death.

IDLE HEROINE

Behind her Dresden cups she's out of place.
The splendor of that heart needs nobler spending:
To be sung of and died for without ending,
Such loveliness belongs to all the Race.
And all that hope desires is in her face.
The dying brave of war she should be tending,
Who, at that haunting beauty o'er them bending,
Foreknowledge of all heaven well might trace.

I see her not behind the trivial glass
And trifling china. In far hills forlorn,
Fast-spurring deep through that disastrous pass
Where heroes heed the sound of Roland's horn,
With banners streaming wild I see her come
Where the last bugle's sounding the charge home.

464

THE GALLANT

I watched Humanity go by.
No anguish brought a bitter cry;
Some sang, and some were hushed as night.
With wondering awe I saw this sight.
At first I could not tell or see
How much alike they all could be;
But learned this universal host
Carried the battles it had lost;
Forever of his life a part,
Each wore his woundings in his heart.
Beneath the ragged coats, the plumes,
Under the glories and the glooms
Lay the dead hopes each pilgrim bore;
The mystic loves that were no more;
The longings wild that had been vain;
The days that could not come again,—
All bearers of the Might-Have-Been,
The hero and the heroine!
Not without pride and tears could I
Behold the Gallant going by.

CAESAR'S WIFE

With Julius Caesar on a far campaign,
His wife Calpurnia craved companionship,—
Possibly more. To wish for him were vain. . .
But that tall guard with a barbarian's grip
Might make the night less lonely. Nor was he
A marble statue with her beauty by.
Although her guardian he was meant to be,
Once on his watch she called him with her eye.

Yet each beheld a vision intervene:
They saw the valiant spirit of Caesar stand
As they had always known him, and had seen
Him dauntless front all dangers. Then her hand
Rose to forbid the guard, to thwart her will,—
For Caesar absent remained Caesar still.

CATHEDRAL AND SONG

He passed the great cathedral.
The city lay below.
Its glory had been growing
Out of the long ago.
The city gleamed beneath him;
The mighty shrine he passed.
Of all that glimmering splendor
Nothing would ever last.

And he, too, was to perish.
His days could not be long.
No legacy had he to leave
Except a little song.
Yet when the city lies in dust,
Its shrine no light can give,
Or music to a listening world,
His little song will live.

CONQUEST

I was a soldier, and a Roman one,
Clanging down martial corridors to fame,
Blazing against the thunder and the sun,
My eagles made far-terrible my name.
In clashing combat, brother to red Mars,
Kingdoms to deep oblivion I hurled;
My legions conquered under Gallic stars:
Mine, and the might of Rome, dismayed the
        world.

But suddenly I came on power more vast:
They failed me then,—my strength, my legions
        true;
A conqueror, I trembled at love's charms . . .
All I had dreamed was triumph faded fast,—
All I imagined glory,—when I knew
The mystery of Egypt in my arms.

465

IN CAVALIER DAYS

The dark-panelled door of the Hall has swung wide,
And forth strides the Cavalier, booted and spurred,
His wife and his daughters, a-flutter with fear,
Clasp his hands, kiss his cheek, call him every name dear.
His servants stand anxious, and awed at the men
All mounted and waiting, so silent and stern.
He sees his wife's tears in her dark eyes divine.—
Then a stirrup-cup's drunk of the battle-bright wine.
With a jest and a laugh and a wave of the hand,
And a merry "Good-bye!" he is off with his band
For the front of the fray! Through the avenue's gloom,
With the glitter of steel and the toss of the plume,
He shoots like a meteor through the black night;
Before him is darkness; behind him is light.
On, on speeds his charger; while humming behind
Roll the hoofs of his followers, swift as the wind.
They clatter down causeways, over bridges they roar,
Through Marston they gallop, and come to the Moor;
Where, cold as the steel they so dreadfully wield,
The Roundheads are stubbornly sweeping the field.
He's up in his stirrups, his sword flashes high,
The Cavalier turns to his men with a cry,
"For God and King Charles!" So, fiery and brave,
They charge to their glory, they charge to their grave!

That night, saddle empty and darkened with blood,
The Cavalier's charger comes home through the wood.
Fast, fast has he galloped in piteous dread
From the wild roaring marge of the battle-front red.
The servants all gather with whispers and cries,
And aprons are lifted to tear-streaming eyes.
Before the Hall steps the horse trembling stands;
While, trembling also, the beautiful hands
Of the Cavalier's wife strokes his mane and his head,
Yet because of his spirit, so brave and so bright,
Forever he lives in her love as its light.

AUTUMN MOONRISE

The west's far glory of wild roses
Has tinted all the world with gleams
Of light that tenderly discloses
The beauty of its glimmering dreams.

A haze is on the hickory trees;
The rising moon has bronzed the beeches;
Wafted are haunting spiceries
Of honeyed grapes and misty peaches.

The moonlight on the cornfield broad
Silvers the tattered tasseled tops;
Heavy with summer sweetness stored,
An apple in the orchard drops.

On many a far-off trampled nation
This harvest moon has looked and seen
Wide wakes of ashen desolation
Where ramping, wild-hoofed war has been.

O Land our hearts have ever cherished,
A fairer beauty robes your form
Because of those, your sons, who perished
To shield you from the dreadful storm.

A SONG OF HOPE

O gallant Heart, defeated,
Now gazing toward the west,
Where this day's splendor crumbles,
Disastrous and unblest,—
Look, till the deathlike darkness
By stars be glorified,
Until you see another dream
Beyond the dream that died.

FORT SUMTER, 1861

Full many a beauteous morn had come
Roseate o'er the river-foam,
To wake the city from her dreams,
Asleep between the sister streams;
To sweep afar by dune and cape
In light their darkness to drape;
But never yet had dawned a day
More tranquil on the tranquil bay.
Yet as the red behind the pines
Glowed into delicate crimson lines,
High in the morning heavens stark,
From Johnson, on James Island dark,
There rose a shell that tore the dawn,
And burst with dreadful menace on
The brave Fort in the harbor gray,
That watchful, silent, waiting lay,
A creature sinister at bay,—
With iron fangs already bare,
Defiant even in despair.

O Pity, on thy white throne, weep!
Slowly the lines of daylight creep
Up through the eastern forest wall;
Sweet mated birds begin to call:
But thunder rolls along the deep,
The forts are hidden in a pall,
And little is discerned, save
The alien flags that proudly wave.

HAROLD AT HASTINGS

He at the foot of the royal standard fell,
Unconquerable but by death. O this
Remember, who to life must say farewell:
If it be noble, the expiring breath
Can be triumphant victory; for death,
Met in a quiet home, or in wild war,
To valor always is inferior.

I.

Two maids gazed on the gleaming lists
Where knights, in fair array,
Were chafing for the bugle-blast
To call them to the fray.

Blue banners, pennons vert and white,
O'er many a dais did wave;
And, viewed by glimmering Beauty rare,
For battle burned the Brave.

II.

Then Blanche, whose radiant haughty brow
Black tresses garlanded,
Marked on a helm her jewelled sleeve,
And musingly she said:

"Sir Hubert strives amain for me;
His fame shall be my own;
And I am his is he shall gain
A terrible renown.

He wears my sleeve, and he shall wear
Hy heart if he prevail;
Love is for them who triumph here,
But not for them who fail.

I cannot love the vanquished; I
A conqueror's bride shall prove;
And he must bring me victory
To whom I yield my love."

III.

Then Regan, beautiful and bright,
Blue-eyed and yellow-haired,
Looked on her lover; and her heart
Its tender trust declared:

"He goes, my Harold, to the fight
With Valiance divine;
My image in his heart he wears,
And his is graved on mine.

My love is with him in the lists;
Together we may fall,
Together we may overthrow
The doughty knights and tall.

But if he fall or if he win,
Love lives this conflict through;
For he will bear him like a knight,
And, I, through all, be true."

IV.

The knights have shocked, the lists resound
With din like wintry hail,
Though sunshine blazons tawnily
The lances and the mail.

And helms are hewn, and casques are hacked,
While Blanche and Regan gaze;
And Blanche burns with imperious pride,
But wistful Regan says:

"O come what may upon this day,
No stroke of sword or lance
Can love defeat; nor glory gained
Love's oriflamme advance."

V.

Humbled to dust in yonder lists
The good Sir Hubert lies;
And the sad rose of wounded pride
Blanche wears, and vails her eyes.

How still is he! Some mighty blow
Has cleft the sleeve which bound
The glittering helm . . . But who is this
Who has his heart's queen crowned?

To Regan, Harold straight has brought
The prize for which he strove:—
Sir Hubert dies in yonder 'lists,
And with him dieth love.

To win the black-haired Blanche, he died.
But Harold and his bride
Live in the joy of them whose love
Is not the whim of pride.

UPON THE VERGE OF DARK

Upon the verge of dark he set
As brave a foot as ever yet
Invaded unknown country where
Foes might be ambushed everywhere.

Upon the threshold of the night
He stood as if he stood in light;
And on the marge of final shade,
As in the sun, was unafraid.

Beloved and young, it was his lot
To meet the darkness. Ah, grieve not
For him who passed with dauntless mien
The portals of the dread unseen.

Or was it that his valiant eyes
Visioned beyond our shrouding skies
A special glory, past the gloom,
For a good soldier coming home?

472

For her alone he drew the blade,
Casting the scabbard from his side;
His hand her guiding heart obeyed,
And terrible her name he made
Ere for her love he died!

But all the splendor of his fame
No victory o'er her grief has won.
Though kindled by his glory's flame,
Her heart breaks when she hears his name,—
Her valiant, vanished son!

But he keeps conquering through the years
The bitter hearts of former foes;
This victory shall dry her tears;
For as her heart his emblem wears,
The world his grandeur knows!

THE CONFEDERATE DEAD

Although the Flag they died to save
Floats not o'er any land or sea,
Over eternal years shall wave
The banner of their chivalry.

Lost in the silent Past profound,
Their war-cries to the dead belong,
Yet poets shall their valor sound
In music of immortal song.

Save that for them I nobly live,
Bear life, as death they bravely bore,
They need no glory I can give,
Whose fame abides forevermore;

Whose fame fades not in marble arts,
Nor sleeps within the Past's dim night;
Heroes who live in loving hearts
Are templed in Eternal Light.

BRAVE LAD

My lad who will be daring
Adown life's winding trail,
For naught on earth he's caring
Except to find the Grail.

I cannot hold him longer
Beside me, safe and hid;
His heart—than mine that's stronger—
How can my love forbid?

He turns him toward the foe-land,
Where clangs the certain fray;
Hearing the horn of Roland,
He mounts and spurs away.

How paltry is all censure
Upon a brave deed done!
The hills I dared not venture,
His chivalry has won.

The darkness and the danger
Call to him more than home;
To lands where I'm a stranger
Through passes drear he'll come.

Far valiant quests divining,
He's gone into the gloom,
His hand, a sabre shining,
His heart, a gallant plume.

BRAVEST

Although your life you gave,
You would not be so brave
As one I'm dreaming of:
Who, with eyes undismayed,
Could see the Great Dream fade,
Watching the death of love.

474

DISFIGURED

I loved you then when you went
In your perfect strength to the war,
But your broken body is dearer to me,
And I love you more as you are!

For others your beauty is gone
Or marred by the half-healed scar;
But you are my soldier who fell at the front,
And I love you more as you are.

There's a cross on your wounded breast
That the bandages hide, and a star
On the shattered shoulder I dare not touch
Who love you so as you are!

Your strength is gone, and the light
From the eye that could see so far
When we wandered the hills in olden days,
But I love you more as you are.

For out of the battle you brought
Courage no weapon could mar:
I dreamed not love's depths until I had learned
To love you more as you are!

BRIDE OF VALOR

Long had I thought that peace was to be found
After the battle; in the windless dells
Leeward from strife, where one hears but the sound
Of drowsy birds and mellow evening bells;
There in white ease and languor, from surcease
Of struggle, might I come upon her form—
The silent angel that I pictured Peace—
Nor even thought to meet, save after storm.

But Peace is Valor's bride. Who to her comes
Will likelier find her in the perilous dark
Of duty; where the maned sea-breaker foams,
Standing with him who helms his driven barque:
Who dauntless dares life's lightning and its thunder
Is resting in her starry bosom's wonder.

THEY FELL IN FRANCE

Strong soldiers of the sky,
We feel you marching by.
Through you the world's wide life is glorified.
We know for whom you gave
Glad youth unto the grave;
We know it was for us you fought and died.

When bright-lipped bugles sang,
Forth into line you sprang
With ardent strength to meet the foe's advance,
With song and happy laugh—
And now your epitaph
Are those few mighty words, "They fell in France."

Great hearts who now are gone,
Warriors, whose wars are done,
A faithful vigil over you we keep.
Our love's remembering you
Is lasting tribute true,
Good soldiers, sleeping now your battle-sleep.

Somewhere your legions bright,
In everlasting light,
Are by the Captain of All Souls reviewed;
Your radiant ranks arrayed
Where splendors never fade,
In powers of eternal life renewed.

Though grand your victory
That set the chained earth free,
Your sacrifice a nobler triumph gives:
By you are hearts made pure,
And faith established sure;
And by your spirit Honor's spirit lives.

The dreadful path you trod
Led upward unto God;
And you shall lead us in the days to be.
Ever you march again,
O tall, resplendent Slain!
And following you shall be fidelity.

476

Your courage high survives
In each true heart that strives;
Who dies a hero's death retells your story.
Where flags of Freedom wave;
You'll always lead the Brave;
And where you are shall be the home of Glory.

STRENGTH

Not in a night, not in a day arrives
The spirit of triumphant fortitude,
The hardihood that overcomes the world.
When you go forth to meet your enemy,
Be compassed by your allies of the past,
The army mobilized each day you live,
The friends that throng to aid you in your need:
The years in which you lived undauntedly,
The days, the nights, the patient moment's power,
The little brave decisions that make strength.
So when the imperious challenge summons you,
To some great conflict with a dreadful foe,
Let all your life make answer ,"I am ready."
—If otherwise, vain will be sudden valor,
Born out of sudden swift necessity,
And frustrate final desperate courage . . . But
If at the stormy bugle-blast you rise
Strong-girded with the gathered strength that comes
From life's uncounted loyalties of heart,
And fealties of long ago,—fear not;
For to all tempests you are adamant,
And master of the mightiest enemy.

FINAL HOPE

If I can only have my will,
Before I shall my singing cease,
The trembling chalice of my verse
With sweet wildflowers I would fill,
Love-gathered from the field and hill,
From ferny slopes of stream and rill,
Hoping that they may bring you peace,
And make you keep your spirit still.

477

BLOOD ROYAL

Disdainful was my heart and black;
Before me lay the downward track.
I know not how the thing befell
That kept my soul from death and hell,
But suddenly there woke in me
Awareness of my pedigree,
Remembrance of my heritage,
Illustrious through every age.

I am a son of God who made
The morning light, the evening shade,
Who throned the mountains in the sky
And set the wild sea's boundary,
Who hung the stars with mystic art,
Who touched to life the human heart
And gave man power to feel and see
Those tokens of his majesty.

I claim all noble hearts as kin;
Mine is all valor that has been;
King David was my ancestor;
'Twas I that he was singing for.
My sister was the Orleans Maid,
Whose courage keeps men unafraid;
And when One died on Calvary's Tree,
My Brother gave his life for me.

Inheritor of their renown,
How can I live like knave or clown?
Caesar once faced his killers grim;
Can I turn coward after him?
They burned alive my sister Joan;
She upward looked and made no moan.
Lo, I must stand as they have stood,
Nor stain the honor of our blood.

BULL'S ISLAND'S BEACHES

Stripped to the screaming hurricane,
Bared to the black, inrolling sea,
Naked to moon and sun and stars
In lone and daring liberty,
The front-beach, harried by the gales,
Is hard and shining, clean and bright
Far up to where the pines emerge
From the dense beach-wood's glimmering night.

To leeward, on the languid shore,
Behind the island's dusky screen,
Ignobly peaceful stretch away
Quiescent marshes, still and green;
There many a waveless current warm
The sallow, balmy shore-line brims;
And there is silence; though the sea
To windward, wildly, grandly hymns.

The dauntless beach that fronts the surf
A tawny hardihood achieves;
And gallantly, and gloriously
The tempest's epic wrath receives:
The listless shore behind the isle
Is supine, soft with placid dreams,
Hushed, dimmed; and stilled with lassitudes
From fair but stagnant-hearted streams.

To brave all suns and winds, to take
Heroic strength from each of these;
To suffer anguish, yet to scorn
The languor and the rancèd ease
(Such as the back-beach drowses in);
Against the tyrant storms to stand,
Calm, valiant, failing, triumphing,—
Alone can make Life's meaning grand.

OUR SOLDIERS

I. The Volunteers

They are with us, whatever else departs;
They bivouac in all our noblest dreams.
In martial beauty marching through our hearts,
Each like a flag of freedom for us gleams.
They are our heroes. Valor is their story.
We lift our hearts to listen to it, knowing
Forever they shall shed the light and glory
Of splendid manhood into battle going.

II. The Fallen

The patriot's diadem of fame is theirs,
Glory's resplendent and eternal crown,
Unfading, unforgotten through the years.
In all our hearts their record, written down,
Shall be remembered by our love and tears.
Whatever comes, secure is their renown.
—What tribute can we offer to these Brave?
A love that understands what love they gave.

HEROES

Gravely and nobly by their memory moved,
Over their fate shall wistful poets grieve;
In their stern fate the doubter shall believe;
By mourning Beauty shall their deeds be loved.
Valor and strength the thought of them will give;
Fame on their brows her coronal shall set;
All save their courage will the world forget,—
Among the perishing their souls will live

To be brave dreams returning with the rose,
And autumn's raptures burning in her leaves,—
Recalled among sweet long-ago farewells:
And so remembered, as on summer eves
To thrill the silence, when tall spires close
The glamour and golden tempest of their bells.

480

SEPTEMBER MOONRISE

That west's far glory of wild roses
Has tinted all the world with gleams
Of light that tenderly discloses
The beauty of their glimmering dreams.

A haze is on the hickory trees;
The rising moon has bronzed the beeches.
Wafted are haunting spiceries
Of honeyed grapes and misty peaches.

The moonlight on the cornfield broad
Silvers the tasseled tattered tops;
Heavy with summer sweetness stored,
An apple in the orchard drops.

—On many a far-off trampled nation
This harvest moon has looked, and seen
Wide wakes of ashen desolation
Where ramping, wild-hoofed war has been.

Fair Land, our hearts have ever cherished,
A fairer beauty robes thy form
Because of those, thy sons, who perished
To shield thee from the dreadful storm.

Peril is passed because they braved it;
Our Land they have established sure.
The Flag is ours because they saved it,
And, 'neath it, made our homes secure.

TIDAL RIVER-MOUTH

I said, "It is like love," as I watched the river
Give all her beauty to the boundless main.
And when I saw that mighty flood deliver
The ocean back, I said, "Like love," again.

BEATTY OF THE BATTLE-CRUISERS

I.

If you're looking for a fighter and a scrapper on the sea,
Just call on David Beatty, and he'll entertain you free.
For if in all the ranks of war you want to find a man,
There's Beatty of the battle-cruisers, leader of the van!

II.

I'm nothing but a bosun's mate, a-serving of the King,
But equal to an admiral in knowing of one thing:
That if there is a chance to be where hell is busting through,
This Beatty will be mixed in it, to whip the devil's crew!

III.

Round Heligoland he swept to lure the sulking Germans out
They came to smash him roundly, but he put their best to ro
He sent some back to hiding, and some never saw the shore
For the *Mainz* and *Ariadne* and *Cologne* will sail no more!

IV.

Then came their sneaking by night to raid our coastal towns
To shoot at sleeping children and the young lambs on
    the downs;
The *Seidlitz* and the *Moltke* and the *Blucher* creeping nigh
But they reckoned not on Beatty with his battle-cruisers by

V.

The *Seidlitz* and the *Moltke,* oh, a pretty race they ran,
When Beatty in the roaring *Lion* led the English van!
But the *Blucher,* mauled and battered, never crossed the
    Dogger Bank:
Deserted by her comrades there, she shuddered, rolled,
    and sank.

VI.

The *Seidlitz,* all aflame was she, fast burning in her flight;
The *Moltke* beat her into port,—for so these Germans figh
But I hardly blame their running. When our guns began
    to shout,
" 'Tis David Beatty after you!" they burnt their boilers out

When Jutland came,—that fight in mist,—that battle
  'gainst the shore,
'Twas Beatty, David Beatty, was to lead our line once more!
Though many brave were in that fray, the bravest was
  this man,
Our Beatty, rushing to the front his battle-cruiser van!

Then on that gray November morn that Kaiser's navy came,
The vaunted German High Seas Fleet, surrendering in shame!
A craven crew that meekly steams between our mighty lines.
And to our Grand Fleet Admiral their blooming fate assigns!

So if you love a fighter and a scrapper on the sea,
I'd name you David Beatty first, for such a man is he;
And if in all the ranks of war you're looking for a Man,
Here's Beatty of the battle-cruisers, leader of the van!

"HAVING DONE ALL, TO STAND"

In pain and grief to be
A patient one;
In clanging strife to be
A valiant one;
With every joy to be
A generous one;
At Beauty's shrine to be
A worshiping one;
In doubtful dark to be
A vigilant one;
With those I love to be
A gentle one;
In times of triumph be
A humble one;
In hours of wild dismay
A steadfast one;
And to all song to be
A listening one.

483

RIDERLESS HORSE

With stirrups wild flying,
With bridle a-stream,
A riderless horse
Has rushed into my dream,
No hand on his bridle,
No spur in his flanks,
No master to guide him,
No place in the ranks.

He has burst out of battle,
All blood and all foam;
His heart is aflame for
The hills of his home.
He brings us a message;
For all it is plain:
He carried a rider,
Nor bears him again.

The riderless horse
Of my dreaming has passed,
But left me a vision
Forever to last:
The valiant vanguard
That bore the brunt well,
The flag that was riddled,
The hero who fell.

OUR GRATITUDE

Now you have gone from us,
What can we say?
Now you have left our earth
For Heaven's day.
You made our pilgrimage
Calmer, more dear;
And left in death itself
Nothing to fear.

THE KNIGHTHOOD OF HEART

Who dreams of King Arthur
And taketh his part,
On him is conferred
A knighthood of heart.

In the hands of the Valiant,
To the eye of the Brave,
His lances are gleaming,
His banners still wave.

In the tone of the Steadfast,
His voice can be heard;
In Silent Endurance
Complaining no word.

In following Arthur
Unfearful through gloom,
How bright to his faithful
His sword and his plume!

And now in new glory
That armor is worn;
In wars of the spirit
That weapon is borne.

In a life beyond life
The King acts his part,
Conferring on heroes
A knighthood of heart.

IF YOU WERE GONE

Even in light without you I am lost;
And I would know that all my life were done
If in the dark I turned to touch your hand,
And found that you were gone.

I GUARD THE DOOR

Think not that I am far away
When fighting on some foreign shore:
Rifle in hand I watch and wait
Outside your door.

I am at hand, however far
From home the Flag beloved we bore;
Ceaseless the vigil that I keep,
Guarding your door.

Trenches of Flanders, fields of France,
Or soaring as the eagles soar,
It matters not; it means but this:
I guard your door.

And when you gather to the hearth
As darkness shrouds the wood and moor,
Fear not, for in that night I stand
To hold the door.

On the red frontiers of the fight
I shield your safety evermore;
And I shall stand, or I shall fall,
Guarding your door.

STRONGER

I do not think it any less or more,
This anguish, than it was long years before.
But if I live with grieving any longer,
I think that of us two, I shall be stronger.

OUT OF THE VALLEY'S SHADOW

Condemned to encounter sorrow's sword of flame,
Into the Valley all alone I came;
Into this valley one must come alone,—
A solitary place of sand and stone.
Had no one seen this wilderness before?
Had no one borne the anguish that I bore?

But there were mortal tracks in the waste sand
Of this incredibly sad and lonely land.
It was as if, even from the long ago,
Here battles always wavered to and fro.
All, all humanity before my day,
Predestined to meet grief, had come this way.

And then the meaning of it dawned to me:
Life is a land of old catastrophe.
Not alien I, but only come at last
Where multitudes preceding me had passed.
And here and there, and round and round about,
Valor had challenged Grief, and fought it out.

By grim old relics I became aware
That many a heart, grief-stricken, had been here.
Here lay abandoned, by tall peaks of doom,
Hacked lordly helm, sword, shield, and lance and plume.
Hung on a thorn by a mournful mountain-side
Was a withered rose that had been wordly pride.

Sorrow was the wild foe they had to slay;
And, having triumphed, they have gone away
Into a land where love is lord forever;
Where, for this desert, they have found a river;
For warfare, peace,—serene and glad and strong;
For grief's mute discord, many and many a song.

AH, CONQUEROR!

Glory to them who fought the field and lost!
Not only those who in wild battle fell,
In beauty of tall manhood, blood-embossed;
Of all whose hearts were valiant, I tell:
The flier, plunging down the screaming skies;
The lover, learning that he comes too late;
The mother, tearless o'er her babe that dies;
The champion strong, condemned to watch and
    wait.

Anguish was theirs, defeat, and overthrow.
But let no mournful bell their story toll;
Theirs is the noblest saga that we know.
Glory to them who never reached their goal!
Ah, conqueror, what trophy can you show
To match the splendor of a dauntless soul?

PIONEER MOTHER

She gazed across the casket
With wild grief's tearless eyes,
And said to me, her only son,
"No good man ever dies.

"Now you must be a man like him,
And stand as he has stood.
There is not anything that's worth
The worth of being good".

Even in shock my mother looked
Strong as a white oak tree.
"Cunning Comanches killed my man,"
Was all she said to me.

It was not all, for now that I
Am gray, with dimming eyes,
I never, never can forget,
"No good man ever dies".

SECOND MARRIAGE

Now am I one with Music:
Melodious are my days
With voices that I love to hear.
My ways are lyric ways.

With hymn and carol brightened
My journey has been fleet.
By Life I'm serenaded,
And all her songs are sweet.

Yet I'd not listen longer
To Music, but would hark
To stillness of the mystic shade,
To muteness of the dark.

I, in that quiet coming
To shadow from the sun,
Shall fall in love with Silence,
And she and I be one.

WHITE APPAREL

O who are they in white apparel clad,
These spirits calm, unspent in life's campaign?
Though they all anguish and all wounds have had,
Sorrow, their mightiest foeman, they have slain.
They are the hearts that out of grief have come,
Advancing to the last. The fire and sword,
The vigil lone, the loss of friends and home,
Even the loss of love they have endured.

Why are they robed in white? Because they passed
Out of the Valley's shadow, and they stand
Dauntless upon the hills of vision vast.
And from another and more radiant land
Tomorrow's light of glory now is shed
On them who would not linger where they bled.

489

RIDING AWAY

Riding away as to bugles of old
Into a region all sunset and gold,
Into far realms romantic we see
Stuart and Johnston and Jackson and Lee.

Riding away, O they're riding away,
Robed in the splendor they gave to the Gray.
Tinged with love's glamour and tinted with gleams
Into the sundown they're going like dreams.

Into the twilight they ride undismayed:
Night, by their coming, is nobly arrayed!
Warriors gallant, from all their great wars,
Unto the evening arriving like stars.

Riding away! Is it far that they ride?
Whom can we follow? Who trust now to guide?
Where shall we find such brave convoy as they
If from our lives they are riding away?

Robed in the glory they gave to the Gray,
Riding away,—yes, they're riding away
Into a place whence love never departs:
Out of the wide world and into our hearts!

ALL I KNOW

Give me not fame or wealth or power!
Upon that road I long to go
Which brings me to life's noblest hour,—
When love is everything I know.

THE CAVALIER

Before you, sounded trumpet-tones,
And sunward thronged bright sabres bare:
Behind, were ruinous landscapes fair,
Mirth, tears, and dust of falling thrones.

O noble Soul, a purpose stern
Was alien to your gallant life;
He only conquers in the strife
Who to the God of Truth can turn;

Can kneel to pray on bloody sod,
Then face the foe with fearful zeal,
And in the fevered battle feel
The calm of him who works with God.

The noon-clear principles of Right
We from the Puritan demand;
From you, like evening o'er the land,
Are gifts more beautiful and bright:

Glamours that haunt the summer air
With dreams of early love, with hopes
Faded on far-off morning slopes,
That make the Past beloved and fair.

VALIANT HEART

Since in her grief she never wept,
What she has borne no one can tell.
O Valiant Heart that always kept
Your crown of thorns invisible!

SOLDIERS

They are with us, whatever else departs;
They bivouac in all our noblest dreams.
In martial beauty marching through our hearts,
Each like a flag of freedom for us gleams.
They are our heroes. Valor is their story.
We lift our hearts to listen to it, knowing
Forever shall they shed the light and glory
Of dauntless manhood into battle going.

The patriot's diadem of fame is theirs,
Glory's resplendent and eternal crown,
Unfading, unforgotten through the years.
In all our hearts, their record, written down,
Shall be remembered by our love and tears.
Whatever comes, secure is their renown.
What tribute can we offer to these Brave?
A love that understands what love they gave.

THE OLD KNIGHT

"He was a doughty knight who, long ago,
Fell in a famous jousting." Thus I read
The ancient epitaph. No more was said.
And yet from this terse hatchment one might know
The story of his life and death, I trow:
The vigils that he kept, the foes he sped,
The glamour of his fame about him shed,
The conquering plume at last in dust laid low.

Trumpet and banner, lance and shield and knight—
Ladies who leaned to watch with lovely glance—
Gone, gone are they with all their glorious strife.
Yet there remains so much that we can write:
"Before he fell, he broke a gallant lance
For Beauty, in the Tournament of Life."

THE LAST TOURNAMENT

Tall queens I saw at life's last tournament
Their beauty darkened all—except one knight.
No combat had there been. No blood was spent.
Yet more than martial was that hero bright.
Then I beheld him as victor hailed
By her who was most beautiful. She gave
Her hand to him whose honor had prevailed,
While all hearts honored Beauty and the Brave.

It was a vision of the time to be,
A nobler morrow, when, Might's banners furled
Forever, peace shall come to land and sea,
And Love be splendid sovereign of a world
Where glorious spirits only are renowned,
Where only he with grace of heart is crowned.

SOLACE FOR WOUNDS

For wounds, you ask, what solace shall atone?
The loneliness of love that cannot be;
The cold unbroken tears grief sheds alone;
The traitor's triumph; and the victory
Of selfish friends; the darkness on before;
The failure of the strength; the fading roses;
The trouble in loved eyes; the mystic shore
Of faith receding as the voyage closes.

Against this long grim discipline for death
One saving recompense there is: the right
To know that merely by this mortal breath
Your honor stood; to know that in the night
Of sorrow and despair, while others wept,
A long watch for the morning star you kept.

WOUNDED STRANGER

As by the evening waves a watch I kept,
Marking the distant shores and all between,
Tall graceful yachts in quiet beauty swept
Safe to their berths . . . For an hour they had been
Out to the bar and home . . . Then on the rim
On the mysterious and fading blue
A battered hulk appeared, begrimed and dim,
Survivor of far storms we never knew.

When hearts come home, judge not by beauty only,
But by the voyage, the hazard, and the war
With elements primeval; by the lonely
Watch in the reeling dark without a star.
Not to the trim bright yachts that knew no danger:
My tribute goes to the valiant wounded stranger.

BLIND

Once when I heard a blind musician play,
I pitied him for all he could not see:
Through forests dim the light of breaking day;
The high blue moon, with cloud-ships sailing free;
The glory of sunset; then the stars to make
Magic of all the heavens . . . I yearned he might
Look on the beauty that we know; could wake
From darkness to the splendors of the light.

I did not pity him long . . . For, sightless, lone,
He with a wizard's wand created fair
A world more beautiful than I had known;
Of lands undreamed of I became aware;
Of fabulous seas, beyond all mortal fashion . . .
Then for my own blind self I felt compassion.

494

AMPLE FOR GLORY

I was haunted by the spacious names of old
That roll like music and that sound of glory:
Marathon and the Field of the Cloth of Gold;
Arbela, Agincourt, and Senlac's story;
Wild Chalons; Orleans and the warlike Maid;
Blenheim and Ramillies and Malplaquet;
Waterloo, where the Corsican essayed
To hold inexorable fate at bay.

But ample for glory is the narrow trench;
Or the destroyer's bridge above the foam;
Or a tree in the jungle's green and feverish stench;
Where the hero is, splendor will find a home.
Would you behold high Honor? See this man
Crouched in a tiny foxhole on Bataan.

WHERE WATERS REST

Beneath the pines' heroic crest,
Below the rapids in the glen,
Deep in a fragrant fern-fringed fen
Is a still place where waters rest.

Torrents, once tawny, lose their zest;
Here sound and motion drowse and cease,
Far in this haunt of ancient peace,
To wildbirds known, by wildflowers blest.

When daybreak comes, or when the west
Makes radiance for all to see,
Glimmers the stream's felicity
In silence where these waters rest.

Peace can by beauty be expressed:
An oriole in his glory glows;
The cardinal becomes a rose
By this calm place where waters rest.

A meadow-lark with golden breast
Broods on her young above the pool;
A vireo warbles soft and cool
And joyously where waters rest.

Where ferns a fairy home have blest,
A little while to cease their flowing,
Between their coming and their going
The waters find this place to rest.

Deep in basaltic rock recessed,
Where glimmering hummingbirds can dart,
This is a place to heal the heart,
This halcyon place where waters rest.

With royal mien and lifted crest
A maharaja father quail,
A maharani mother quail
Lead their brown elves where waters rest.

An angel voice says, "Love is Best";
As I approach this tranquil place,
I think of beauty and of grace
Serenely where the water rest.

Here all dissension is repressed.
Under the chestnut oak, the shade
Is deep as is this mountain glade
This gentle place where waters rest.

May you be always love-possessed;
And with your spirit, heart, and mind
God grant that you may always find
A still sweet place where waters rest.

BLACK ANGEL

Black Sue Alston's taught me well
How to save my soul from hell;
And I listen to her voice,
For it makes my heart rejoice
Thus to find her seeing through
Thunderclouds to sky that's blue,
Darkness to the light that's true.

"I must take the sinner's part;
I must hold them to my heart."
So she tells me, meekly willing,
Her high humble task fulfilling.
As a comrade she is known.
Leading others to the Throne,
She has never walked alone.

Lost in misery and shame,
To her home a woman came,—
I had passed her by with scorn.
But Sue loved that life forlorn.
My heart questioned why she should;
My eyes asked her how she could;
Her voice answered, "Jesus would."

With a gentleness of tone
To lost little children shown,
With the sinners she is talking,
Unashamed with them is walking . . .
Shining, shining in the night,
Angels black and angels white,—
All are Children of the Light.

THE KING'S SON

Scene: Twilight in the King's gardens at Jerusalem.

Time: Shortly after the death of the son of David and Bathsheb
  (A murmur of conversation approaches, and David and Bathshe
  enter, conversing in subdued tones; they walk slowly up and dow
  pausing as their speech demands.)

David.

> Now I am coming home from lands remote,
> From a lost battle like a vanquished king,
> And from the bourne of sorrowful high thoughts.

Bathsheba.

> And I from Beauty's promise unfulfilled,
> From dreams faded and flowers fallen asleep,
> And from a light that was exceedingly sweet.

David.

> As a lone ship returning through the mist,
> After its sleepless plunging on the deep,
> Through days and nights, in far-away strange
>   seas,
> I come to life again.

Bathsheba.   *One* comes not home!
> The springtime cannot bring me back my blossom,
> Nor any night my lost and shining star,
> Nor all the winds my snowy little sail!

David.

> O I behold in this the western way:
> Glory descends and into darkness goes
> With fellowship of withered dreams and
>   thoughts,
> With autumn and with sunset. From this hour
> I am a lonely river of the night,
> Upon my bosom starlike memories,
> But borne through darkness to the dark
>   away.

Bathsheba.

> Think you the hills were conscious of a flight
> Passing above them through the shadowy air?
> A touch of spirit wings beneath the stars?
> Last night I saw the cold pure lilies wave
> In the rapt peace of moonlight.

500

id.

                    And I marked
Visions of distant battles calling me.

hsheba.

  The garden-trees were trembling, and sighed
  Like weary watchers.

id.

                    Tumults did I hear,
  And shouts of warriors that did summon me
  To the fierce front and bade me swiftly come.

isheba.

  O David, leave me not! War yields no love,
  Whose power only can sustain me now.
  The sorrowing have comfort, or they die.
  Such loneliness is death, when Death has borne,
  Like a strange heartless ship, a loved one
        far
  Beyond the skyline and the bounds of sight.

id.

  If I remain, shall we not speak of him?
  What will avail save sunset, when we go?
  No morning light for him shall dawn; no noon
  Shall steep the broad fair world in happy
        light;
  No evening lift her tremulous tapers tall;
  No gathering stars for him shall make the
        night
  A glimmering camp of God where bivouac
  A host with silver spears and gleaming
        shields.
  Darkness and silence have laid hold on him,
  And even love must grope to find her way.
  Yet for thy sake will I a little while
  Tarry with thee and pain.

isheba.

                    David, my King!
  Was ever one so loved as he was loved,
  And could not live? What had he done,
        to die?
  Why should this Terror ambush our little
        child?

Through him Death smote at us. His sword
    surprised us.
Our hearts had been at revelry; we were
    dancing
And singing riotously when we came
Suddenly on life's end 'mid flowers of
    May.

David.

As soldiers seeking for a comrade strayed,
After a vague night of carousing wild,
And unaware of death's swift passing, come
Suddenly on their friend in a gay wood,
Cold as the drenching dews,—so did we
    chance
On death's fell work, that undoes all we
    do.

Bathsheba.

                       (A sound of music is heard)
Hark to the music of the minstrels' harps
Melodiously wailing through the halls
Like sea-wind or a song of long ago,
Or breezes through the cedar-scented heights
Of lofty Lebanon . . . Think you he hears?

David.

Not even kings can tell, such lands may lie
Twixt us and him.

Bathsheba.

                    But love forgets not love.
Perchance he knows us speaking of him still,
Or the far voice of evening waters here,
Or liquid language of the twilight wind,
Calls unto him with music through the sky.
O should there come a crying in the night,
How can we rest, knowing our little one
Went out alone into that very dark?

David.

I cannot know this depth of mother-love;
Yet strong men keep the faith beyond the
    years.

My love for him shall wait through all my
    days
Unchanged, save by its sorrow nobler grown.
This sinless love of children is a gift
Left by some wandering messenger of light.

hsheba.

It is God's love . . . David, I had a love,
But lost through thee and sinfully forgot . . .
How dearly has Uriah been avenged!
O but for blinding passion, we had seen
There is a deeper love than love's
    possessing,
A path to glory that no victor knows:
And it is found in love's renouncement
    high.
I am a woman, and I see it now;
Soul-cleansing death my vision has restored.
My child is dead, but I am made alive
And pure through sorrow to remember him.

vid.

Remembering, what have we at last to hold?
Mists that the morning whirls in scorn away,
Leaves that can never hide the bloom's sharp
    thorn,
Thoughts vain as tears o'er vanished
    loveliness.
I care not for the past. The child is
    dead.

hsheba.

Yet is that past the solace for my grief,
Since then he lived. Let us forget the end,
Recalling but our love's delight in him.

vid.

Rather would I foresee the evening hour,
The setting sun, the shadows and the silence,
When I shall go to him. To me he shall
Never return. But unto him I go.

We are forbidden access to him; yet
There comes an hour when barriers shall
    fall,
And we shall be as in a world of light.
Bathsheba.
O mystic meeting! David, shall we find
Him wandering in those lilied fields of
    light,
Or playing with the children of the sky,
Or sleeping beautiful beside a stream,
Like some fair blossom flowering on its banks?
If this we knew! Then our last sun's
    going down
Would bring us joy, if unto him we went
Through the deep final darkness unafraid.
David.
God, God forgive us! Scarlet is my sin;
Wash me, and cleanse my heart that I may
    meet
This child, this love, this starry sentinel
On the waste ultimate shores of bleakest death;
When all things mortal fail, perhaps he'll be
A light, a hand, a voice, and love's own
    strength.
Bathsheba.
I know he lives—and somewhere we shall
    meet.
(They pass slowly through the darkened garden, and their voices
away as they enter the palace.)

THE HARRIETTA GATES

Beyond these gates in Wonderland;
The Past is wakened fair:
The Sleeping Beauty smiles again,
With roses in her hair.

This is no place of glamour gone;
I see it gleam and glow—
The trembling loveliness and grace,
Sweet as of long ago.

These are the gates to Wonderland;
Beyond their magic bound
Love's is the only language heard,
Music the only sound.

Calm in the loveliness that comes
From Nature, still and sure,
The live-oaks and magnolias tower,
Their massive charms endure.

And bowered in a blossoming
Fairer than orchids yield
The white home in her beauty stands
Beside the wide rice-field.

Here love has wrought a miracle
With nature and with art,
And built of all things beautiful
A home dreamed by the heart.

And better than the beauty rare
Beyond the magic gate
Are the true hearts and generous
That for their friends await.

Beyond these gates gleams Wonderland
All tender, true, and fair.
Behold the end of all the world—
Of all the world of care!

BACKWOODSMAN

Whenever he goes to the city, people know
He's a backwoodsman, and they pity him
For what he is, for what he cannot be.
He never can keep the smooth mechanic pace
Of the multitude; and even to cross a street
Bewilders him. For the wife he dearly loves
He buys a ring of brass—assured it's gold,
And for himself a watch that will not run.
Getting in the way of those on business bent,
He is shoved and hustled. If a shower comes,
He is likely to stand under a gutter spout.
Amazed by all the myriad sights and sounds,
He is abashed at his own ignorance,
And full of wonder and mistakes. He looks
In awe upon the city's commonplaces.
Naïve as a child, he tries to join
In all the meretricious merriment
Of commerce and the panoply of trade.
And if he is polite in a woodland way,
Men think his courtesy mere awkwardness.
And if a strumpet smiles at him, he smiles,
Thinking her gracious. All who see him, smile
With quiet scorn, feeling how much they know—
Princes of Babylon, and he a stranger,
A stranger and a fool in a foreign land.

And yet, if those who hold him in contempt
Could visit him at home, they soon should find
His wisdom matching theirs in a different way,
Him their superior. All Nature's moods
He registers like a barometer.
Of deep concern to him are winds and stars;
Momentous are the seasons and the tides;
He understands the portents of the skies,
And knows the import of the changing voices
Out of the forest calling. Friendly to him
Is solitude's immense primeval hush.
He loves a storm, and even is at home
Deep in the dim and meditative night.

And he can read the mystic pages old
Of Nature's green gigantic book—a dower
Far more authentic than all else we have.
The music and the stillness of the wilds
He comprehends; and he can tell what bird
Sings in the wilderness, though far away.
By the turned leaf, bent grass and faintest tracks,
He knows what shadowy wild thing here has passed.
With such a man of self-sustaining strength
Even an urban arch-sophisticate
Feels foolish, and a stranger in a land
More lordly than the country he has known.

POET BELOVED

(To Daniel Whitehead Hicky)

If in some time of terror, all we see
Of Georgia's loveliness Fate should destroy,
From the blue mountains to the violet sea;
If all the native beauty we enjoy
Were vanished: all the dewy trees that tower;
The streams that sparkle in the morning light;
The wildrose vales; the upland fields that flower;
The marshes dreaming in the arms of night:—

Though all were lost, 'twould not be gone forever.
The immortal faculty to live again
The magic of your music would restore.
For you confer on hill and field and river
Such beauty by your song that they attain
Eternity they never had before.

EMMA SABINE

It were better not to linger where he lies upon the hill,
For your waiting will not wake him, those wild pledges to
fulfil.
Come away to life and laughter; leave him lying lone and
still.

Emma Sabine with her soldier was a sight we loved to see.
But he died—the preacher told us, that the whole world
might be free.
Emma Sabine, in your freedom, will you deign to walk
with me?

On the mound the bronzing beech-leaves make a blanket
from the cold;
In the west the autumn sunset flaunts her colors red and
gold;
Now the farmer turns him homeward; now the sheep are
in the fold.

Emma Sabine, there is no one on that hill your heart to
greet;
For his heart is frozen colder than the dead leaf in the sleet.
Yesterday shall sleep forever; but tomorrow may be sweet. ...
Come you back to love and laughter, to the poppies and the
wheat.

GIVING

If beauty is withholding beauty, why
Should it be worshipped? Does it ever bless?
How generous are earth and sea and sky!
Beauty that gives itself is loveliness.

ARLINGTON BRIDGE

There is, across Potomac's stream,
A mystic bridge (yet all may see)
From Northern dream to Southern dream
Leading from Lincoln up to Lee.

It spans the gulf that sundered wide
A Nation in her mad distress,
Symbol that now alone abide
Forgiving and forgetfulness.

From Lincoln leading up to Lee,
From Lee to Lincoln leading down;
Each lived and died for liberty;
Immortal is their world-renown.

Not victory but valor gives
The hero in our hearts a shrine;
Say not in yours that Lincoln lives
Alone, and Lee alone in mine.

Ask not whose was the nobler love,
Or who was right, and who was wrong;
Remember only how they strove
Like men, and suffered, and were strong.

Calm in the Temple of the States
The soul of Lincoln lingers on;
And Lee's great spirit consecrates
His homeland heights of Arlington.

Foes of the past, now brothers all,
Your chieftains by the peaceful river
Upon you, as their comrades, call
To clasp in love your hands forever.

INGA

Inga is Saxon,
Is flaxen,
But not of her beauty
She's vain.
Yet often, again and again,
As if it were love's joyous duty,
Of Olaf, her man, will she boast,
Her Olaf, the faithful strong keeper
Who signals to ships on the main
From that stormy coast;
Her Olaf the Keeper
Of the tall lonely lighthouse
Protecting from peril the otherwise lost.
He keeps the light burning;
He keeps the light turning;
And when his stern work is fulfilled,
The tumult and peril are stilled,
With the lightning, the mad hurricane,
The surf driving in like wild rain,
The breakers that bellow like thunder,
The tawny sand scudding thereunder,—
Then in her sweet naïve way
Will Inga delightedly say:
"Since you ask why my love is like wonder,
Since you ask why so happy I seem
I will try to interpret my dream.
I will tell you all that I can—
For a husband God gave me a man."

FOREVER

A song that's hushed makes music still for me
Over life's silent land, its voiceless sea;
Because love made its light forever mine,
A star that's set will always for me shine.

IRISH POLICEMAN

You say, "He's an Irish policeman,
Patrolling our drab city street."
But Belfast and Connaught and Ulster
Are all on my regular beat.
You think I'm at Fiftieth and Broadway,
But I'm nearer my home in Tralee.
There's a Darling in Donegal waiting,
With her heart full of love,—all for me!

And deep in my soul is Killarney,
Erse, Kildare, and Kilkenny, too;
And some of my people fell fighting
With our hero, King Brian Boru.
The mountains of Moreland and Wicklow
Are mine; and the Shannon in flood
Is coursing through more than her country:
She flows through my body like blood.

And as on my beat I am strolling
I listen to dapper pert fauns;
To elves, to the Little Men laughing;
To brownies, gnomes, imps, leprechauns.
While I may return to my Erin
In some far romantic tomorrow,
Being Celtic, the fairies will friend me,
Right here, and so save me from sorrow.

SECOND MILE

Compel me for a mile to go:
Your order strict I will obey.
Submissive to you will I be
Through all that dusty, weary way.

A second mile? Come, take my hand!
With yours my heart flies joyously!
We'll sing and dance together; for
The second mile is love's, you see!

A CHARGE

Light that for me must die,
Dawn to the blind man's eye,
Shine where no path is seen,
Show where brave deeds have been!

Youth that must leave me soon,
May they receive your boon,
Who in good works are strong,
That they may labor long!

Joy that from me must part,
Enter the broken heart,
And to the vanquished give
Hope that they still may live!

Love that from me must go,
Ah, that it must be so!
Speed, speed from coast to coast,
Help him who needs you most.

Love, Youth, and Joy, and Light,
Pass not into the night!
Unto my brother come,
Enter his heart and home.

PERMANENT WAVE

As my train sped through Lula,
A tiny Georgia town,
Dreaming amid the quiet hills,
Unknown to earth's renown,
A little girl stood waving
At my proud heedless train;
I had just time to wave to her,
And see her wave again
When she was lost forever
Behind a low green hill,
But I shall always see her there,
Smiling and waving still.

HER LOVE
(J. H. C.)

Of her one thing we are forever knowing:
There shines not in the spacious sky above,
Or glows on earth, or on wide waters flowing,
A wilder, deeper loyalty of love.

Her constancy a watch on us is keeping;
Steadfast, unfailing gleam her guardian lights.
Her love, a valiant sentry never sleeping,
Patrols our dangerous days, our perilous nights.

If we were ever lost, her care would find us.
Her life tells nothing but devotion's story,—
Whose beauty and fidelity remind us
That she gives more than we have need of glory.

THE POETS

If from our sphere the lofty bards were taken,
If from our life their light extinguished were,
With whom might we in darkness then confer,
With whom rejoice, if by their joy forsaken?
For us they toiled; for us they laughed and wept;
Unfadingly their dreams illumine Thought;
Mightily grasping Truth, they homeward brought
Ultimate secrets that the far bournes kept.

In every hour of life we can rejoice
In bringers of flaming tidings from above,
In all whose souls for us were sacrificed;
In Dante's dream divine of death and love,
Melodious Milton's rolling organ-voice,
The brain of Shakespeare, and the heart of Christ.

513

OUR GARDEN

My garden is upon a height
Above my shadowy river.
There, when I work, there comes to light
What I thought gone forever:
Ashes of campfires, arrowheads,
Artistic shards and glimmering beads
Of those who watched my river flow,
Beautiful in the long ago.

My river? Rather it is ours.
Between the cypresses I seem
To vision Indians gathering flowers;
And when I see in memory's dream
A brave, than whom none could be bolder,
A shaggy buck upon his shoulder,
Into my blossoming garden come,
My heart keeps saying, "Welcome home!"

VIRGINIA DARE

The glory of being a firstborn is your song,
Virginia Dare! All loving memories throng
About your life, and to your name belong.

You were our Nation's dawning, come to bless
With beauty all its tawny wilderness,
Bringing to shaggy shores blithe loveliness.

A special splendor and renown you gave
To Roanoke Island, primitive and grave;
And on that beach each blue and breaking wave

Offers its tribute, hailing you the queen
Of all that without you had never been.
The mystery of another Eve you mean.

THE LONG HUNTERS

Let us always remember with honor the Long Hunters,
For they were the hardiest of all our hardy pioneers.
When such a durable one left home and headed
      westward
Into the haunted and unknown primeval forest,
It might be a year or more before he would return.
He lived alone in the wilderness and on the wilderness,
And you know it takes a resolute man to do that.
A man had to be a man to be a Long Hunter.

Old Meshach Browning of far Western Maryland
Was such a man, and dauntless Lou Whetzel,
And the Virginia Bledsoes, who made Tennessee;
And tall Tom Spencer, who lived in a sycamore;
And bold Jim Brady of the Pennsylvania wilds.
We Americans should remember with honor our
      Long Hunters,
For they were the young nation's uhlans, the outriders,
The discoverers of empires that slept secret, lonely,
      and lost.

Mortal Toils

THE EVERLASTING LIGHT

I

That night, as I was going home,
I heard a man cry, "Christ has come!"
Unheedingly I passed him by,
Thinking he spoke a bitter lie,
Or was profane, or drunk, or both.
To hear such folly I was loth,
And hurried on, for I was late.
But just outside my garden-gate,
Near the white lilac bush that grows
Beside my yellow Banksia rose,
I saw a woman on whose face
There shone a light of utter grace,
As if to her bright angels brought
Dreams that illumine life and thought.
I did not know her, but she came
Running to me, and called my name,
Gently as a loved sister would.
Amazed and half-afraid I stood.
"The Master's come!" she cried. Such joy
I never saw in girl or boy,
In man or woman since my birth . . .
Something was happening on the earth.
Something was happening in the sky:
Sidereal music, rolling by,
Set all the heavens trembling.
I even heard the silence sing.

II

Now all this while a Light kept growing,
Wave after wave resplendent flowing.
I left the street and neared my door.
The heavens a bridal beauty wore
That was not sunset's pageantry,
Or any light from land or sea.
And, somewhat fearful to behold
The wide world burning into gold;
And fearful, too, to farther roam,
And fearful, too, to enter home,

Lest those I loved should think me mad
At all the tidings strange and glad
Upon the earth, I stood me still,
Wondering if I had done God's will;
And if His mercy I should find
For sins of body, sins of mind;
For all I might have been; for being
Nothing in His just sight all-seeing.
And all the while the Light kept beating.
And from it there was no retreating.

III

It was a miracle Christ wrought,
This all-divulging Light He brought;
A strange intolerable Light,
That left no shadow of any night
Even in the heart's deep passageways.
Its luminance was not the day's.
All saw themselves; each saw the other;
And love's light showed him as a brother.
The nearer Christ approached to us,
The more we looked inglorious.
We were not judged that judgment day,
Or we were judged in a new way.
God's coming was in mercy meant,
And not for pain or punishment;
His only purpose, to restore
To life the loving heart once more.

IV

The Light, that everything revealed,
From which no secret was concealed,
The Light, the Light compelled confession.
To tell the truth became a passion
As strong as love when love is true.
We heard what no one ever knew.
For all whose lives had been concealment
Stood naked now in their revealment.

The Light was agony because
Each saw himself for what he was.
To tell the truth was all his need
To any one who would give heed.
And those who told their lives became
Absolved of punishment and shame.

V

There was my neighbor, Johnny Waite,
Who met me breathless by my gate.
Johnny had always had his way
With wine and women. He was gay
And sordid. Now, in sweating dread,
"What shall I do?" he wildly said.
"Ah, God, that Christ should come again!
Upon life's dunghills I have lain.
I cannot meet him cool and clean;
Only a wild boar have I been.
Feeding my heavenly soul on husks,
I am all odor, bristles, tusks.
I know that each of us should be
A music in life's harmony.
I've given my music to the vain
Revels of bacchanals profane.
How can a man get ready now?"
Dim anguish glimmered on his brow.
"My money does not count in this,
Or wine or song or harlot's kiss.
My heart is all begrimed, defiled.
Ah, God, to be a little child!
I'd give my all to be once more
The little child my mother bore."

As arrogant as Johnny is,
I stood and heard him tell me this.
But even as he told me all,
I saw a miracle befall:

I saw his heart go white and clean,
And beautiful as it had been
When o'er her child his mother leant,
Above his slumbers innocent.
Then he went singing down the street
With joyous voice and dancing feet.
The burdens old in secret borne,
The lies, like heavy armor worn,
Were laid aside. How young he stood,
Emerging from sin's solitude;
In Christ's forgiveness strong and free,
How like the child he longed to be!

VI

There came a girl of faded gown,
And more than faded her renown,
Who'd sold her heart for sordid gain.
She called herself La Belle Lorraine.
Leaving a brilliant evil place,
All sorrow mirrored on her face,
From which the beauty and the grace
Had long since gone, toward me she stole,
As if I'd power to make her whole.
As if toward me her heart were homing,
Sinful myself, I saw her coming;
Yet even far-off my soul recoiled
From one so brazen and so soiled.
Wearing the withered rose of shame,
Gently and sad toward me she came.

"My heart is breaking with the pain
To tell my tale. I am Lorraine,
Who once was young and innocent,
Whose spirit was for heaven meant.
I see myself as I am seen:
Wicked, repellent, and unclean."
Now she was weeping quietly
That all should know, that all should see

How sin and sorrow, shame and tears
Transformed her likeness into theirs.
"O Christ forgive me!" then she cried.
"It was for such as I you died.
I am another Magdalene.
Your love alone can make me clean."
Yet even as she staidly wept
A glory through her grandly swept,
Purging away all evil there.
All that remained was pure and fair.
And lilies on her breast she wore
To tell she was not as before.
Beautiful as a star at even
She rose from earth and entered heaven.

VII

Not always did the Light discover
A sinful maid or guilty lover;
Not always did its poignant flame
Disclose dishonor, greed, or shame.
It showed my heart a dusty clod;
But beauty, innocence, and God
The hearts of little children held.
From them no penance was compelled.
No lust or hate their hearts concealed;
There was no sin to be revealed.
To them the Light came but to bless,
For they had nothing to confess.

VIII

One man we knew who had the wild
And rainbow fancy of a child,—
Our well loved poet, who had sung
His songs to us and kept us young.
He laughed; he led us by the hands
Into authentic fairylands;
And to our dusty eyes unfurled
The bannered beauty of the world.

He sang to us and stilled our fears;
He sang and loosed our hearts in tears.
Telling us that our love's divine,
For it he built a glimmering shrine.
We saw an astral splendor burn
In him. He taught us how to turn
From loveliness that's only feigned
To loveliness that is ordained.

Living as if he were attended
By spirits out of heaven descended,
Sometimes he seemed a fay. So mild
He was, some thought him but a child;
But thrilling tidings kept him glad,
Trustful and unafraid. He had
The magic phantom hand of art,
The wizard surmise of the heart.
Believing things he could not see,
Through vision came to verity.
Of joy he knew the poignant pang;
Sidereal music through him sang;
Through him far intimations swept.
Upon Night's naked breasts he slept;
And, wakening, he took for flight
The Morning's mighty wings of light.
All loveliness delighted him:
The gulfs of noontide, blue and dim;
The bud of darkness, mystic, tender,
Whose opening is the dawning's splendor;
The haunting wildwood, and the wan
Beauty the evening's builded on;
The frost-flowers on the window-pane,
The hush of lilac-scented rain;
The little bird that sings so late
That it must wildly love its mate.
And Nature mothered him with wild
Compassion, for he was her child.
With tenderness more deep than shade
Her hands upon his eyes she laid.

Now he came by in gracious power,
His faith fulfilled in that dread hour.
And when the Light went through his heart,
Each of the other seemed a part.
He always had been like a portal,
Leading to life and love immortal.
Not what we kept, but what we gave
Alone has power our lives to save

IX

Whenever to our town had come
The great of earth, they felt at home
Because our clubs had entertained
These guests until they felt they reigned.
But now what could we say or do?
Not even the Chamber of Commerce knew,
Whose pallid president I met,
His broad face lined with care and sweat.
Long since he had laid by his hoard;
And he was chairman of the board
Of many a corporation great,—
The owner of a vast estate.
Yet on that memorable night
His was a pitiable plight.
For all his power ill sufficed
Against the majesty of Christ,
The glory that has other birth
Than any glory known to earth.
And used to power, and used to pride,
With the world always on his side,
He paused beside me in the way,
And I was stunned to hear him say,
In language that he might have sung
(It was the Light that loosed his tongue):
"How solidly they fall who stand
Too solidly upon life's land!

They build themselves. It is their fate
Massively to disintegrate,
Subsiding in elaborate power.

They fall much farther than they tower.
Too solidly I stood. I never
Saw the white lilies by life's river;
I never tiptoed, peering over
Life's wall into love's fields of clover;
I never leaned to see the dust
That is the end of every lust;
Nor ever lifted to the skies
The worship true of wondering eyes.
Behold in me Success; behold
The sorriest story ever told.
I've lived for nothing loftier than
To victimize my fellow man.
Life is love's gift of fellowship;
I've made of life a business trip;
And all my many mighty labors
I've spent defrauding all my neighbors.
Ambition is the avarice
For which we pay the highest price.
Of all God's glory round me glowing
I've never come to any knowing.
My grimy useless story told
Is nothing but a greed for gold.
My futile history plainly proves
A man *becomes* the thing he loves.
I am but riches time has tarnished,
A tomb whose outside's gaily garnished.
O not in houses, not in lands
Our blessed hope immortal stands;
Shall have for us the power to save."
Yet even as he so confessed,
Into his eyes a look of rest,
Of vision clearing, came, and grace
Deep from his heart shone in his face.

He who was dead arose to live.
Christ can such resurrection give.

X

A little down the street I strayed,
When once again I was waylaid
By one whose beauty always had
Made life more beautiful and glad,
Had given aspiration, till
Grief had with her its selfish will.

"O I have sinned beyond the rest,
For more than others I was blessed.
My husband loved me. When he died,
I in my sorrow took such pride
That I enjoyed grief's luxury.
My selfishness I could not see.
Of all who grieve, I should have borne
My sorrow nobly, should have worn
My cross in secret, while I gave
Myself to life, not to the grave.
'Let not your heart be troubled.' He
Gave that command to you and me.
But I paraded in my tears.
Now would I pay my sin's arrears
Thus humbly. Only those who come
Out of their sorrow can find home.
God cannot meet us in our night;
We must go forward toward the light,
And as we reach that frontier land,
Mercy shall take us by the hand.
All human tribulations prove
That broken hearts pour out most love;
Grief to all life this glory lends:
That in pain's empire all are friends;
When there is naught our way to mark,
We gather closer in the dark."

Restored, refreshed, I saw her gleam
A girl again, with a girl's dream.
She like a precious jewel glowed,
A jewel on a queen bestowed.

XI

And here and there, and now and then,
Among the women and the men
Confessing, came a spirit bold,
Who dauntlessly his story told.
Who seemed to feel he had some claim
To be absolved from sin and blame.
Such was our well known naturalist,
Who thus apologized to Christ.

"God, what a sinner was your child,
With wayward heart and lips defiled!
Your old commandments he has broken;
Vainglorious words his ways have spoken;
Yet they were not his spirit's token.
Rarely did he obey Your will;
And yet, from many a lonely hill,
Your hand had heaved, he marveled how
Your valor did the valleys plow,
And lift the mountains' cloudy brow.
He never saw a wildflower beaming,
He never saw wild starlight streaming
But of Your love he fell a-dreaming,—
As to him came a sense of awe
At majesty and ancient law,
Feeling more deeply than he saw.
At loveliness his tears outwelled;
And always in his heart he held
A shrine apart, wherein he wept
For all the rules he never kept.
Lord, now the great account is given,
This child of your must needs be shriven,—

Failing in all things saving one:
He saw You in the lordly sun,
In mystery Your might divined,
And was not to Your magic blind.
He heard You in the thunder's roll,
And felt You plotting in his soul
For reverence and self-control.
In beauty that Your mind had made,
He listened to the words You said,
Alive among the living dead;
Visioned in all things fair Your face,
And in all wonder sought Your grace,
Nor looked on love as commonplace.
Almighty Love, that never mocks,
Creator of this paradox,
Let him be tenderly compassioned,
This dusty angel by You fashioned.
O generous Christ, all wise and mild,
Accept this sinner—and Your child."

And as he spoke, I saw his tears.
He had not wept through all his years.
The Light burned through him, strange and wild,
Transfiguring him. No more defiled,
He stood a shining figure lone,
As if he gleamed beside the Throne.

XII

There was a lawyer in our town
Who had a dubious renown,
I mean Tom Alden. All his brains
He sold for power and for gains.
A spurious patriot, he bought
The votes of others, and he fought
Against all noble change that meant
That he thereby might lose a cent.
He owned a wide and mouldering slum,
Where he himself would never come,

But fattened on the heart's despair
Of those who wept and rotted there.
Wherever sin and sorrow lurked,
A lover of the dark, he worked.
Out of the alms' box he would steal
The widow's mite, nor guilty feel.
We knew Tom Alden for a thief
Who never grieved, yet had one grief:
That he could not abscond with all
The earth possessed since Adam's fall.
Yet who should come to me, afraid,
But this same felon, and he said:

"My day is over at this hour.
I am a weed. Christ is love's flower.
O look into my heart and read
The history of a hideous weed.
I might have been a mountain pine,
But am a poison ivy vine.
I am a pestilential thing,
Abhorrent to my Christ and King.
I have a heart as hard as any's.
I stole the widow Warren's pennies.
I've filched the orphans' bread and meat,
And given my spirit dust to eat.
Behind the bank vault's many locks
There is a stack of bonds and stocks
That represent my infamy.
Ah, who but Christ would pity me?"

He spoke and, shuddering, turned aside.
But Heaven's gate is very wide;
And ere Tom Alden left that night
Within his eyes I saw a light,
A far dawn breaking, that would bring
Peace to a spirit suffering.

XIII

Miss Margie Mays for countless years
Had taught our children. All her tears
Had been for other people's woe.
She went wherever love can go.
Her gladness was for others' joys.
Mothering all our girls and boys,
She had no time to sin at all,
But like an old rose by life's wall
Still kept on blooming, though 'twas late,
And winsome made time's garden gate.
She had a heart that sang love's song;
She never wrought another wrong,
But like a warbling rivulet went
Through life's dark woods of discontent.
Of worldly goods, of earthly fame
Nothing she had, yet had a name
For selfless living. I was near
When the great Light made her appear
Not as a teacher, worn and gray,
But as a rose at break of day,—
For immortality arrayed,
By Love, for all her love, repaid.
Her life for others she laid down;
Imperishable her renown.
Peerless on love's high altar lies
The gift that is a sacrifice.

XIV

There was a person on our street
I never thought that night to meet,—
The famous Dr. Vanderveer,
Whose very name inspired fear.
O none denied his brilliant mind;
And little children thought him kind.
But he derided faith, and stood
In unbelieving hardihood.
He was a scientist, a man
Whose spirit was pedestrian.

531

Searching for fires of truth, he came
On ashes only, not on flame.
Reading the world's stupendous story,
He found the facts but missed the glory.
Denying all he could not prove,
He smiled at chivalry and love;
Or if he thought of love at all,
Knew it as biological.
His soul had red and hairy hands,
And if one wept, he thought of glands.
He hated laughter, song, and tears,
The visionaries and the seers.
But most he held in high contempt
The poets for the dreams they dreamt . . .
Seeing one star (and that was faint),
He thought he viewed the firmament.
A sailor merely, he'd deny
That mountains climb into the sky;
An inlander, who could not be
Persuaded that there is a sea.
Having no power to divine,
He made within his heart no shrine
For beauty. And it was a place
Too grimed to entertain a Grace.
He fed his soul as swine are fed;
With weeds her brow he garlanded.
Feeling life should be disenchanted,
He never flowered, though firmly planted.

And now, with faltering step and slow,
With shoulders drouped and head bowed low,
Toward me he came, with face of stone.
Faith in himself was dead and gone.
He said: "In vain, in vain I strove
Against the mighty law of love.
I see the armored cruiser quail,
The dreadnaught shudder in her mail,
The wild destroyer reel and sink:
There is no Force that shall not fail.

532

Now, now I feel Christ's power divine.
Ah, could I make that power mine!
God, let me worship at love's shrine.
I've lived in pride, and lived in vain.
Christ comes to let me live again."

And even in his meek despair
The famous Dr. Vanderveer
Transfigured stood before us there.

XV

And there was one through fortune proud
And nature, far above the crowd.
Her fatal memorable grace,
The beauty of her ruinous face
Betrayed all men. What she loved most
Was conquest, and the conqueror's boast.
Toward luxury her soul was bent;
From cocktail unto cocktail went;
And measured life by baubles hung
(That had been hearts). She was so young
Yet old in wiliness; she proved
How false love is as she had loved.
Yet Sandra, shorn of mystery,
Out of the darkness stole to me.
To me she came. I hardly knew her,
But through her tears I listened to her.

"Men thought me beautiful," she said;
"But all the while my heart was dead.
I dangled lovers in the mad
Voluptuous triumphs that I had.
Luring them on with sweet delays,
I was a strumpet in my ways;
For never once an honest thought
Possessed my mind. The pain I wrought
Gave me delight. No fiend of hell
Enjoyed men's anguish half so well

533

As I. And never in my life
Had I a thought to be a wife,
A mother. What I loved was power,
That stained my beauty hour by hour.
A glamour girl they labeled me.
The hideous hag that now you see
Is the real Sandra. But the Light,
Revealing me, restores my sight:
My vision true that once I had
To wed a simple sterling lad.
Promiscuous, a queen I reigned;
Myself I lost, and nothing gained.
Can I be this? Ah, look not long
Till I again am well and strong.
Christ, Christ, restore me. Your estate
Is boundless, as your love is great."
Her beauty, that had been of earth,
Mysteriously had another birth,
Divine translation in that hour
Her contrite heart awoke to power.
Dissolved to dust was all her pride,
And she stood shimmering like a bride;
Or as the forest or the sea
Wakes to a glorious life to be
When the full moon begins to shine
And the whole world goes argentine.

XVI

Then suddenly as if in fright
Ran Arlie Bates into the Light;
And he in torment writhed to feel
That poignant luminance reveal
His deep besetting sin: he ne'er
Had soul enough to really care.
For he was neither ice nor fire,
Was neutral even in desire.
The Light of God tore him apart
Who had a hollow for a heart.

Said he, whose life had thus been cleft,
"Of all I was, there's nothing left.
If I had wildly loved, I know
I never should have felt this woe;
If I had hated, I had been
Less futile, colorless, and mean.
To everything in life lukewarm,
I never felt the generous storm
Of sacrifice; my ardor idled
As selfishly through life I sidled.
The faith that can dim mountains move
Is just another name for love;
And not to care enough, I call
Far worse than not to care at all.
Who saves himself alone shall be
The least in heaven's company.
Could anything on earth be less
Than I,—who now my sin confess?"

The Light, that burnt him out to naught,
A magic from his ashes wrought:
Out of his darkness and his shame
Christ kindled love's immortal flame.

XVII

All night, all night, and without rest,
Women and men their lives confessed;
About the world a murmur ran
Of man confessing unto man
The inhumanities of old.
Myriads of wasted lives were told.
I heard but few of these, but all
Told the same story of our fall
From loving-kindness, and the plan
God had, and always has, for Man.

XVIII

And then I heard a voice above
Earth's silence sing this song of love:
One could be, with a voice like hers,
On earth one of God's choristers:
"Each human heart a jewel is,
Hidden until it burns with Christ.
Our jewels are lost in the night,
Are darkened; and only by light
At length can their beauty be known.
Then the rose in the ruby is blown;
In the sapphire sparkles the ocean deep,
And the turquoise cradles a sky asleep
In the tender twilights of tone.
On the beryl's shrine is the springtime shed;
In the agate the autumn is red.
As an angel, of wonder aware,
Adown the white shimmering stair
Of the amethyst's crystalline door
A violet glory is led.
Through the opal a far moon will roam,
As over a wild seashore,
Through clouds that curtain her western home
She sinks to the foam.
O Master of love and of light,
O Giver of glorious day,
Not less than these jewels we pray
Deliverance out of the night.
From the dim and the ignorant thought
Bring us forth as these jewels are brought;
By the might of Thy mind we were wrought;
Leave us not in the darkness alone!
More precious are we in Thy sight,
Are we, Thy children, Thine own,
Our radiance yielding more perfect delight
Than the wizard starlights of stone."

Whose voice, like bird-songs after rains,
So worshiped Christ? It was Lorraine's.

XIX

Christ came. He shone. He did not stay;
For our old world had passed away.
Where once the palace and hovel stood
Were broad estates of brotherhood.
By Him all men were changed because
Each saw himself for what he was.
O such a light Christ shed, its glow
Could through the heart's deep darkness go,
And lay all bare, and bring to be
One comradeship from sea to sea;
As back the clouds of darkness roll,
One brotherhood from pole to pole,
And peace and love in every soul.

XX

A little while ere birds awaken,
And dewdrops from the leaves are shaken,
By winds of morning, hale and clear,
I heard a singer coming near,
Like a rivulet down a rosebay slope,
Singing this song of joy and hope:

"Peace is beginning to be;
Deep as the peace of the sea
When stars their faces glass
In its blue tranquility:
Peace, and the passing of pride,
With love alone for our guide;
Peace, and the passing of fear.
The lilies of mercy we wear;
Joy, and the splendor tall
Of the Angel of Love over all.
Brothers and sisters are we;
And we see what we had not seen;
And we are what we have not been:
Brothers and sisters are we,
Building without a stain
Life and the world again."

He came on stupendous
And burning wide wings,
Like the vast rose of light
That the sunsetting brings.
In splendor and beauty
And silence He came:
The sea rolled effulgent;
The mountains took flame.

But never a sunset
Had beauty like His.
We trembled; we questioned:
Was our reason amiss?
Was the Great Doom at hand,
And this sentinel lone
A watchman to guard
Till destruction was done?

But soft from all lands,
And from ships on the sea
Arose a sweet music
Of spirits set free.
O never was heard
So rejoicing a sound
For liberty given
To them who were bound.

Then laughed the sad captive;
Then upstared the slave;
Then settled the fortress,
And opened the grave.
Men ran about crying
From home to glad home,
"The Conqueror's coming;
The Conqueror's come!"

Then the armies disbanded;
The navies no more
Were a threat to the sea
And a dread to the shore.
All barriers olden
That held friends apart
Quite vanished, and left us
All brothers in heart.

Ah, Mercy eternal,
O glorious hour!
Glad, sinless we stood
In the Conqueror's power.
And we danced, and we sang
On the hills, by the sea;
For the Spirit of Love
Had set the world free.

WHAT LITTLE THINGS

What little things the heart remembers!
The fervid heat was late September's.
A sultry haze made dim the meadow.
The sycamore's pale dappled shadow
Could offer only stifling shade.
The airs were all asleep, or made
A burning breeze, almost aflame,
As from the fevered fields it came.

Then from this blazing pitiless glare
I turned into a dingle, where
Down mossy rocks a little stream
Came singing in a silver dream . . .
Upon the harp he harped upon,
Where rhododendrons hid the sun,
Under the shade's deep barriers,
A woodthrush played cool arias.

THE DAY OFF

I will do nothing today;
I will only be:
I will be one with the sky
And the earth
And the sea.

I will forego all toil,
Ambition forego;
Forsake my exhausting strife
With its pride
And its woe.

I will do nothing at all.
It will be sweet
Not to consider campaigns
Of advance
Or retreat.

On Nature's breast will I lie
While she sings to me
In voices of winds and birds
And in waves
Of the sea.

I will not go anywhere,
Though all the world goes.
I will be dreamfully still
As a rock
Or a rose.

Tomorrow there will be time
To gird and to strive.
I will do nothing today
But to love
And to live.

RESTORATION

Before they came, this yard, this place
Belonged to Nature. Here they stayed.
Home was to them this little space.
Here love was known; here children played;
But now of them fades out each trace,
And all their work is now unmade
By golden rod and Queen Anne's lace.

When they were gone, the yard grew rank;
Fennel and jimson weed took over;
With moss the walk was green and dank;
Uncut were hedge, and grass, and clover;
Deep in the earth the step-stones sank . . .
Of such wild solitude the lover
A tall stag from the bird-bath drank.

But mourn not for this ruined shrine;
For Nature will reclaim her own.
Already hickory, oak, and pine,
Dogwood, and holly trees have grown.
This spot could not be yours and mine
Or theirs forever: 'twas a loan
From Nature: all to her assign.

This place is silent save for songs
Of mated birds. And down the years,
As more to Nature it belongs,
Her heart, that never knows despairs,
Will hide the wounds, and right the wrongs,
Until a forest reappears,
Brightened by fairy wildflower throngs.

HER REWARD

Out of Parting's mortal pain
Hers is this immortal gain:
Though her soldier-son depart,
Comes a hero to her heart.

THE GARDEN

Radiant and winsome she gleams,
Bright, friendly, yet calmly sequestered;
Reticent, virginal, wise,
Reflective, most patient through power;
Having nothing to do
With vanities, prides, and vexations;
Having nothing to say
To the foolish, the flippant, the froward;
Having nothing to think
Of the trivial, transient, ignoble;
Having no slightest concern
With the hoof-hearted hurry of Progress.

Always and only engaged
With the major issues majestic;
With Beauty eternal concerned,
With blossom and pregnance and fruitage;
Steadfast, demure, subdued
With the deep-hearted joy of creating;
Thoughtful of life and of love,
And resigned to death's mystical meaning;
Laying sweet hands of hope
On the sure, the immortal, the lovely;
Charged with tremendous tasks
And addressed to miracles chastely.

Through the still portals of dawn
And the glimmering casements of evening
Hears she the Message from Far,
Accepting, approving, fulfilling;
To her compassionate care
Is entrusted the timidest flower;
Yet is her ministry felt
By the oak and the pine monumental;
A child of the Flesh and its frailty,
Into the garden I wander,
Seeking the pathway to peace,
Nor elsewhere on earth do I find it.

For in the garden I come
To gentle and infinite wisdom,
Tolerant, constant, detached,
At toil through the daytime she's singing;
Exquisite, magic, serene,
In the glamour of pendulous moonlight.
Holding patents and deeds
And parchments and grants and free-
    warren
Out of the ancient years
From the Lord and the Maker of all things;
Calm with the surety of one
Who labors with God as his helper.

ACCEPTANCE

The tall trees, how calm,
And how quiet the grass;
Then came the wild storm.
I felt its force pass.
Designed to destroy
All this stillness of joy.

As if it were duty,
As if a wand waved,
By bowing their beauty,
The tall trees were saved.
By bending, they broke
The hurricane's stroke.

To frustrate the gale
That can never long last,
To make tempest's fail,
Bow low to their blast;
And the ruin essayed
Will by yielding be stayed.

THE HAUNTED HOUSE

One after one I hear them softly closing,
Inviolately, with the hush of doom,
The doors behind me in the House of Life.
And I shall never see those rooms again.
There was the one of wildrose dreams of youth,
Where love's untroubled wonder made divine
And mystic with new meaning all the world.
Fair from its perfumed casement Beauty leaned,
Summoning Strength to enter and be glad.
Who enters finds that even lyric love
May be to death addressed . . . That door is
  closed.
And in another room dwelt Pride of Fame,
In haughtiness of vivid beauty burning,—
A ruddier constellation than the rose.
Her eyes were gorgeous ambushes of pain.
And from her room a stairway seemed to lead
Starward, even to the loftiest throne of thought;
And up and down went ministers of mind,
Having the speed and language of the light.
But soon I found the stairway's sudden end,—
Learning how swiftly earthly glory fades
On the eternal threshold of the stars.
And many rooms there were, and many doors.
All, all are closing with the dreadful might
Of gentleness . . . Hope's door is open still,
Shedding its wistful beam far in the dark,
Now that the haunted house is solitary,
Mantled in silence and in mist asleep.
Hope's door is last; and it need never close;
For evermore to the heart Hope's voice is saying:
"Fear not; arrayed for change immortal, you
Shall radiantly quest that luminous bourne
Of all lost lyric love and every longing.
It is not far; you shall not fail to find it,—
That ancient and tremendous Portal fair,
On Everlasting Beauty opening."

REVELATION

Behind the brooch, the jeweled bar,
In all your beauty bare you are.
Forgive me if your loveliness
Allures me more than any dress.
I see your hair, your eyes, your lips,
But only vision breasts and hips.
What can be wrong in longing to
Behold the beauty that is true?
Come glorious from God's great hand,
His masterpiece for me might stand,
Breathlessly beautiful and near,
Wild, native, sweet, disclosed, and clear.
The loveliness that we might see,
Withheld, has not a right to be.
The heart must ever weep the most
For beauty that is loved and lost.

Dull in the rock the emerald gleams;
The pearl, dim in the oyster gleams.
The rose, close-curtained by the night,
Forfeits her virtue to delight.
The blue-eyed violet wears no cloak;
Naked and noble stands the oak.
The diamond in the blue earth veiled
Her radiance to reveal has failed.
No mask the artless lilac wears;
All that the lily is—appears!
Her mystery to manifest,
The waterlily bares her breast.
Deep in the darksome Modoc mine
The Burmese ruby cannot shine.
No meretricious mantles cover
Hale stargrass, daisy, jasmine, clover.
How frustrate at the husk to stare!
What bliss to gaze on beauty bare!

PROUD BARQUE

How often has he sadly wondered
Of the goal and the fate
Of that magical proud barque
That passed him as the dusk was growing dark,
When, shipwrecked, he lay floating on a spar,
His only light the setting evening star.
But his peril had no power to make her wait,
Nor to his hailing would she hark,
But hastened on her swift and radiant way,
Her bourne some lordly city, river, or bay
Unknown to him,
Beyond a wild sea strange and dim.
From her exalted course
She never wavered or turned.
Though he lay spent,
On nobler emprise was her genius bent.
She saw and knew his desperate need,
But gave no heed.
It was if she burned
With dedicated grace
(Such was her speed),
Bearing great tidings to a mighty king.
By him she drove apace,
As if so save
Old empires from the grave,—
As if her bright arriving well might bring
Salvation to doomed nations shuddering,
Waiting her coming as a time to sing.

So to his fate she left him long ago.
Nor shall he ever know
If she has found
The prize for which her beauty had been bound.
Imperious, impetuous, and swift,
She left his life to drift
On the sea, in the night alone.
He knows not whither she has gone,
What treasures she recovered from what coast.

But he is troubled in his heart and mind,
Knowing that nowhere shall she ever find
A glory equal to the glory lost
When she left love behind.

RADIO

O not a word and not a thought
In the wide world shall come to naught;
No little love with sails of white
Shall vanish homeless in the night.

This wind that moves with fluting song
My plumed and purple pines among
Shall wave dim palms in tropic nights,
Shall storm the white Himalayas' heights.

And every dream I mourn as dead
Or lost is lyrically fled
Out of my heart into another's—
While I have taken home my brother's.

At length shall break on Hatteras
The wave that Breton sailors pass
Blue rolling westward, or shall run
To thunder on the dreadful Horn.

The tingling air is thrilled with spirit;
The universe I can inherit.
Mysteriously great and near,
Creation's throbbing heart I hear.

Of those elusions, farewells, flights
That dim my days and haunt my nights,
In all the lonely strength of wings
Some heart shall make recoverings.

WOMAN

To save the Race, most sovereignly endowed,
She is deserving to be very proud.
For her to be a miracle to man,
Eternity would be too brief a span.
The guardian of life's unfading flame,
Of all to be the glorious source and frame,
Its solemn mystery to love she gives,
And in her loins alone the Future lives:
Sleeping in her unborn are tribes and nations;
In her abide the coming generations.
Her breasts are pointed rosebuds, and her eyes
Are invitations into Paradise.
All Eden's on her flowery bridal lips;
Love's deeply heaving ocean's in her hips,
And immortality between her thighs.

TWO AND THREE

Two wandered to the greenwood,
The deep wood, the wildwood,
And wild with love were they.
One with the forest's mystic mood,
In silence and in solitude.
O long they stayed, as lovers should,
Nor had they lost their way.

O deep in love were they!
Such love no heart debases.
Under wide azure spaces
Two wandered to the places
Of woodland airs and graces.
Long, long were their embraces,—
And three came back that day.

THE GOLDEN BIRD

Not a wave on the river had changed.
Not a leaf in the forest had stirred.
But, lovely, as lonely I ranged,
A music supernal I heard.
As if all the beauty beyond
Our capture had utterance found.
From all other singing apart,
I listened alone with my heart
To life's glory no longer deferred,
To the voice of the Golden Bird.

Not a star in the firmament faltered;
Not a wildflower faded or fell,
And yet my whole being was altered
As under a magical spell.
I was where I never had been.
I saw what I never had seen.
My whole life had listened in vain
This joy of the soul to attain;
No dream could the wonder foretell
Of my saying to sorrow farewell.

Not the wild note from Orpheus' lyre,
In the gloom, from love's mystical chord
So could answer immortal desire;
Not the awful and beautiful word
That Lazarus harked in his sleep,
In his dreaming eternal and deep;
Not the anthems of shore and of sea
Can ever make music for me
With the ecstasy on me conferred,
Like the voice of my Golden Bird.

TO HART

The music of all that is joyous and free;
The beauty of all that the eye cannot see;
The dawn of deep wonder that love brings to be;
The spirit of all that is dearest to me.

COUSIN GEORGIANA

I

When Cousin Georgiana from New York
Came for a visit, all of us were scared,—
All except Dollie, who'll be five next June.
Our Cousin's name was awesome to begin with;
Then there was something large, if artificial,
In her importance. She had taken on
A metropolitan air, and was a contrast
Between the city's notability
And the little obscure farm on which we live.
Of course, we knew the difference, but she seemed
To be Fate's delegate to drive it home.
She made us feel that Christmas and Santa Claus
Lived where she came from; and the clothes she wore
Made all our things more homespun than they were.
She once had been to Rome; and had even been
To Boston. And of course our hearts were proud
That we were kin to one who knew the world
Beyond our garden and our humble yard,
In that great life beyond our little lives.

II

But Dollie, with a child's naïvete,
Which is unspoiled native sagacity,
Took her quite casually, was unimpressed;
And to our horror she seemed positive
Great Georgiana was inferior,
And that it was her task to teach her things.
Dollie just took our Cousin's hand, and said:
"You must see Mopsie and the babies. Come;
It's almost feeding time, and they're so sweet,"
Leading her to the pigpen! "We have lots
Of things to make us happy. Iffen you don't play out,
I'll show them to you: yonder's the piedied heifer
That we call Bess; and that's the little runt bull
What will not grow. O Cousin Georgiana,
Let's climb for cherries! Don't you like to climb?
I reckon that the city has no trees.
Over the hill we all go blackberrying.

I'll take you there, for you don't have all this
Where you come from." And so they toured the farm.
When Cousin Georgiana said goodbye
After her visit to her country cousins,
Not one of us could quite help noticing
How long and close she held our Dollie to her.

VISITOR

If love should ever deign
To visit you, you could
Render his coming vain,
Live on in solitude.
But should you ask him in,
He will not come alone;
To far lands he has been,
And all things he has known.
O should you welcome him,
With him will come wild tears,
Shadows from marshes dim,
Doubts, hesitancies, fears.
All these with him shall come,
And wondrous joy beside
To consecrate your home . . .
'Tis wisdom to decide
O take this comrade true
Though you must take with him
His mortal retinue,
Haunting and strange and dim.
Be brave, and bid him hail,
And of your life a part:
Without him you shall fail,
Showing a coward's heart.
Stand not from him apart:
Be brave, and bid him hail.

ROADSIDE SPHINX

Beside the highway's thronging crowds
There is a place concealed,—
The glimmering marsh that stretches mute,
Veiled, latent, unrevealed.
The sky above, the fields about
Lie open. It is sealed.

The tide may take great tidings in,
But brings no message out.
The dark enigma's undivulged
Of what it is about.
No mortal man can understand
Its silence like a shout.

I see the wild geese flying over,
The sea-gulls wheeling white;
The world around is full of day,
The marsh is full of night.
It has old secrets of its own
Of sorrow and delight.

Although surrounded you may be
By road and clanging mart,
Clandestine marsh, you have a life
Dim, occult, and apart.
Nothing is so mysterious,—
Except the human heart!

FAME

Of fame's austere
Illustrious power
He has the crown,
He wears the flower,
Who kindles fair,
With fragile art,
The flame of hope
In a frozen heart.

552

O PASSIONATE HEART!

O passionate Heart, to you
This tribute true!
Selfless and masterly,
Free as the wild bird free;
Incautious, gallant, wild,
Nature's most precious child;
Your soul is too profound
To be orbit-bound.
You live to bless,
To give your loveliness
To a world but half-aware
Of the meaning of your air.
Your valor to earth brings
Beauty that sings.
O lovely Morning Star,
Wounded you are,
But still your spirit's bright
After grief's cruel night.
Always and ever your story
Shall be nothing but glory.

THE LAST

That morning like all other mornings broke
Over the fragrant wildwoods, where the flowers
Asleep in dewy loveliness, awoke,
To make wild rainbows in those glimmering bowers
Looking for the last time on all he loved,
The last of all his Race, a monster stood
Pathetic, where his mighty kind had moved
For ages through the forest and the flood.

The world like Eden gleamed, a fairyland;
There was no sound of earthquake or of war;
No sin or shame a single heart had planned;
But the Inexorable spoke from afar;
And unseen spirits, hearing that command,
Led to his doom the mailèd dinosaur.

ROSE BY THE RIVER

For the first time alone,
With free hearts unsundered.
How wild were the woods
Where we joyously wandered!
And how wild were our hearts,
After waiting and waiting,—
Love blessing, approving
Our spirits for mating!

Now no land and no sea
Our spirits can sunder:
And ours will be always
The rapture, the wonder!
My Flower Unfading,
My Rose by the River,
The glory you gave me,
You gave me forever!

SYMBOLIC SEA

I doubt if there could ever be
A symbol of inconstancy
So perfect as the changing sea.

Here are the arms, alluring, white;
Here is the promise of delight;
Here all the wonder hid from sight.

Her glimmering breasts gleam through the foam
Her wild voice calls for me to come;
Her arms are wide to take me home.

Heartless she is, yet deep and wise;
Deceptive are her occult eyes,
And treacherous her luring thighs.

I do not know why this should be:
But life reveals to you and me
Some women cruel as the sea.

RIDERS

Ride out, young rider. The world is awaking;
Glad voices are calling you forth to the trail.
The mist on the mountains is bright with daybreaking;
The wild birds are warbling from hilltop and swale.
For you beauty beckons, and glory is gleaming;
For you the gold trumpets, the banners that wave;
For you love and honor, fulfilling your dreaming;
For you the adventures awaiting the brave.

Ride on, strong rider. The morning's behind you;
The stern path's before, through the desert's wide
    pallor.
Hold fast to the trail; for no searcher could find you
If once you should stray. And you'll need all your
    valor.
Still sing your tall song though your dawning-hopes
    languish;
Still bear the noon's hammers of heat on your brain;
Still keep on your riding through dust and through
    anguish,
Against the bleak wonder if all is in vain.

Ride on, old rider. The twilight is bringing
The hues of the gloaming to tint the far mountains;
His vespers the shadowy veery is singing,
Now evening has deepened the voice of the fountains.
Now fever relents as the miles are diminished;
The muscadine fragrance of darkness is shed.
All perils are passed, and the journey is finished,
The stars are arriving, and your home-lights ahead.

YOUR VOICE

For melody I need not make a choice;
For I have you to make my heart rejoice.
Like seawind or a song of long ago,
All music's in the beauty of your voice.

LOVE AND SORROW

When shall Love and Sorrow kiss,
Kiss and clasp each other close?
When each of the other knows
All its beauty and its bliss.

Love that has not sorrow known,
Is untried and is unsure;
Sorrow is by Love made pure,
Glorified by Love alone.

When a Love and Sorrow part
In some hot rebellious breast;
There is aching and unrest;
And there is a broken heart.

But the hour of all the years
Deepest, purest, and most sweet
Is when Love and Sorrow meet;
And embrace amid their tears.

Love, the beautiful and bright,
Joins us to life's joyous day;
Sorrow, in her silent way,
Reconciles us to the Night.

SUNDOWN

For feet, a hill that's steepening;
For eyes, a dusk that's deepening;
For hands, a toil that's ending;
For strength, a sleep for mending;
For fear, a quiet stilling;
For faith, a deep fulfilling;
For ears, a music failing;
For pain, a peace prevailing;
For hearts, a joyous homing;
For love, a glory coming.

LIMITS

Joy, how far can you go?
"As far as the shade,
Where the flowers fade.
In the light,
By the light,
For the light was I made."

Grief, how far can you go?
"As far as the dawn,
Where hope is born,
That night is mine
Where no stars shine.
But I die with the dawn."

Love, how far can you go?
"Through all light and all shade,
Past all things made,
And deep beyond death;
After these tears,
And the failure of breath,
In other spheres,
In other years,
Deep beyond,
Deep beyond,
Deep beyond death."

UNCONCERN

Wounded, through shadows wending,
The broken hearts go by,
Broken beyond all mending . . .
And one of them is I.

Bright wine in sunlight quaffing,
The hearts that know not rue
Are singing and are laughing . . .
And one of them is you.

557

TOUCHDOWN

A hush is on the bleachers; even she
Who wants to ask a question, silent is,—
A miracle of feminine control.
Clear come the signals from the quarterback;
The leonine ends are trembling in the leash;
A sudden deeper hush, as if of doom . . .
Then treads the tempest wildly, warily;
The hurtling hurricanes of flesh and blood
Converge dynamic toward the fullback grim,
Safe in whose mighty arms the ball is clutched . . .
Bickeringly for a second he is poised,
Waiting his interference . . . Then he's off,—
Sheer naked strength of body, helmed by
The dauntless pilot of the heart of youth.

Downfield they stream, a broken battleline;
And now a runner, lithe and powerful,
The fullback grim,—eluding, checking swift,
Through breathless gaps, and dodging foe by foe,
Following his interference, deftly darting,
Amid the shouts and waving of thousands, mad
With glory manifest, crosses the line,
And straight behind the goal-posts rests the ball.
Where late the tempest trod in tumult wild,
Strewn lies the field; for in this gallant game
Ten men go down that one may cross the line,—
Ten sacrifice themselves that one may win.

And on life's playing-field all is the same.
Let any man look back the way he came,
Down which in pride his difficult way he won
To fame and honor. Selfless comrades there,
Intrepid, valiant, instant, chivalrous,
Broke his rough passage; they to ward from him
A plunging peril, threw themselves before
To take the shock, while he unscathed sped on
To glory and the goal . . . His heart knows well
He never had a fell antagonist
But he had ten staunch henchmen, giving o'er
Their lives, their hope of glory, dreams of fame,

All for his sake; to dust unknown going down,
Quite vanquished for his sake; quite doomed that he
A diadem of splendid fame might wear.
Let him who wears that jeweled golden crown
Remember them who for his glory died.

TRANSMUTATION

Nothing was ever lost
That came to her:
All cargoes to her coast
She minted into gold;
By magic she could mold,
Changing the lovely
Into the lovelier.
Out of her grief and woe
Garlands she wove;
Gallantly wore them
As if they were love.
Out of her tears she sang
A silvery stream;
Out of a hope long lost
A shining dream.
And when joy came to her,
Her only thought
Was to be sharing it
Lest it be naught.
Gain in her loss she found;
Jewels in dusty ground;
By love's transmuting might
Turning all dark to light.
By her all things were made
Flowers that will not fade.

THE LAST TRIUMPH

O Erie, Lake Erie, I fear me for thy child;
For Man his mighty hand has laid upon her tresses wild.
She wrestled him with foaming thews to stay his raping shock;
But like Andromeda she's chained fast to a somber rock.
He made her wed obscurely a chimera in a cave:
A dynamo, an octopus her beauty bright he gave.
She who was fit to mate the skies, the thunder, and the sun—
To immemorial freedom born, to bondage has been won!
Niagara, Niagara, proud princess of the air,
Is now the pliant mistress of a monster in a lair.

And thou, deep vault of heaven far, the sapphire throne of God
The mind of Man toward thee has turned a comprehending no
He mounts the storm, he climbs the clouds; the dizzy void he gair
To jest among the rainbows and to romp through radiant rains.
He steals a kiss from sleeping Dawn. Beyond the sunset bars
He holds a tryst with Hesper in the country of the stars—
Serene along the thunder rides; he startles systems old;
He'll rob the moon of silver, and the sunrise of its gold;
Among the Pleiades he plays, and on the sky's blue sward—
Makes Hell's last gulf his highway, and the stars his boulevar
While to that green dim netherland beneath the lonely foam
Intrepidly, audaciously, commandingly you come!

O ancient Nile! O magic Nile! O mystic river old!
The mind of Man is bidding thee gray secrets to unfold:
The sepulchres of Nilish kings that mountains stood upon
Are rushed to garish light at last beneath an alien sun;
For all that Man has buried deep, and all that God concealed,
Shall by a man be hunted down, and to the world revealed.
With canopy and blazonry and glittering sad array
Forth from their tombs the Pharaohs march into satiric day:
Obscured by silent centuries, asleep, they now awake;
And the Sphinx begins to tremble, and the Pyramids to quake.

Whose voice is on the vibrant air—celestial casual talk—
Now Auckland chats with Albany, Calcutta with New York?
Who through the dead Sahara leads the living sea afar,
Till down the desert commerce rides to dim Arabia?

560

ho brings in tropic Panama the Jungle to his knees—
vorcing mighty continents, and wedding mighty seas?
vader of the inviolate, reducer of the strong,
viner of dread mysteries, singing his triumph song,
ae Tyrant comes! Cliffs crumble, and the outflanked forest reels;
ae tempest takes the tether, and to tacit labor yields.

long array, in solemn ranks, in splendor trooping dumb,
hold gigantic gallant powers, the quelled and conquered come!
hold subjected oceans vast, and vanquished lordly tides;
amed lightnings led submissive home, like captive haughty brides;
splendent rivers shackled fast in bonds none shall release;
ill cataracts that signed a truce, proud hills that sued for peace;
ae bridles round their heads are bound; they quiver 'neath the reins—
l Nature in barbaric pomp, close-leashed and brought in chains.
he mountains match to music, and the sea in harness bright;
id even Death's beleaguered in his hold in ancient Night.

it O, brave binder of the winds, brusque beckoner to the sun,
every close encounter drear, remorseless champion!
hou hast unhorsed the hurricane, and solved the chasmed skies,
rmounting and prevailing and victorious and wise;
iscoverer of God's designs, relentless, unappalled,
remendous Tamer of the world, one giant goes unthralled:
ear Gladiator, grimly proved, by gorgeous conquests crowned,
orger of fetters for the earth, behold, thyself art bound!
hy flaming, restless-ranging heart, does it obey thy will?
Conqueror of conquerors, thy spirit canst thou still?

PRAYERS FOR YOU

Hoping life's fevers I may thus allay,
For you my prayers arise both night and day;
They are so constant that I cannot say
When I begin, and when I cease to pray.

FOREIGN WAR BRIDE

Your Land, My Land,—O what are they but dreams,
Rainbows and gorgeous shadows of the mind?
Your hills are higher? Ah, but see my streams!
And here you miss what in your land you find?
Missing one country, desolate we roam:
Where love abides, there is the heart's true home.

Your Flag, my Flag—Beneath one flag we meet,
Its domain all unseen, but fairest, best;
The message that it waves, all hearts repeat
If they are loyal to that realm blest.
Where we in quiet joy walk hand-in-hand,
And love is lord, there is our Native Land.

Only one kingdom is for you and me,
Only one blossoming field and waving wood,
Eternal hill and everlasting sea,
Its flag the banner broad of brotherhood.
Only one land our emblem floats above,
The country of the heart, and peace, and love.

BEAUTY'S STATION

The soldier to his grievous wars has gone
To make the world attentive to his might.
The scholar past the midnight labors on
That men in him may see and worship Light.
With stubborn aim the toiler in the mart
Heaps gold on gold, that others may perceive
His valiant power, and, with envious heart,
Shall in his pyramids of dust believe.

But Beauty makes their triumphs seem as naught.
Her affluence puts others' wealth to shame.
Hers are by right the treasures all have sought:
Illustrious, who never strove for fame;
Most eloquent—who never spoke a word;
Victorious—yet in her hand no sword.

"The Avon's pacing slow along,
That, as I hold thee, cradles Song . . .
Green to the tide the willows sweep,
A shadowy tryst the birches keep,
A wild bird's singing in the sun,
The dew-drops down the grasses run,
And Nature's tremulous to tell
Of thee, my child, some miracle.

From the vast future comes to me,
Like the choiring of shore and sea,
Far music. Through my deep of soul
I feel it like the thunder roll.
And nearer now! My being shakes,
The music like an ocean breaks,
And floods with glorious grief my heart,
O Baby, tell me who thou art!

In Bethlehem, did Mary mild
Wist of the wonder of her Child?
Heard she His voice o'er dying Rome
Calling His wandered millions home?
And shall my little one—nay, nay,
Forgive the thought, dear Lord, I pray:
I only long to know that he,
O blessed Christ, may follow Thee.

This little head that lies upon
My bosom,—ah, when I am gone,
Where shall it rest? Uplifted now
These dewy lips, this pearly brow,
These angel eyes.—I cannot see
What Time, sweet child, will make of thee,
Only I hear great music sound;
In thee its voice may yet be found."

THE BALLAD OF GOD'S BENISON

Once as I was kissing my wildwood elf,
Who should chance by but the Lord himself!

The heavens did not tremble nor the stars plunge
    down.
God looked quite peaceful, and He did not frown.

But we were frightened, my elf and I.
As we sprang apart, she began to cry.

And it was not because we had really done wrong;
In a way, we were worshiping, singing love's
    song.

But saints are indefatigable, zealous, undefiled;
While we were little children, playing wild.

We feared most because when God arrived
We were not ready, we were not shrived.

We were not working against evil and ill.
But we were just loving as lovers will.

But O the wild heart that soars and sings
When it might be doing such righteous things!

And O all the dancing, the laughing delight
When we might have been battling for the Right!

In my cold hands I twirled my hat,
Wondering why the universe did not fall flat;

Wishing we were anywhere but in God's sight;
For His coming brought a special light

That made all the wildwood burn like a rose,
And our hearts' secrets could disclose.

God raised His hand, and I fell prone,
Feeling I was facing then the Judgment Throne.

And down fell Violet, my darling sprite,
And we wept as all mortals must in God's
    sight.

My Violet prayed. Ah, she loved me well!
We waited the blow . . . But no blow fell.

What this might mean I could not guess
Until I felt God's hand caress:

One hand on Violet, and one on me.
O strange and tender mystery!

O Voice of Love that to us spoke!
Our hearts with gladness almost broke.

"On wings of light to earth I've ridden
To tell you love is not forbidden;

I come to say, even out of heaven,
True love need never be forgiven;

To tell you who the outcasts be,
Who get no mercy out of Me:

The loveless have no share, no part
In the compassion of My heart."

We heard with joyous strength and awe,
"Love's the fulfilling of the Law.

I love all mortals, great and small,
But I love the lovers best of all.

Love on, my children, with never a fear;
For as you love, you draw more near

To my Throne of Grace, where the angels stand,
To the place in Heaven that is Holy Land."

Then God was gone, though on sky and hill
His light of glory lingered still.

He came and He went with no alarms,
Leaving glad Violet in my glad arms.

ETERNITIES

When the guns of Antietam
And Gettysburg rolled,
The plowman plowed
His field as of old.

"Our dreadnaughts are sunk!
We are ruined now!"
"Johnnie, Johnnie,
Have you milked that cow?"

Over that hill lie
Ten thousand dead . . .
"Sweetheart, tell me
Again what you said."

Though they butcher their brothers
In God's blue air . . .
Still life is good;
Still love is fair.

The sea is a shambles,
And the sky above;
The earth's an abattoir . . .
The war-giants work
But to destroy . . .
But there is love;
And there is joy;
And glad old toil
In the home and the soil;—
Which shall abide
After folly and pride.

TWO LOVES

One gave me all she had;
Yet her love left me sad.
One brought me bliss because
She gave me all she was.

THE SISTERS

In the station-crowd at dusk,
With everyone intent on home,
With young fathers leading little boys by the hand,
And anxious mothers gathering in their broods,
And day-laborers in their grimed clothes,
Their heavy tools stained with clay and rust,
Their faces fatigued, their eyes weary for rest;—
In all eyes I saw, wistful and joyous,
Like a thought of happy refuge,
Home ahead.
Among these suddenly appeared
The faces of two women.
Ah, how different from the others!
They were not sad and anxious and troubled;
Black-robed they were; and their hoods
Were lined with white.
Quiet their beautiful faces,
Glowing with peace,—
Peace not of earth or of time.
If angels had suddenly alighted
There on the station-platform,
They would not have seemed stranger,
Or more remindful of all
That may come after this thronged life—
'Twas but a moment I saw them, those beautiful faces.
But in them I had seen
Home ahead for them too,—
A home in the heart of God,
Eternal, divine.
Indeed, from their celestial eyes,
They may now have found that home,
Here in life; for with them
So calm, so wonderful,
Nothing would seem a miracle,—
Not even peace on earth.

ALWAYS BELOVED

Westward there is a wood that shields
My ancient, quiet, homeland fields.
Southward the dreaming river bends
In a wide beauteous curve that blends
With marshes glimmering out of sight.
Fields, river, wood are my delight.

I love the waters, trees, and sod.
Not less than love was his who trod
On moccasins these homeland trails
Beneath the mosses' mystic veils.
Upon this place the same stars shine
On what was his, and now is mine.

Not less another's joy shall be
Who in his turn shall follow me;
Shall roam with joy these wildwoods dim;
These fields shall be beloved by him
Until, his little visit over,
His home shall have a different lover.

SMILE UNRETURNED

Deep in the eye of azure
That on the world looks down
There is a distance, a distaste,
The shadow of a frown.
Reproachful looms the mountain;
Rebuking rolls the sea;
Reprovingly the river runs:
They're all upbraiding me!
And honorable is their wrath,
Since for a little child
My heart had no responding grace
To offer when it smiled.

APPEAL FOR A LEGACY

Should that day come
When we must part,
O leave to me
Your valiant heart!

Of your estate
Naught else I crave
But constancy
In being brave.

O great is my
Necessity!
Your dauntless courage
Will to me.

To gold I give
No longing heed:
Your fighting heart
Is all I need.

FEAR

I saw a sweet Cambodian girl,
A dryad of the hills.
Like a wild deer she ran from me,
Leaping across the rills.
Was it from me she fled away,
Was it from me she ran?
Or would her terror be the same
At sight of any man?

God grant that I may never cause
A human heart to fear,
Or bring to any pilgrim heart
Fever it cannot bear.
I long to be a refuge calm,
A shrine to which may come
The fearful and the wandering
As if I were their home.

569

DICTATOR

"I will pull down my neighbor's house
That I may build my own.
I will kill him that I may harvest
The seed he has sown.

I will slaughter his wife and babes;
Then I will take my ease
Where he planned to rest after toil,—
Mine being his peace.

I will blacken his world that my own
May the brighter be;
I will ruin his homeland's freedom
That I may be free.

While he lies rotting away,
I will prosper and laugh;
On his fields and vines will I feed;
His wine will I quaff.

And my children shall have the toys
That his children had;
So shall I comfort my soul,
And make my world glad."

But God, with a withering smile,
Considered the villainous dolt
As out of His wrath He forged
His thunderbolt.

And the heart and the head and the reins
Of the fool were riven;
For no man shall have on earth
A beastly heaven.

AT ANKHOR VAT

I did not know that,
Moldering in the Cambodian jungles far away
In Siva's ruined temple of Ankhor Vat,
Two huge hamadryads,
Lush and lascivious,
Had made their holy mating-place;
And that this was their sacred time
To create life, to be alone,
Permitting none to come,
Terrible, sublime,
Lethal and vigilant,
With sex their religion,
Against the world they held their wild love-home.

The fault was mine.
Mortal and ignorant, I intruded
Into this perilous serpent-shrine.
Outraged, the furious female
Lashed amain.
There was no need for her to strike again.
I barely saw that venomous face and flat,
And therefore even to this lonely day
I lie far, far away
In solemn Ankhor Vat;
While, quite beyond my sight,
In the mysterious jungle night,
The glimmering huge hamadryads
Perform their secret and their sacred rite.

THE ARROWHEAD

() more than beauty in this stone I trace—
A wild sad meaning in its glimmering grace:
Wrought for eternity, I here behold
The sign and symbol of a vanished race.

SISTERS

How placid was she as a wife,
Yoked to a dray-horse all her life!
Her sister gave her hand and heart
To a starry lad who from his birth
Of the sweet wildwood was a part.

One wife was staid and true and dull;
And one was gay and beautiful.
Now, which was which I let you guess;
I only know that one endured,
And one was vivid loveliness.

A man will on his wife confer
His nature, all reserved for her,
Far more than poverty or wealth.
One feeds the hogs at pasture-bars;
One dances with the silver stars.

MY BROTHER

There was a day when either he or I
Might have been taken. Little boys were we;
And on life's road, the braver pilgrim he.
Yet it was willed that early one should die
And one should journey all the way alone.
Thus all alone this journey have I made,
And though to be like him I have assayed,
I have been my poor self, he being gone.

Even as a child he did surpass me quite
In virtue and in hardihood. My dream
Was to be like him, and my chief delight
Was to be with him. Then death's sullen stream
Swept us apart. Ah, had he stayed with me,
I had fulfilled a better destiny.

JUDGMENT

Before the throne of God
Two souls to judgment came,
And one unworthy stood:
On Heaven he had no claim.
But she, before God's face,
Undaunted said, "I come
Before Eternal Grace
With one who brought me home.
Although he has been wild,
Forgive him, Lord." She seemed
Only a little child,
Yet like an angel gleamed.
"Along life's wildest coast,
The black and bitter strand,
I would have wandered lost
Had he not held my hand
With love that made me feel
He never would let go.
Dear God, to you I kneel
For one who loved me so."
Then said the Lord of Heaven,
Of Earth and Sky and Hell,
"All things shall be forgiven
To one who loved you well."

THE CROWN

Of fame's austere
Illustrious power
He wears the crown,
He bears the flower
Who kindles fair
With fragile art
The flame of hope
In a frozen heart.

573

DIALOGUE

I. Her Spirit

"O whither now, wild Spirit, through the gloaming?
The sky has faded, and the night is coming.
Too lonely is the dark, too far the way.
Ah, whither, glorious Spirit, are you roaming?"

II. His Spirit

"I cannot rest until I find the Place.
All beauty's for me in one haunting Face.
All splendor in one Soul my soul shall find;
And in one Heart the meaning of all grace.

And once, upon my everlasting quest,
In dreams I saw Her in the luring west
At sundown, when the golden gates were wide.
My soul in music then her soul caressed."

III. Her Spirit

"O Spirit, turn you now! Look and behold!
I am your Rest. Mine are love's gates of gold.
Our meeting is the end of all your questing.
God made my wings your longings to enfold!"

LONELY SOUL

From every other spirit sundered far,
All unattended, kinless, insular,
As solitary as a single star,
By isolation orbited apart;
Disjoined and kithless, with no heart-to-heart
Relation to another,—with its chart
Unique, and singular its lonely goal;
None other like it on Time's ancient scroll,—
The human soul!

ALONE

My mortal foe am I;
None else can harm me.
Nor can a friend or foe
Arm or disarm me.

I am my dearest friend.
Who can assail me
If I am true as steel?
Friend, do not fail me!

I am mine enemy,
We cannot ever part:
Life's only battle's fought
Out in the heart.

I am my joy and grief,
Silence and song;
I am my conqueror,
My saviour strong.

I am my destiny:
In my arena small
I all alone must fight,
Triumph or fall.

CINDERELLA

Though she goes in rags and tatters,
Yet she is a princess born,
And she speaks of splendid matters
Though her vesture is forlorn—
Even the body, fading, sad.
But she's radiant and glad . . .
And in a day, a month, a year,
Cinderella Soul shall wear
A gown to match her beauty bright,
Woven of celestial light.

OUR PRETTY NELL

When laughing Nell trips down the street,
And we come out to see her,
We wave and smile, and every one
Loves her and longs to be her.

In flowered frock and pretty hat
She has a way of being
A morning glory in her grace,
That we rejoice in seeing.

She never strives for dash and show,
But she is always beaming;
Hers is a beauty past all art,
Beyond all rainbow dreaming.

We take delight in winsome Nell.
To us she's always bringing
The image of a lovelier life,
That sets our hearts a-singing.

She lilts her joyous way through life.
She has the gift of blooming,
As if she were a fragrant rose,
Our barren world perfuming.

So, blessings on you, pretty Nell;
Afar through life you'll carry
That winsome charm that you'll confer
Upon the man you marry.

Our prayers and hopes will always be
That he'll be gentle to you.
There's so much heaven in your heart
An angel well might woo you.

No: all is over, over.
She longs not even for her lover.
Say, "See, your love lies dead"
Instead.
You say, "She's sleeping."
Behold my weeping
Then you will know
How vain your lying is, how vast my woe.

THE CANDLE-LIGHT OF MEMORY

By candle-light our hurrying race
The childhood of its love can trace;
For many a knight adored the grace
And beauty of his lady's face
By candle-light.

By candle-light the bride was led,
And candles shone beside the dead.
How many a welcome has been shed,
How many a farewell has been said
By candle-light!

By candle-light of memory
Loved faces of the past I see,
My buried dreams come back to me
By candle-light.

By candle-light there rise and glow
Lost visions of my long ago;
Glamour and love and beauteous woe;
'Tis best to have such come and go
By candle-light.

THE WAYWARD ARE THE WISE

I

Watching two spirits on their pilgrimage,
I saw how one pursued the narrow way,
Austere and righteous; often in a rage
With one who turned aside to laugh and play.
Before them both was the same vast Unknown:
And one refused love's natural bread and wine
With prudish scorn and pride. One aim alone—
To gain a paradise—was his design.

The joyous spirit dallied. God had given
So much he could not pass its beauty by,
So much on earth he had no need of heaven.
He wandered down unsanctioned paths to try
To find all wonder, mystery, and grace
His Maker offered for his glad embrace.

II

Sometimes I think the wayward are the wise.
Men have forbid them, but they have not missed
Love's gifts beneath life's strange and pitying
    skies.
Their ardent arms have held, their lips have kissed
Beauty whenever Beauty turned her face
To them in Time's grim desert; and they drained
Love's honeyed chalice with high hearts of grace.
I cannot find their radiant spirits stained.

Their hearts wear mortal colors, rich and warm
Because they took life's deep designed delights;
Of passion they have known the splendid storm.
And while the sterile slept, they have known nights
When rapture wild and beautiful and strong
Made their souls one with music and with song.

DEATH'S RIVAL—LIFE

"So the jade all your hopes has been jilting?"
Inconstant! But I will be true:
My dark rose of love, never wilting,
Is dewy forever for you.

"Her blue wild bright orbs flash the number
Of changes of heart that she knows;
My eyes are of night and of slumber;
My love, of immortal repose.

"For your vigor this Amazon clamors;
Her calls on your strength never cease:
Do you weary of passionate glamours?
The passion I give you is peace.

"Your grief on my bosom to smother,
My breasts make a vale full of sleep;
Like me you shall not find another
Whose heart is so mystic and deep.

"For others she's busy adorning
Her beauty . . . But faithful I'll prove.
To live is to suffer her scorning;
To die is to clasp me in love."

THE CROWN OF LIFE

The Mortal and the Immortal held debate
Within me, asking who are wise and great.
"Those who transcend in power wear the crown,"
The Mortal said; "for mighty is their state."

"But with such conquerors all is not well,"
I heard the Immortal to the Mortal tell.
"Life's glory at its highest and its best
Is to be loved, is to be lovable."

SONG OF THE MARCH

March—march—marching along—
I am but one of the millions that throng—
Every one singing his favorite song . . .
What shall mine be?
Say it of me,
"He loved to tell of the stricken and strong."

Fair, fair, fair is the sight
Of the young lovers who take their delight
Where roses blush, and the moonbeams are bright .
Shall this my rune
Be of love's moon?
Rather I sing of the dead in the fight.

Wild, wild, wild is the way.
Whither we go, not a leader can say.
Some of us curse and some of us pray.
What shall I do?
Ever say you,
"He hymns our heroes who fall in the fray."

Oft, oft, oft we rebelled,
Shuddering sore at the bludgeons that felled . . .
But there were those whom our courage compelled . .
Them I would hail;
Though we may fail,
Theirs were the hands that our banners upheld.

Fierce, dim, mad is the joust . . .
Gallant we tourney, for tourney we must!
Hot through the heart goes the merciless thrust.
What shall I tell?
Splendid we fell!
Proudly I'm hailing the dead in the dust.

Strong, strong, strong as the oak,
Blinded, but not to be crushed by a stroke—
Knowing a grief that their lips never spoke:
Them I acclaim
Singing their fame:
Nothing's so brave as a heart that is broke.

Night, night, night on the road,
And we are far from a friendly abode.
Weary the burden is, sharp is the goad.
What shall I sing?
Only this thing:
For valor only true honor's bestowed.

Far, far, far is the Place
Where we find resting, and hard is the pace . . .
I am but one of a migrating Race . . .
Minstrel am I;
Say, till I die,
"He would be hymning our Valiant's grace."

Reel—reel—reeling ahead . . .
Who is our leader? And are we misled?
On the rough road there are tracks that are red.
What shall I say
Of the long way?
Mine is a song of the feet that have bled.

Vast, dim, vague is our host,
Wavering sadly by river and coast;
Some cry, "The mountain can never be crossed!"
What shall I cry
Through the dark sky?
"For the brave spirit no battle is lost."

March—march—marching along,
I am but one of the millions that throng,
Every one singing his favorite song.
What shall mine be?
Say it of me,
"He loves to tell of the stricken and strong."

"IT IS OVER"

Coming out of her room, the surgeon said,
"It is over,"—speaking without an appropriate dread.
Quizzically absorbed in the scientific alone,
He had no tinge of terror in his tone.
"You must not grieve," the nurses said to me . . .
Can sea-birds' voices still the raging sea?
For my heart in wild wrath was crying, crying,
"Must life and joy and love always end in dying?
Is silence the close of every song we sing?
Our hatchment a scabbarded sword, a folded wing?"
"It is over," they gently said; "it is over, over."
It was well to speak gently thus, I being her lover.

What is over? Life, loving, life's pain, our comrade-
        time,
Hand-in-hand a vale to traverse, a mountain to climb?
"It is over!" on Calvary the Master cries;
But He meant His immaculate lonely sacrifice.
Her journeys with me are over: to Paris and Rome;
And then to bright Bali; and, last and best, home.
And we said when we entered the portal, "It is over,"—
We who had wandered afar the world to discover.
And we were like children who leave a great darkness
        behind;
At last we were free from the world, in our joy confine
Now me she awaits in more glorious liberty
When that which is over for her is over for me.

INSPIRER

Rather than song or singer,
O would that I might be
Of golden dreams the bringer,
That wakes the artist to his art,
The star, the flower, the loving heart
That sets the music free.

582

NATIVE LAND

We are no strangers here. Our native land
Is earth, and here is all the joy we know;
Here all the sorrow. And we understand
Her steadfast mountains and her streams that flow.
This is our home; and let it be confessed
No other shows us fields and flowers more fair;
On nature's bosom only can we rest,
Drowned in night's dusky hyacinthine hair.

Our songs are taught us by our ancient Mother,
Love, laughter, tears,—the harvests of the heart.
To her we owe our all, and to no other;
Of her dim origin we are a part;
Authentic as her mountains and her sea,
We share her far mysterious destiny.

FLOWER OF THE SHADOWS

I found a blossom beaming
In the shadows, all alone,
Where never a star was gleaming,
Where never a sunbeam shone.

I marveled how the flower
Could rise with radiant grace,
A fragrant tiny tower,
In such a darksome place.

The shades were all around it;
The shades were overhead;
And in an hour I found it
When light in me was dead.

Fair are the blooms of meadows,
That in the sunlight ope;
Fairer the flower of the shadows,
The blessed Flower of Hope.

DESTINY

If Longstreet had come up at Gettysburg,
And Lee had won, I never should have turned,
Far to the North, far from my ruined home,
To keep this rendezvous with Fate—and you.
I should have lived the old plantation life,
Under the live-oak dreaming out my days,
Unconscious of the tragedy I was
Because I had not found you. It is strange:
Sometimes from death and dim disaster rise
The flowers of the future that we wear.

And you, beneath your cool New England pines,
Had never known me; and the dream we share
Had never come to birth; this ecstasy
Had never had a being. On the shores
Of this your homeland you had been alone,
Your child of wonder evermore unborn.
O never for two souls are battles won
Or lost perhaps. And yet this truth remains:
Life could have no meaning for our hearts
If Longstreet had come up at Gettysburg.

LONG INHERITANCE

He suffers from the Long Inheritance,
This dreamer who shall never live Today.
His heart beats with his forebears far away;
He walks with the old dead. Our proud advance
To him is the prolonging of a dance
After the guests are gone. We hear him say,
"They had a nobler grace, a better way
Of life than all our pride and circumstance."

Clasping his irrecoverable dreams,
In twilights of the past he lingereth,
With glamours faded by unflowing streams,
With Beauty sleeping in the arms of death.
He is of Yesterday . . . You who would be
In no wise like him, love and pity me.

PITY

Pity no man who feels the glory old
Of sunset and the rose of dawning dim;
Who drinks dark wine of evening. All the gold
Of autumn is love's legacy to him.
Temples and shrines by lesser men profaned
Are by his coming consecrated. He
Shares in the splendor of the silver-maned
Sea-breakers and the stars above the sea.

But pity most the man who turns aside
From beauty, with his hooflike heart unstirred;
A heart to which all wonder is denied.
Hearing high music, he has nothing heard.
Behold in him one whom the gods forgot,
Who looks on majesty and sees it not.

THE HIGH MOTHER

Ere I had learned to stray, she took my hand;
And led me where the shy wildflowers blow;
To misty glens where warbling waters flow;
And many an elfin scene and wild we scanned;
My future as her chosen child she planned,
Telling my heart sorrows that it must know,
What hopes pursue, what joys it must forego;
And mysteries she made me understand.

She left me long ago; and yet it seems
As Beauty she returns, and noble feeling,
With starlight through the dead vast darkness stealing;
Moving as music through my deepest dreams . . .
More than all earthly love she is to me
The spirit of my immortality.

FORGIVE! FORGET!

Forgive! Forget! The hour is passing by;
The fortune of the future waits thy word.
After the storm is heard the singing bird,
After the rain appears the happy sky;
Not long do Nature's aspects hold regret.
Forgive! Forget!

Forget! Forgive! Remembering the Past,
Far, silent land in memory's moonlight fair;
That shadow on its landscape like despair
Is by regret for unforgiveness cast.
Only by love's forgiveness can we live:
Forget! Forgive!

Forgive! Forget! It is the nobler part.
These are the only cures for heartache ills;
These are the graces of the strongest wills,
These are the powers of the humblest heart.
Ah, spend them ere love's moment shall have set!
Forgive! Forget!

ALL SAINTS' DAY

I dreamed I stood among the saints of God,
Though how or why I joined that company
I could not tell, since I had always trod
Life's soiling dusty way most mortally.
But now I was in glory. Music rang
From multitudinous harps' celestial gold;
Myriads of voices in their gladness sang,
And light and song and joyance starward rolled.

But suddenly I forgot the splendid song,
Being awestruck by one who stood apart,
Idly regarding our resplendent throng.
"O God!" I cried, "who made the human heart,
Our heaven is a lamentable coast
To him who finds not here the one loved most."

586

MISTAKEN

The mountains made him and the sea;
The rivers gave their strength to him;
The morning gay, the evening dim
Helped mold the man he was to be.

And they who sleep upon the hill
Awake in him to dare and do;
They prove again that they are true,
And that their strength's abiding still.

He is of all the world a part:
The deeds by others nobly wrought,
The dreams to him by beauty brought
Have fashioned limb and mind and heart.

The sunlight made him and the shade,
Thousands of seasons come to flower;
Thousands of hearts have wrought his power,
And yet he says, "I am self-made."

PAVILION IN THE NIGHT

O beautiful pavilion in the night,
With multitudious torches, gay with revels,
With sounds of music's wildly sad delight,
With voices of angels calling, voices of devils;
From your enchantment, brilliant in the dark
Of mystery, I saw a Figure come,—
One of the revelers. And I could mark
A quiet longing in his face for Home.

As grateful, from the tumult and the glare,
As one who leaves a glad exhausting dance,
Breathes with hale joy the dewy deep night air,
Hearing the white stars choiring old romance,—
When from Life's gay pavilion I shall fare,
My heart shall know divine deliverance.

SHADOW-STARS

See yonder evening stream:
    There are two stars within the waters deep,
Two shadowy stars come down to earth to dream,
    Come down from heaven to sleep.

Out of the night-lands, a wind
    Wakens a wave: —spent are the tranquil charms,
Yet the dim stars are driven til they find
    Rest in each other's arms.

The wind goes o'er the hill.
    A moment only throb they, heart on heart,
A moment, and the waters wild are still
    And they once more part.

A moment, and in vain
    The Wave of Life disturbs the twilight stream:
The stars sink back to sleeping once again,
    Into the ancient dream.

O MARINERS!

"Death is a voyage," I heard it lightly told,
"Across an ocean conquered by the heart
Of faith, that finds beyond, the realms of gold."
But in this world death has no counterpart,
And abject is each poor analogy.
From mariners upon that mightier main
We have no tidings of discovery . . .
We only know that they come not again.

Da Gama, to what vaster Orient—
Magellan, to what fabulous ports of morn—
Came you on circling death's Dark Continent,
Came you on rounding death's stupendous Horn?
They for Eternity were outward bound:
Great as the quest should be the glory found.

DOUBT

In some black hour you may have your way,
But you are doomed from birth. You stand alone,
And none shall grieve when you are dead and gone.
Though you have power to menace and to slay,
In league against you is the rose of May,
A thousand daffodils against your thorn,
And love and laughter 'gainst your lonely scorn.
You are outnumbered by a great array..

The stars are for me, and the marching sun,
The order that the farthest planet knows.
My faith, Imposter, makes your strength forlorn.
Behold my allies gathering one by one:
Out of the dust, the summer, rose by rose,
Under the night, the trumpets of the dawn.

THE GREAT CONCERNED

Compassionate Ones, though few,
Our lives are saved by you . . .
Concerned with others only,
How beautiful and lonely
From the hoof-hearted herd,
At pity's gracious word,
From mercy's mystic verge
You radiantly emerge!
Intent on our distress, on our despair,
You are the Ones Who Care.

Ah, Merciful Ones, your story
Burns with a strange wild glory:
All grief is understood
By your deep love's disquietude.
You Pitying Ones, how bright
You make our mortal night,
As toward tomorrow's dawn
Your vision leads us on!
For others only you have always yearned:
You are the Great Concerned.

589

BY THIS RIVER

Lay down, my soul, your burden by this river;
Too long oppressed by all your care, behold
The beauty that is yours, and yours forever.
The music of the birds is more than gold.
The wildflowers wait like fairies to attend you.
Here in the shallows, on the sandy bars,
The water-harps sing melodies to mend you,
O Broken Heart! Here, underneath the stars.

When the dark comes, a deeper peace than day's
Shall be divulged. For love is of the night;
And through the secret and mysterious maze
Of shadows wild will bring to you delight.
Upon her naked breasts, when dark is deep,
You shall know rapture, peace, and innocent sleep.

APPEAL FOR A BEQUEST

Should that day come
When we must part,
O leave to me
Your valiant heart!

Of your estate
Naught else I crave
But constancy
In being brave.

To answer my
Necessity,
Your dauntless courage
Will to me!

To gold I give
No longing heed.
Your fighting heart
Is all I need.

HOW OLD?

How old am I?
How old are you?
Though years be many,
Or years be few,
Of age, one thing
Is always true:

You and I are,
Each day, each year,
Old as our doubt,
Old as our care,
Old as our malice,
Hate, and fear.

But heaven keeps
The balance just:
Life's flowers are taller
Than its dust:
We are young as hope
And love and trust.

REQUIREMENT

What is required of us? What now must we
Suffer that love may not be perishable?
Render that love may not be ruinous?
What flower, far in the dark fields of pain,
Must be by us gathered immaculate?
What unknown seas, what dim and perilous shores
Must witness us? What silence must we keep,
What song sing in the night when others mourn?

Dear Heart, no peril and no strife forlorn,
Only to love as God would have us love;
Only to love as we ourselves would love:
Only to love that Love may never die.

591

FORGIVENESS AND THE FALLEN PINE

I

O beautiful dark Pine! O tall and strong!
Returning to the storm's black wrath a song
Like love triumphant over death . . . I thought
Your mettle all unconquerable,—wrought
To utter hardihood. But you are gone,
O fallen, fallen, fallen champion!

II

O Tree of murmuring music, I was born
Under your shade. For each of us the dawn
Opened her gates of rose and ivory;
Fair was the west arrayed for you and me.
O naught for me your place can ever fill
Within my heart, or on this lonely hill.

III

And you were comrade of my nobler mood:
My trust in you was like my faith in God;
My bravest thoughts aspired because of you;
And in your might my dreams of strength came true;
Your beauty made belief in Beauty mine,
O beautiful, beloved, and broken Pine.

IV

That little tempest harrying through the land,
How could it fell you? Who can understand?
But,—hold! 'Twas trouble in the heart . . . Ah,
    hold!
Despite your gallant bearing, brave and bold,
E'en as I watched and loved you day by day,
A secret sorrow stole your life away.

V

O should they fail me whom I trusted most,
Swiftly I could forgive the loved and lost,
Whose trouble of the heart no mortal knows,
Whose hidden wounds no tempest shall disclose . . .
—After their fall, if then, indeed, I live,
It must be to forgive, forgive, forgive.

STARS AND TOWERS

That was a glorious star that fell!
Learn from it to sustain this shock:
Not on the rock,
Not on the rock impregnable
We build our lives, our loves;
But on the sand that shifts and moves,
And their intransience proves
Through all our days and hours.
So is it that with all our powers,
With all
Our masterly designing,
We rear but vulnerable towers,
Most exquisite and tall,
But fated soon to fall.
Our beauty covers only flesh and bones.
Dauntless we build the thrones
We shall be soon resigning. . . .
And yet, though all is dust,
Subject to moth and rust,
Glory we build, and splendor proud and strong
That thwarts Time like a song.
We love because we must;
And in that which we know will fail
We have to trust.
All life to dissolution tends;
Our knowing this a tragic beauty lends
To our pathetic dust;
Our cup of anguish is a Holy Grail.
Life's dying lights that shine
Illumine nobly and compassionately
How many a hero,
Many a heroine!
On life's disastrous brink,
Even though the lofty cliffs begin to cave,
And the towers sink,
We set our gallant flags to wave,
Riddled and memorable,
Winning no triumph save
By being brave.

UNANSWERED

It fell to me
To entertain our Justin, who was three.
So, taking her tiny hand in mine,
She fluttering like a fairy by a pine,
To a glass case I led,
Where perched a wood-duck—dead.
Stale in a static beauty without strife,
Lacking the fluid magic of life,
In ineffective glory sinister
He glassily peered at her
With bright disastrous eyes . . .
In innocent surprise,
And seeing the window open, and the blue sky,
"Why doesn't he fly?"
She questioned wonderingly.
And with a quick stupidity I said,
"Because he's dead."

"And what is 'dead'?" she asked   .   .   .
How I was tasked!

Nor then, nor through the long, long years between,
For all I've heard and seen,
I have not found what death may really mean.

Is it a plunging to abysmal night?
A calm ascending toward a larger light?
Or, after blindness, is it more than sight?
A far retiring into dreamlands deep?
A tranced listening to the runes of sleep?
I've paced imagination's pinnacles,
Peered from high casements of the spirit's walls,
And listened at the posterns of all Thought,
But back to Justin have no answer brought.

THE GRIEVING HEART

As one by one my talents fail,
And momently my powers depart,
Lord, leave me till Thy summons come
    A grieving heart.

My grieving heart! My power to feel
The pain that stabs my brother so;
Ah, mystic poignancies that I
    Would not forego.

O Christ, whose pitying love has brought
The dead to life, we share Thy power
When we have caused our love to shine
    In some dark hour.

On those who sink beside the way
To let those win the race who can:
O Master, make of me a Good
    Samaritan!

And I shall find by sorrow's stream
Flowers of beautiful faith and pure,
That, nobly worn, will be a crown
    That shall endure.

A PRAYER

I hope that peace and joy may be
Comrades to keep you company;
That love alone in you may reign
With everlasting beauty . . . Then,
That you may have no pain or fear,
I pray a strange and tragic prayer,
A wild appeal, yet true and deep,
For the dear one my heart adores:
I pray that God will safely keep
You from a longing for my love
As I have always longed for yours.

INSIGHT

By gazing on the dusty clod
If you can plot the course of God;
And in the mud and slime can trace
The waterlily's coming grace;
Feel in the bare and lonely tree
The slumbering spring's divinity;
Beneath the seal that winter sets
The breathing of the violets;
View in the tiny acorn brown
The massive live-oak's old renown;
Can feel the love of God beneath
The mailed and mighty stroke of death;
If you can find the undefiled
In yonder sad corrupted child,
If through abhorrences you can
See a dim Christ in Caliban,
And by the promise in a soul
Vision it beautiful and whole,—
I'd say you had a gift to give,
And should a little longer live.

WOUNDED STRANGER

As by the evening waves a watch I kept,
Marking the distant shores and all between,
Tall graceful yachts in quiet beauty swept
Safe to their berths. For an hour they had been
Out to the bar, and home. Then on the rim
Of the mysterious and fading blue,
A battered hulk appeared, begrimed and grim,
Survivor of far storms we never knew.

When hearts come home, judge not by beauty only,
But by the voyage, the hazard, and the war
With elements primeval; by the lonely
Watch in the reeling dark without a star.
Not to the trim bright yachts that knew no danger:
My tribute goes to the valiant wounded stranger.

NOT FOR LONG

Westward the moon is sailing white,
And I am all alone with night.
Upon a hill above the town
I watch the homing moon go down
In darkness but for its own light.

I hear the birds of marsh and wood
Make music in night's solitude.
I watch the pine-trees, rank on rank,
Behind whose host the wild moon sank.
I watch the planets, silver, nude.

O what to me are moon that sets
And night-birds voicing old regrets,
Or hills, or stars, or pines that wave?
Love to my longing once you gave.
And now your love forgets, forgets.

The trembling earth is turning fast;
Tonight shall soon become the Past.
For me there can be no tomorrow
Save one of darkness and of sorrow:
I had your love—that could not last.

I had your love to keep me strong,
To fill my silent life with song.
But now I feel its tide no more;
Its waves forsake my lonely shore.
I knew your love—but not for long.

Now in the night, mysterious, late,
I stand as at a garden's gate,
Bereft of bloom by wintry snows,
Where once my own Beloved, my rose,
For me with all her love would wait.

MERCERSBURG CENTENNIAL ODE

For centuries, upon this lonely hill,
The woods were waving, and the woods were still.
Here glowered the wilderness; and here were heard
The howling wolf, the wailing whippoorwill.

In sleeping beauty, all unknown, unsung,
On every hand the glimmering wildwoods hung;
And all this pageantry that gleams for us
Was radiant here while Eden still was young.

Before Columbus and his caravels,
These green hills stood, primeval sentinels;
As still they stand, rapt listeners to hear
The glamour and golden tempest of our bells.

Unchanged are they as an immortal soul:
They guard the dawn; the sunset they patrol,
Where aye in triumph, toward the north and west,
The maned sea-breakers of the mountains roll.

But the spirit of Man for change must ever quest:
A mortal malcontent, she knows no rest;
She heeds the bugles of the dawn; she heeds
The tawny mystic trumpets of the west.

To make the uttermost parts of earth her throne,
She led her children to this frontier lone,
Where wild beasts dwelt, and where, with shadowy art,
The savage shaped his implements of stone.

The pioneers against their foes prevailed . . .
Ah, but the soul has frontiers, vast and veiled;
And they who in that land are luminous
Shall as the saviors of the Race be hailed.

Long ere the beacons on our mountains burned,
Imperial spirits had so deeply yearned
Over humanity, that on this hill
They were a light toward which the nations turned.

And men as noble, in a royal line,
Treasured this heritage of yours and mine,
Guarding the sacred flame. A thousand years,
Even from today, shall see its beauty shine.

From men like these we learn of long renown:
All earthly glory to the grave goes down;
But he who lifts a light to guide a soul
Shall wear the stars' imperishable crown.

We learn, wherever men like these have trod,
That love is virtue's most compassionate mood;
That grace alone confers nobility;
That they who live for others walk with God.

The splendors of a hundred years depart,—
Leaving one talisman to guide the heart:
The truth that nothing that we know endures
Save God, and sacred love, and sacred art.

The evening of our century fulfils
Its morning hope. A grander age God wills;
And as the heralds of that fairer day,
The stars are all arrived above the hills.

APOLOGY TO LIFE

If in the beauty of your presence bright
Our laughter fails, and falters our delight,
It is because a shadow far we see.
In fields of flowers, blithe Persephone,
Singing and gathering blossoms long ago,
Suddenly knew our thought and felt our woe,
And all her blooms let fall, amid her bliss,
Discerning the disastrous face of Dis.

GOD'S HIGHWAYMEN

I

In carrying more than mortals can
John was an ordinary man;
Of cares, he was a caravan.
He staggered onward in the sun;
But for his load, he might have run;
How shamblingly his pace advanced
When joyously he might have danced!
He reached the wood at last;— and then
They ambushed him—God's highwaymen!

II

Ah, when he reached the wood at last,
Delicious rapine followed fast,
Pillage divine, celestial rape,
From which no mortal could escape.
Their purpose steeped his heart in dread;
He shivered, trembled, cried, and pled;
Had he a chance, he would have fled.
A mirthful, tolerant, lawless clan
Now had him sure,—and had their plan
To sack the precious caravan
Of this unhappy Everyman!

III

Burdened, unarmed, he faced about;
A tall Oak robbed him of his doubt;
A Hickory hale the thieves among
Deprived him of his weakness strong;
A Holly stole his fine disdain;
A Dewdrop plundered him of pain;
The agate of his heart, they say,
A Sunbeam melted quite away;
His hate he suddenly let fall
Because he saw a Cardinal;
Huge Elms—those burly buccaneers—
Despoiled him of his priceless fears;
A Laurel leaned to him and took
His aching eyes, his anxious look;

600

From him a Cedar lifted soft
A burden that had bent him oft.
A debonair and lissome Stream
The luggage of his self-esteem
Laughed quite away; and from him bore
Pity of self, a tragic store.
A spirit of wild glamour came
And filched his sordid greed of fame;
A splendor-coronetted Pine
Has made him all his pride resign;
A lithe Birch spirited away
Forgetfulness to kneel and pray;
A poignant Perfume merciless
Preyed on his paltry thriftiness . . .
He laid sick hope that had been sleeping
Upon a Greensward's quiet keeping.

IV

O what a raid on John to stage!
O buccaneering! brigandage!
Disaster on disaster came:
Into her secret halls of flame
The stately sorrow that he kept
Closest his heart, a Wildrose swept;
His anger—he was sore beset—
He yielded to a Violet;
To many a joy his sad farewells
He lost to golden Jasmine-bells;
Surrendered to a spray of Rue
The dream that never could come true;
And with a virgin Lily left
A love whose heart long since was cleft.

V

Stripped, rifled, raided, and profaned,—
His wealth evanished,—what remained?
A dewy respite deep; a sense
Of all relaxed that had been tense;

Once more the blue of God above,
A white star looking down like love;
A delicate wild stillness sweet
In which the heart finds far retreat;
A tide of beauty flooding fair
With waves of wonder, drowning care.

VI

Pillaged and joyous, ruined, glad,
Free, naked, reft of all he had,—
John Everyman, from yonder wood,
Carried no more than mortals should:
Carried a heart for life made strong,
A hope, a faith, a friend, a song.

VII

O Traveller somewhere on the Way,
May God's good thieves your path waylay . . .
—And this with all my heart I pray.

DUSKY EVE

I heard dusky Eve consoling
One who'd had a bitter loss:
"Chile, for each one Jordan's rolling,
And we've got to get across.
I know how your soul is aching;
I don't blame your tears that fall;
I know how your heart is breaking.
You just cry and tell me all.
You'll be better for the weeping.
Soon your tears will all be dried.
Soon your sorrow will be sleeping,--
If you will not cry inside."

602

IMMUNITY

Give me, O Life, your bitterest cup to drink,
Though its wild rancours course like sudden shame
Through honor's heart, I shall not from it shrink,
Although its poison harries all my frame.
My peers before me bravely drank it down,
And were not troubled any more again.
They wear an iron but eternal crown
Who have survived the ultimate of pain.

That cup will yield me, after bitterness,
Peace in the heart and quietude from fear,
Freedom from hope,—the worst and best being known.
I shall not hatred feel or love confess,—
Being past both. Nor shall I dread to hear
Life's horn of battle— Roland's having blown.

DESIRE AT SUNSET

still to be one with delight, and with wonder to start
the thrush's veiled song, though its beauty is breaking my heart;
nd to be of the music and wildwood and magic an intimate part!

hen arose my first star, softly flaming above my first wave,—
he splendor and awe of that moment are all that I crave;
l life's glory I'd give if that passionate grace I could save.

s in the beginning I burned, ah, still let me behold
ith rapture the fabulous banners of sunrise unrolled;
nfailing to feel in the sundown death's majesty old.

o love the illustrious pageantry blazoned by night;
o find in life's shadows the heart's most victorious might;
the dark to discover more truth than is found in the light.

ive to the dark tides of Being,—the ebb and the flow;
ware of life's mystery always; and joyous to know
e were God's and beloved, when we came,—and not less when we go.

EXILE

So we were married, and I brought her home.
But after a little while she could not bear
The country that I loved. The big dark pines,
That kept on looming loftier in the dusk,
Gave her, she said, the shudders. The old owls,
The oaks' dim oracles, made her afraid.
The sounds and silences that I could read
Were to her mind mysterious. I saw
Her longing for the city and its ways.
Yet she was very gallant for a time.
But once she said: "If we stay here, I know
The gray moss will be growing on us both.
It takes a savage to love the wilderness,
And you can't love it here as you love me."

So, from the old plantation, cityward
We came, leaving the hollies and the oaks behind
To sentinel the home that we had left;
Leaving the wild birds singing on the boughs
Of blossoming dogwood,—how I envied them!
Leaving the Negroes in the cotton laughing,
The river flowing placid at our doors;
The sibilant whisper of the growing corn;
The hounds to hunt without my hearing them;
The jasmine and the woodbine, that would toss
Saffron and carmine showers, stayed in air,
The wild azalea flaming in the woods,—
We unbeholding. And I left my gun
Hanging forever lonely in the hall.

About me now the buildings tower; the cries
Of many voices sound, but make no song
For me, a woodsman lost in Babylon.
And yet above me still the pine trees soar,
And still I hear the music of their harps.
I cannot see for all that I have seen:
The shadowy deer, furtively stealing forth
To roam the dewy country of the dark;

The old wild gobbler, that all night has slept
In starlight, in the shrouded cypress crest,
Sail to the ground at sunrise in the wilds.
And sometimes, when the wind is in the south,
I know I smell the jasmine in the swamp,
And hear the mallards clamoring in the marsh.

BEFORE MY TIME OF TROUBLE

Before my time of trouble
All Beauty made me glad;
My joy it would redouble,
Exalting all I had.

But since o'er hill and meadow
I take Man's destined way,
I now am in the shadow,
And now in sun and May;

And Beauty still is magic,
However I may roam.
But O it can be tragic;
For sometimes it will come

Upon me in my sorrows,
The vision to disclose
How red will be tomorrow's
Regalia of the rose,—

While for a sign and token
Of love that will not stay
My heart must wear the broken
Dead rose of yesterday.

605

THE OTHER CITY

There is a city all the world would reach,
Where Joy's broad ocean rolls on Pleasure's beach,
Where love and laughing respite give the sense,
For all our toil, of having recompense.

And She is there, the woman of his songs,
And He, the lover after whom she longs.
Some thither speed, soft-cushioned, urbane, dull,
Lustful to reach the city beautiful.

Some strangle in the swamps and dim morasses,
Beset by jungle-claws and scything grasses.
Deep in the goblin dark some lose their way;
Beleagured in the wilderness they stray.

But many come: the crafty reach this goal,
The beautiful, the hero high of soul.
Then of each mortal pleasure will they taste,
From flower to flower importunately haste.

Their hearts to madness does the moon allure,
A universal virgin paramour.
But soon, ah, soon they search the sea and sky
As if some other city to descry.

Each will be asking: "Tell me sister, brother,
Is this the city, or find we another?"
With haunted eyes they scan the shore and sky:
All that earth gives them will not satisfy.

Ah, soon from Beauty, Strength impatient turns;
And soon for more than Strength tall Beauty yearns.
Alone they go; their spirits cry and call
For something that transcends the physical.

Somewhere, they dream, another city stands,
Immaculate, not made by human hands.
Strength turns from Beauty, longing for release;
And Beauty finds in Strength no perfect peace.

With eyes and heart of hero enterprise,
Famished of soul, they search the sea and skies,
Beyond the utmost shoreline and the tides,
To find that place where fadeless love abides:

Those alabaster walls, those fountains singing,
Those silver bells at evening softly ringing—
They can be found, in all their beauty whole:
Who finds that city builds it in his soul.

STRONG IN HER SORROW

Now it has come to her,
What can I say?
I unto God will go,
A prayer to pray

In a deep wood I love,
A shrine apart:
Nothing is here between
God and my heart.

And my heart cries to Him,
"Lord, hear my cry!
There is no mortal more
Helpless than I

To give her comfort now,
Or on tomorrow:
God, make her stronger than
Even her sorrow."

And He the gift has given,—
Lest her heart break;
And lest I too should die
For her dear sake.

OBLIQUE

O often have I prayed, and thought
An answer from the skies would come;
Yet heaven would be deaf and dumb;
The firmament no answer brought.
But then in glad surprise I found
My comfort coming from the ground.

Sometimes I have besought the great
To lend their aid that I might bring
Life's flower into blossoming.
I waited; and they let me wait.
But in my need a humble friend
Brought all my trouble to an end.

In night, in solitude I groped
Another's sympathy to find,
Till to the dark I was resigned,
Thinking that I had vainly hoped.
But, come from realms to me unknown,
I felt love's hand upon my own.

The flight of angels never seems
To be direct. We look before.
But a surprise they have in store:
Not here, but there, the glory streams.
To tell their course in vain we strive;
We only know they shall arrive.

LION IN THE NIGHT

Who wakes in the wilderness when night is done,
Fancying himself the lord of all the land,
May see what was not there at set of sun.
And tremblingly will come to understand
The peril that has passed him in the dark,—
Tracks of a mighty lion in the sand.

TOO LATE

Her sad heart keeps saying to her,
With the hours and years growing dim,
"In the far lost glad days that were,
I could have been kinder to him."

He says, "Now forsaken I live,
All alone by life's lonely sea;
She kept all that love had to give
That would have meant mercy to me."

When famished with thirst he implored
His desperate longing to heed,
Her love-brimming chalice to hoard
Meant more to her pride than his heed.

Now fallen's her fragrant red rose,
And the wildflowers fade in her lane.
Now with tears and with anguish she knows
That a miser of love is profane.

THE CROSS

Dark shadow of a shameful death,
Symbol of terror and disgrace
Among the ancients of the earth!
How oft on thee was bleakly reared
The passion of a hopeless face,
Fell Cross of anguish, grim and feared.

But love hath made thee pure and fair;
Strong men from thee receive their might;
To thee our children come in prayer;
In thee we seek and find our best;
Within thy shadow is our light;
Upon thy bosom is our rest.

THE VALLEY OF THE SHADOW

I

On the road to El Dorado lies the Valley of the Shadow,
On the road to El Dorado, to the country of the blest.
It is called the Vale of Sorrow; and today—or else
tomorrow—
We shall find that Land of Sorrow, lying lonely in the West
Mother Eve and Adam knew it; every mortal eye shall view
it,
For the path of life runs through it, for the worst and for
the best.
Veiled stream and misty meadow on the road to El Dorado,
Called the Valley of the Shadow, we shall find them
without quest.

II

In that Valley there are flowers never blown by morning
showers,
Never closed by evening hours, astral blossoms tall and fair.
Wanderers in that Valley's starlands gather white mysterious
garlands,
Wearing them as toward the farlands of their journey they
repair.
And the perfume wafted sweetly heals the spirit's wounds
completely,
Dries the saddest tear-drop fleetly, and bestows a solace
rare . . .
Astral beauty, mystic powers have the Valley's wondrous
flowers,
Blooming in no earthly bowers, never blown by sun and air.

III

Bright above the shadowed Valley all the hosts of heaven
rally,
Blazing fair and mystically, intimate with things divine . . .
They are shining, they are singing, guidance and compassion
bringing,
Low above the Valley winging, chanting hymns as in a
shrine.

Close they come and close they hover like a sweetheart over
                              her lover—
Can it be that they discover all your trouble and all mine?
Else why should they yearn and dally over the solitary
                              Valley,
In compassion lyrically toward that Shadowland incline?

IV

In the Valley of the Shadow on the road to El Dorado,
In the Valley of the Shadow there are hymns unheard
                              elsewhere;
For the harps with music waking are the hearts of mortals
                              breaking,
Melodies immortal making, through the darkness coming
                              clear;
Through the pale illustrious glory of the Vale with shadows
                              hoary,
Telling sorrow's poignant story, and love's triumph over
                              fear.
On the road to El Dorado, in the Valley of the Shadow,
On the road to El Dorado, beautiful the hymns we hear!

BELOVED OF ANGELS

It seems the least in all the night,
This humble star. Its modest light
Is almost darkened by the blaze
Of lordly planets. It displays
Only an unassuming gleam,
A little candle in a dream.
But all the angels love it best;
God looks on it, and it is blest.
This quiet star, what can it be?
They say it is Humility.

BECAUSE

Because he loved them well
In days no more to be
Beyond all else they have
A magic wild for me:

The voice of a little child;
The wind that bends the mast;
The tawny thunder of
The grouse that rises fast;

The solitary state
Of the great rosebay's pomp;
The horse he rode; the hound
He followed through the swamp;

The poem that he kept
Upon his desk; the song
That quieted his heart,
Surging and wild and strong;

The fiery funeral old
Of forests in the fall;
His hunting-horn that hangs
Silently in the hall;

The meditative night;
The rosered dawn; the deep
Hour of twilight, full
Of intimated sleep;—

For me they hold a charm
All other charms above;
It is because he found
Them worthy of his love.

A CHILD

His little feet have turned aside
Ere yet they learned to stray;
What flower or toy or shining light
Has lured him far away?

Life's thronging, dusty wayfarers
Their course still journey on;
Few, few indeed are those who miss
A tiny traveller gone.

A little while with us—and then
His feet forsook the path:
This flower, faded by earth's strife,
A heavenly springtime hath.

And we who live to mourn, we must
Fulfill as best we may
The beauty of his childhood's dawn,
The briefness of his day.

His feet from us have turned aside
But love can lead us still;
And he it is we hope to meet
Beyond life's sunset hill:

He who was love's bright sun to us
Through every hour's delight,
At closing of Life's day shall be
The first star of the Night.

LONE EAGLE

It was not that he did the thing,
Nor was it yet the thing he did:
The man became a hero when
He tried to keep his glory hid.

613

A WILD FLOWER

Immortal in its little mortal hour,
Returning all the roses lost and wild
That long ago had bloomed for me, a child—
Far on a distant hill I found a flower;

With colors shy, and luring faint perfume;
With dewy gown, and virginal surprise,
And wonder of the world in childish eyes,
And timid beauty, half-afraid to bloom . . .

One was to me as this frail flower now:
Beloved and beautiful, a mortal rose . . .
The flower of her face a far land knows,
And other fields the lily of her brow.

VIOLET

She's melody beyond all mortal reach;
Her beauty does not to our world belong.
Her face is language, and her look is speech;
Her smile is music, and her words are song.

If virtue is withholding beauty, why
Should it be worshipped? Does it ever bless?
How generous are earth and sea and sky!
Beauty that gives itself is loveliness.

HUNTER GONE HOME

Master of Medway, the pineland is waking,
Glinting with dew at the rising of morn;
The mist on the myrtles is bright with daybreaking;
The bay-leaves with silver are shining and shaking;
The hunters are coming with hound and with horn.

Master of Medway, the wild birds are singing;
The tall pines are touching their harps of the sky;
Far over the Delta the mallards are winging
As down the old wood-road we hunters come swinging
With jesting and laughter and hopes that are high.

Master of Medway, an old stag is started!
Down by the river sequestered he lay.
Gallantly now he will prove he's great-hearted . . .
But our loved Master from us has departed,
And from Life's Hunt he has ridden away.

Master of Medway, you've gone on before us!
We in Time's forest forsaken shall roam.
Strong was the love that forever you bore us;
Only one thing shall to gladness restore us:
When the Day's done, to rejoin you at Home.

NIGHTS NEVER LINGER LONG

Nights never linger long;
Days are more brief than song.
Regard the hills, dear Heart;
The mountains and the sea;
Remember me.
Look at the stars, my Own
And do not miss the moon;
For even perfect love
Will be gone soon.

RETURN

With Joy I walked. The blissful world
Had never been so gay;
The birds had never wildly sung
So sweet a roundelay.
The flowers in all the fields rejoiced
As I went forth that day.

With warier step, with mystic eyes,
The world unseen to mark;
With heart more poignantly aware,
With ears more keen to hark
A deeper music, I came home
With Sorrow, through her dark.

WITH US FOREVER

O may we still have them, the gallant, the generous-hearted,
The dauntless illustrous ones who gave life for our lives?
Are they lost to us, desolate? From us forever departed?
Is there aught of them out of the shadows that nobly survives?

The tawny wild music sonorous, the monuments splendid.
The honor, the glory, the tributes magnanimous paid
(They were modest of heart, these heroes whose epic is ended
These cannot return them, who in all memorials fade.

Yet there is a simple, a wonderful, way to restore them
(O hasten, my heart! Not a moment in sorrow we'll spend):
Come, take up the arms of the spirit. Your champion bore them
Fill his place in life's ranks, and so be his valiant friend.

Grief is not the road that shall end in your mustical meeting.
Only live for him bravely, and he in your heart shall abide.
By fulfilling his chivalrous dreams, his triumph completing,
You shall have him forever, your Darling, who for you has die

ASTRAY

If he who once so gallant strode,
So certainly upon life's road,
Assured and strong,—
Now falters, now bewildered goes,
And is like one who never knows
Right ways from wrong;

Remember her who was to him
A steady beacon in life's dim
Wilds full of dread;
Brief candle burning in the dark,
She was to him a torch to mark
The night ahead.

Together far they safely came,
She guiding like a sacred flame
By vale and hill:
Till death her shining course forbade.
—Her love was all the light he had—
Or ever will.

SECOND DAWN

I dreamed that from that other world unknown
My Love returned. It was in deep of night.
Though every star was on her silver throne,
No constellation as my Love shone bright.
O then I asked what wisdom aye has failed
To answer: "Angel, in that first strange hour,
When you did cross life's frontier vast and veiled,
What felt you then? What saw you? What new power

Suddenly gave you immortality?
O tell me, for I soon shall pass that way."
My Love replied: "Of all the bliss to be
I must not tell. Rejoice to hear me say
At death I saw, as at true love's awaking,
Only an immense dawn, in glory breaking."

617

F. H.

O thou with the unlifted eyes, and face
Starry with recollection and the light
Of beautiful unhappiness, time brings
Not loss but sure reward. Thy heart has dreamed
Of beauty that thine eyes will never see,
Has listened to the voices of the Past,
And answered them: has heard life's sorrowful
Sweet music softly grieving on the night.
When the grey years have gathered and stolen up
To gaze into they memorable eyes,
Thou shalt behold the fair long time ago,
And those well loved. The shadowy quietness
Will bring the lost days back to thee, and they,
Arriving silently with faces bright,
As wistful stars in some still river's tide,
Will look on thee, will understand, and love.
It is thine hour. God will permit thee then
To touch the hands of dear remembered friends,
Old childhood playmates with soft waving hair,
That blows through the low sunset on thy face,
Ineffably caressing. Then thine eyes,
Beholding loveliness will be lifted to
Fields deep in flowers, lotus-blossomed strands,
Sweet indolent valleys sinking to the sea,
Beyond blue mountains in the luring west.
I see thee near the unillumined land
Radiant, and as a rose immaculate,
Exhaling beauty dying in the dark.
It is thine hour of hours. And from that dream
Unto a deeper dream thy spirit glides;
Not as those who from transient visions start,
For then their love, earth-born, must rise and go,
Wounded, into the darkness of the night.

THE SOLACE OF THE HOURS

Thou in the Shadowy Hours, remembering,
Wilt see return in many precious ways
Unbroken dreams of far-off summer days,
The luring mysteries of dawn and spring,
The holy passion for the star, the flower,
The tenderness of some far farewell hour.

Thou in the Wistful Hours wilt dream and bless,
And when the sunset kindles and rolls by,
In deep delicious stillness thou wilt lie,
Folded as in some long-ago caress,
Upon the breast of Mercy, while thy sight
Falls on beloved faces in the night.

Thou in the Mystic Hours wilt see the Veil
Rent, and the solemn beauty that appears,
Eternity, so idle with her years,
The ancient loveliness that grows not pale;
The wise, sweet angel musing on men's faith,
The Angel Beautiful, the Angel Death.

Thou in the Pitying Hours wilt lend thine ear
To all the sighings of the world; to tears
Falling, and men long weary of the years,
Voices of sadness, shudderings of fear:
To thy still peace will the lone mourner turn
And in his sorrow beautifully burn.

Thou in the Mortal Hours wilt feel the high
White aspirations to the silent stars;
The loss that blesses and the gain that mars,
Wilt yearn for that Lost Face beyond the sky
Grieving, and know that grief is vain;
Wilt fear to die, yet find in death no pain.

Thou in the Silent Hours beneath the sky,
The calm years for thee this great gift will keep,
Upon the Twilight's breast to fall asleep,
On the deep bosom of the Dawn to lie,
While dreams flow on through quiet vistas grey
Like silent streams to Silence borne away.

IN A GARDEN

Around our garden, sweet and wild,
    In softest waves the pinewoods move:
I hear thy voice in them, Dear Child,
    And in their silences, thy love.

Beyond the pines the white beach runs,
    Beyond the beach, the marsh, the sea:
Beyond our world, the stars, the suns,
    Beyond thy life, my thought of thee.

I stand where love and sorrow meet,
    And where the sea-wind o'er thee blows:
Now in our garden, wild and sweet,
    Thy heart is risen in yonder rose.

Thy heart is risen unaware,
    For thou no more awakeneth:
Because of life, so fair, so fair,
    So beautiful because of death!

My heart forgets the tears, the grave
    In love's diviner mystery.
The pines against the sunset wave,
    And I am one with them and thee.

FIVE

Some in the morning sing; some, all day long.
Some, wakening late, will sing at evensong.
Some never sing. Alas, death strikes some mute
Between the lifted finger and the lute.

SUNSET

O beautiful sorrow of sunset,
    We turn, we turn unto thee:
From the winds o'er the summer lands blowing;
    In the days that will never more be:
As the meeting of many bright waters
    That deepen the blue of the sea,
O Ending of love, O Beginning
    Of rest, we turn unto thee.

(Ah, the wonderful pang when we realize
    That Sorrow forever is ours;
Her presence is felt in each farewell,
    Her strength in the fading of flowers:
In the loved ones long folded to Silence,
    In the bourne that love cannot unveil,
Where the faith of our childhood lies buried,
    With the hearts of the friends who fail.)

To the golden, mysterious westward,
    Through the way our eyes cannot see,
O beautiful sorrow of sunset,
    We turn, we turn unto thee.

WAYWARD CHILD

Unless we find the missing one,
His loss will all our dreams unman;
For he is all that we have done,
That we have been, since love began.

CLOSED GATE

The saddest thing in all the world
That I have known by land or sea
Is that a gate once opened wide
By love is closed to me.

SIGN IN THE NIGHT

She looks serene, as if no anguish ever
Could have invaded her strange perfect peace.
Hers seems contentment that could last forever
Tranquility that would not ever cease.
Languid the roses in their beauty hang
In her still garden, and she seems to be
Like them; for surely for her never rang
Passion's wild bell that sets love's music free.

Yet in the night, when she is all alone,
The woman of her weeps; and though there sounds
No loud lamenting, not a single moan,
Yet the still air with sorrowing resounds;
And you may read, by Fate's dark finger scrolled,
Signs on her shore where once love's ocean rolled.

DESERTED

Over the fields and the far lonely strand
The barren broomgrass waves, the lost winds sigh;
Gray-shrouded oaks and rustling laurels high
To sentinel the desolation stand.
The wild sweet woods are deep on either hand.
Beneath the tranced and trembling southern sky
There is a beauty here that cannot die,
For love makes beautiful a ruined land.

I saw a mourner in that solitude,
And the mute twilight seemed to search his face
With anguish dim. Faint with vain tears he stood,
A loneliness, and of that scene a part;
For he beheld the tomb of all his race,
And gazed upon the burial of his heart.

THE GREAT OF HEART

They have no time for hate.
Naught can dismay them.
Malice would make them late.
Fear would delay them.

They are the arrowy ones,
Beautiful, blinding;
They wreck all cruel thrones,
Seeking and finding

All who are being driven,
All who are hounded;
Give them a joyous home,
By peace surrounded.

Look, wonder, and behold
What ardor burns them.
Theirs is no search for gold;
Love, love concerns them.

INDECISION

They stand before the gate of Paradise,
That portal fair beyond which there is peace:
From the gray deep below, the lonely seas
On earth's wild shores in homeless longings rise.
"O let us haste within," the lover cries,
"Within the gate is rest, and tumults cease."
But she, far-gazing, doubted; and her eyes
Shadowed her uncontrol. The very trees

Of Paradise are trembling lest she turn;
The winds of God consent not; in the night
They thunder; at her pause the sea-waves mourn:
The stars with dazzling pangs flame with new light
On the fair way, imploring, lest the gate
Close with a sigh upon them, desolate.

623

DISCOVERY

Adventurers depart for lands unknown;
Under strange skies they sail. Their questing feet
Startle new mountains, immemorial, lone,
The wings of their wild inquiry are fleet
Over lost oceans, plunging on the shore
Of solitude. Forever outward bound,
Till they behold what none has seen before,
They rest not till they find what can be found.

But in the ancient Homeland of the Heart
All is familiar from the long ago.
There is no lonely grief, no joy apart.
Myriads have gone, and myriads will go
The way we journey. All we here discover
Is known to every mourner and every lover.

KINGDOMS PASSED AWAY

Long had he, as a soldier, known the shock
Of battle, and the brazen voice of death,
Whose merest whisper rives the granite rock
Of valor. Well he knew the rancid breath
Of bellowing guns, and often had he knelt
By dying comrades; in a maddened flood
Had seen tall thrones swept headlong, and had felt
The crash of falling kingdoms in his blood.

But all these seemed as naught when he descried
The end of Beauty's infinite estate:
He, gazing on the glory as it died
In one adored, by grief made desolate,
Saw, like the doom in splendid sunset skies,
Love's noble empire fading from her eyes.

624

THE VISION OF DAGONET

When to the court of Arthur, fair Elaine,
Who died of hopeless love for Lancelot,
Was borne, a sense of pathos and of pain
Stilled all the careless voices of Camelot.
"Behold the Lily Maid!" "Was ever yet
So deep a love as this?" "Can it be well
Ever to love?" "How bitter with regret
Must Lancelot be." "Such rue no tongue can tell."

But Dagonet, Arthur's fool—and very wise,
Said to himself, his countenance alight,
Scorning their lamentations and their cries,
"She greatly loved. Now in eternal night
Starlike she reigns forever, and her story
Tells all there is of life's wild grief and glory."

MORNING SONG

A song-sparrow in the earliest morning sang
In natural ecstasy. Then it was still.
And nevermore all day that music rang.
Though countless lyrics came from vale and hill,
That single one I could not hear again;
Though more than all the rest it meant to me:
The light of love, compassion for all pain,
Like choiring anthems of the pines and sea.

So once a little child, whose life left mine
Had brought me joy: she never knew her noon,
Life's afternoon or evening. Love divine
Was hushed for her, so silenced and so soon!
Only a morning song was hers, and yet
She made me music I will not forget.

625

VISION

With magic hand he paints the picture, seen
Deep in the soul-recesses of his dream;
With passionate clairvoyance piercing keen
The veil of things, the vesture, to the gleam
Of the vision's heart. Or if a truth there be
That he would tell us of life's wondrous story,
He with power of beauty and deathlessly
Will chant it forth with banners streaming glory.

And though his words be wild, yet all he sings
Is understod by children, and by those
Who see a mystery in dawn's yellow wings,
Who fell a delphic meaning in the rose,
To whom the mountains in the moonlight stand
For other mountains, in another land.

NATURAL BRIDGE

Before Columbus and his caravels,
It towered in the wilderness alone,
Lulled by the murmur of its ferny dells,
This dream stupendous of eternal stone.
The naked savage, pausing on the trail,
Stood reverent at this primeval fane;
His weakness worshiped strength that shall not fai
Abiding while the sun and stars remain.

By love and awe to make this marvel mine,
This slumbering beauty o'er wild chasms flung,
I come to wonder at this ancient shrine
That God upreared while Eden still was young.
Always the work of His almighty hands,
Amid our palaces in ruin, stands.

626

FLOWER OF JOY

"These are the flowers of joy," the angel said,
When in a vision I was walking with him
Down pathways in life's garden sweet and dim:
"White Innocence that lifts a fragile head,
And Faith, uplooking where the heavens shine,
Fair Hope and Patience, blooming many an hour,
And Sacrifice, yon dark and noble flower,
And starry Peace and Truth and Love divine."

"And which brings deepest joy?" I asked him then,
Looking about me with uncertain eyes;
And he with certainty at each again
Replied: "The marvel flower that never dies—
It brings most joy." He pointed to the slope
Were radiant gleamed the unfading flower of Hope.

A SONG AFTER STRIFE

Once in the woods the wind that had been raving
Suddenly slept. The flowers that widly danced,
The trees with arms and tresses madly waving
Now beauteous stood, and quietly entranced.
Then in the silence following after strife,
Holding an ancient magic that I knew,
Full of rich music from the heart of life,
A bird-song sounded sweet and clear and true.

So in the storm of days that round us sweeps
Come moments of great stillness, when we hear
Music from out life's mystic astral deeps
From beauty that eternal is and near.
The song of peace and joy that gently swells
Is the true meaning that life's tempest tells.

627

QUANDARY

If to the shore I go, I'll miss the hills:
The rustic roads that clamber to the crests,
The music of the laurel-shrouded rills
That lure me on to wilder, lonelier quests;
As odorous as Eden in the night,
The ardor of the aromatic air;
The solemn strength of stone; the mountain-light,
Transfiguring tawny beauty everywhere.

If to the hills I go, I'll miss the shore:
The curlew's wild contralto in the hollows
Amid the dunes that hold the deep in place;
The azure over azure evermore;
The water-harps' soft tenor in the shallows;
The thunder-maned sea-breakers' rolling bass.

BRAVER WAY

How often in his anguish he has said,
"O if the swift dark way I homeward take,
She would be free in joy and peace to wed,
When I am sleeping, never more to wake.
So wild the glory that we share, I know
She would not wed another while I live.
Would she find greater splendor if I go?
If this last token of my love I give?"

I do not dread the night. But I must fear
Her heart would grieve, her little hand would grope
To find my hand, lost in that darkness drear.
Darling, I will stay with you, and must hope
My love for your proud waiting will atone.
I will not ever leave you all alone.

TAJ MAHAL

When we appraise the harvests of our joy,
Transient they seem and meagre. It is willed
Silence is barren when the laughter's stilled.
If bliss makes aught, it is a fragile toy,
That we in merriment may soon destroy.
Out of our gladness little can be build;
Felicity is in itself fulfilled.
Not toward eternity delights deploy.

Grief is the mighty builder and the wise.
From anguish to illustrious beauty born,
Out of life's darkness, towering for the morn,
The glory of this fane ascends the skies.
On majesty they made, we see them fall,—
The eternal tears that wept the Taj Mahal.

BATTLES

Grieving, I read of battles long ago,
Of hosts that met in sanguine onsets wild;
Of the poor futile dead, the friend and foe,
Of the beauty of tall manhood's grace defiled;
Of Varus and his legions, fallen afar
In the Teutonic wilds; and of the doom
Of Harold; of the setting of the star
Of Cleopatra's hopes at Actium.

Yet daily, and in our dangers all alone,
In more than mortal combat we have part.
And no historian has ever known
Of the antagonists that storm the heart;
Of the armies fled; of the dreadnaughts of the soul,
Sunk where the great deeps of the spirit roll.

629

ONCE IN THE MOUNTAINS

Once in the mountains, thrilling a fragrant glade
With silver music, laughed a crystal brook;
Its high-born home in beauty it forsook;
Immaculate at heart, through sun and shade,
The ancient country young again it made.
From lonely pine and hill-hung star it took
In the stiller pools clear images. Its look
Was lyric, as of things that cannot fade.

But then it grew a stream, and then a river,
With flow profound. Yet the deeper, darker tide
Had lost its laurel-loveliness forever;
A sombre heart homed in its bosom wide.
Ah, long ago, far childhood's hills among,
We, too, were joyous, beautiful, and young.

PRAISING THE DARKNESS

Thank God for darkness and the bitter hour!
What hero or what heroine was made
By joy and laughing ease? Life's deeper power
Finds its release in sorrow and in shade.
Ah, only those who have of woe partaken
Are of all human trouble made aware:
The better angels of our hearts awaken
Only when we are wounded to despair.

Behold the Taj Mahal. Its beauty rose
From anguish dreaming on a loved one dead.
Deep in his night, and hemmed about by foes,
Milton sublimely sang. The faith that led
Our Master on his lone immortal way
Had strength and hope, but grief far more than they.

630

BEAUTY IN STORM

One night I dared the storm, and with the dark
Kept awful pace, not caring where we went.
Black-browed above me was the monster bent,
And sword-sharp flashes showed the wildly stark
White trees where thunder once had burst . . . No barque
Takes the high seas in splendid banishment,
More dauntlessly, where death is imminent,
Than I drove bleakly toward some fatal mark.

Ah, brave I thought myself, and proud until
In the black pall enshrouding earth and sky,
A rift was rent, through which there shone all still
A star immaculate . . . O then did I,
With Beauty breaking my rebellious will,
Struggle against the storm, and dread to die.

SAINTS

I look on them with wonder and with awe,
The saints of earth. Have they a better guide
Than any that has journeyed at my side?
And do they see a light I never saw?
Even from dark adversity they draw
Radiance of virtue. Ever they abide
Serene, although on stormy gulfs they ride,
Who know and love and live Eternal Law.

Marking a beacon that is hid from me,
They hear a voice that unto me is dumb;
The harbor they behold, I cannot see,
And to the faith they feel, my heart is numb . . .
Yet if I follow them, may it not be
That to the bourne they reach, I too shall come?

THE SOUTHERN ROSE

To those who loved and waited, and to those
Who watched by their dead heartsides desolate:
To those who stood beside the closing gate
And bravely said farewell, and saw it close:
To the proud heart of our dear Southern Rose,
Through all the moaning night immaculate;
To those who waited faithful, and must wait
To meet their lost ones where the Lily blows.

Now in the darkening day's farewell embrace,
I see her stand, pale Spirit of our wars;
Beautiful in the twilight is her face.
With the serene arrival of the stars,
God suffers her to grieve, to glide away
Quietly into the quiet evening gray.

MEMORY OF THE HEART

The mind remembers all things. To forget
Is never possible. Life's joys and fears,
All that delighted us, all we regret,
The mind will hold forever. For our years
Are pages written down, are records kept.
We read our childhood and our youth. We turn
To that strange page, telling when first we wept,—
Learning of grief; then came of love to learn.

The guardian of our annals is the mind,
The faithful keeper of our history.
There all things saving one thing you shall find,—
And that is what is best in you and me:
For gratitude, the memory of the heart,
Is our mortality's immortal part.

THE CHOICE

If Love comes to your door, you may decide
That you this royal guest will not admit,
That all alone in peace you may abide,
Sterile and safe, your rosy lamp unlit.
Is it not wiser so? He comes attended
By blinding beauty, immemorial pain,
By wildest joy; and by a vision splendid
That will not ever let you rest again.

Alas, poor Heart! Which is the better way?
The silence and the calm, the heart asleep?
Or, glad imperious trumpets to obey,—
Giving your all, your soul in bliss to steep?
Let Love have joyous welcome! You will lose
Life's glory if his entrance you refuse.

THE SOURCE OF SONG

A little child who runs along the shore,
Coming upon an opalescent shell,
Cries, "See what I have found! A mermaid wore
This for a broach!" And who could better tell
What poetry is? Come from mysterious deeps,
Seraphic wonder from the gross concealed.
Where life's wild wave upon love's sea-strand weeps,
To the naïve heart divinely is revealed.

Forever to the soul its voice is singing
Like sea-wind or a song of long ago;
Always to us in beauty it is bringing
The magic that we always yearn to know.
It is a miracle by the spirit made,
A glimmering wildflower that shall never fade.

HIDDEN ORGANIST

Hidden in some high transept of the hills
An organist keeps playing night and day.
Sometimes his music, like the mountain rills,
Is liquid melody—faint, far away;
Again it will be thunder, rolling deep,
Or like the mournful music of the sea;
Then like some elfin aria heard in sleep,
Hymning of joy, of love, of peace to be.

Amid the pines and hemlocks, spruce and firs
This organist, unwearied, is enthroned.
If ever a wind among the mountain stirs,
We hear his music, mystic, organ-toned,
At one with that great rhythm that sustains
The skies, the earth, its hills and seas and plains.

RIVER-BEND

The river makes a glimmering graceful bend
Below my wharf; and there it disappears;
And there my river-world comes to an end, —
And yet begins. For down through all the years,
Around the bend, with a southeaster blowing,
Now a three-master would come riding in;
And now a sturgeon boat with oarsmen rowing.
All life seems here to end and to begin.

I never know what round that bend will come:
A river-steamer, a bald eagle cruising;
A hunter in a long dugout canoe;
Strangers, or my own children sailing home,
An egret white as hope . . . Had I the choosing;
From round that bend my longing would bring you.

THE SLEEPING WEST

The sleeping west
Is calm and bright.
Where tumult flamed
Is tranquil light.
O may you have
A heart at rest
As quiet as
The sleeping west.

SON OF MY HEART

Son of my heart, what shall I leave
　To you as token of regard?
What gold or jewels need I give
　To one already honor-starred?
Only the spirit can survive
　To keep eternal watch and ward.
Son, I shall leave you what will live,
　My bended but unbroken sword.